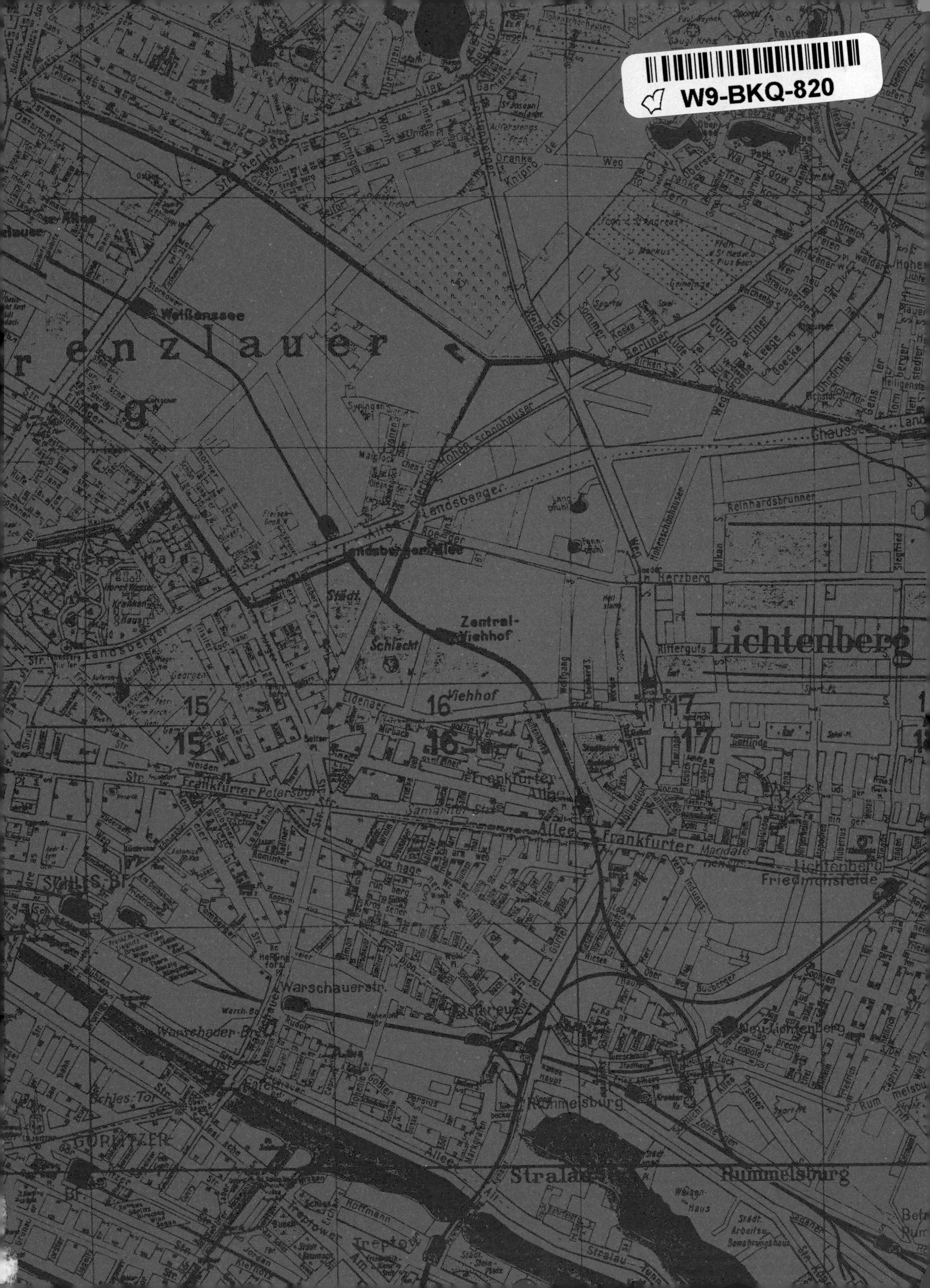
renzlauer
g
Weißensee
Zentral-
Viehhof
Schlacht
Viehhof
Lichtenberg
15
16
17
Landsberger Allee
Frankfurter Allee
Samariter Str.
Reinhardsbrunner
Herzberg
Lichtenberg
Friedrichsfelde
Warschauerstr.
Warschauer Br.
Neu Lichtenberg
Rummelsburg
Stralau
Treptow
Schles. Tor
Görlitzer
Chaussee

Berlin

CITY OF STONES

a work of fiction by
JASON LUTES

Berlin: City of Stones was originally serialized in the comic book **Berlin**, in issues 1 through 8, published by Black Eye Books and Drawn & Quarterly.

The next volume of this trilogy, **Berlin (Book Two): City of Smoke**, is available in many fine book and comic stores or direct from the publisher's website.

Publication design
Michel Vrána/Black Eye Design and Jason Lutes.

Publication history
First edition: February 2001
Second printing: June 2002
Third printing: August 2004
Fourth printing: August 2008
Fifth printing: April 2010
Sixth printing: January 2011
Seventh printing: October 2014
Eighth printing: June 2017
Printed in Hong Kong
10 9 8
ISBN 978-1-896597-29-4

Published in the USA by Drawn & Quarterly, a client publisher of
Farrar, Straus and Giroux
Orders: 888.330.8477

Published in the Canada by Drawn & Quarterly, a client publisher of
Raincoast Books
Orders: 800.663.5714

drawnandquarterly.com

ACKNOWLEDGMENTS

the author would like to thank rachel bers, ed brubaker, michael buckley, stefano gaudiano, lutz göllner, antje guertier, joachim kaps, megan kelso, carolyn lutes, philip lutes, chris oliveros, dirk rehm, kai-steffen schwarz, brian sendelbach, michel vrána, and especially rebecca warren.

Berlin

BOOK ONE

1

ch ch ch ch ch ch ch ch ch ch ch
CH CH CH CH CH CH CH CH CH

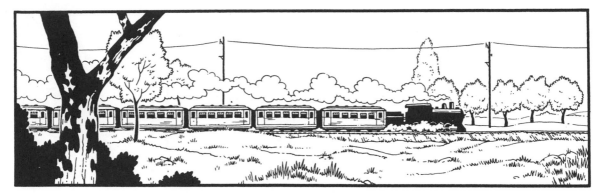

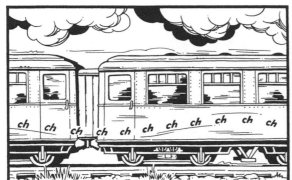

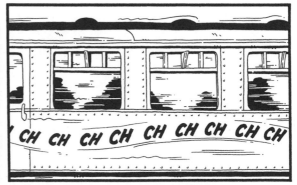

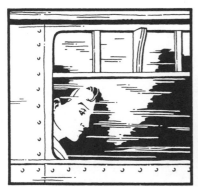

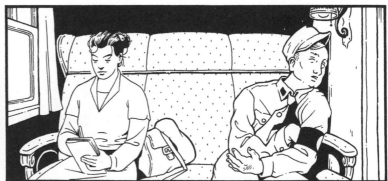

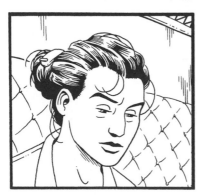

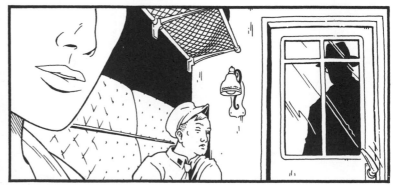

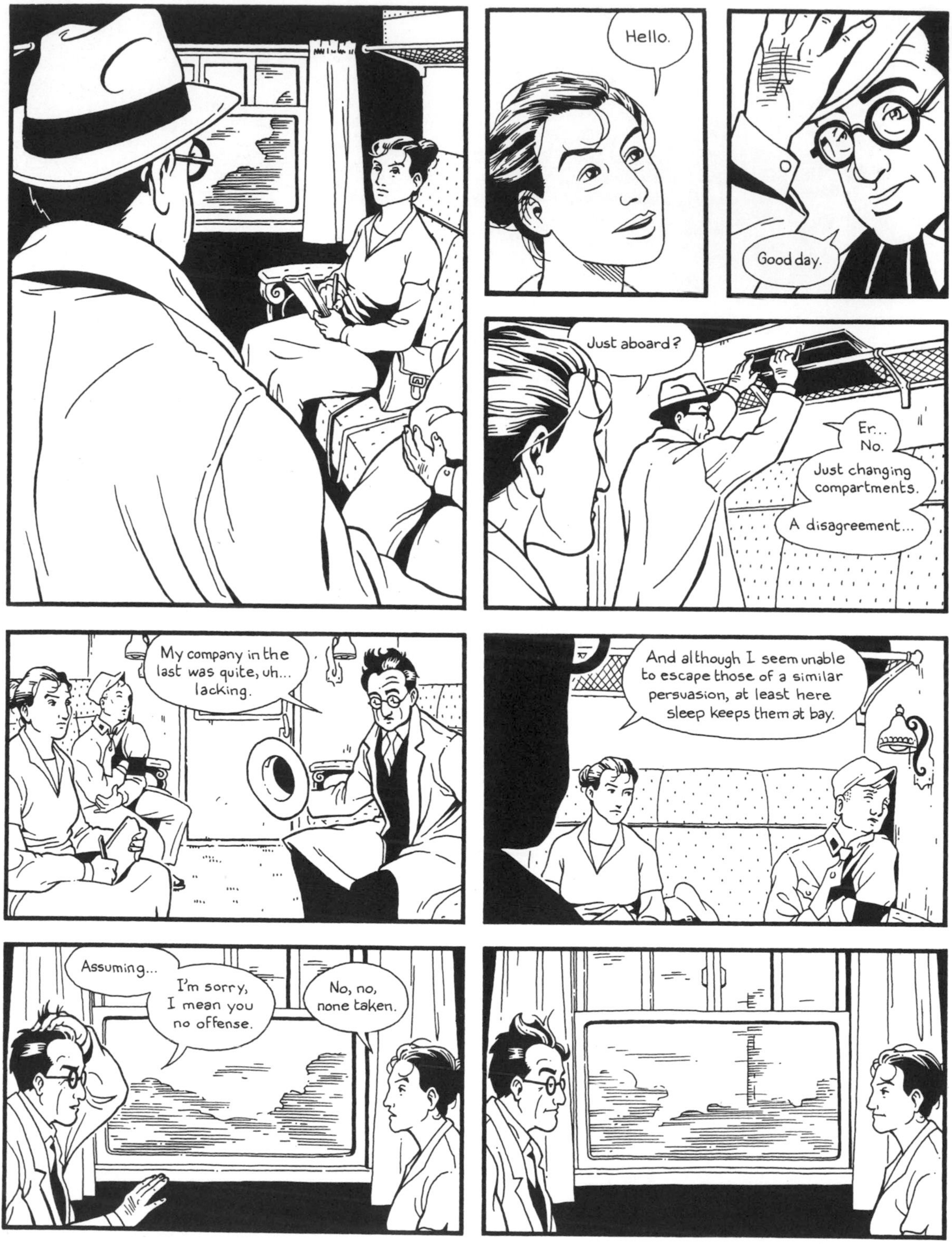
Hello.
Good day.
Just aboard?
Er... No.
Just changing compartments.
A disagreement...
My company in the last was quite, uh... lacking.
And although I seem unable to escape those of a similar persuasion, at least here sleep keeps them at bay.
Assuming...
I'm sorry, I mean you no offense.
No, no, none taken.

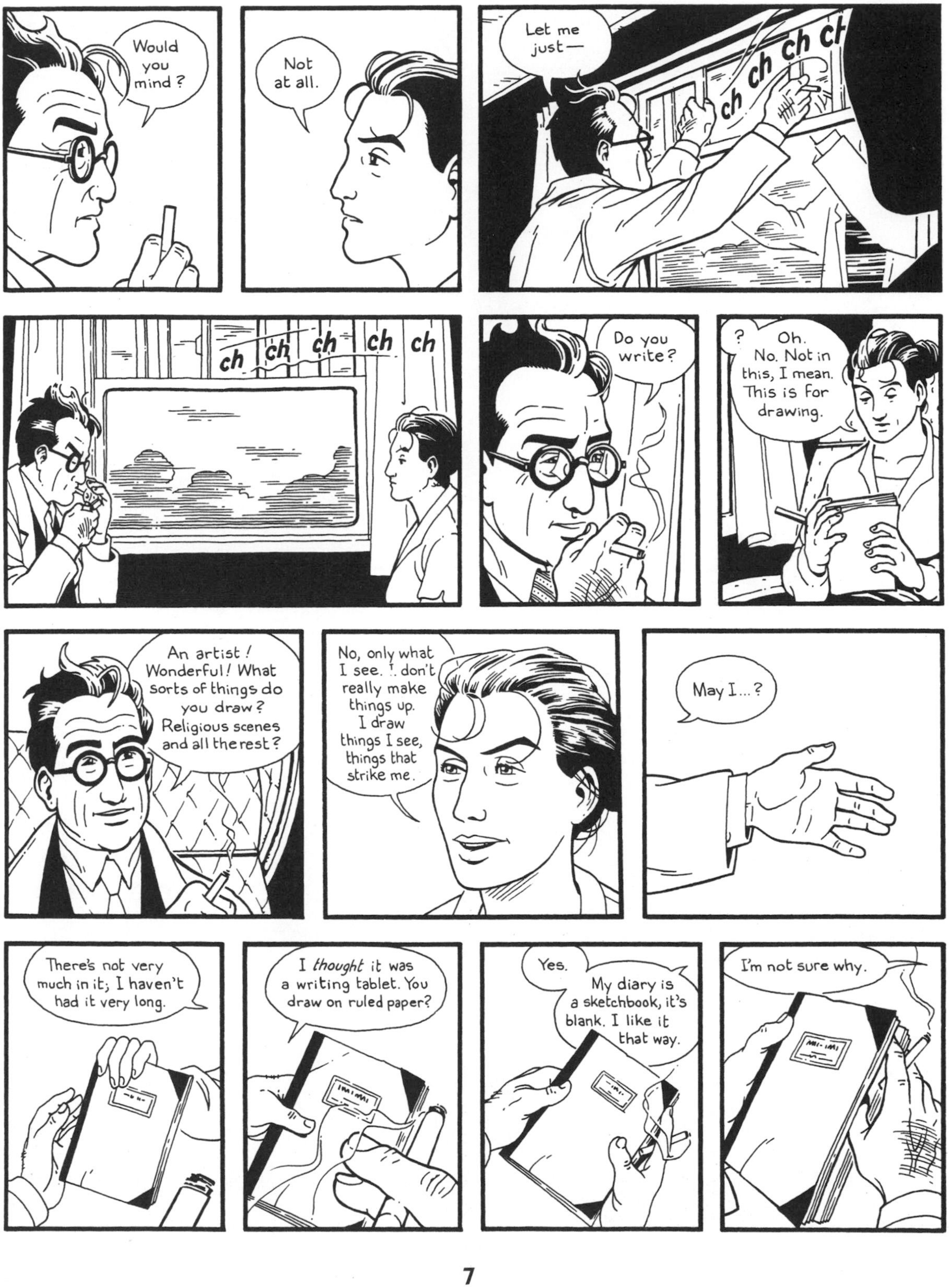

Would you mind?
Not at all.
Let me just—
ch ch ch ch
ch ch ch ch ch
Do you write?
?
Oh. No. Not in this, I mean. This is for drawing.
An artist! Wonderful! What sorts of things do you draw? Religious scenes and all the rest?
No, only what I see. I don't really make things up. I draw things I see, things that strike me.
May I...?
There's not very much in it; I haven't had it very long.
I *thought* it was a writing tablet. You draw on ruled paper?
Yes.
My diary is a sketchbook, it's blank. I like it that way.
I'm not sure why.

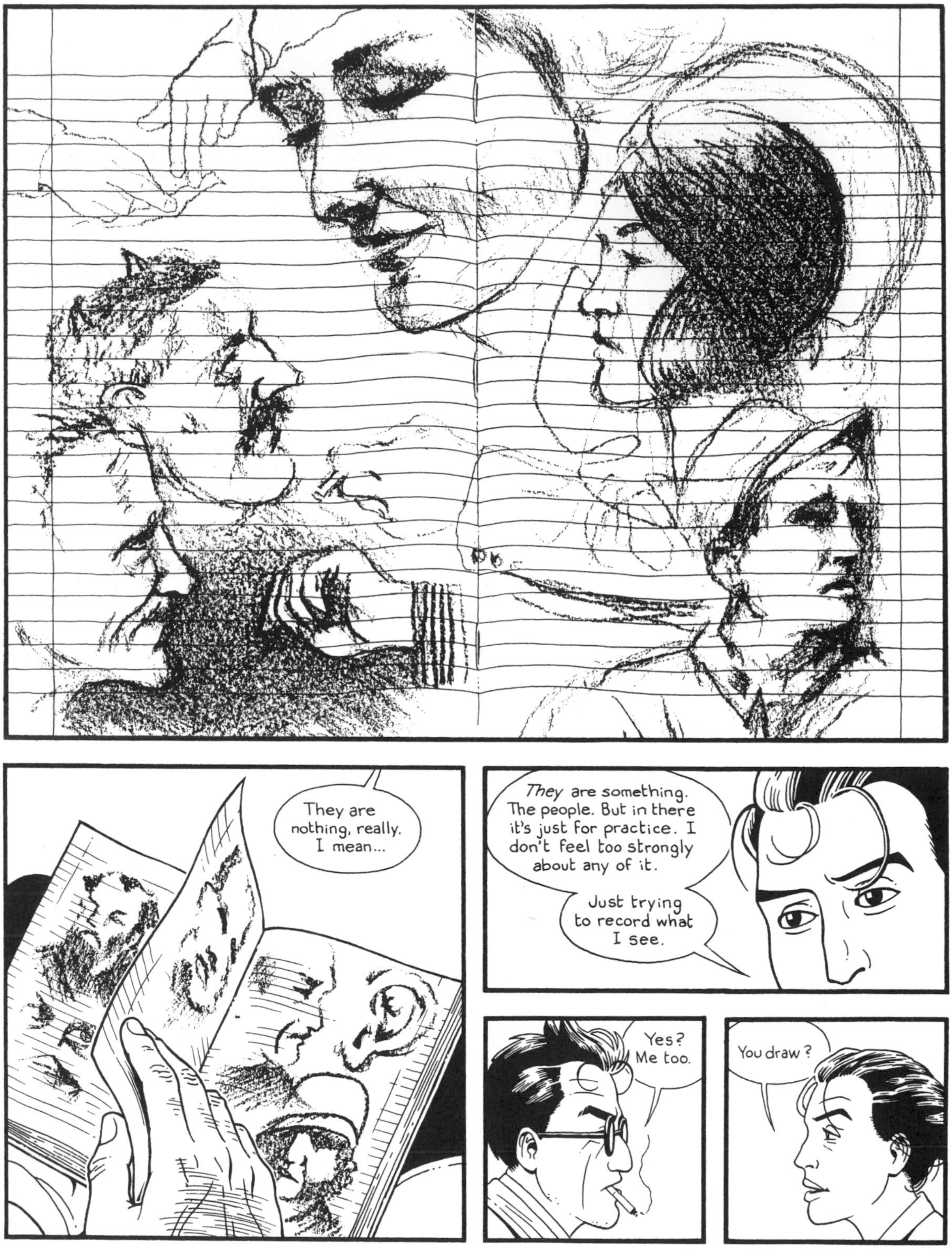
They are nothing, really. I mean...
They are something. The people. But in there it's just for practice. I don't feel too strongly about any of it.
Just trying to record what I see.
Yes? Me too.
You draw?

Ha ha, no.

I try to do it with words. I write.

Novelist?

Journalist.

ch ch ch ch ch

Less eloquent in my language of choice, however.

These are really quite excellent.

That's very kind of you, Herr...?

I'm sorry, how rude of me. Severing. Kurt Severing.

Marthe Müller.

Are you travelling on an assignment of some sort?

Yes.

I've just been checking some background details for someone else's article as a favor to my editor.

And you?

I see by your luggage that this is no small journey.

9

I'm from Köln. I'm afraid I've never been to the city before.

Are you?

Excuse me?

Afraid. Are you afraid?

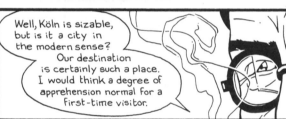

No. Do I have reason to be?

Well, Köln is sizable, but is it a city in the modern sense? Our destination is certainly such a place. I would think a degree of apprehension normal for a first-time visitor.

Our friend here...

His is one among many factions which clash in the streets with increasing frequency.

Communists, socialists, nationalists, democrats, republicans, criminals, beggars, thieves, and everything in between.

All mixed up together—

Are you trying to *make* me afraid, Herr Severing?

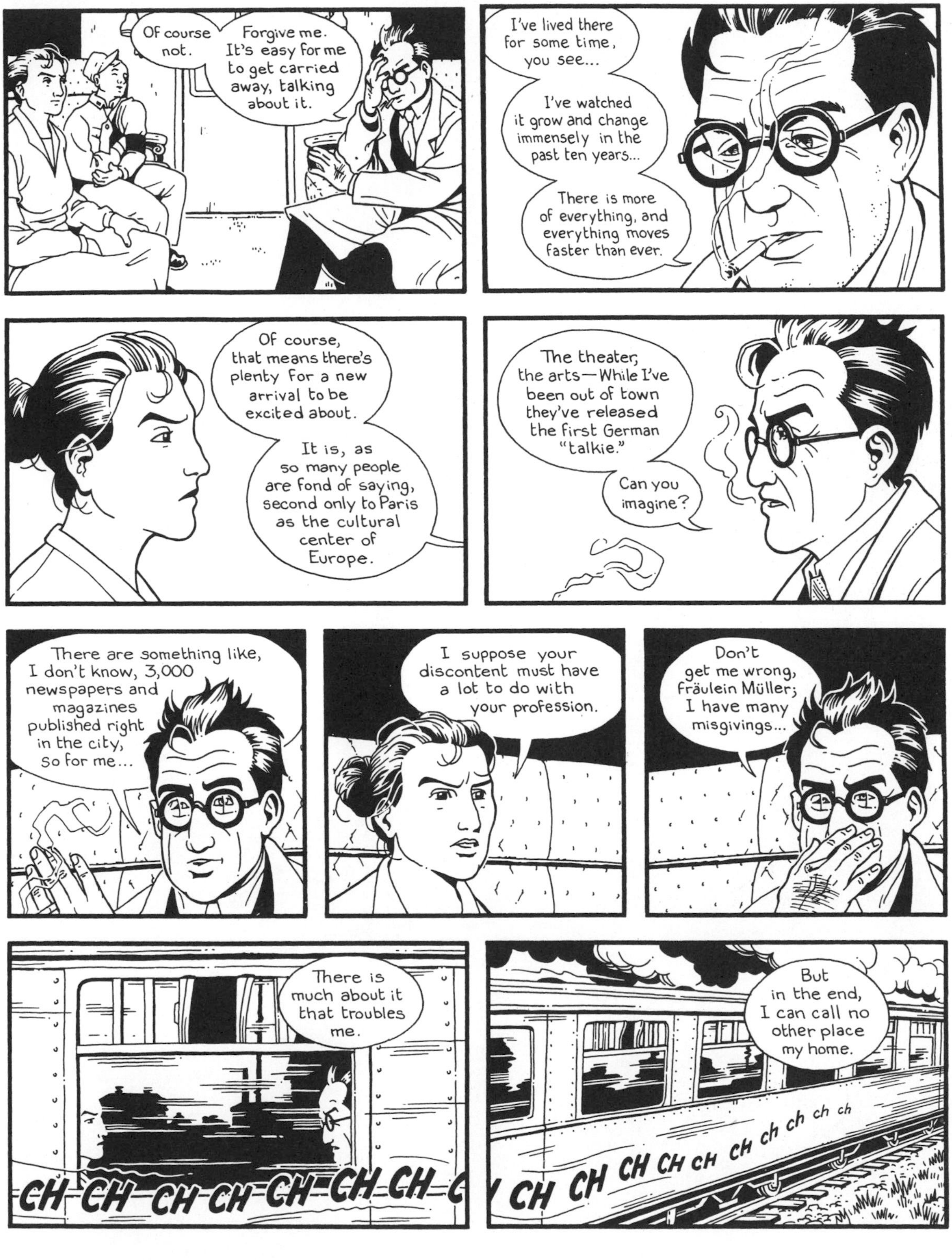
Of course not.
Forgive me. It's easy for me to get carried away, talking about it.
I've lived there for some time, you see...
I've watched it grow and change immensely in the past ten years...
There is more of everything, and everything moves faster than ever.
Of course, that means there's plenty for a new arrival to be excited about.
It is, as so many people are fond of saying, second only to Paris as the cultural center of Europe.
The theater, the arts—While I've been out of town they've released the first German "talkie."
Can you imagine?
There are something like, I don't know, 3,000 newspapers and magazines published right in the city, so for me...
I suppose your discontent must have a lot to do with your profession.
Don't get me wrong, fräulein Müller; I have many misgivings...
There is much about it that troubles me.
CH CH CH CH CH CH CH
But in the end, I can call no other place my home.
CH CH CH CH CH ch ch ch ch ch

CITY OF STONES

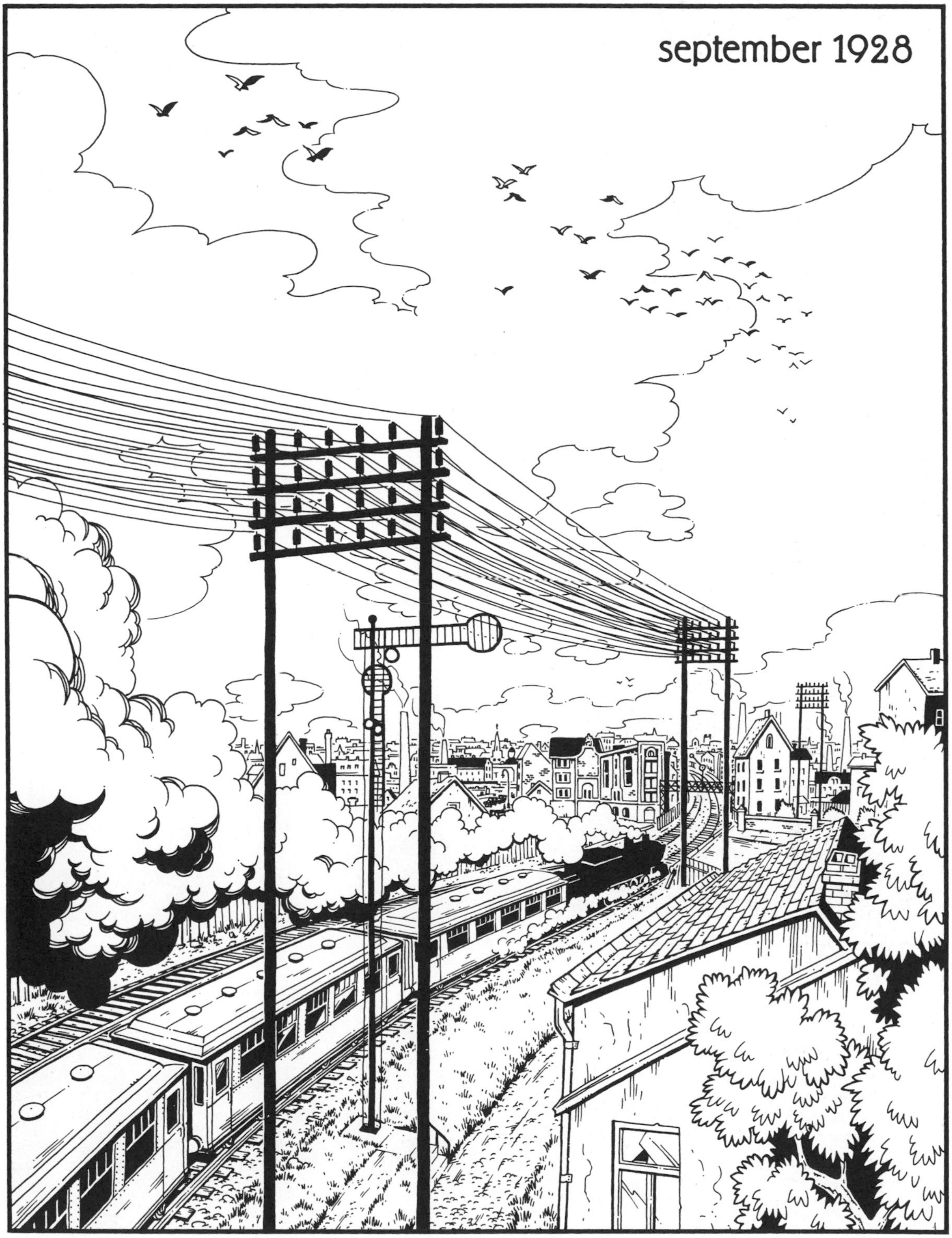
september 1928

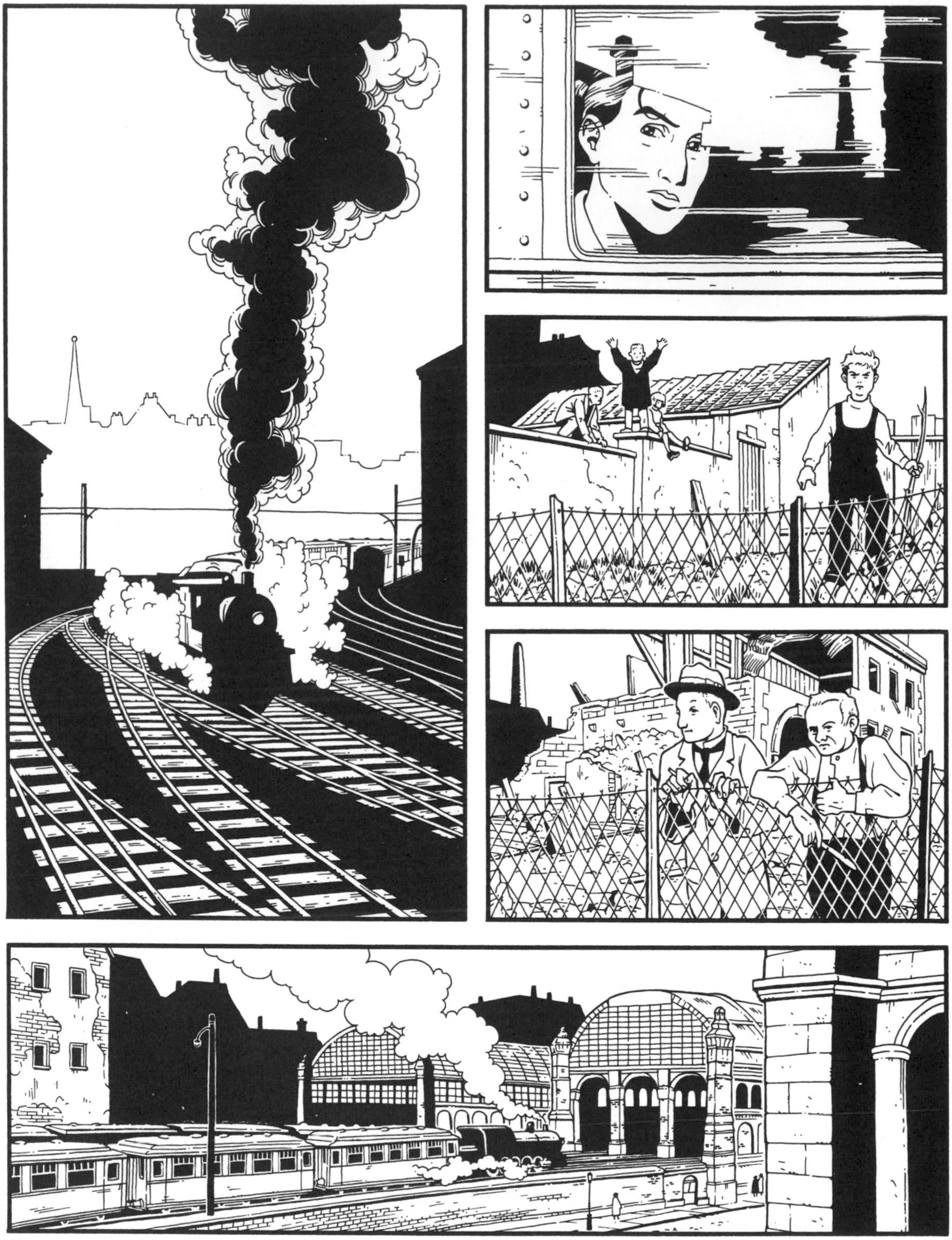

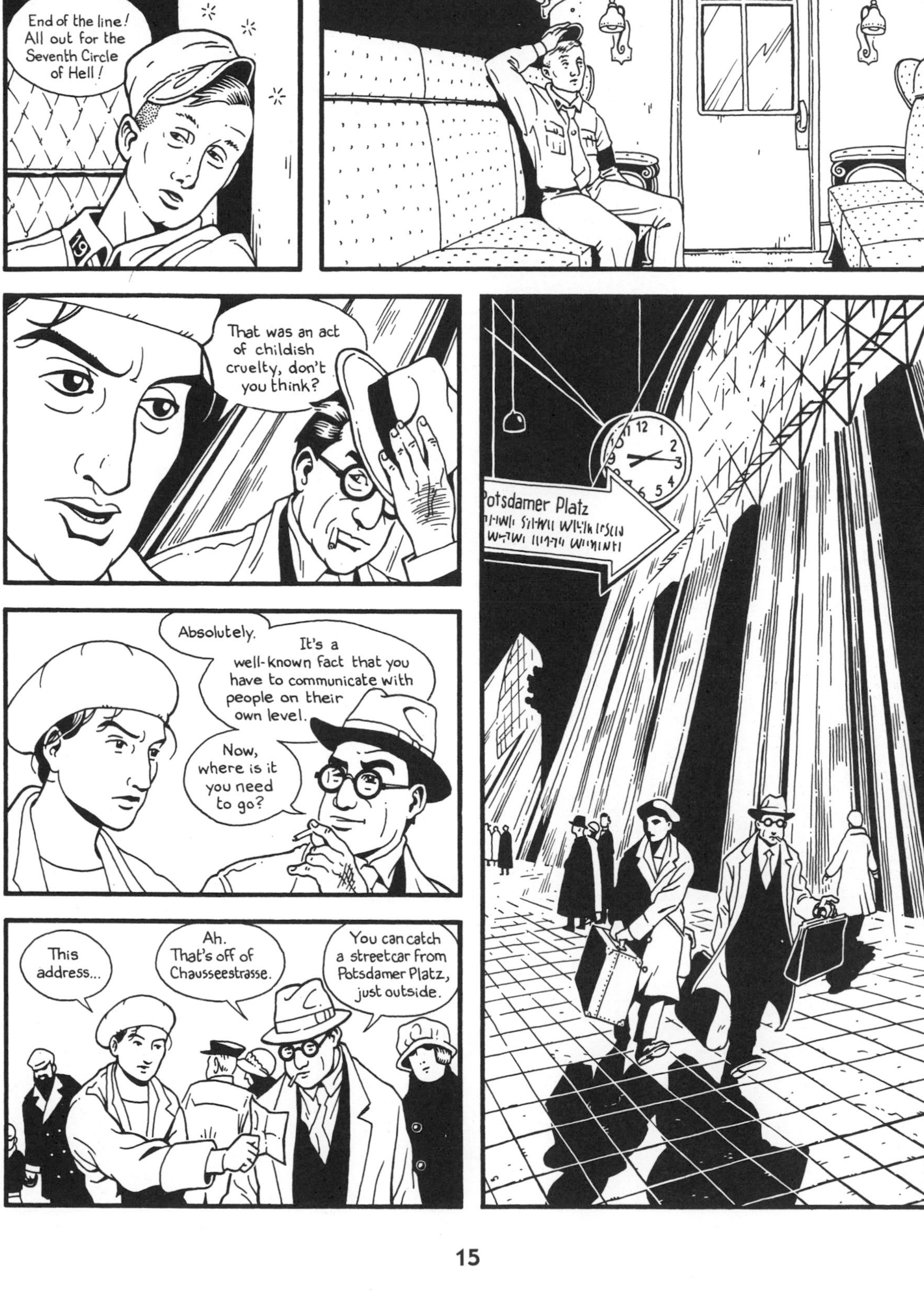
End of the line! All out for the Seventh Circle of Hell!
That was an act of childish cruelty, don't you think?
Absolutely.
It's a well-known fact that you have to communicate with people on their own level.
Now, where is it you need to go?
This address...
Ah. That's off of Chausseestrasse.
You can catch a streetcar from Potsdamer Platz, just outside.
Potsdamer Platz

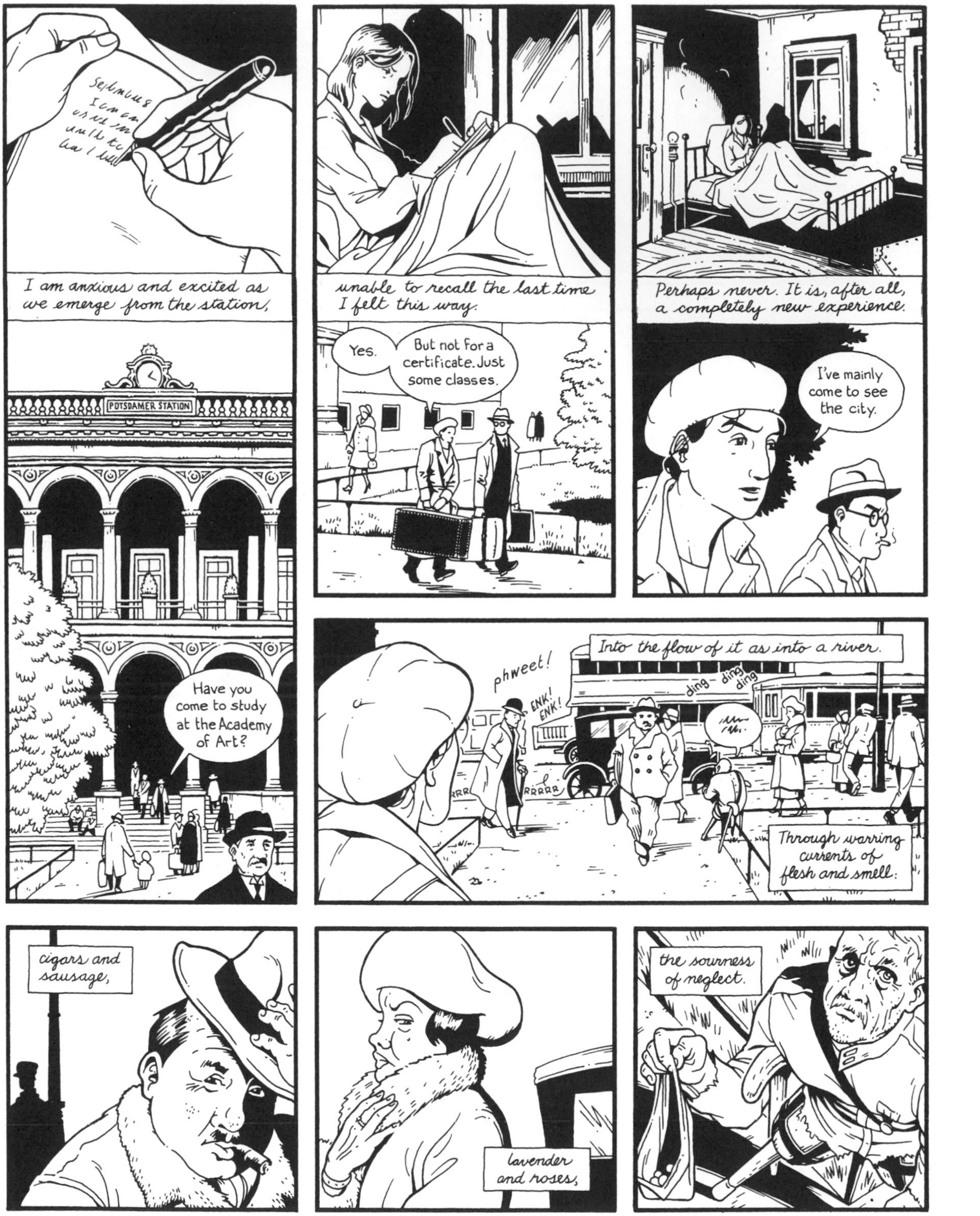
I am anxious and excited as we emerge from the station,
unable to recall the last time I felt this way.
Perhaps never. It is, after all, a completely new experience.
POTSDAMER STATION
Have you come to study at the Academy of Art?
Yes.
But not for a certificate. Just some classes.
I've mainly come to see the city.
Into the flow of it as into a river.
phweet!
ENK! ENK!
ding-ding ding
RRRR
RRRRR
Through warring currents of flesh and smell:
cigars and sausage,
lavender and roses,
the sourness of neglect.

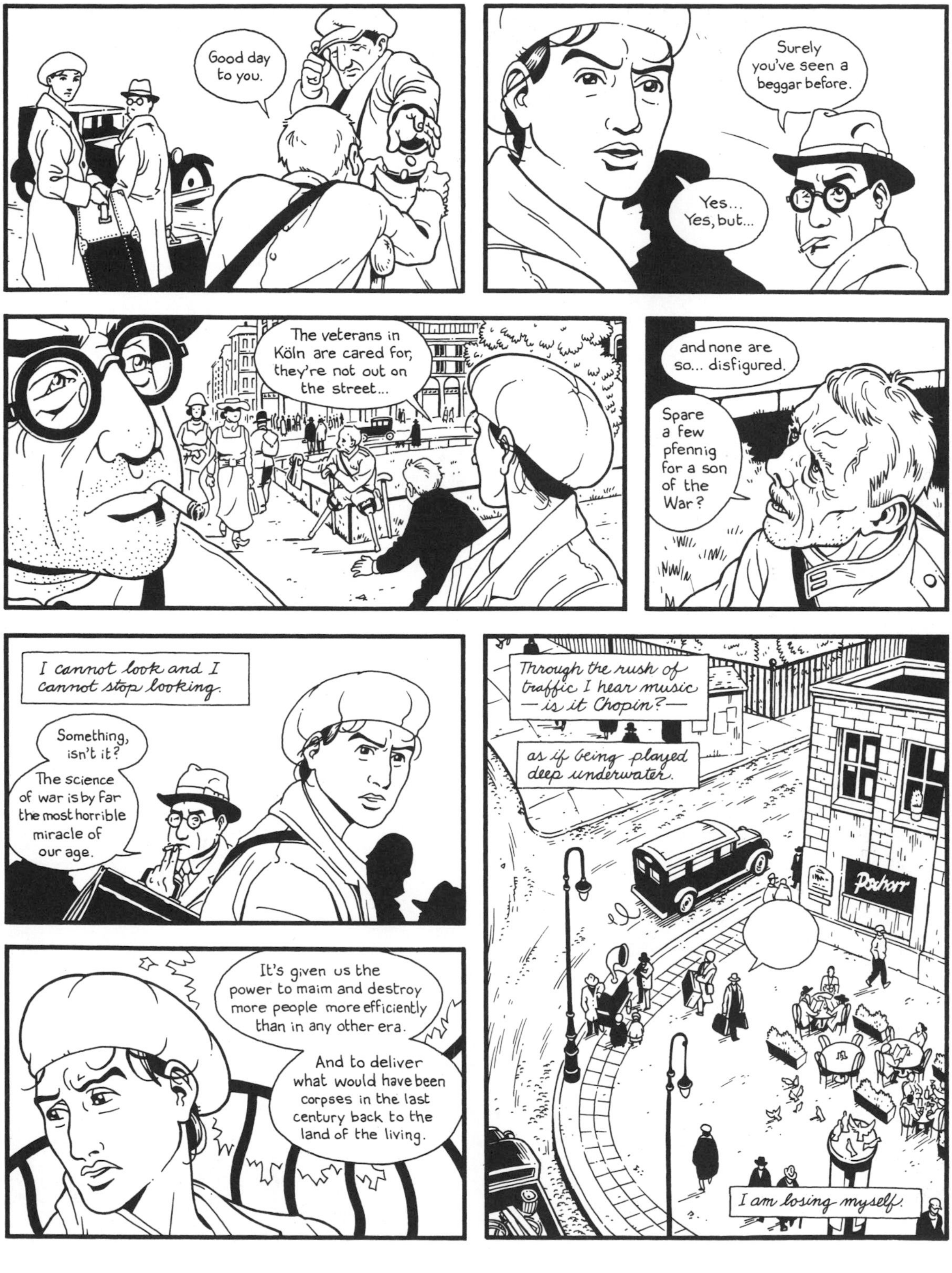
Good day to you.
Surely you've seen a beggar before.
Yes... Yes, but...
The veterans in Köln are cared for, they're not out on the street...
and none are so... disfigured.
Spare a few pfennig for a son of the War?
I cannot look and I cannot stop looking.
Something, isn't it?
The science of war is by far the most horrible miracle of our age.
It's given us the power to maim and destroy more people more efficiently than in any other era.
And to deliver what would have been corpses in the last century back to the land of the living.
Through the rush of traffic I hear music —is it Chopin?—
as if being played deep underwater.
Pschorr
I am losing myself.

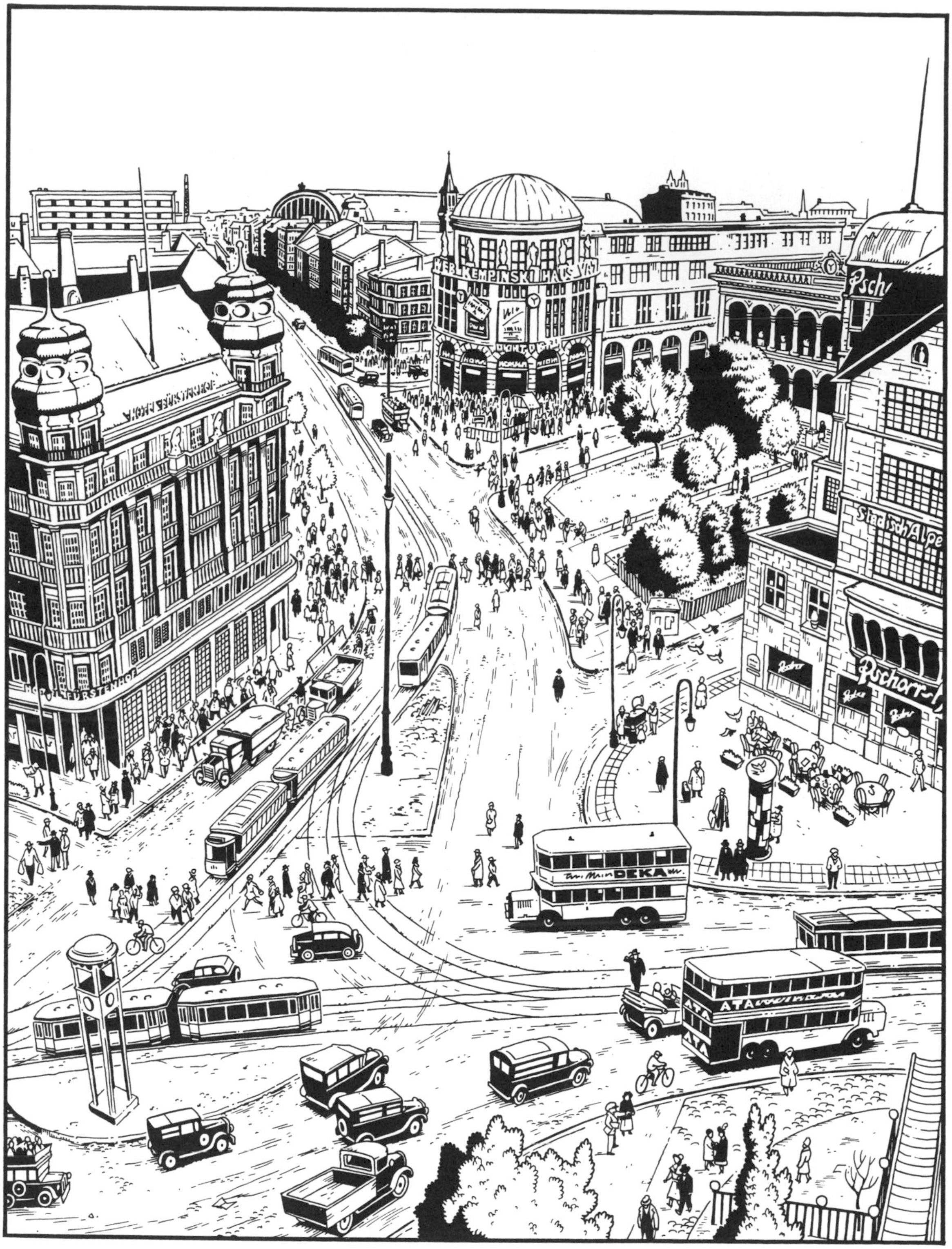
KEMPINSKI HAUS
FÜRSTENHOF
DEKA
ATA
Pschorr

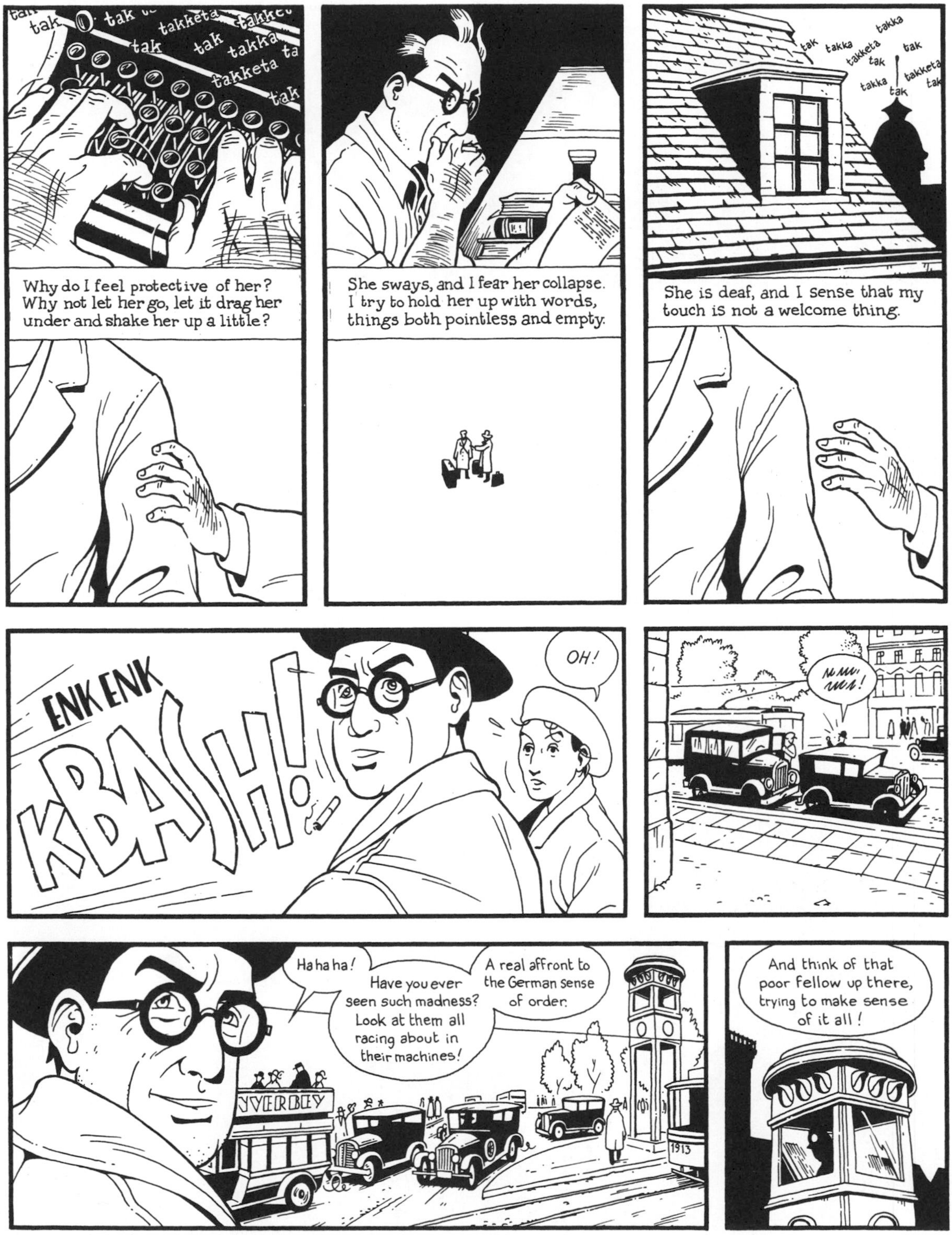
tak tak takketa tak takka takketa tak
Why do I feel protective of her? Why not let her go, let it drag her under and shake her up a little?
She sways, and I fear her collapse. I try to hold her up with words, things both pointless and empty.
tak takka takketa takka tak tak takka takketa tak tak
She is deaf, and I sense that my touch is not a welcome thing.
ENK ENK
KBASH!
OH!
Ha ha ha!
Have you ever seen such madness? Look at them all racing about in their machines!
A real affront to the German sense of order.
1913
And think of that poor fellow up there, trying to make sense of it all!

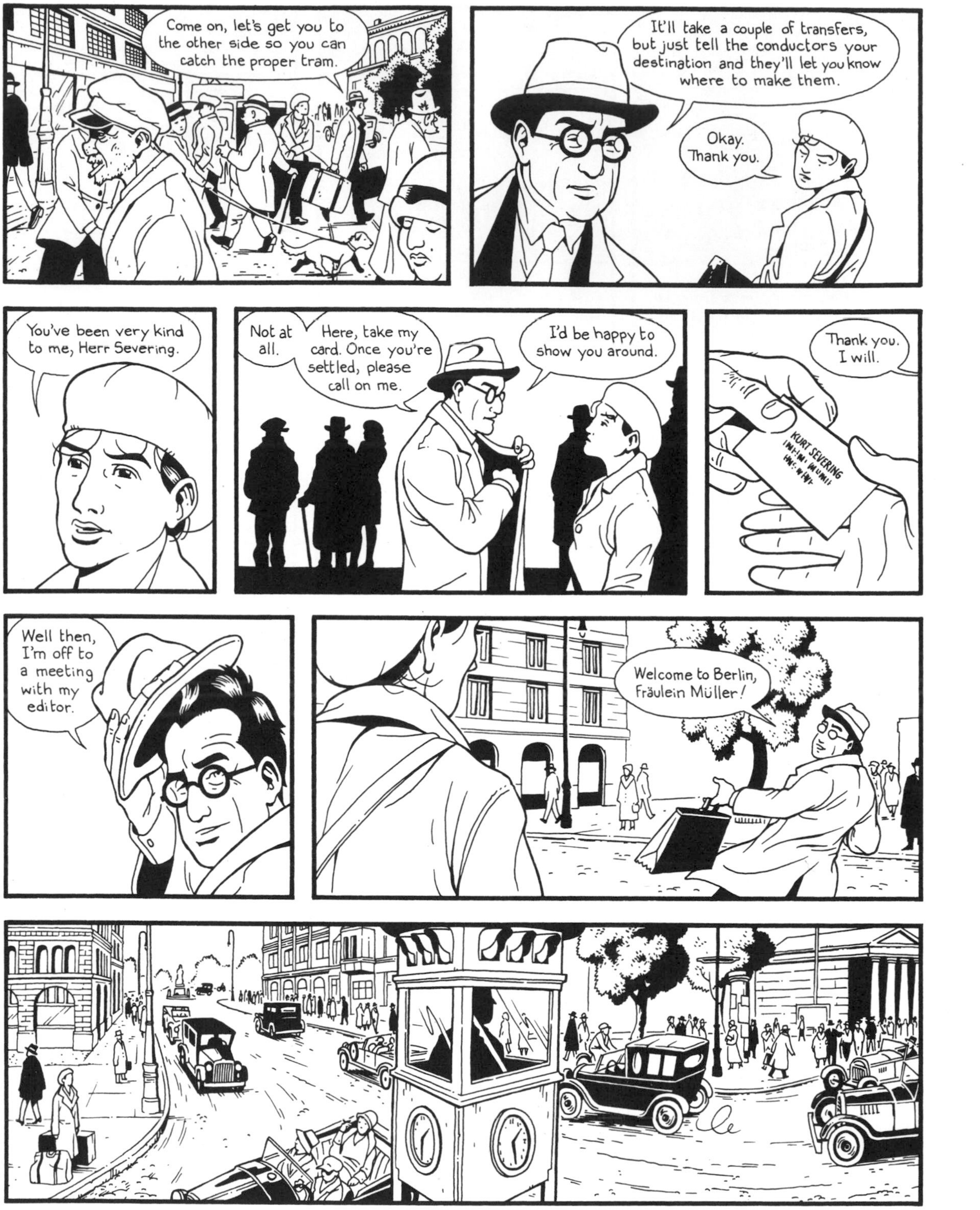
Come on, let's get you to the other side so you can catch the proper tram.
It'll take a couple of transfers, but just tell the conductors your destination and they'll let you know where to make them.
Okay. Thank you.
You've been very kind to me, Herr Severing.
Not at all.
Here, take my card. Once you're settled, please call on me.
I'd be happy to show you around.
Thank you. I will.
KURT SEVERING
Well then, I'm off to a meeting with my editor.
Welcome to Berlin, Fräulein Müller!

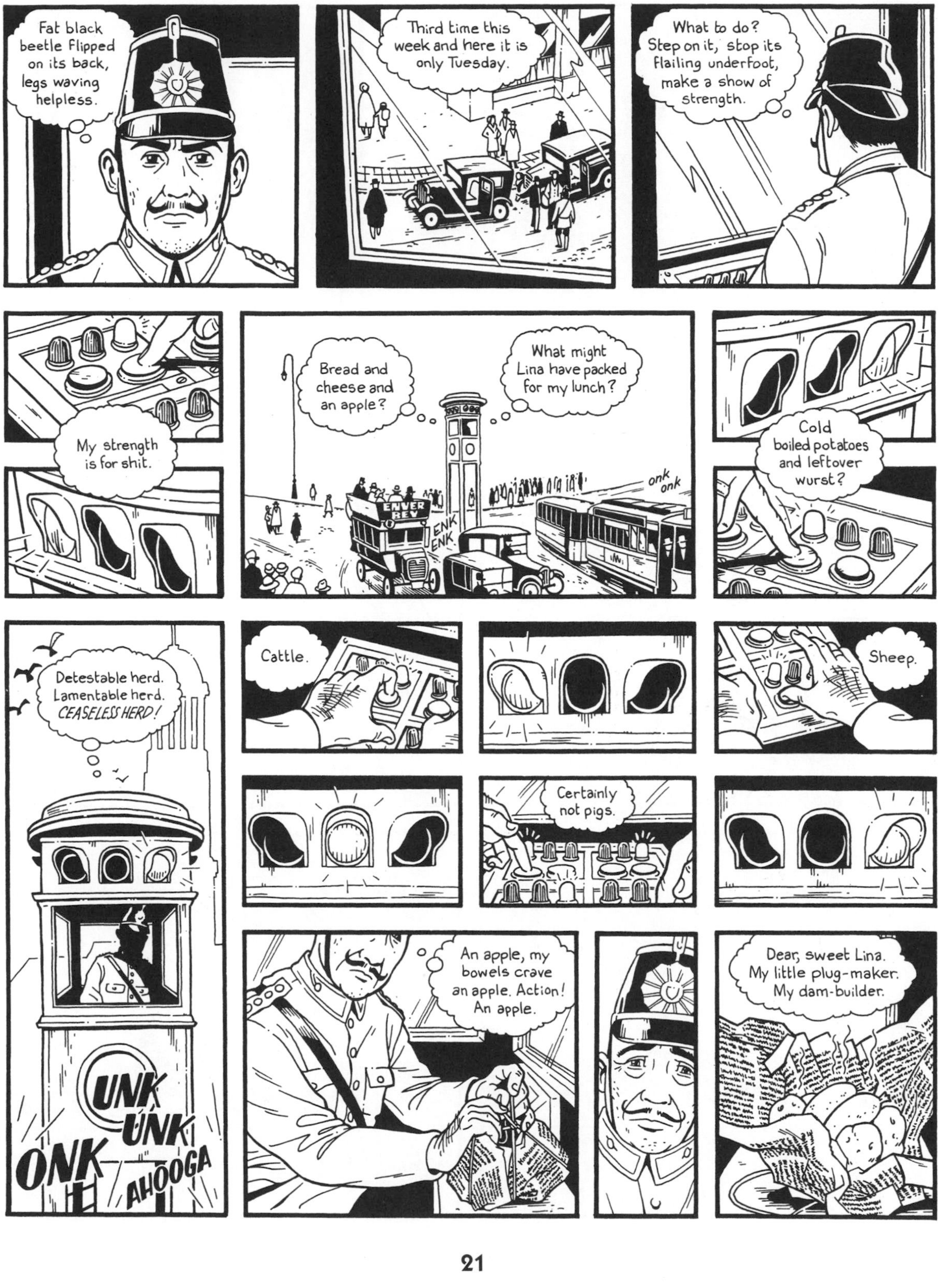
Fat black beetle flipped on its back, legs waving helpless.
Third time this week and here it is only Tuesday.
What to do? Step on it, stop its flailing underfoot, make a show of strength.
My strength is for shit.
Bread and cheese and an apple?
What might Lina have packed for my lunch?
ENVER BEY
ENK ENK
onk onk
Cold boiled potatoes and leftover wurst?
Detestable herd. Lamentable herd. CEASELESS HERD!
UNK UNK ONK AHOOGA
Cattle.
Sheep.
Certainly not pigs.
An apple, my bowels crave an apple. Action! An apple.
Dear, sweet Lina. My little plug-maker. My dam-builder.

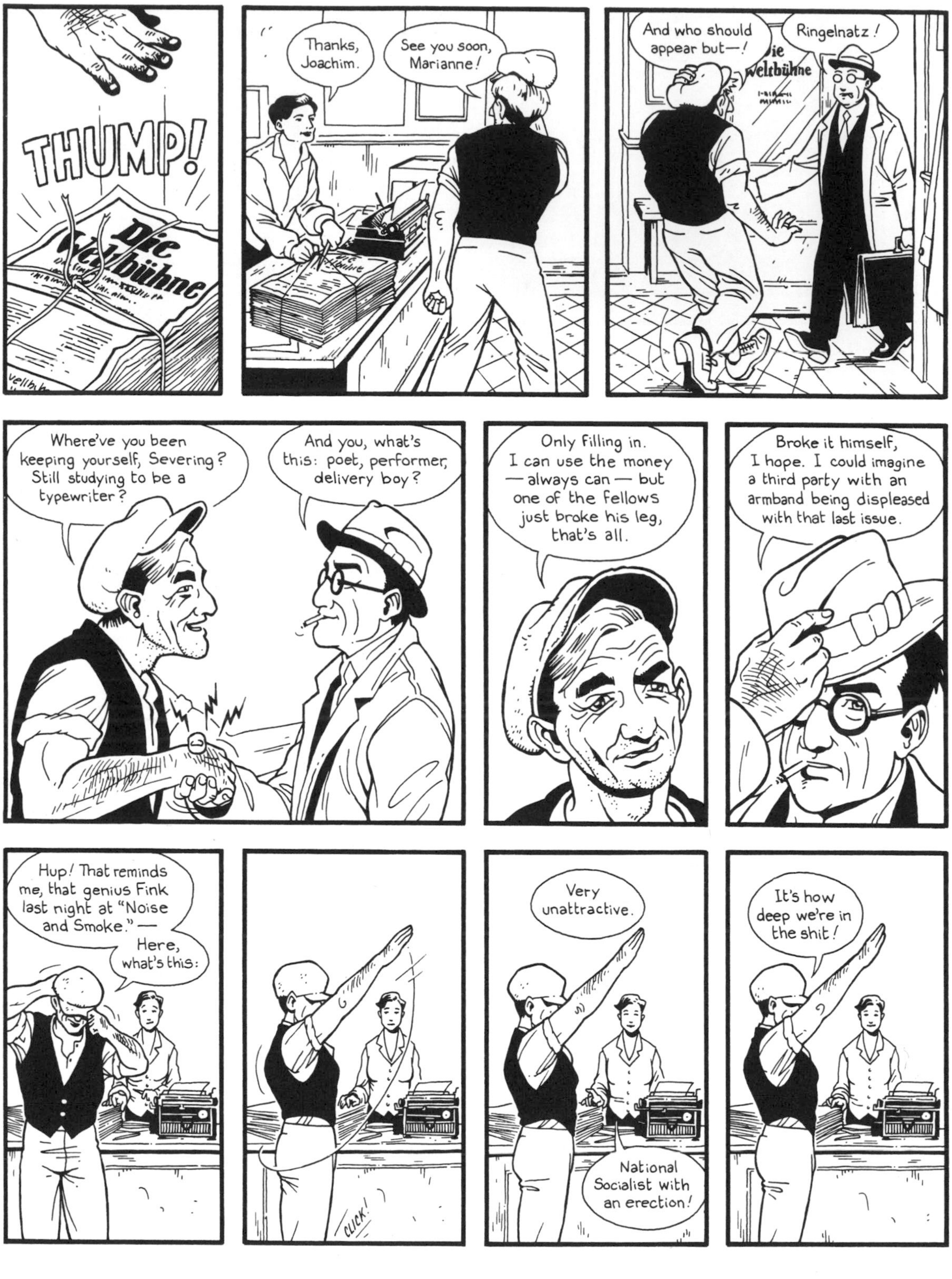
THUMP!
Die Weltbühne
Thanks, Joachim.
See you soon, Marianne!
And who should appear but—!
Ringelnatz!
Die Weltbühne
Where've you been keeping yourself, Severing? Still studying to be a typewriter?
And you, what's this: poet, performer, delivery boy?
Only filling in. I can use the money — always can — but one of the fellows just broke his leg, that's all.
Broke it himself, I hope. I could imagine a third party with an armband being displeased with that last issue.
Hup! That reminds me, that genius Fink last night at "Noise and Smoke." —
Here, what's this:
CLICK!
Very unattractive.
National Socialist with an erection!
It's how deep we're in the shit!

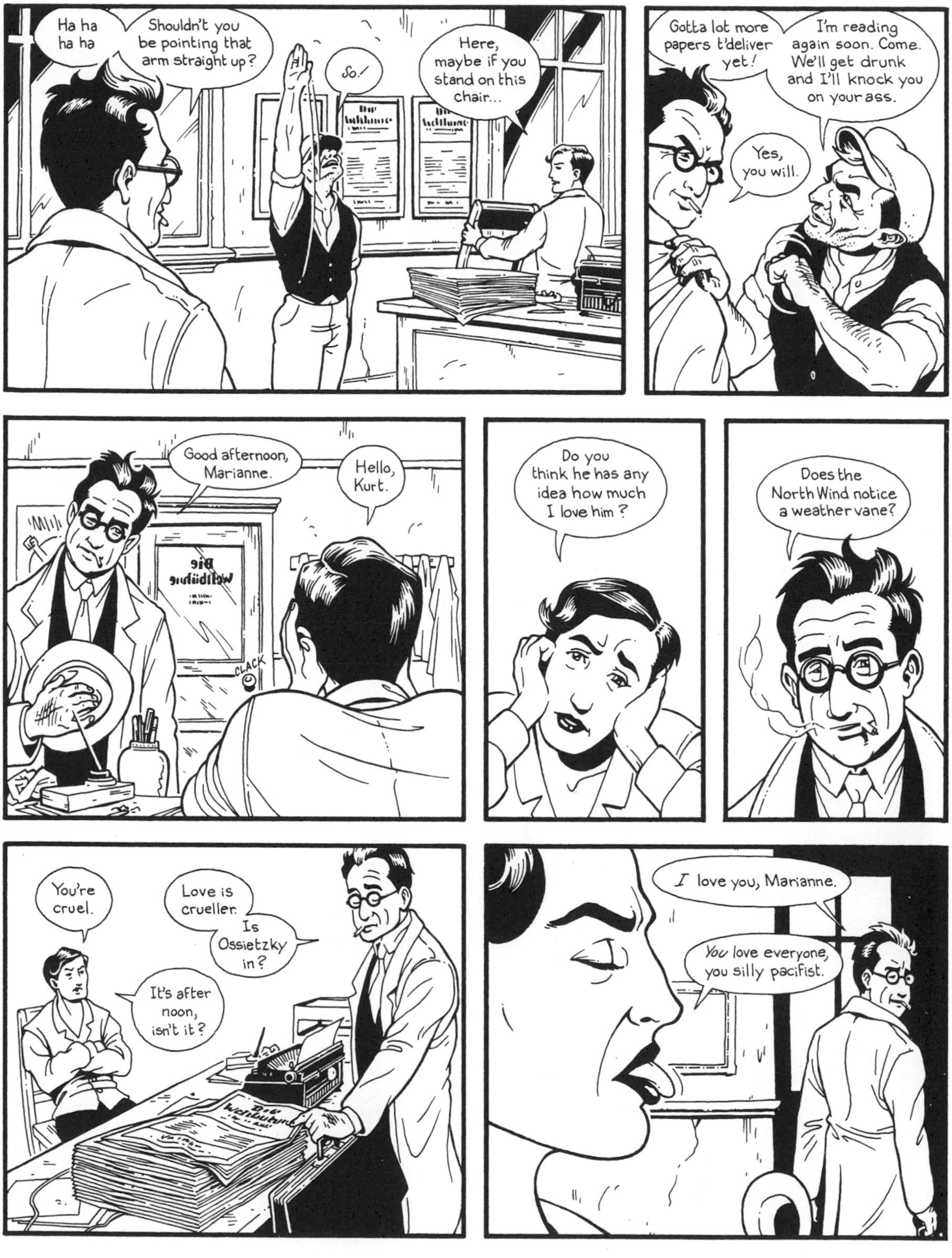
Ha ha ha ha
Shouldn't you be pointing that arm straight up?
So.!
Here, maybe if you stand on this chair...
Gotta lot more papers t'deliver yet!
I'm reading again soon. Come. We'll get drunk and I'll knock you on your ass.
Yes, you will.
Good afternoon, Marianne.
Hello, Kurt.
CLACK
Do you think he has any idea how much I love him?
Does the North Wind notice a weather vane?
You're cruel.
Love is crueller.
Is Ossietzky in?
It's after noon, isn't it?
I love you, Marianne.
You love everyone, you silly pacifist.

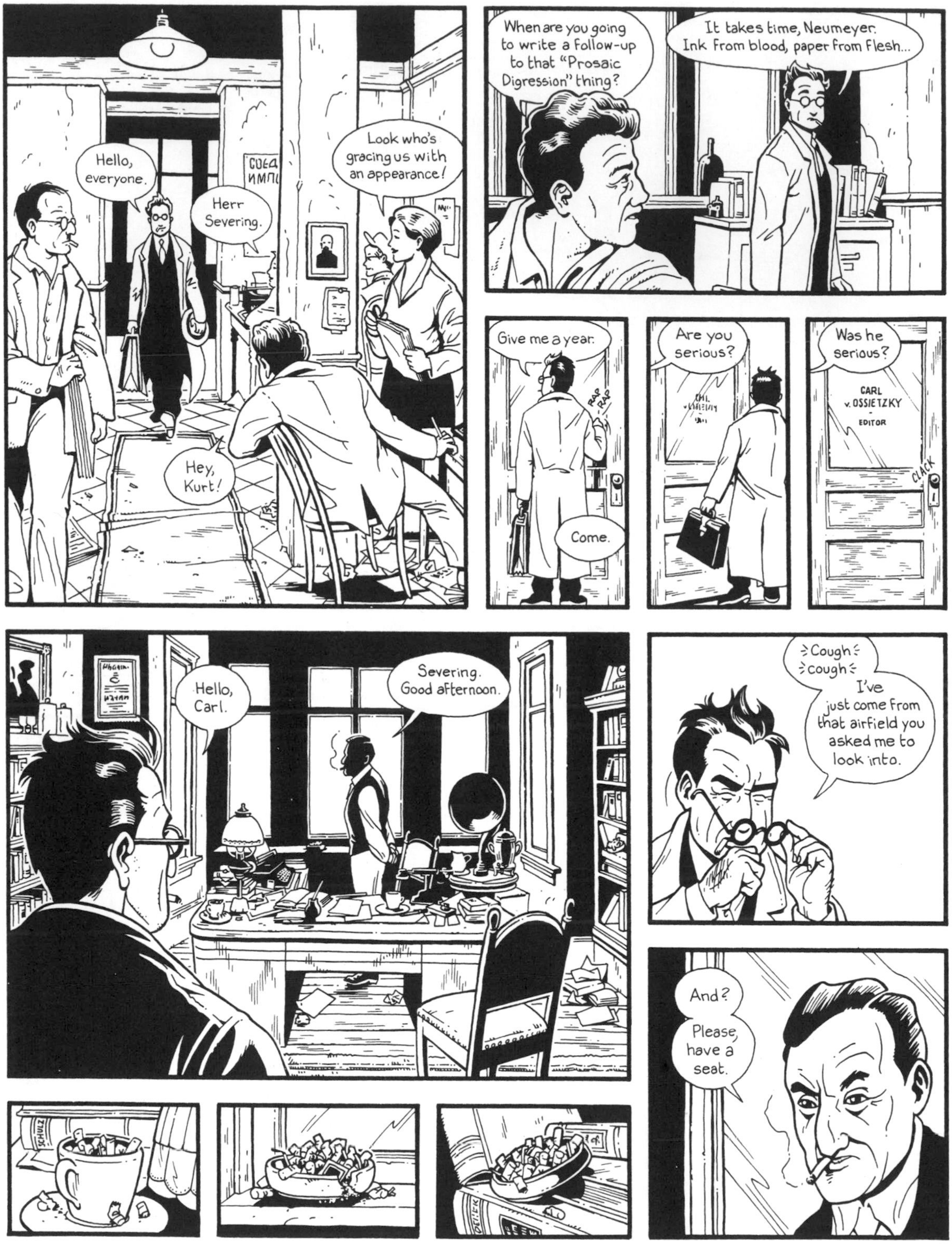
Hello, everyone.
Herr Severing.
Look who's gracing us with an appearance!
Hey, Kurt!
When are you going to write a follow-up to that "Prosaic Digression" thing?
It takes time, Neumeyer. Ink from blood, paper from flesh...
Give me a year.
RAP RAP
Come.
Are you serious?
Was he serious?
CARL v. OSSIETZKY - EDITOR
CLACK
Hello, Carl.
Severing. Good afternoon.
Cough cough
I've just come from that airfield you asked me to look into.
And?
Please, have a seat.

I'll only be a minute, thanks. I haven't been home yet.

Without a doubt, just as Kreiser contends, military planes are being tested there.

I counted around a dozen; there are probably more.

CARL v. OSSIETZK EDITOR

In direct violation of Versailles.

Germany is prohibited from maintaining an air arm.

Articles 198 through 203. Rearmament is illegal, without exception.

Even so, they have done little to conceal their actions.

Kreiser checked the Reichstag's budget commission reports from earlier in the year and found the project duly listed.

It's on the public record, but who's paying any attention to that? Once again it falls to us to remind the authorities of their responsibilities.

Glad to be of help. Oh, here. "Hot off the press."

We've been getting a lot of letters from angry poets thanks to your last piece. Will we be seeing your name on the cover again soon?

Die Weltbühne

Yes, yes. I'll have something new for you before long. I have to run. Good day.

CARL v. OSSIET EDITOR

CLACK

ding ding

37

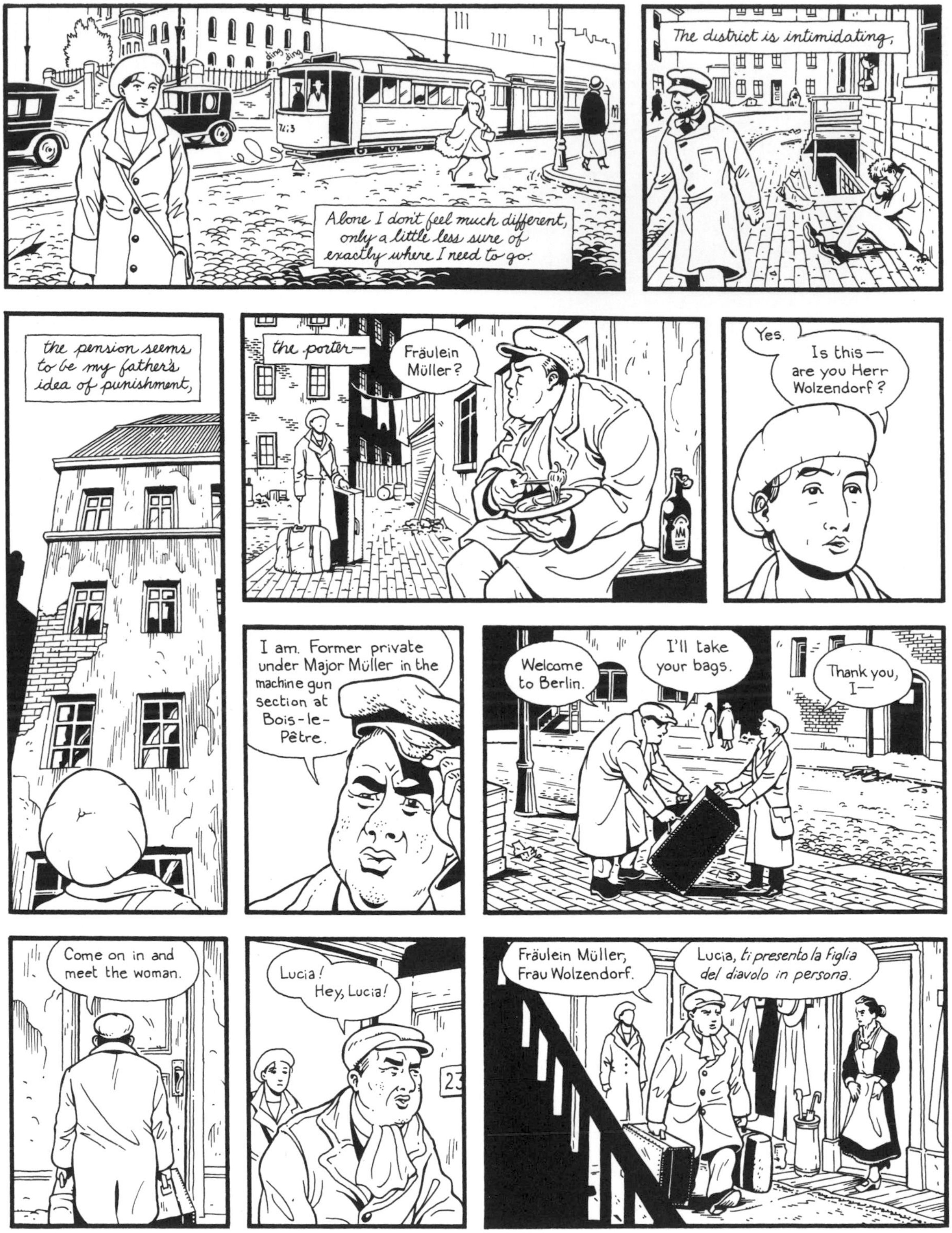
ding ding
Alone I don't feel much different, only a little less sure of exactly where I need to go.
The district is intimidating,
the pension seems to be my father's idea of punishment,
the porter—
Fräulein Müller?
Yes.
Is this— are you Herr Wolzendorf?
I am. Former private under Major Müller in the machine gun section at Bois-le-Pêtre.
Welcome to Berlin.
I'll take your bags.
Thank you, I—
Come on in and meet the woman.
Lucia! Hey, Lucia!
Fräulein Müller, Frau Wolzendorf.
Lucia, *ti presento la figlia del diavolo in persona.*

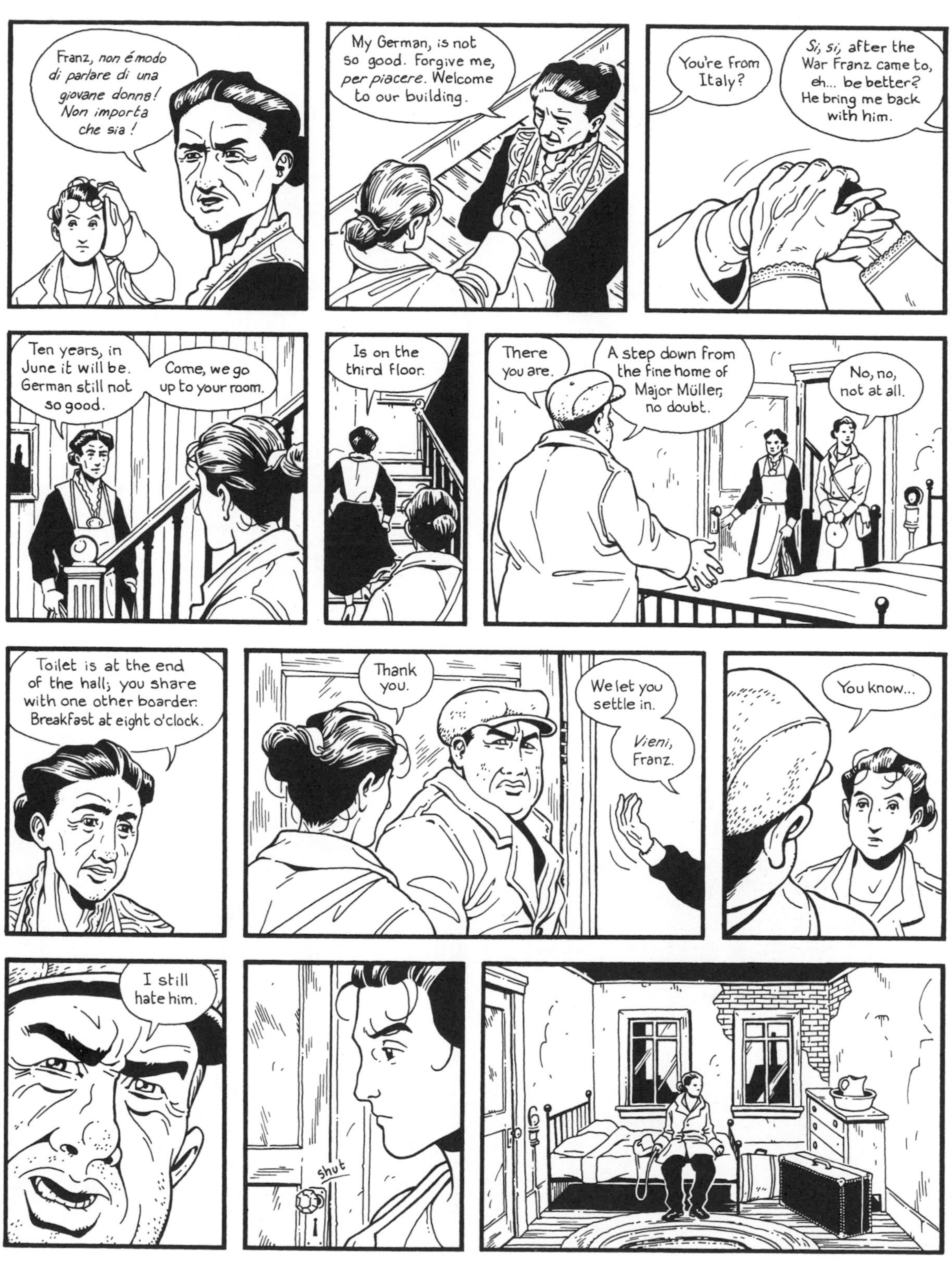
Franz, non é modo di parlare di una giovane donna! Non importa che sia!
My German, is not so good. Forgive me, per piacere. Welcome to our building.
You're from Italy?
Si, si, after the War Franz came to, eh... be better? He bring me back with him.
Ten years, in June it will be. German still not so good.
Come, we go up to your room.
Is on the third floor.
There you are.
A step down from the fine home of Major Müller, no doubt.
No, no, not at all.
Toilet is at the end of the hall; you share with one other boarder. Breakfast at eight o'clock.
Thank you.
We let you settle in.
Vieni, Franz.
You know...
I still hate him.
shut

sleeping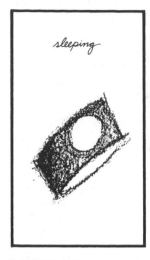

awake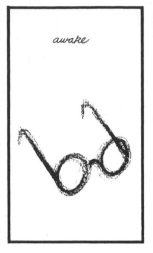

asking

telling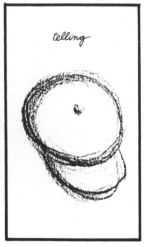

Today was filled with men, each of them seeming duty-bound in some way.

Herr S. was not unkind, but only Frau W. was truly warm.

I can't remember the last time I felt that from someone, and it's even more unexpected here.

From a stranger with as much reason to dislike me as her husband, for who my father is.

At this point in my life, far from what love I've known.

In this city.

28

2

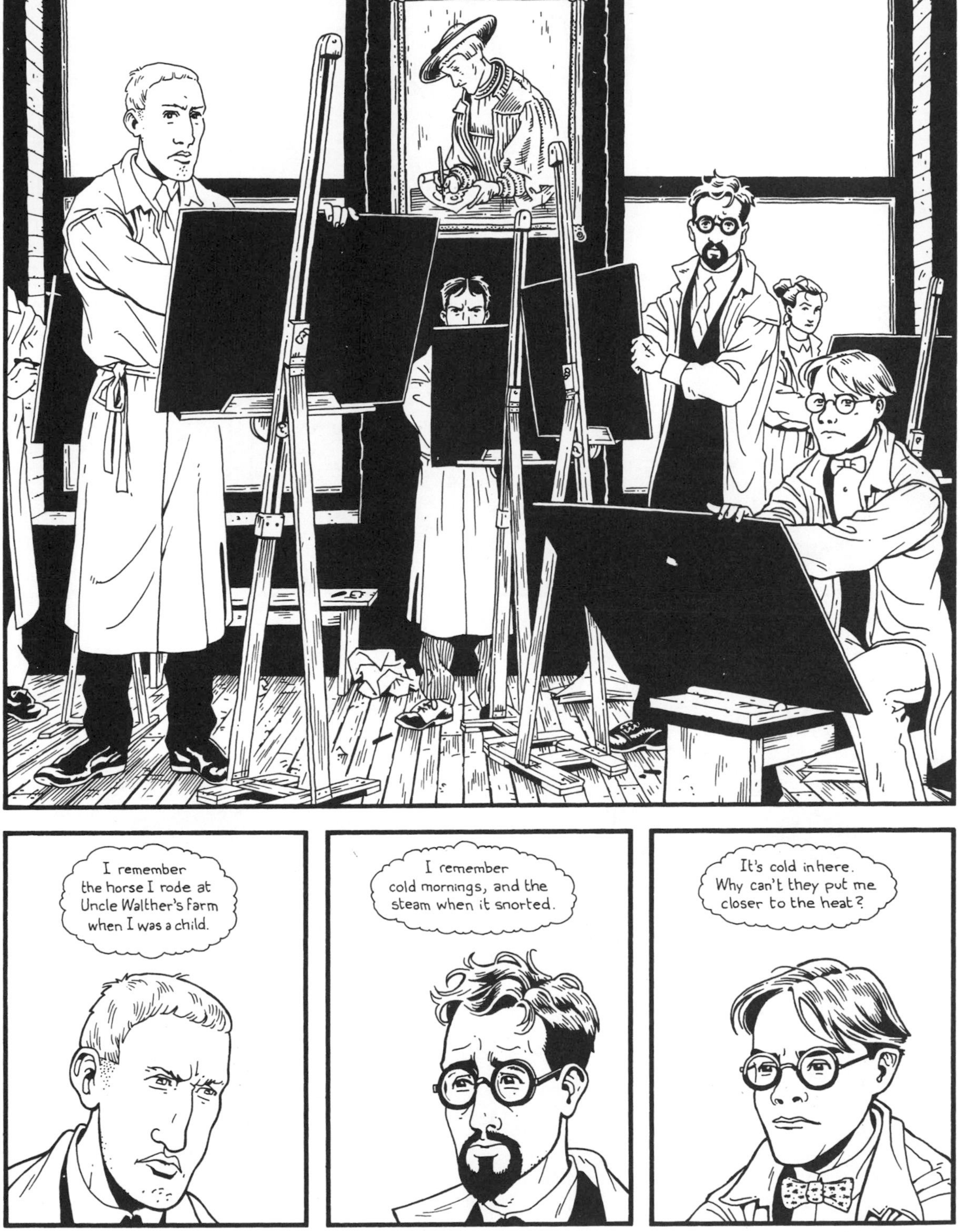
I remember the horse I rode at Uncle Walther's farm when I was a child.
I remember cold mornings, and the steam when it snorted.
It's cold in here. Why can't they put me closer to the heat?

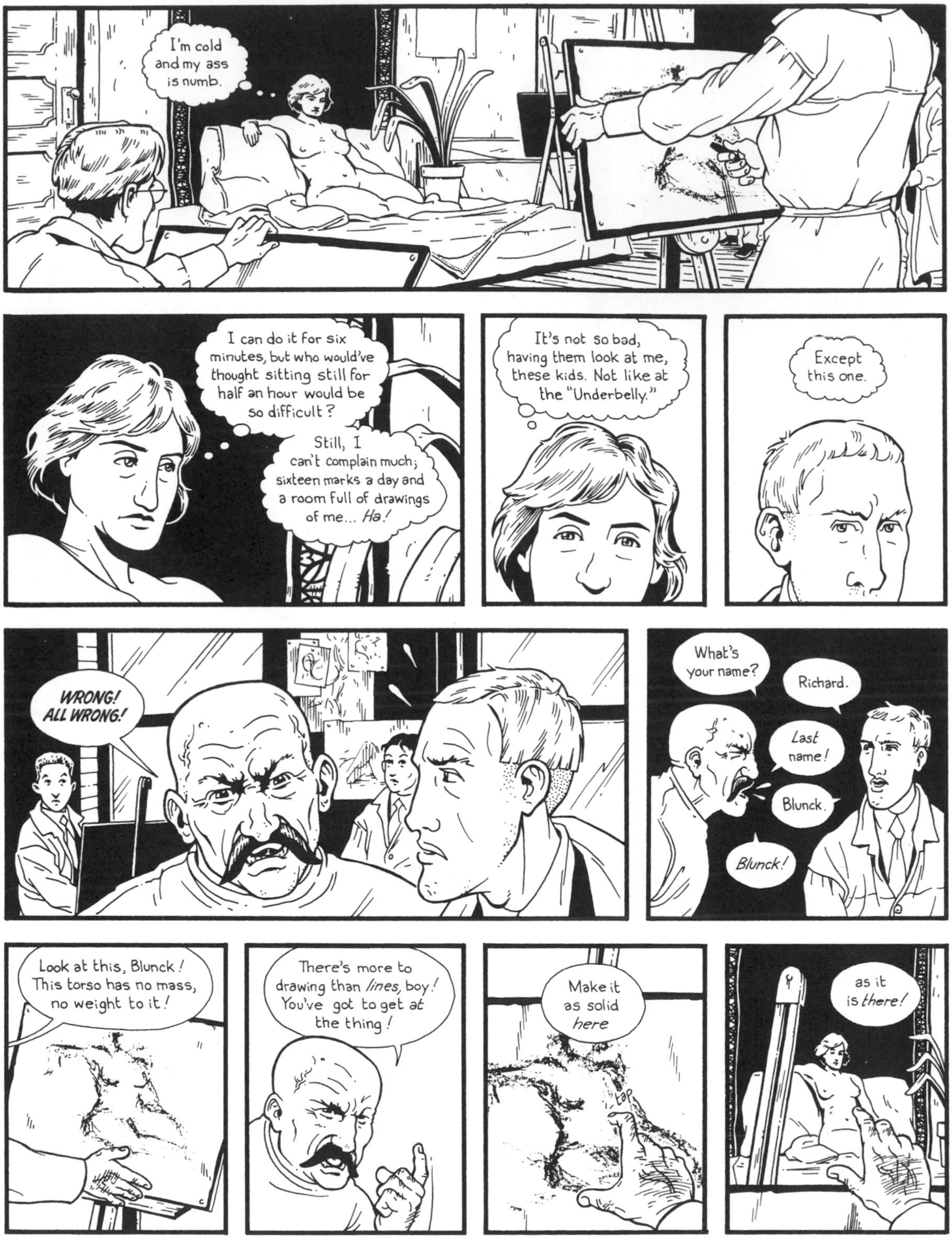
I'm cold and my ass is numb.
I can do it for six minutes, but who would've thought sitting still for half an hour would be so difficult?
Still, I can't complain much; sixteen marks a day and a room full of drawings of me... *Ha!*
It's not so bad, having them look at me, these kids. Not like at the "Underbelly."
Except this one.
WRONG! ALL WRONG!
What's your name?
Richard.
Last name!
Blunck.
Blunck!
Look at this, Blunck! This torso has no mass, no weight to it!
There's more to drawing than *lines*, boy! You've got to get *at* the thing!
Make it as solid *here*
tap
as it is *there!*

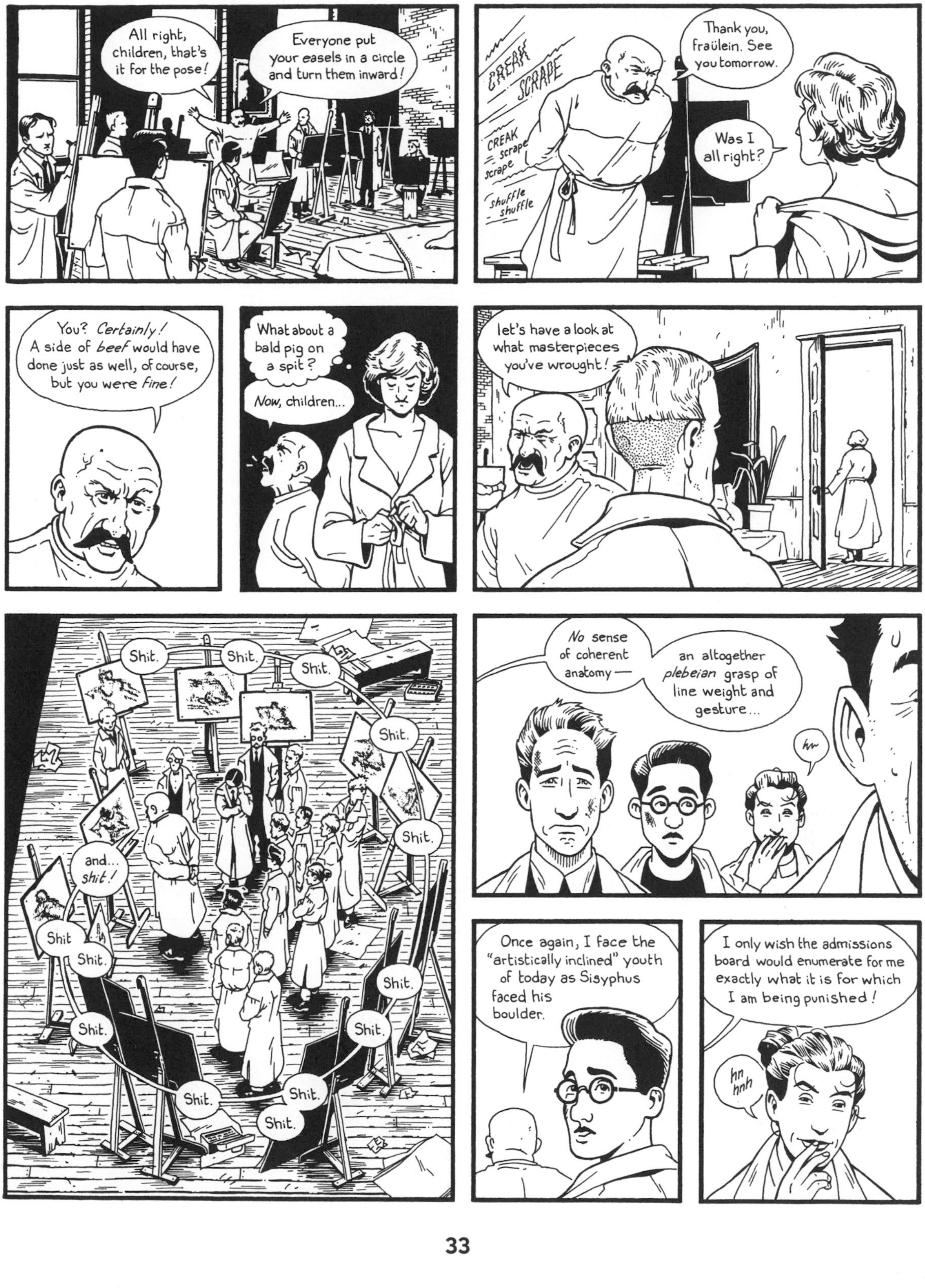
All right, children, that's it for the pose!
Everyone put your easels in a circle and turn them inward!
CREAK
SCRAPE
CREAK scrape scrape
shuffle shuffle
Thank you, fraülein. See you tomorrow.
Was I all right?
You? Certainly! A side of beef would have done just as well, of course, but you were fine!
What about a bald pig on a spit?
Now, children...
let's have a look at what masterpieces you've wrought!
Shit.
Shit.
Shit.
Shit.
Shit.
and... shit!
Shit
Shit.
Shit.
Shit.
Shit.
Shit.
Shit.
Shit.
No sense of coherent anatomy—
an altogether plebeian grasp of line weight and gesture...
hn
Once again, I face the "artistically inclined" youth of today as Sisyphus faced his boulder.
I only wish the admissions board would enumerate for me exactly what it is for which I am being punished!
hn hnh

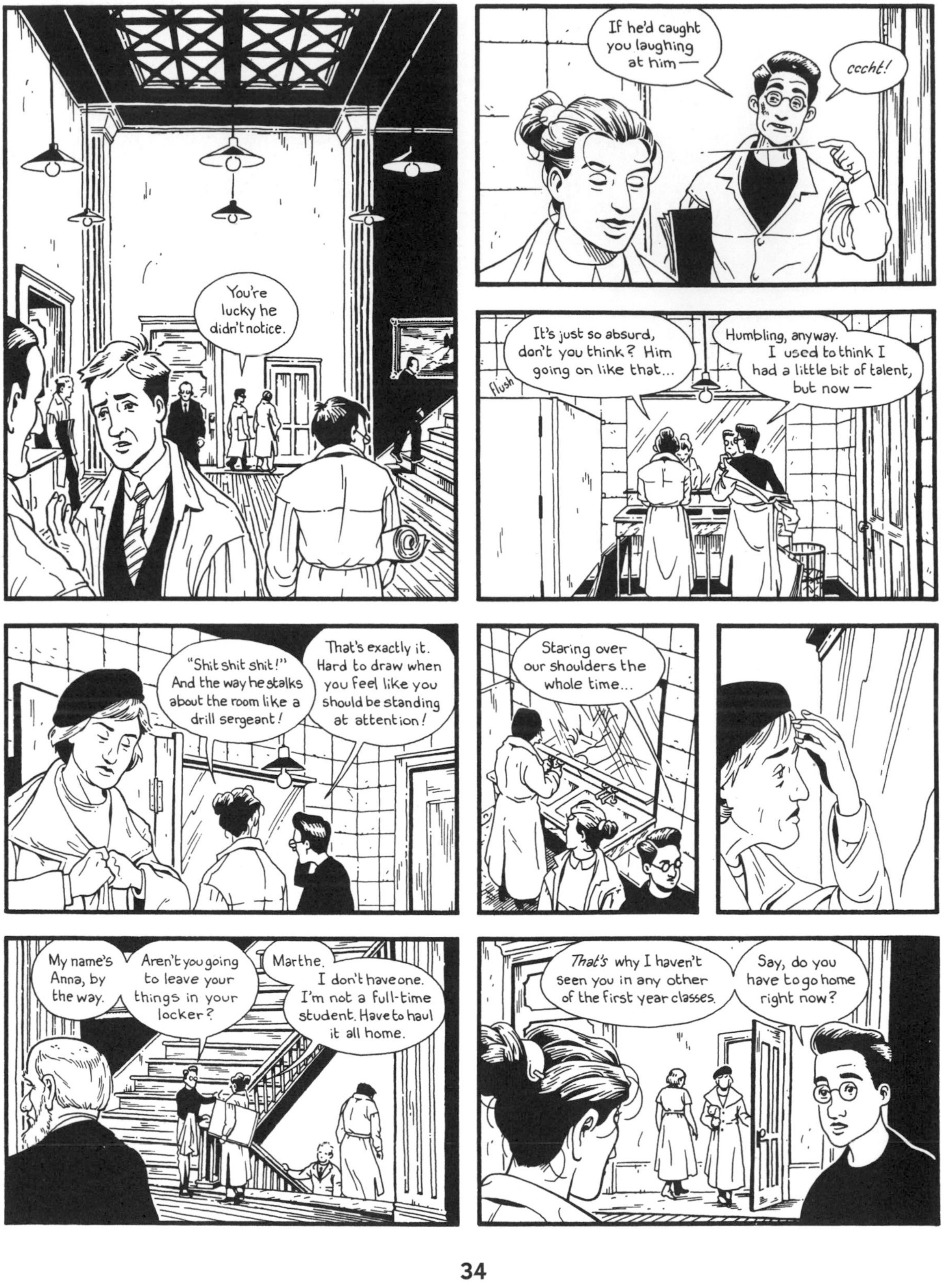
You're lucky he didn't notice.
If he'd caught you laughing at him—
cccht!
It's just so absurd, don't you think? Him going on like that...
flush
Humbling, anyway. I used to think I had a little bit of talent, but now—
"Shit shit shit!" And the way he stalks about the room like a drill sergeant!
That's exactly it. Hard to draw when you feel like you should be standing at attention!
Staring over our shoulders the whole time...
My name's Anna, by the way.
Aren't you going to leave your things in your locker?
Marthe.
I don't have one. I'm not a full-time student. Have to haul it all home.
That's why I haven't seen you in any other of the first year classes.
Say, do you have to go home right now?

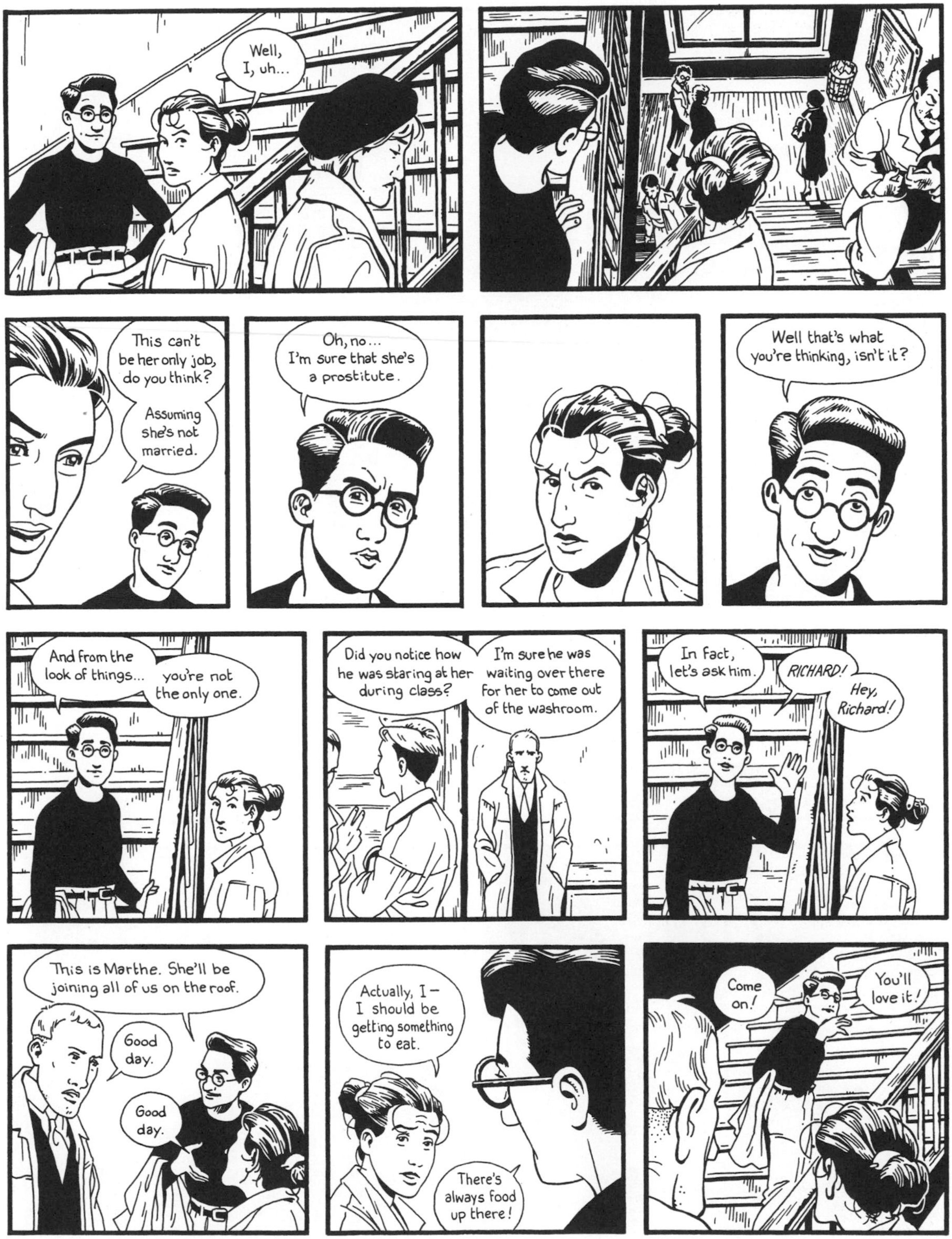

Well, I, uh...
This can't be her only job, do you think?
Assuming she's not married.
Oh, no... I'm sure that she's a prostitute.
Well that's what you're thinking, isn't it?
And from the look of things...
you're not the only one.
Did you notice how he was staring at her during class?
I'm sure he was waiting over there for her to come out of the washroom.
In fact, let's ask him.
RICHARD!
Hey, Richard!
This is Marthe. She'll be joining all of us on the roof.
Good day.
Good day.
Actually, I— I should be getting something to eat.
There's always food up there!
Come on!
You'll love it!

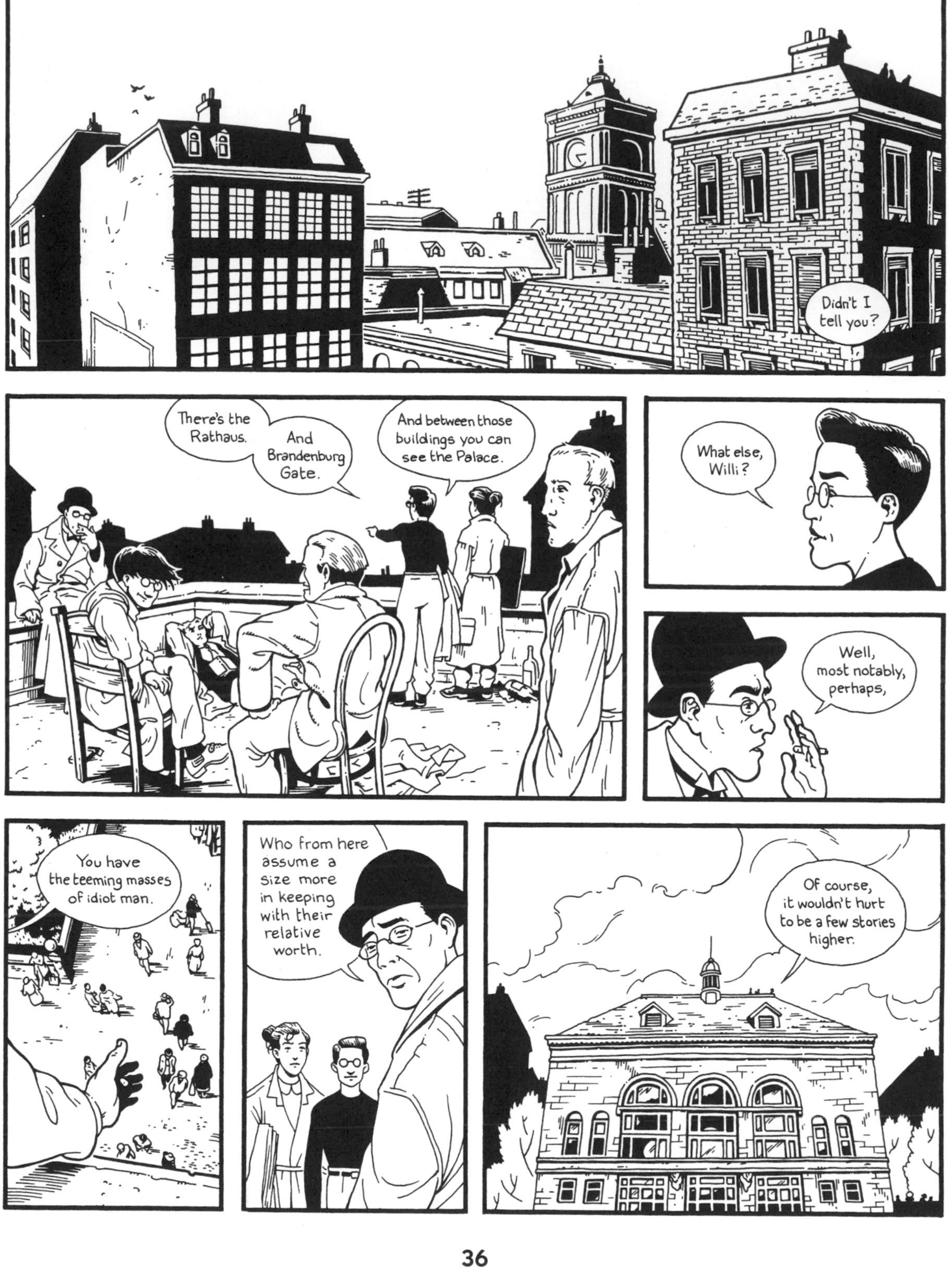
Didn't I tell you?
There's the Rathaus.
And Brandenburg Gate.
And between those buildings you can see the Palace.
What else, Willi?
Well, most notably, perhaps,
You have the teeming masses of idiot man.
Who from here assume a size more in keeping with their relative worth.
Of course, it wouldn't hurt to be a few stories higher.

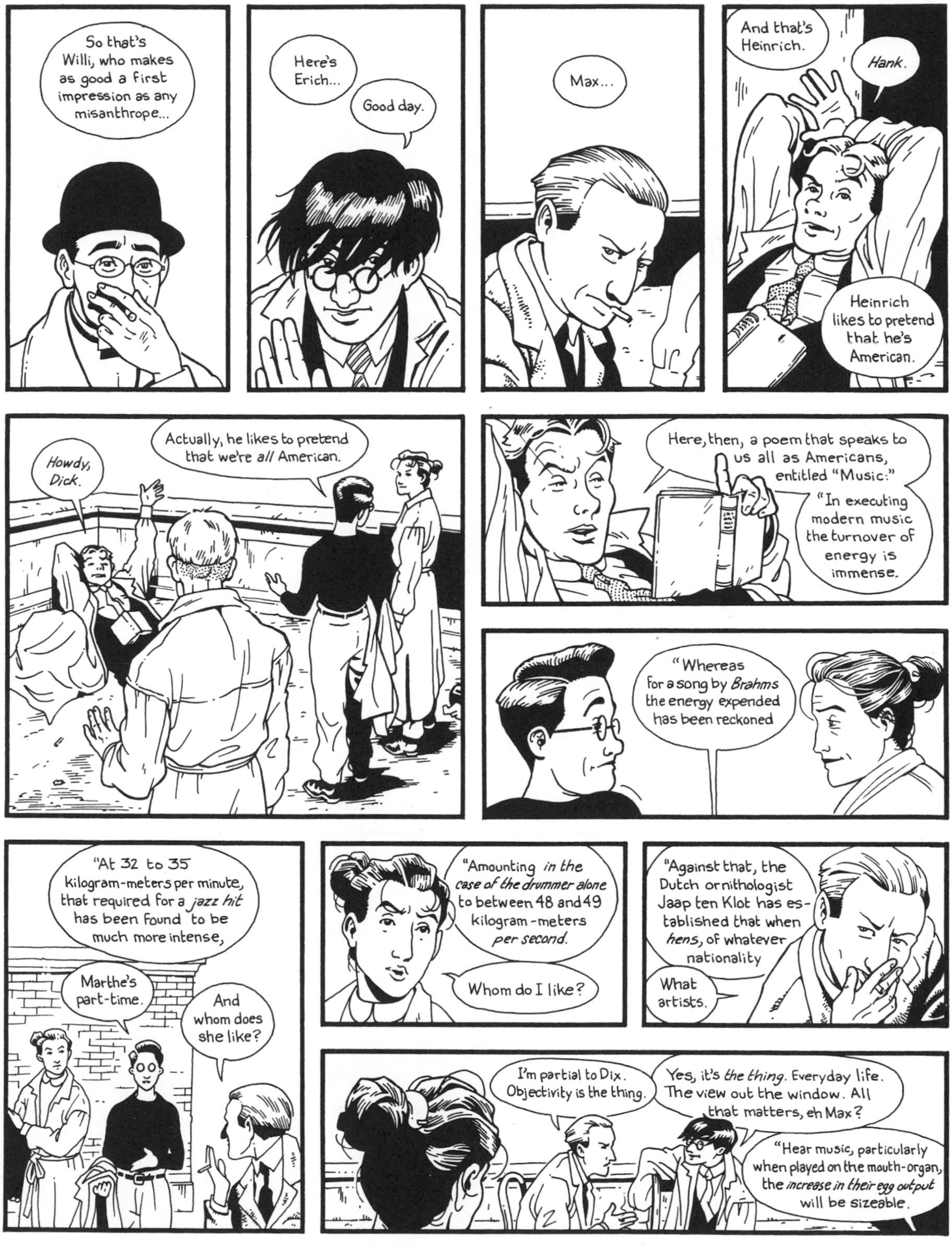
So that's Willi, who makes as good a first impression as any misanthrope...
Here's Erich...
Good day.
Max...
And that's Heinrich.
Hank.
Heinrich likes to pretend that he's American.
Howdy, Dick.
Actually, he likes to pretend that we're all American.
Here, then, a poem that speaks to us all as Americans, entitled "Music:"
"In executing modern music the turnover of energy is immense.
"Whereas for a song by Brahms the energy expended has been reckoned
"At 32 to 35 kilogram-meters per minute, that required for a jazz hit has been found to be much more intense,
Marthe's part-time.
And whom does she like?
"Amounting in the case of the drummer alone to between 48 and 49 kilogram-meters per second.
Whom do I like?
"Against that, the Dutch ornithologist Jaap ten Klot has established that when hens, of whatever nationality
What artists.
I'm partial to Dix. Objectivity is the thing.
Yes, it's the thing. Everyday life. The view out the window. All that matters, eh Max?
"Hear music, particularly when played on the mouth-organ, the increase in their egg output will be sizeable.

"So in view of its admirably hygenic effects on both animal and human vitality"

Precisely. The world in all of its ugliness.

The Expressionists had it all wrong!

—and here's the important part—

Emotion clouds our view of the world as it really is! *That* is what we must document!

"A certain amount of musical activity would be by no means inadvisable."

And what you're exhibiting currently, Max— Is this objectivity or emotion?

But...

...

Wait! Wait, I know, I know!

Where is it, where is it...?

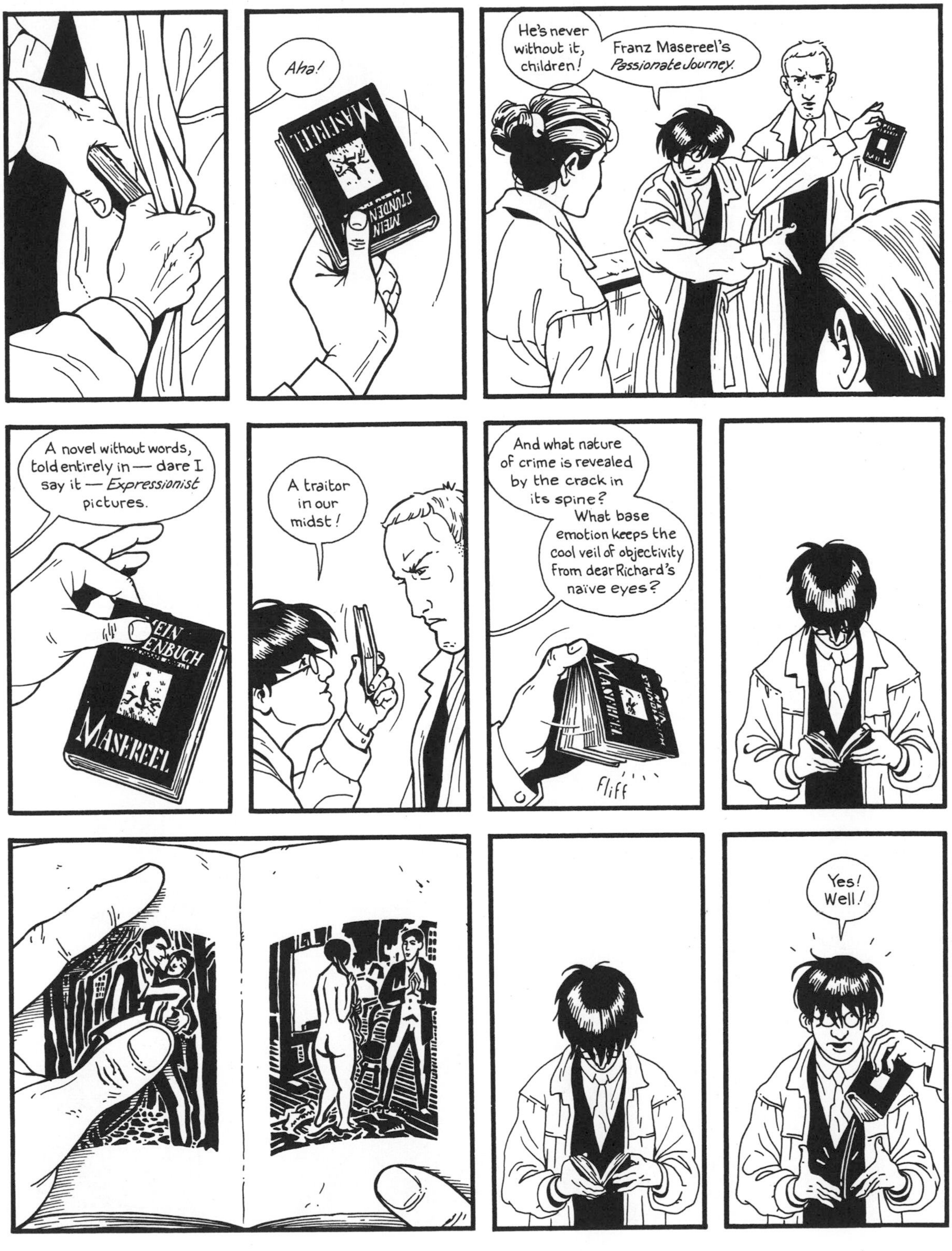
Aha!
He's never without it, children!
Franz Masereel's *Passionate Journey.*
A novel without words, told entirely in — dare I say it — *Expressionist* pictures.
A traitor in our midst!
And what nature of crime is revealed by the crack in its spine?
What base emotion keeps the cool veil of objectivity from dear Richard's naïve eyes?
Fliff
Yes! Well!

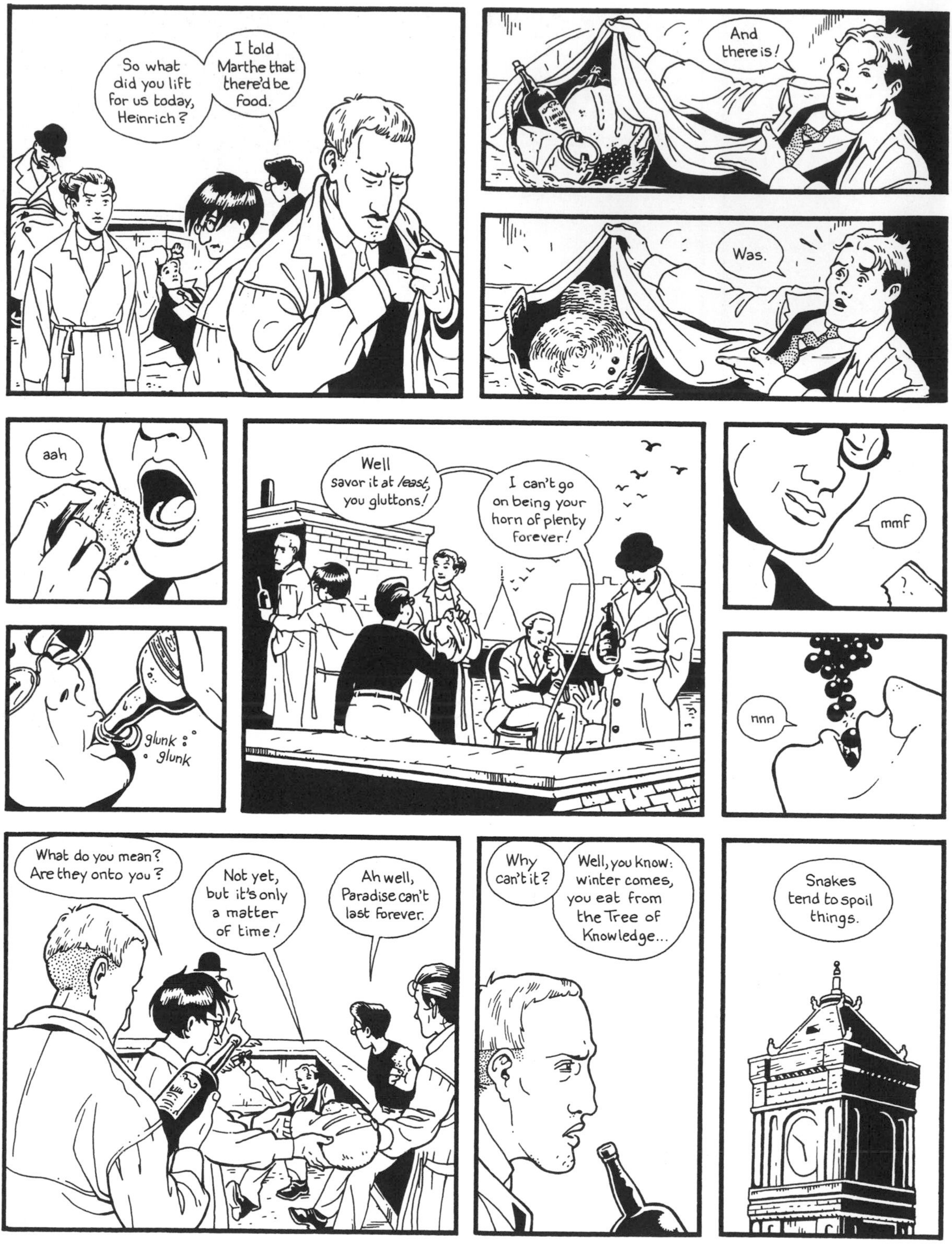
So what did you lift for us today, Heinrich?
I told Marthe that there'd be food.
And there is!
Was.
aah
glunk glunk
Well savor it at *least*, you gluttons!
I can't go on being your horn of plenty forever!
mmf
nnn
What do you mean? Are they onto you?
Not yet, but it's only a matter of time!
Ah well, Paradise can't last forever.
Why can't it?
Well, you know: winter comes, you eat from the Tree of Knowledge...
Snakes tend to spoil things.

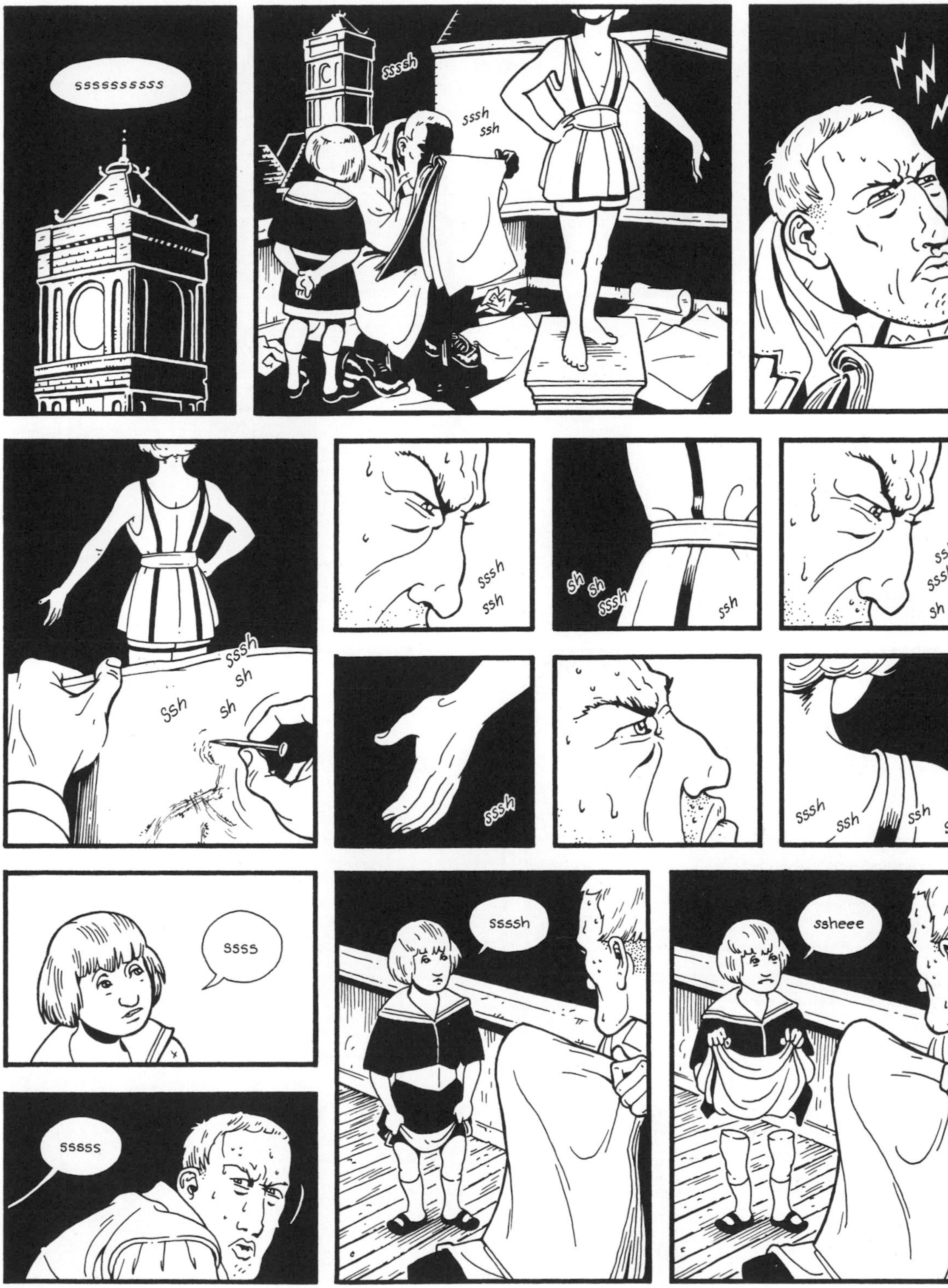
ssssssssss
ssssh
sssh
ssh
sssh
sh
ssh
sh
sssh
ssh
sh
sh
sssh
ssh
ssh
sssh
sh
sh
sssh
ssh
ssh
sh
ssss
sssss
ssssh
ssheee

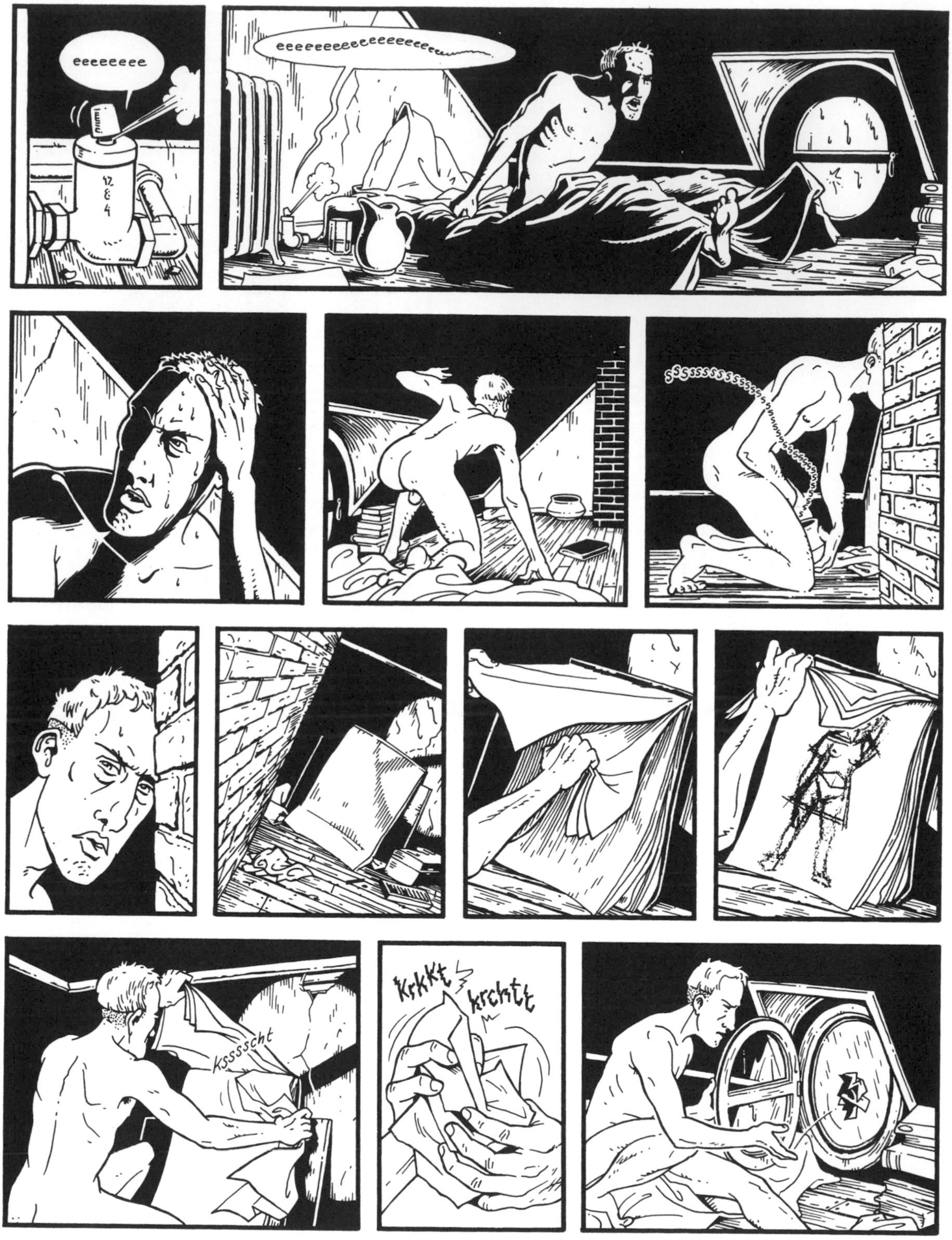
eeeeeeee
eeeeeeeeeeeeeeeee
12
8
4
SSSSSSSSSSSSSSS
Kssssscht
KrkKt
krchtt

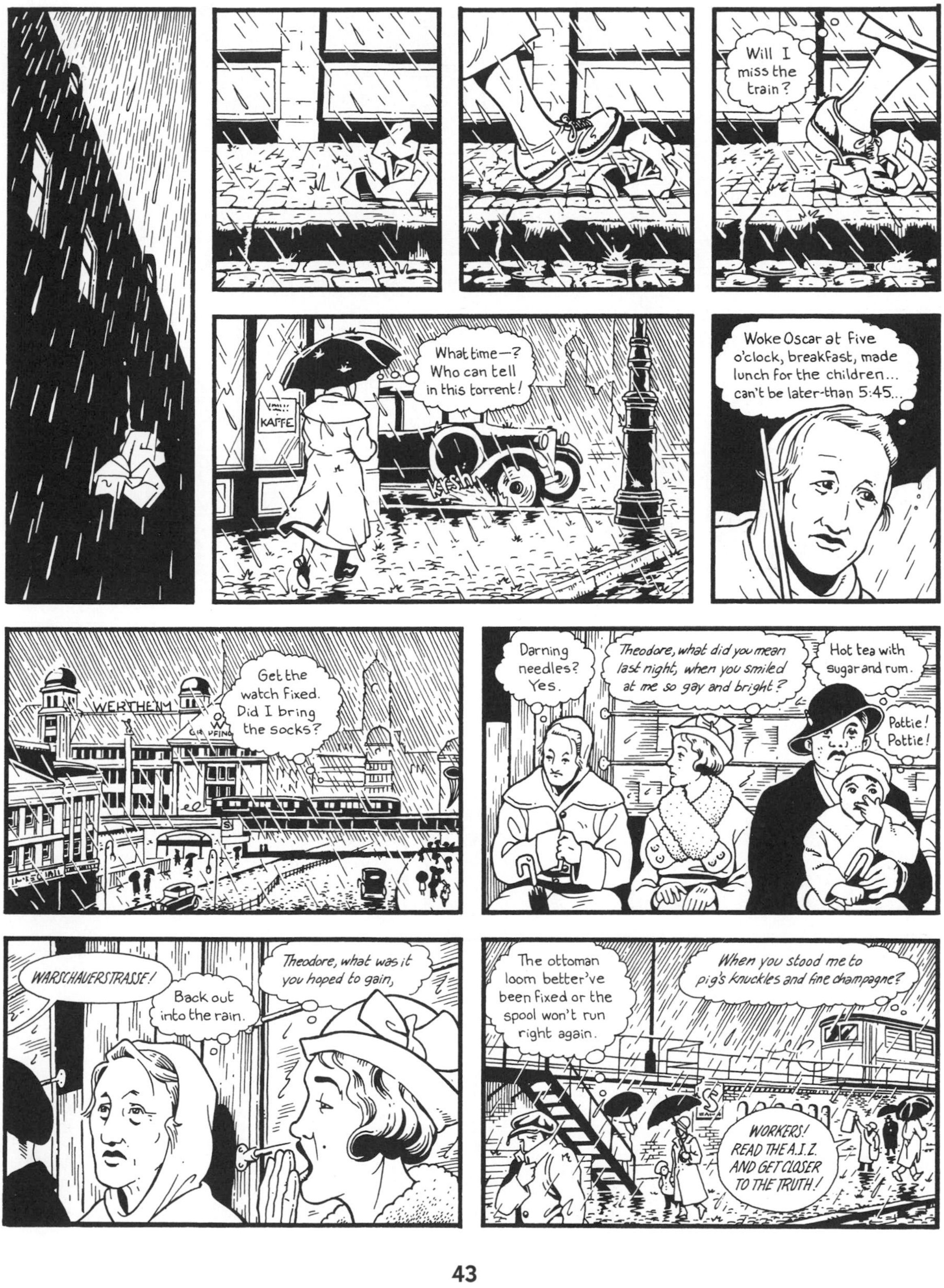

Will I miss the train?
What time—? Who can tell in this torrent!
KAFFE
KRSH
Woke Oscar at five o'clock, breakfast, made lunch for the children... can't be later-than 5:45...
WERTHEIM
Get the watch fixed. Did I bring the socks?
Darning needles? Yes.
Theodore, what did you mean last night, when you smiled at me so gay and bright?
Hot tea with sugar and rum.
Pottie! Pottie!
WARSCHAUERSTRASSE!
Back out into the rain.
Theodore, what was it you hoped to gain,
The ottoman loom better've been fixed or the spool won't run right again.
When you stood me to pig's knuckles and fine champagne?
WORKERS! READ THE A.I.Z. AND GET CLOSER TO THE TRUTH!

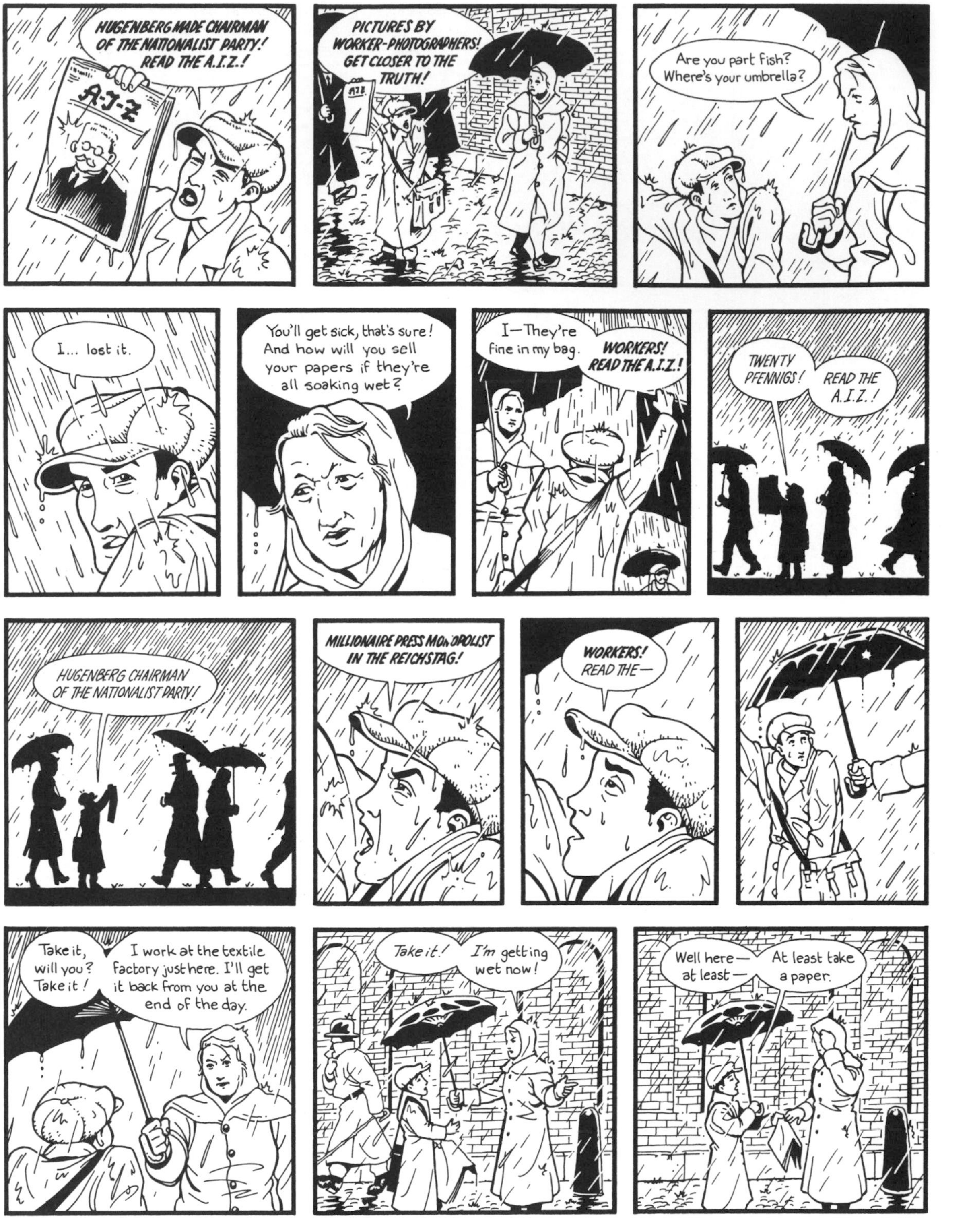
HUGENBERG MADE CHAIRMAN OF THE NATIONALIST PARTY! READ THE A.I.Z.!
A-I-Z
PICTURES BY WORKER-PHOTOGRAPHERS! GET CLOSER TO THE TRUTH!
Are you part fish? Where's your umbrella?
I... lost it.
You'll get sick, that's sure! And how will you sell your papers if they're all soaking wet?
I—They're fine in my bag.
WORKERS! READ THE A.I.Z.!
TWENTY PFENNIGS!
READ THE A.I.Z.!
HUGENBERG CHAIRMAN OF THE NATIONALIST PARTY!
MILLIONAIRE PRESS MONOPOLIST IN THE REICHSTAG!
WORKERS! READ THE—
Take it, will you? Take it!
I work at the textile factory just here. I'll get it back from you at the end of the day.
Take it!
I'm getting wet now!
Well here— at least—
At least take a paper.

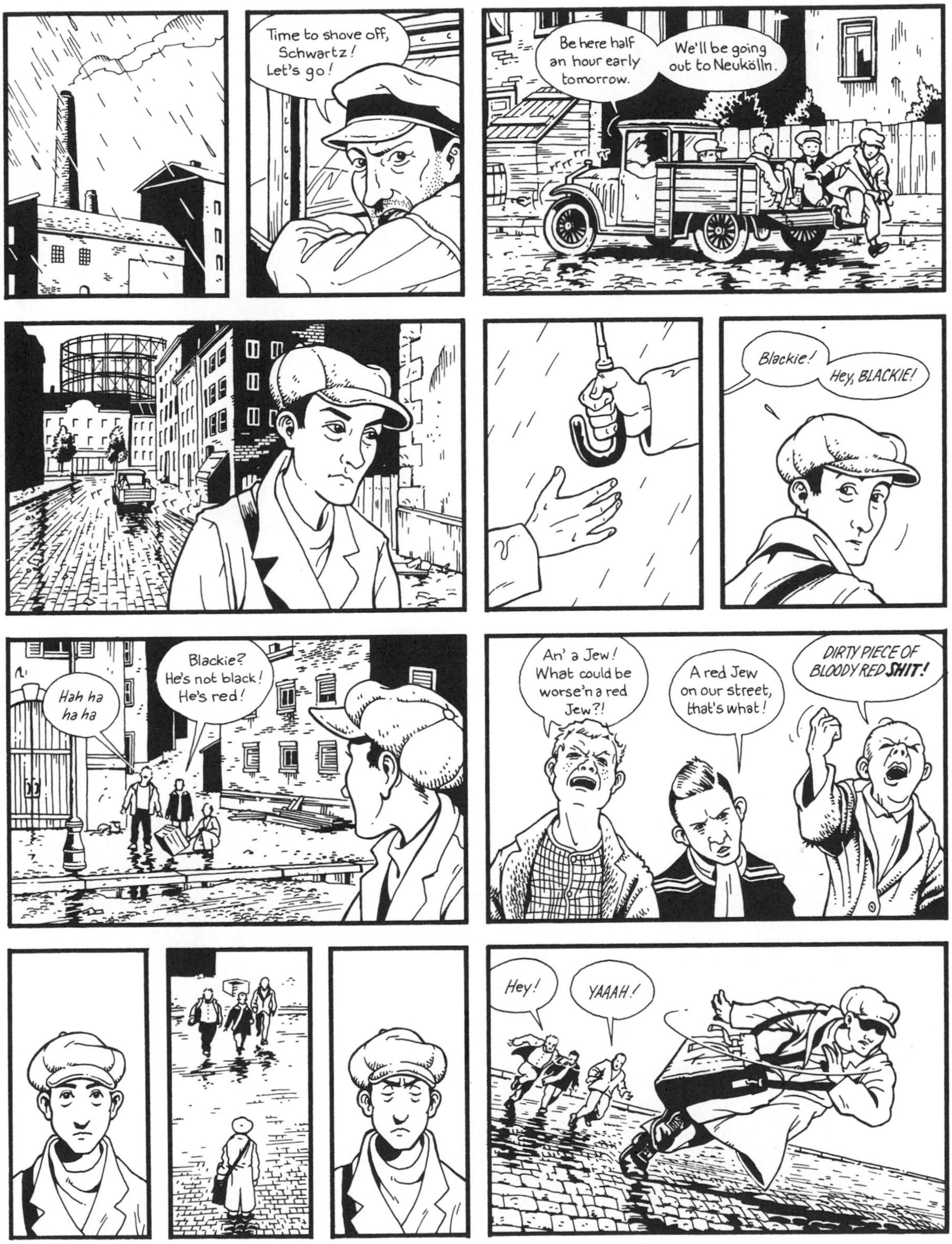
Time to shove off, Schwartz! Let's go!
Be here half an hour early tomorrow.
We'll be going out to Neukölln.
rrrr rrr
Blackie!
Hey, BLACKIE!
Hah ha ha ha
Blackie? He's not black! He's red!
An' a Jew! What could be worse'n a red Jew?!
A red Jew on our street, that's what!
DIRTY PIECE OF BLOODY RED SHIT!
Hey!
YAAAH!

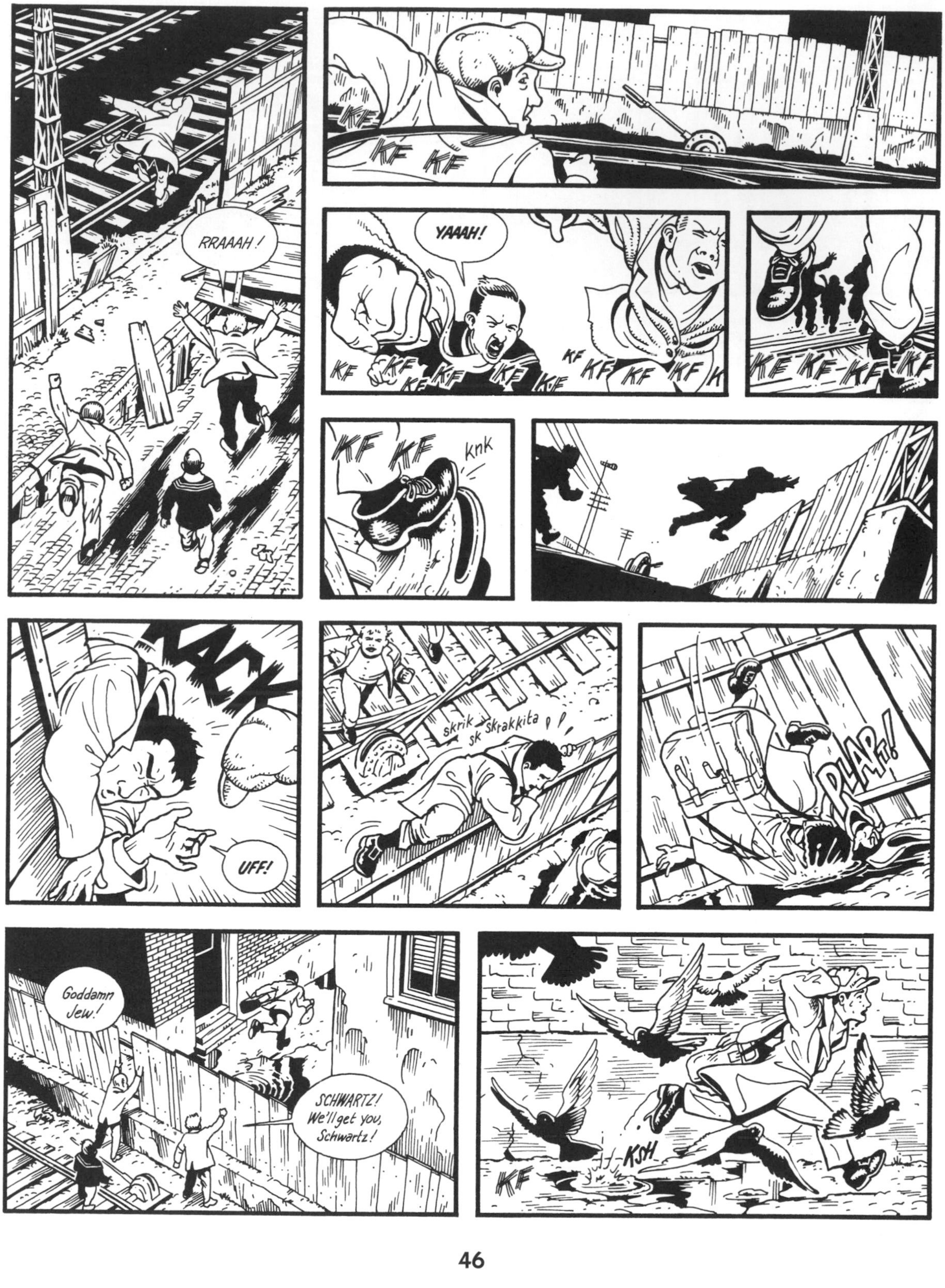
RRAAAH!
KF
KF KF
YAAAH!
KF KF KF KF KF KF KF KF KF KF K
KF KF KF KF
KF KF
knk
UFF!
skrik sk skrakkita
Goddamn Jew!
SCHWARTZ! We'll get you, Schwartz!
KSH
KF

And this candlestick, does it have a mate?

Well, I see it as more of a centerpiece...

In the middle of a mantel, on a coffee table...

Whoever heard of such a thing?

What a ridiculous notion: a candlestick standing alone!

Yes, well you see, it's commemorative, specially made...

the finest silver electroplate.

What happened to you, David, all wet and muddy?

Your mother — Oy, the fit she'll throw, between this and the umbrella!

Have you told her about the umbrella?

No, no, that's for —

Me to tell.

CLACK

JOUDINI
UFF INI & PRISON BURIAL.
·NON 1912·
Circus Corty Althoff

JG & PRISON B

HOUDIN

47

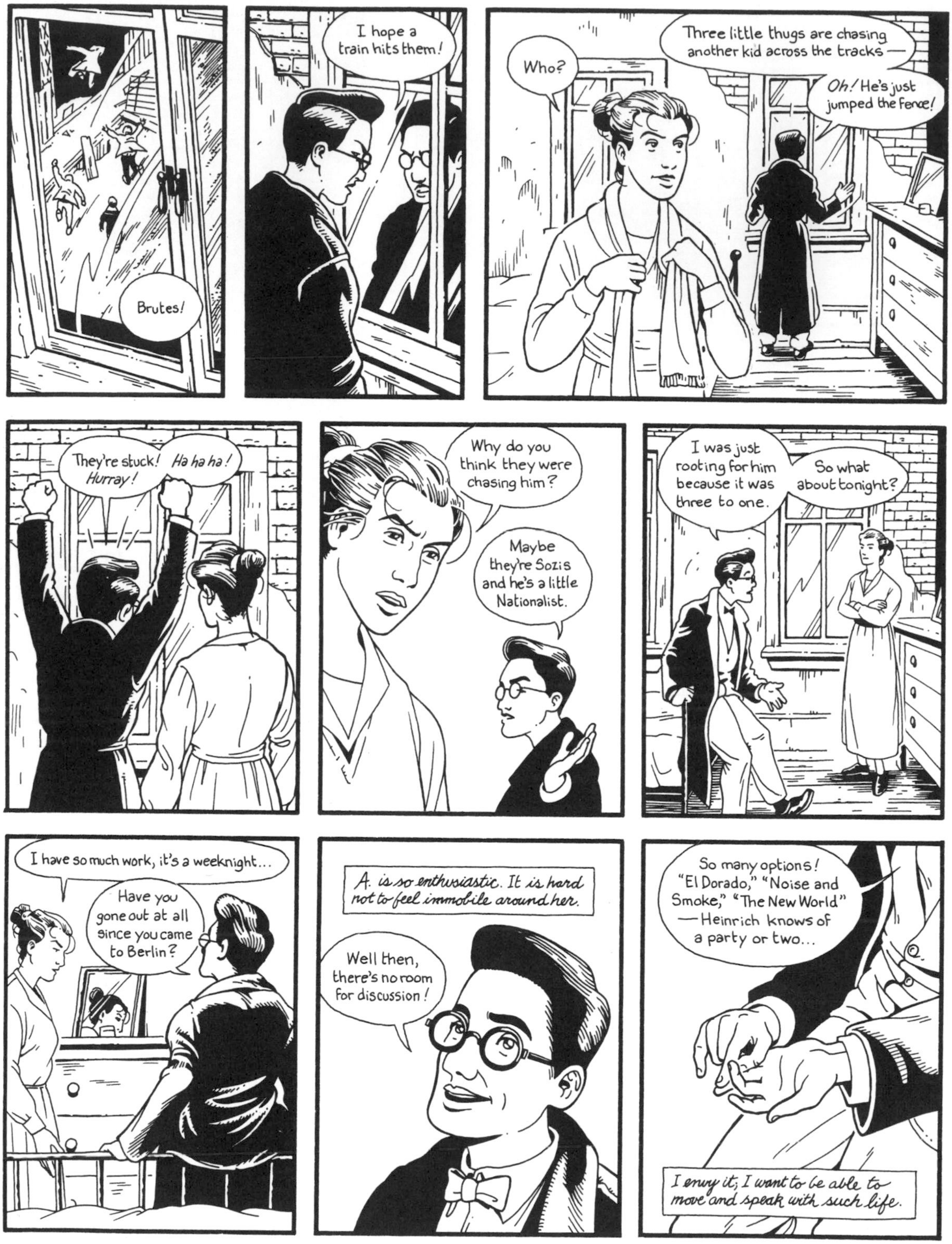
Brutes!
I hope a train hits them!
Who?
Three little thugs are chasing another kid across the tracks —
Oh! He's just jumped the fence!
They're stuck! Hurray!
Ha ha ha!
Why do you think they were chasing him?
Maybe they're Sozis and he's a little Nationalist.
I was just rooting for him because it was three to one.
So what about tonight?
I have so much work, it's a weeknight...
Have you gone out at all since you came to Berlin?
A. is so enthusiastic. It is hard not to feel immobile around her.
Well then, there's no room for discussion!
So many options! "El Dorado," "Noise and Smoke," "The New World" — Heinrich knows of a party or two...
I envy it; I want to be able to move and speak with such life.

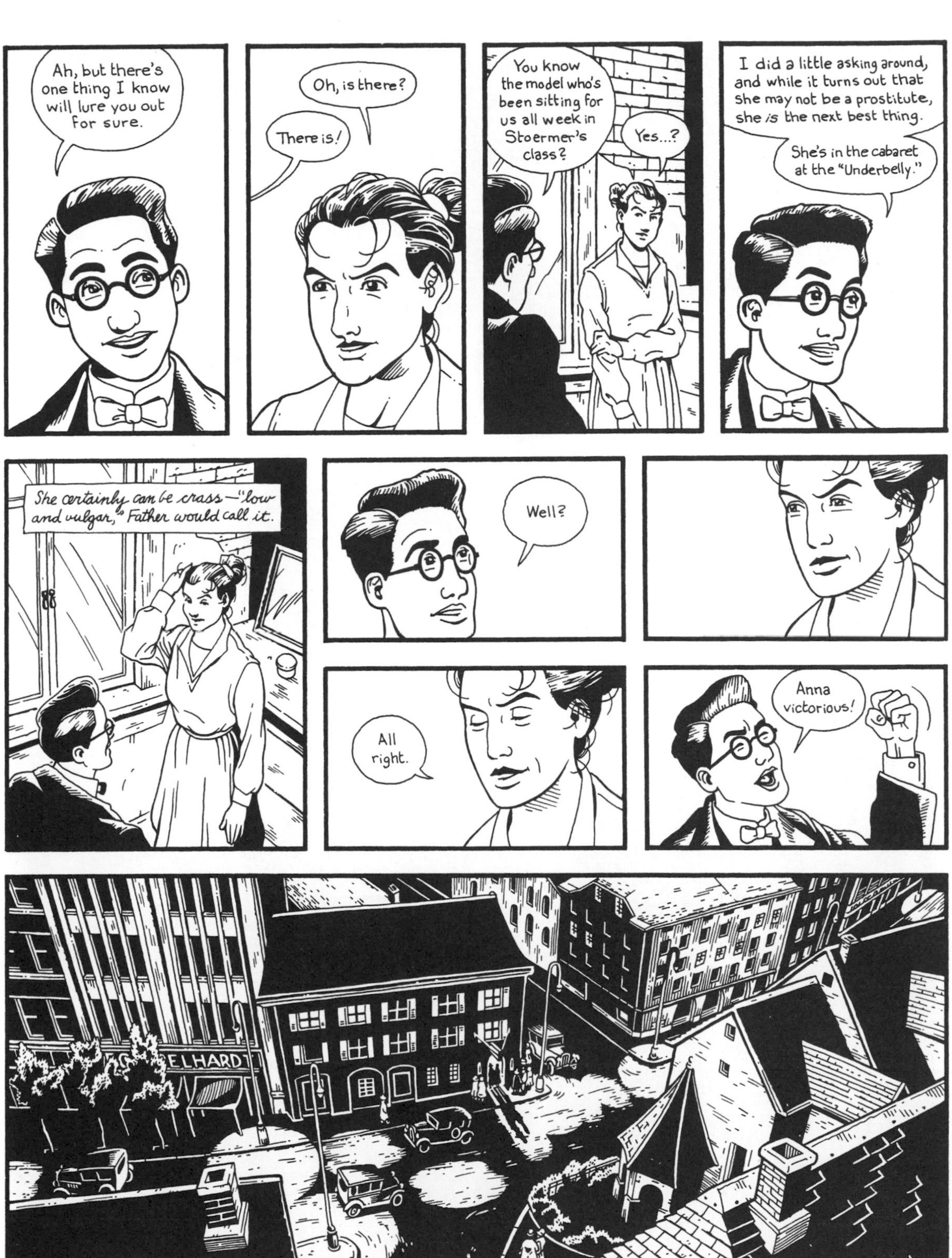
Ah, but there's one thing I know will lure you out for sure.
Oh, is there?
There is!
You know the model who's been sitting for us all week in Stoermer's class?
Yes...?
I did a little asking around, and while it turns out that she may not be a prostitute, she *is* the next best thing.
She's in the cabaret at the "Underbelly."
She certainly can be crass—"low and vulgar," Father would call it.
Well?
All right.
Anna victorious!
ELHARDT

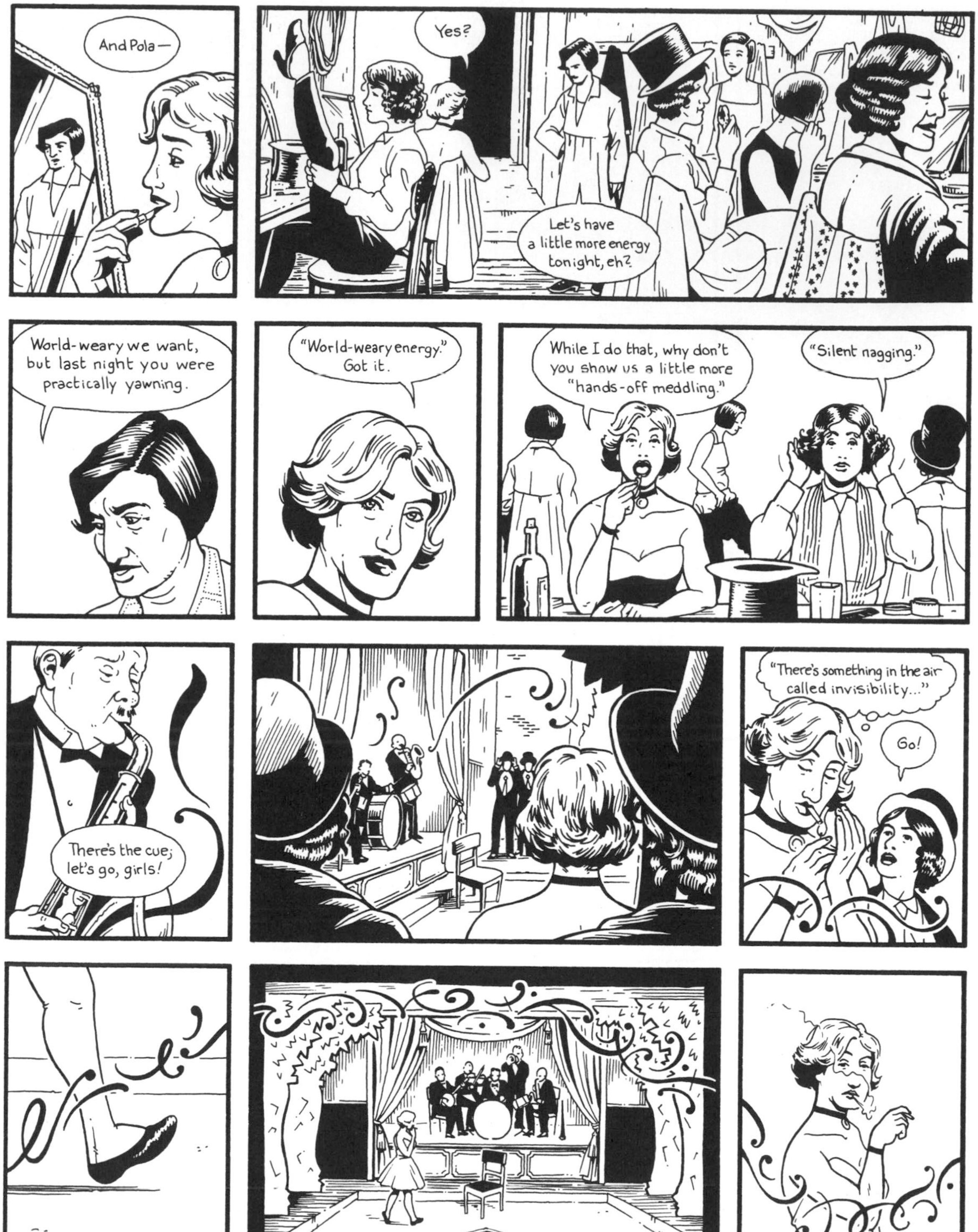
And Pola—
Yes?
Let's have a little more energy tonight, eh?
World-weary we want, but last night you were practically yawning.
"World-weary energy." Got it.
While I do that, why don't you show us a little more "hands-off meddling."
"Silent nagging."
There's the cue; let's go, girls!
"There's something in the air called invisibility..."
Go!

THERE'S SOMETHING IN THE AIR CALLED OBJECTIVITY,
THERE'S SOMETHING IN THE AIR LIKE E-LEC-TRICITY,
THERE'S SOMETHING IN THE AIR,
AND IT'S IN THE AIR, THE AIR.
THERE'S SOMETHING IN THE AIR THAT'S PURE SILLINESS,
THERE'S SOMETHING IN THE AIR THAT YOU CAN'T RESIST.
THERE'S SOMETHING IN THE AIR, AND IT'S IN THE AIR,
AND YOU CAN'T GET IT OUT OF THE AIR!

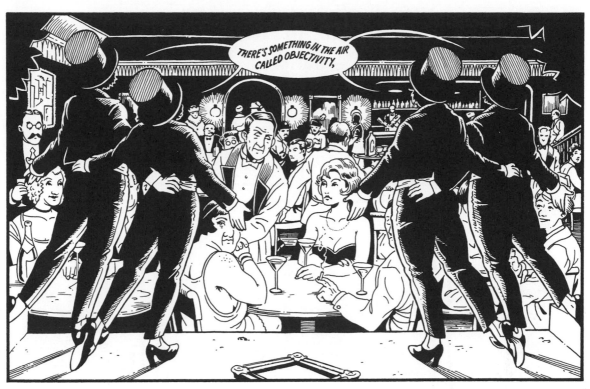

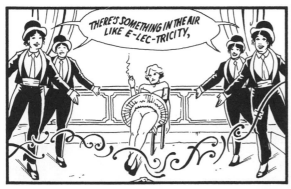

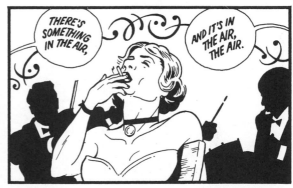

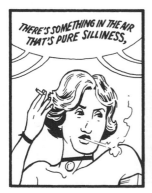

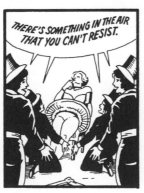

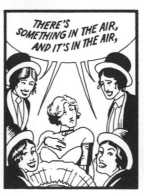

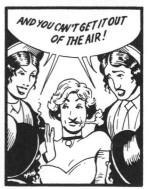

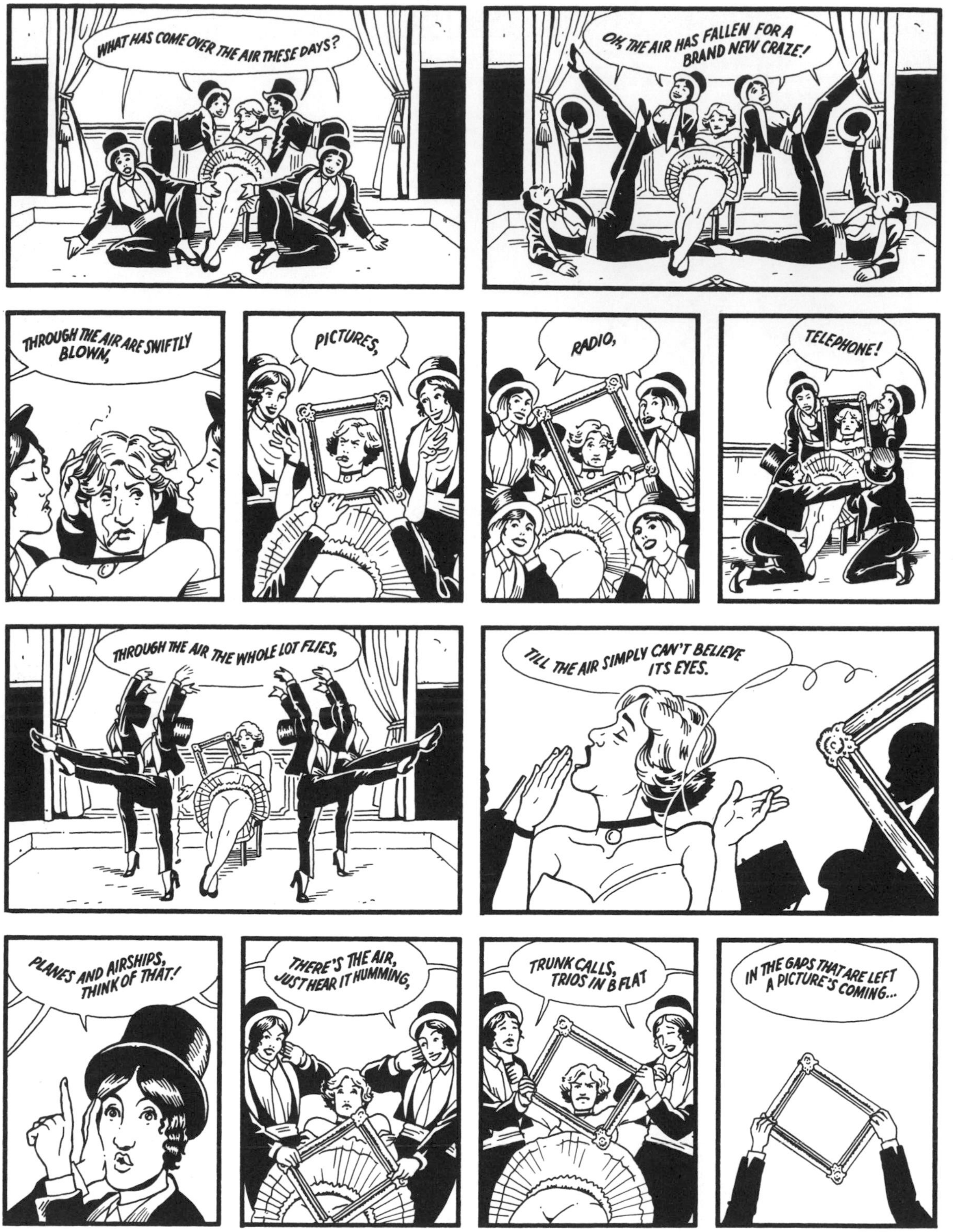
WHAT HAS COME OVER THE AIR THESE DAYS?
OH, THE AIR HAS FALLEN FOR A BRAND NEW CRAZE!
THROUGH THE AIR ARE SWIFTLY BLOWN,
PICTURES,
RADIO,
TELEPHONE!
THROUGH THE AIR THE WHOLE LOT FLIES,
TILL THE AIR SIMPLY CAN'T BELIEVE ITS EYES.
PLANES AND AIRSHIPS, THINK OF THAT!
THERE'S THE AIR, JUST HEAR IT HUMMING,
TRUNK CALLS, TRIOS IN B FLAT
IN THE GAPS THAT ARE LEFT A PICTURE'S COMING...

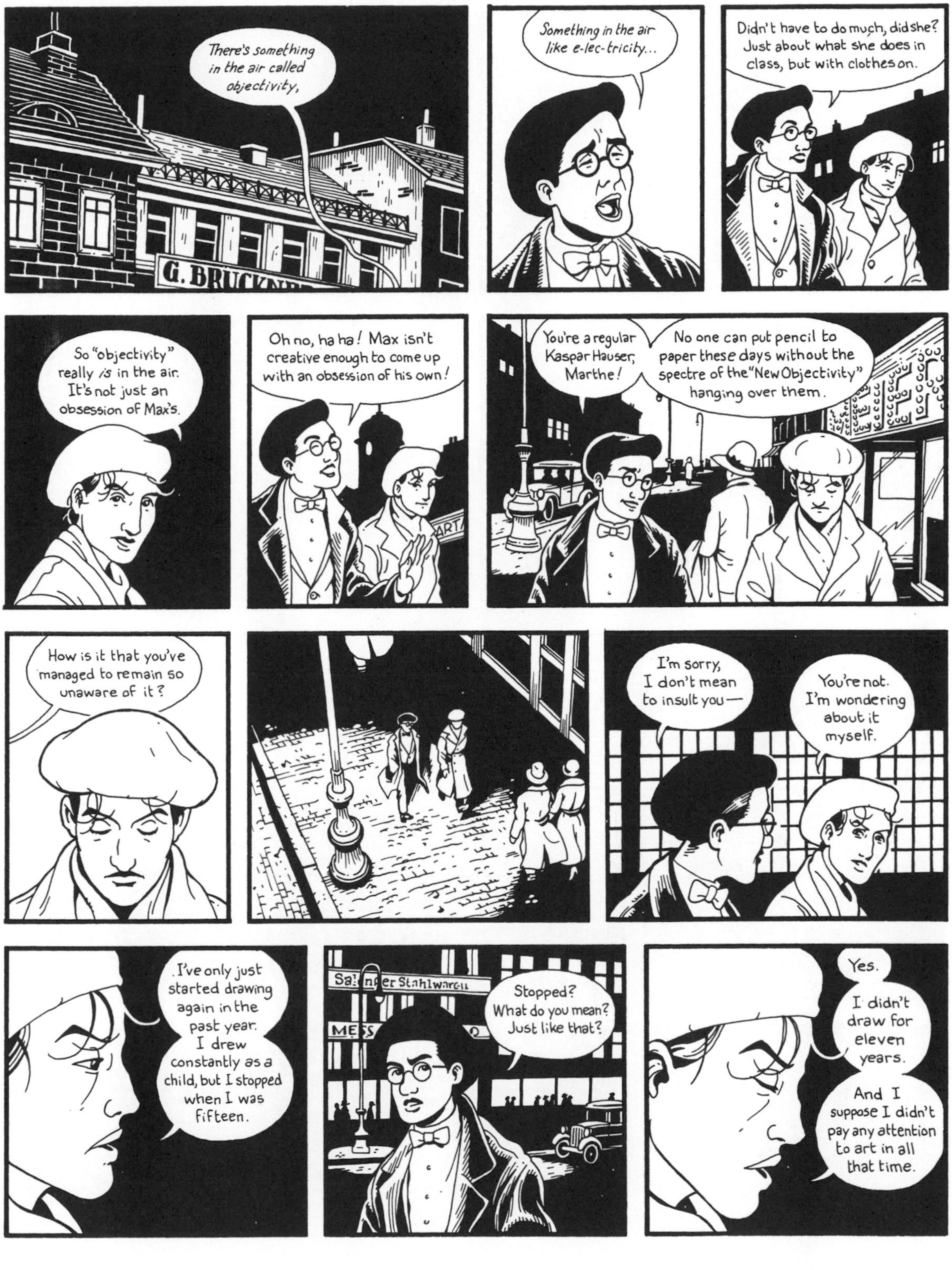
There's something in the air called objectivity,
Something in the air like e-lec-tricity...
Didn't have to do much, did she? Just about what she does in class, but with clothes on.
So "objectivity" really *is* in the air. It's not just an obsession of Max's.
Oh no, ha ha! Max isn't creative enough to come up with an obsession of his own!
You're a regular Kaspar Hauser, Marthe!
No one can put pencil to paper these days without the spectre of the "New Objectivity" hanging over them.
How is it that you've managed to remain so unaware of it?
I'm sorry, I don't mean to insult you—
You're not. I'm wondering about it myself.
I've only just started drawing again in the past year. I drew constantly as a child, but I stopped when I was fifteen.
Stopped? What do you mean? Just like that?
Yes.
I didn't draw for eleven years.
And I suppose I didn't pay any attention to art in all that time.

Eleven years?!?

That's a long time, isn't it? It didn't really occur to me. One day I just started again.

The day my father told me he had arranged for my marriage to the son of one of his business partners.

Then, all of a sudden, all I wanted to do was draw.

And?

Well, here I am. He had no choice but to send me to art school.

Frustrated him quite a bit, but he had no choice. I wouldn't talk to him. I would just draw.

But Marthe, what — what made you stop in the first place?

What has come over the air these days?

The air's fallen for a brand new craze!

Through the air are swiftly blown

Pictures, radio,

telephone!

Through the air the whole lot flies,

Till the air simply can't believe its eyes!

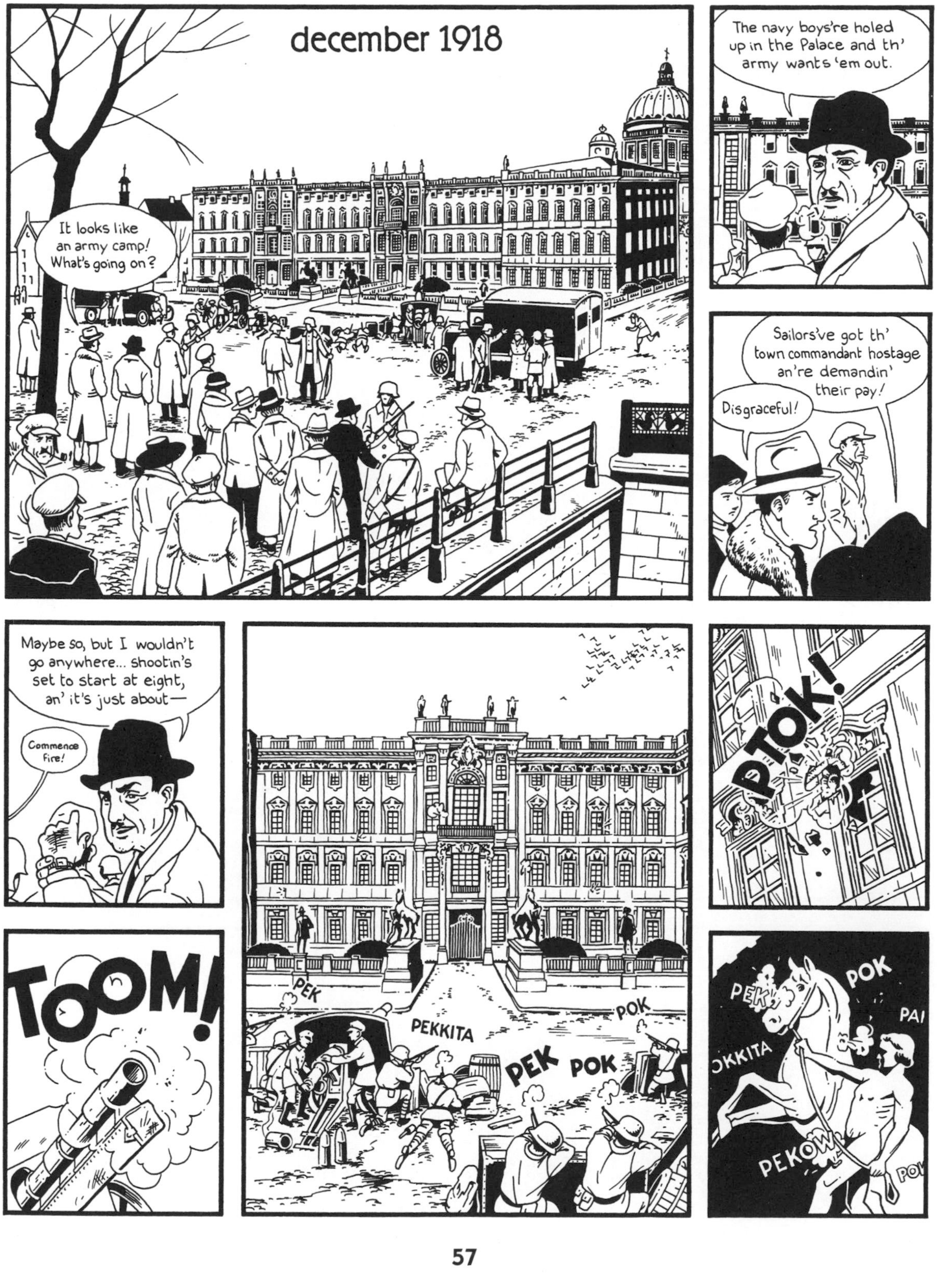
december 1918
It looks like an army camp! What's going on?
The navy boys're holed up in the Palace and th' army wants 'em out.
Sailors've got th' town commandant hostage an're demandin' their pay!
Disgraceful!
Maybe so, but I wouldn't go anywhere... shootin's set to start at eight, an' it's just about—
Commence fire!
TOOM!
PEK
PEKKITA
POK
PEK
POK
PTOK!
PEK
POK
PAI
OKKITA
PEKOW
PO

PEKOW PAK POKKITA POK
POK TOOM! PEKKITA
EK PEK PAK PAK
AKKITA PEK POKKITAKA PEKOW PEK POK
OK POK PAK PAK PAK PKAK POKKIT
KOW
AKKITA POK POKKIT POK PAK EKKIT PEK
PEK POKKIT PAKKITA OK POK PO
PAK PEKOW POKITTA PAK PEKKITA POKKI POK POK PEK OK PAK
TOOM! PEK POKKITA PAK POK PAK PEK
PEK PEK PEK PAK PAKKITA KIT POK PEK PEKKITA
PAKKITA POK KITA POK POK PEK PAK TOOM! POKKI PEK
POKKITA PEK PAKKITA POK PEKO AKKIT PUKKITA AKKIT PKOW POK PAK
PAK POKKITA PUKKA PEK PAK PAK POKKIT PEK
KKITA PAK TOOM! PEKKA PAK PAK POK POK
KKITA PAK CEASE FIRE! POK PEKKIT POK EK POKKA PEKKIT PAKK

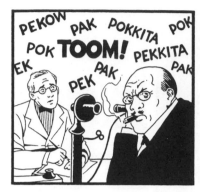

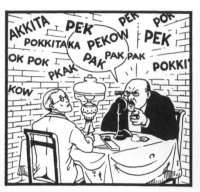

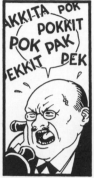

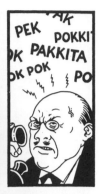

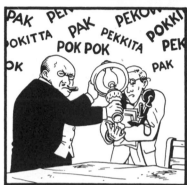

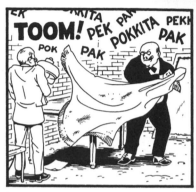

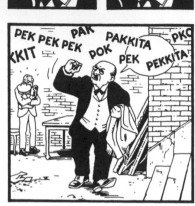

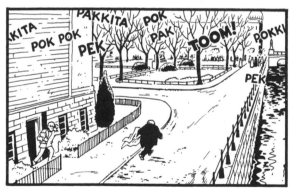

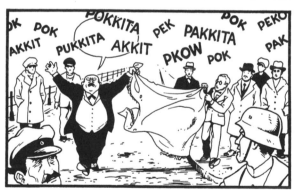

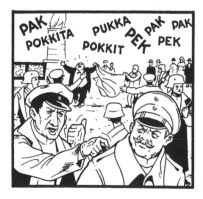

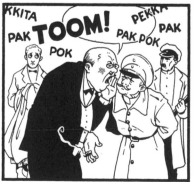

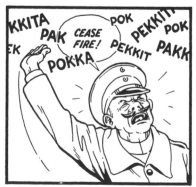

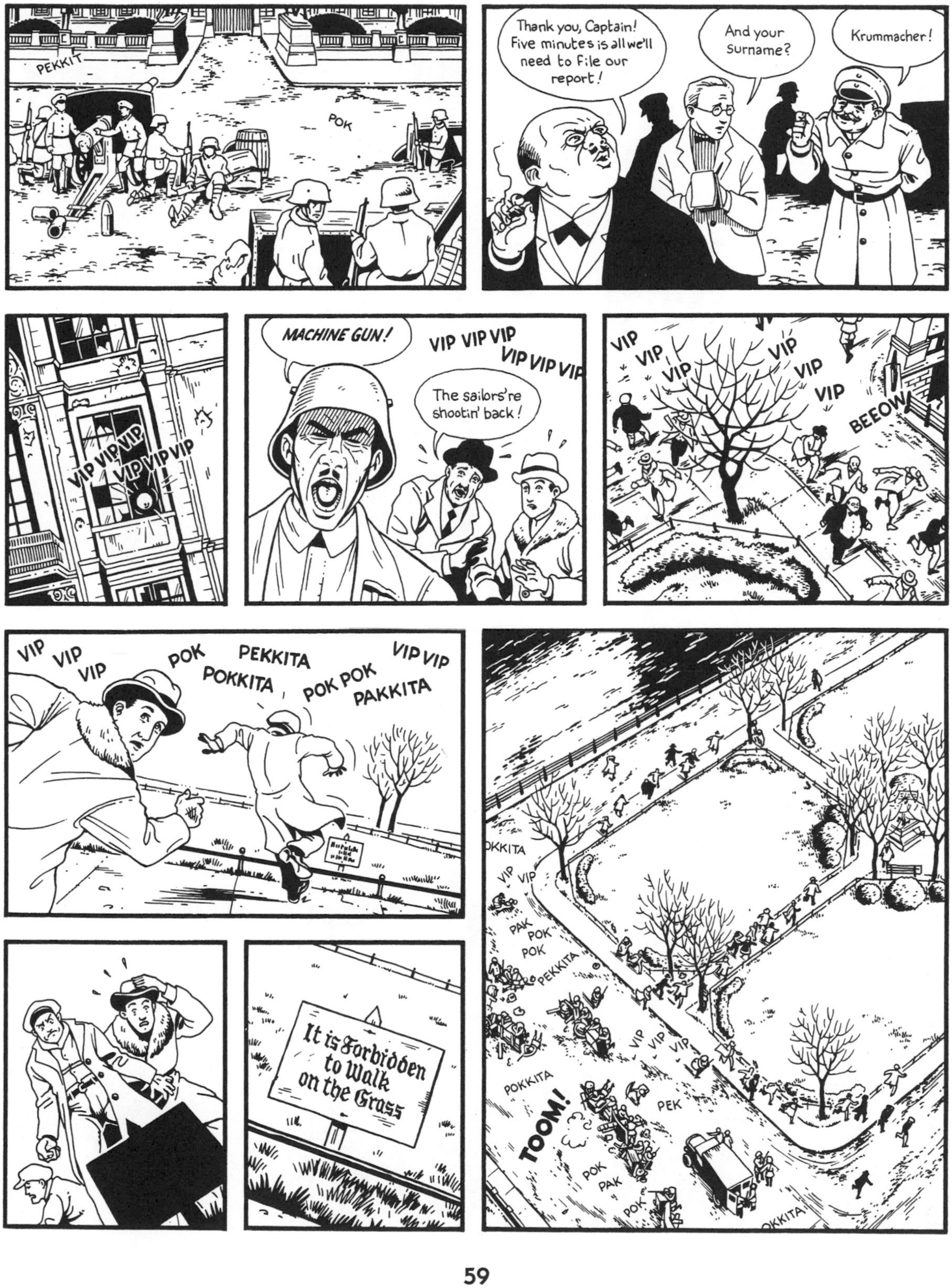
PEKKIT
POK
Thank you, Captain! Five minutes is all we'll need to file our report!
And your surname?
Krummacher!
VIP VIP VIP VIP VIP VIP
MACHINE GUN!
VIP VIP VIP
VIP VIP VIP
The sailors're shootin' back!
VIP VIP VIP VIP VIP VIP
BEEOW
VIP VIP VIP
POK
PEKKITA
POKKITA
POK POK
PAKKITA
VIP VIP
It is Forbidden to Walk on the Grass
OKKITA
VIP VIP
PAK POK POK
PEKKITA
VIP VIP VIP
POKKITA
TOOM!
PEK
POK PAK POK
OKKITA

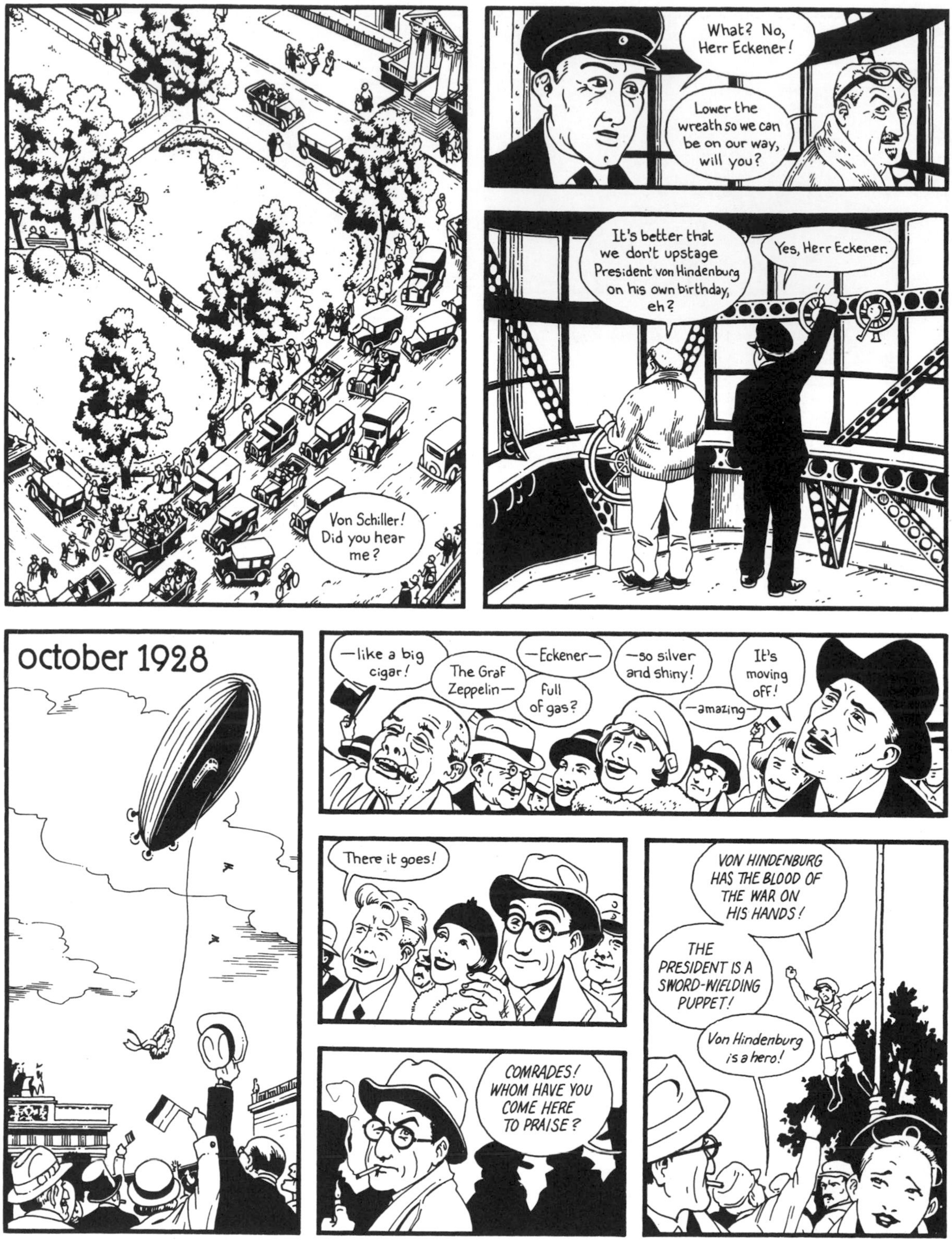
Von Schiller! Did you hear me?
What? No, Herr Eckener!
Lower the wreath so we can be on our way, will you?
It's better that we don't upstage President von Hindenburg on his own birthday, eh?
Yes, Herr Eckener.
october 1928
—like a big cigar!
The Graf Zeppelin—
—Eckener—
full of gas?
—so silver and shiny!
—amazing—
It's moving off!
There it goes!
COMRADES! WHOM HAVE YOU COME HERE TO PRAISE?
VON HINDENBURG HAS THE BLOOD OF THE WAR ON HIS HANDS!
THE PRESIDENT IS A SWORD-WIELDING PUPPET!
Von Hindenburg is a hero!

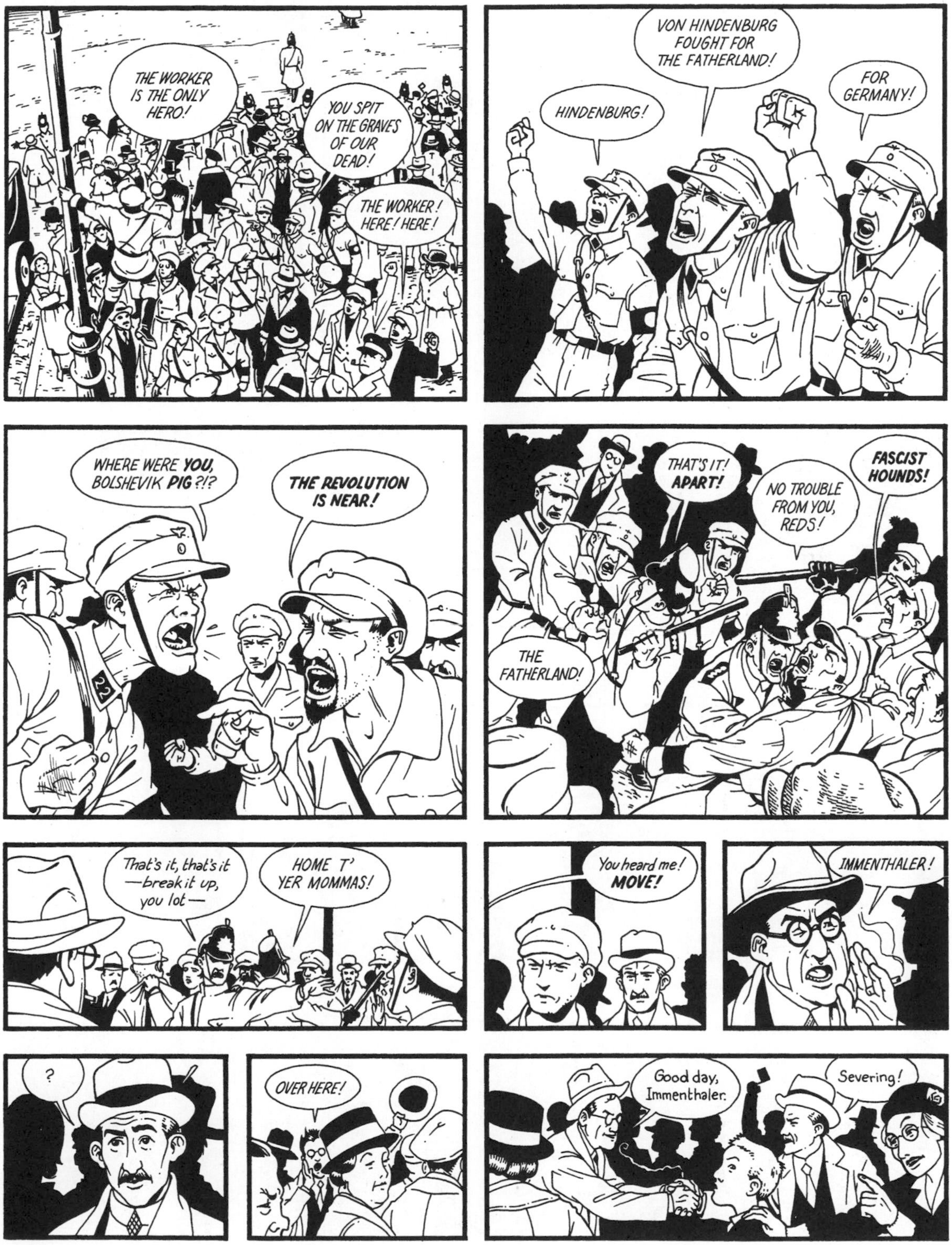
THE WORKER IS THE ONLY HERO!
YOU SPIT ON THE GRAVES OF OUR DEAD!
THE WORKER! HERE! HERE!
VON HINDENBURG FOUGHT FOR THE FATHERLAND!
HINDENBURG!
FOR GERMANY!
WHERE WERE YOU, BOLSHEVIK PIG ?!?
THE REVOLUTION IS NEAR!
THAT'S IT! APART!
NO TROUBLE FROM YOU, REDS!
FASCIST HOUNDS!
THE FATHERLAND!
That's it, that's it —break it up, you lot—
HOME T' YER MOMMAS!
You heard me! MOVE!
IMMENTHALER!
?
OVER HERE!
Good day, Immenthaler.
Severing!

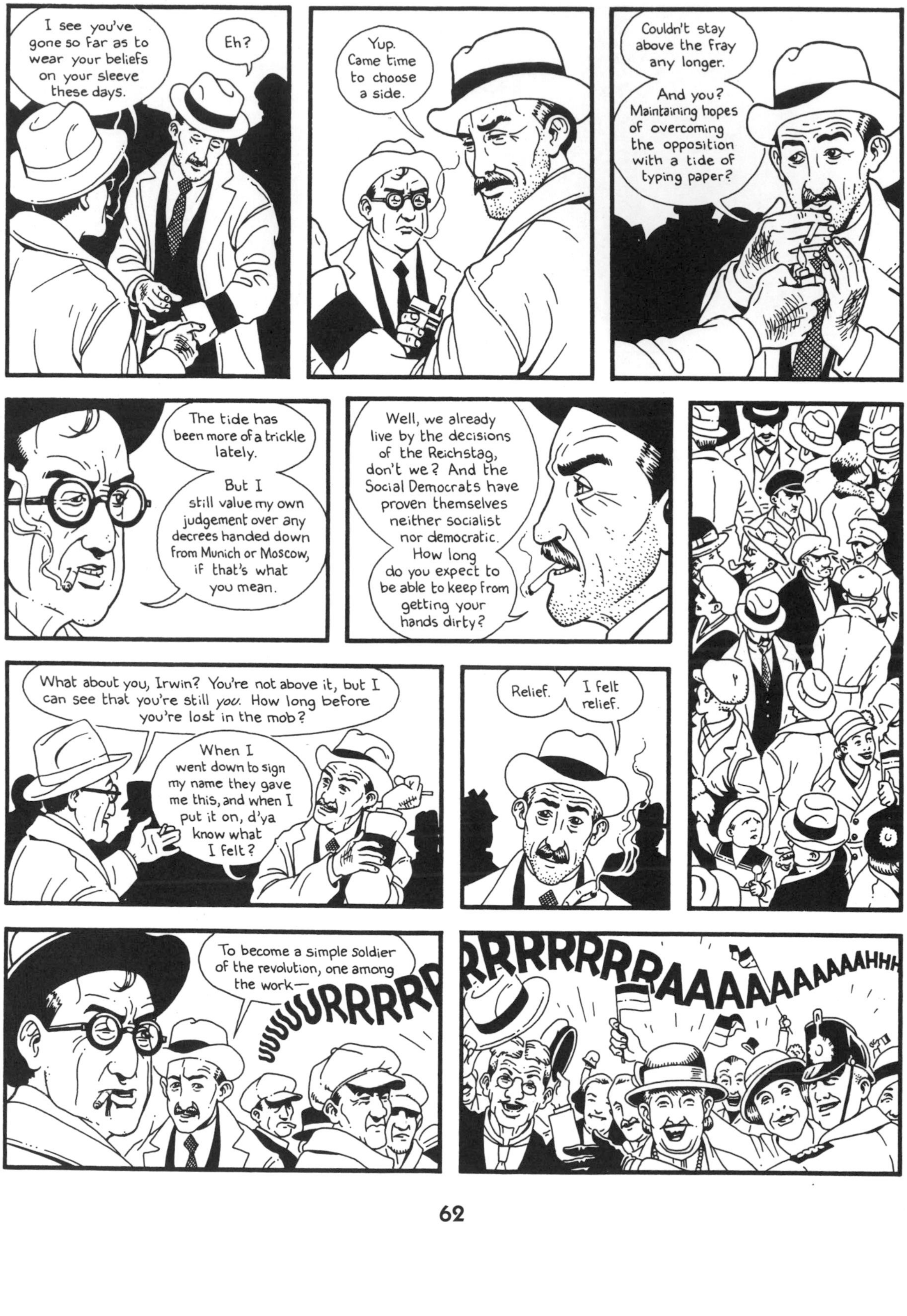
I see you've gone so far as to wear your beliefs on your sleeve these days.
Eh?
Yup. Came time to choose a side.
Couldn't stay above the fray any longer.
And you? Maintaining hopes of overcoming the opposition with a tide of typing paper?
The tide has been more of a trickle lately.
But I still value my own judgement over any decrees handed down from Munich or Moscow, if that's what you mean.
Well, we already live by the decisions of the Reichstag, don't we? And the Social Democrats have proven themselves neither socialist nor democratic. How long do you expect to be able to keep from getting your hands dirty?
What about you, Irwin? You're not above it, but I can see that you're still *you*. How long before you're lost in the mob?
When I went down to sign my name they gave me this, and when I put it on, d'ya know what I felt?
Relief.
I felt relief.
To become a simple soldier of the revolution, one among the work—
UUUUURRRRRRRRRRRRRRAAAAAAAAAAAHHH

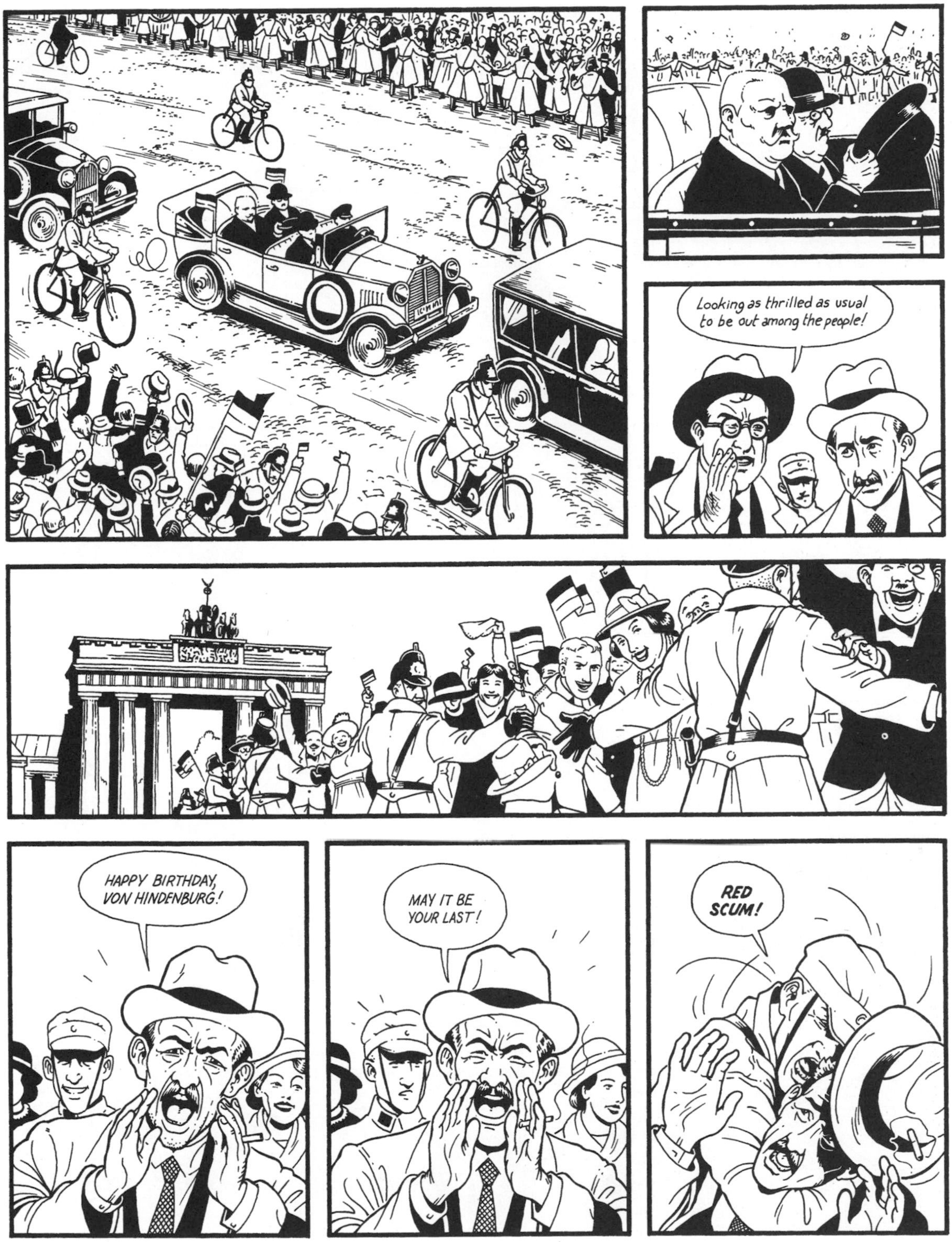
Looking as thrilled as usual to be out among the people!
HAPPY BIRTHDAY, VON HINDENBURG!
MAY IT BE YOUR LAST!
RED SCUM!

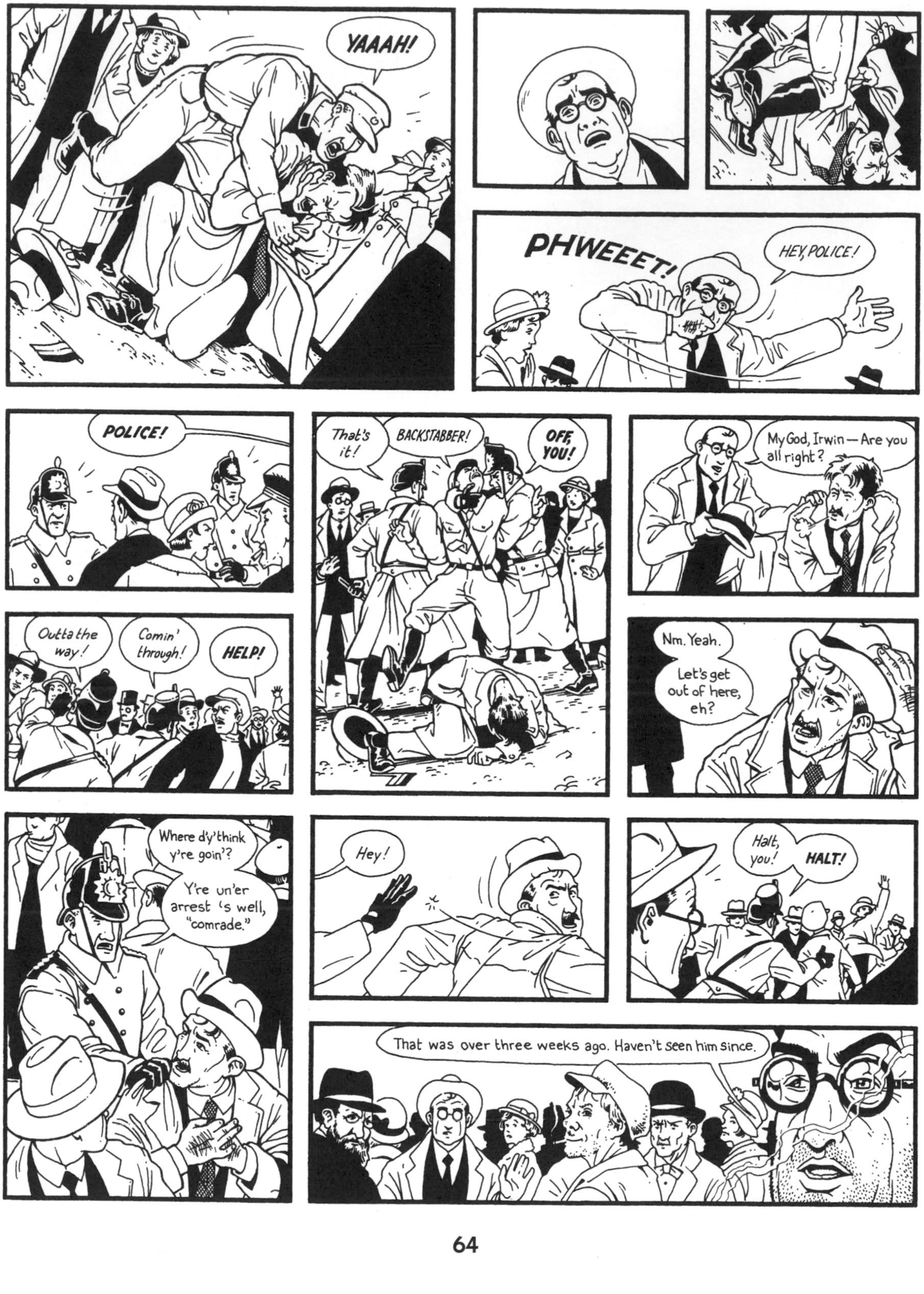
YAAAH!
PHWEEET!
HEY, POLICE!
POLICE!
That's it!
BACKSTABBER!
OFF, YOU!
My God, Irwin — Are you all right?
Outta the way!
Comin' through!
HELP!
Nm. Yeah.
Let's get out of here, eh?
Where d'y'think y're goin'?
Y're un'er arrest 's well, "comrade."
Hey!
Halt, you!
HALT!
That was over three weeks ago. Haven't seen him since.

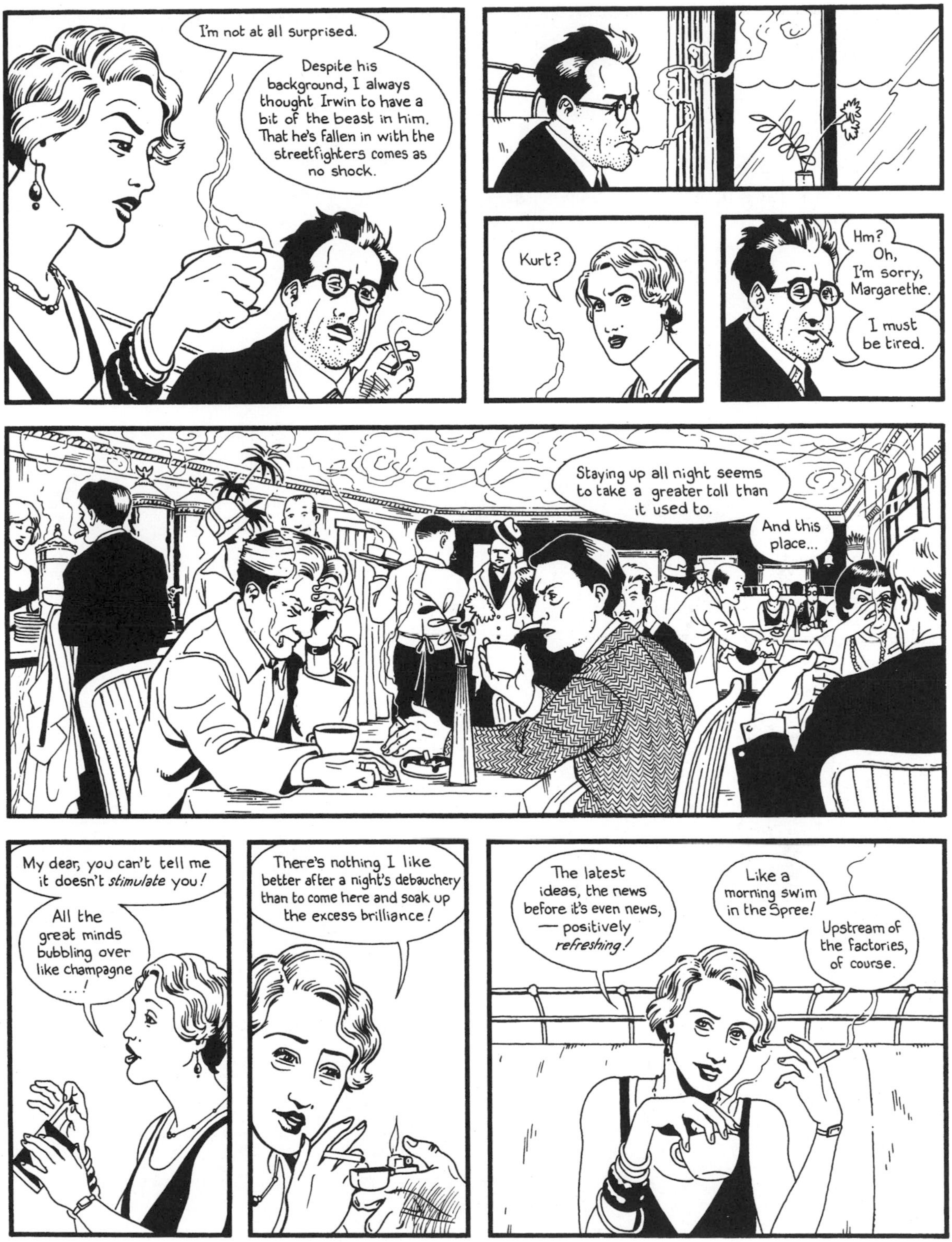
I'm not at all surprised.
Despite his background, I always thought Irwin to have a bit of the beast in him. That he's fallen in with the streetfighters comes as no shock.
Kurt?
Hm? Oh, I'm sorry, Margarethe.
I must be tired.
Staying up all night seems to take a greater toll than it used to.
And this place...
My dear, you can't tell me it doesn't *stimulate* you!
All the great minds bubbling over like champagne ...!
There's nothing I like better after a night's debauchery than to come here and soak up the excess brilliance!
The latest ideas, the news before it's even news, — positively *refreshing*!
Like a morning swim in the Spree!
Upstream of the factories, of course.

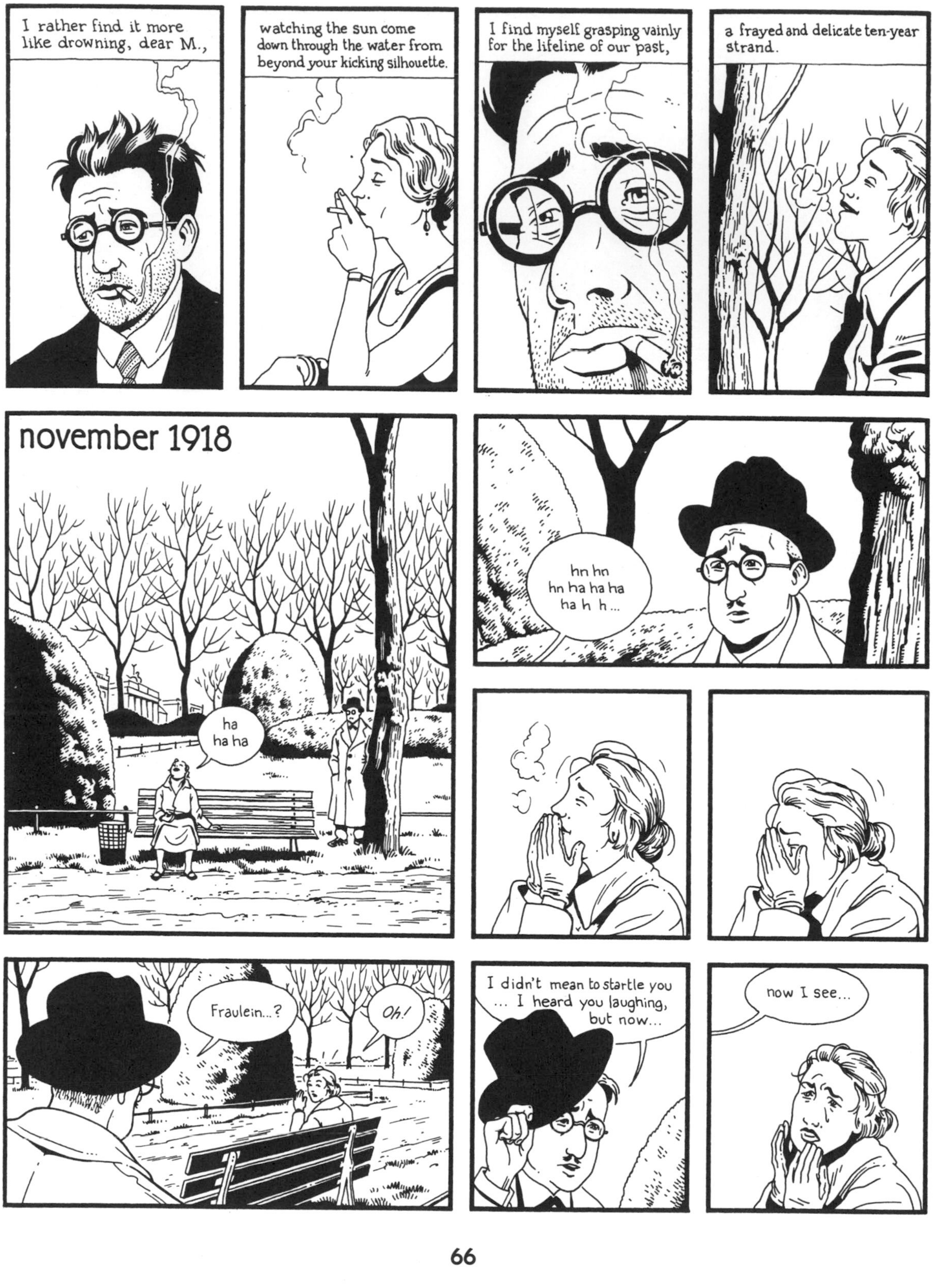

I rather find it more like drowning, dear M.,
watching the sun come down through the water from beyond your kicking silhouette.
I find myself grasping vainly for the lifeline of our past,
a frayed and delicate ten-year strand.
november 1918
ha ha ha
hn hn hn ha ha ha ha h h...
Fraulein...?
Oh!
I didn't mean to startle you ... I heard you laughing, but now...
now I see...

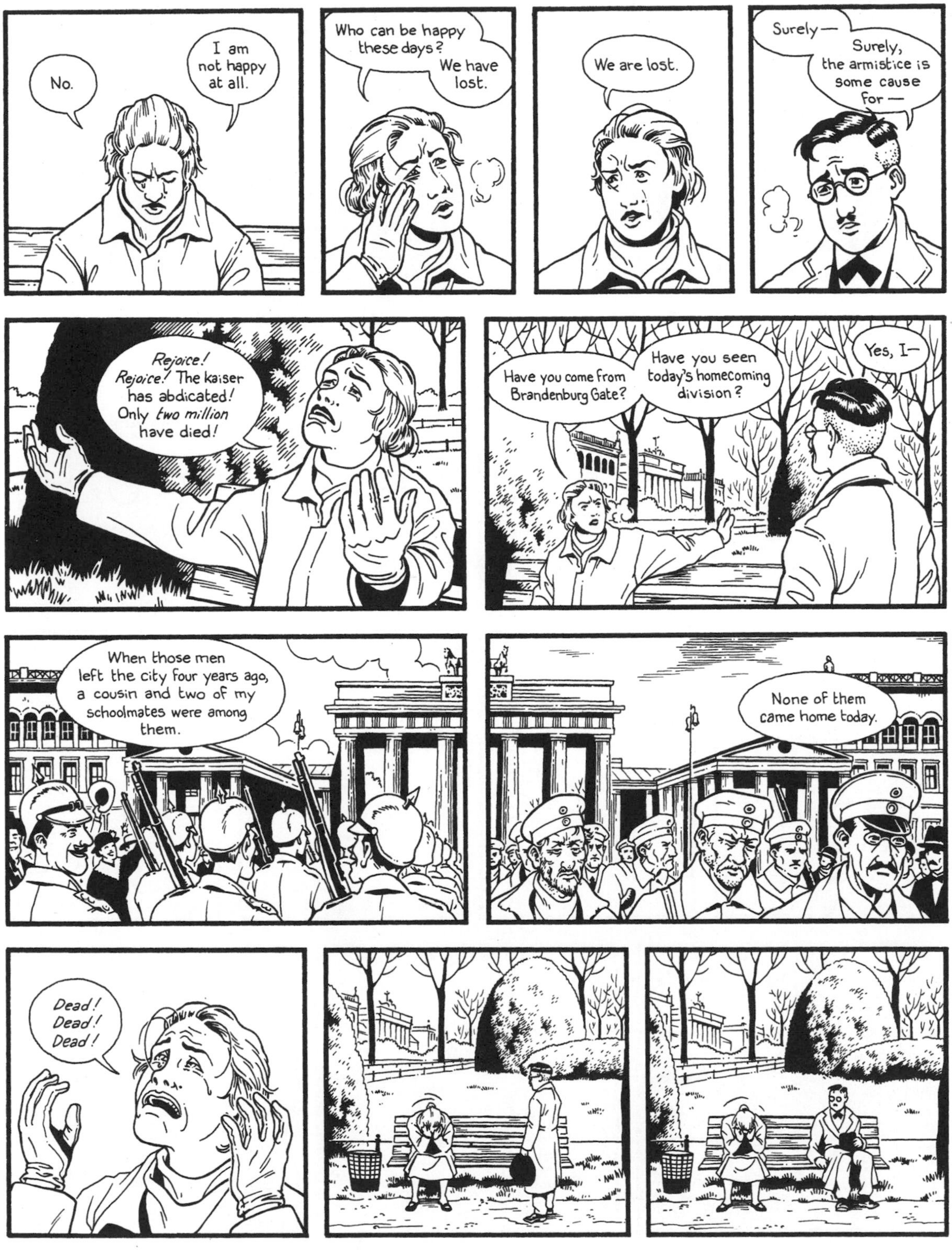
No.
I am not happy at all.
Who can be happy these days? We have lost.
We are lost.
Surely—
Surely, the armistice is some cause for—
Rejoice! Rejoice! The kaiser has abdicated! Only two million have died!
Have you come from Brandenburg Gate?
Have you seen today's homecoming division?
Yes, I—
When those men left the city four years ago, a cousin and two of my schoolmates were among them.
None of them came home today.
Dead! Dead! Dead!

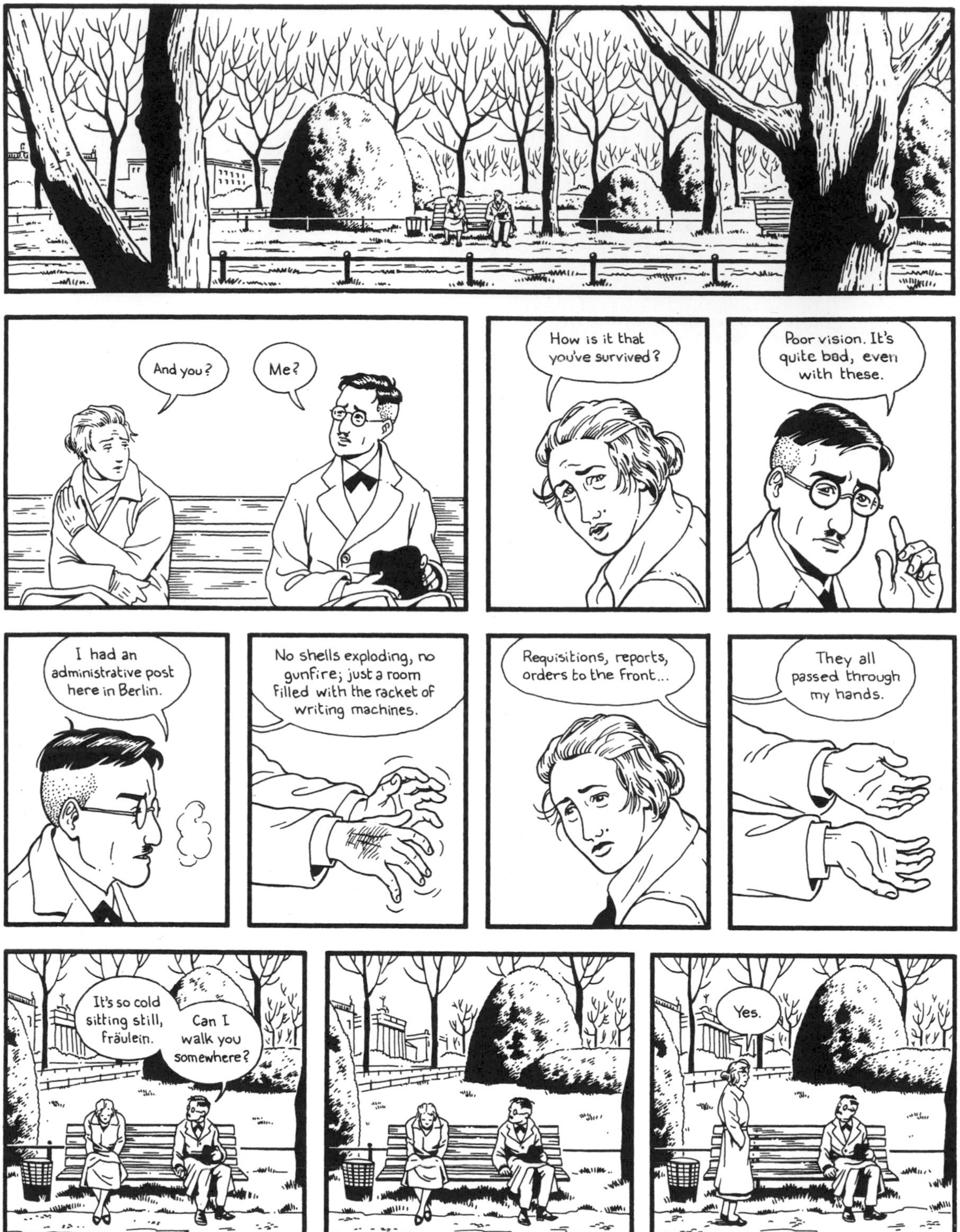
And you?
Me?
How is it that you've survived?
Poor vision. It's quite bad, even with these.
I had an administrative post here in Berlin.
No shells exploding, no gunfire; just a room filled with the racket of writing machines.
Requisitions, reports, orders to the Front...
They all passed through my hands.
It's so cold sitting still, fräulein.
Can I walk you somewhere?
Yes.

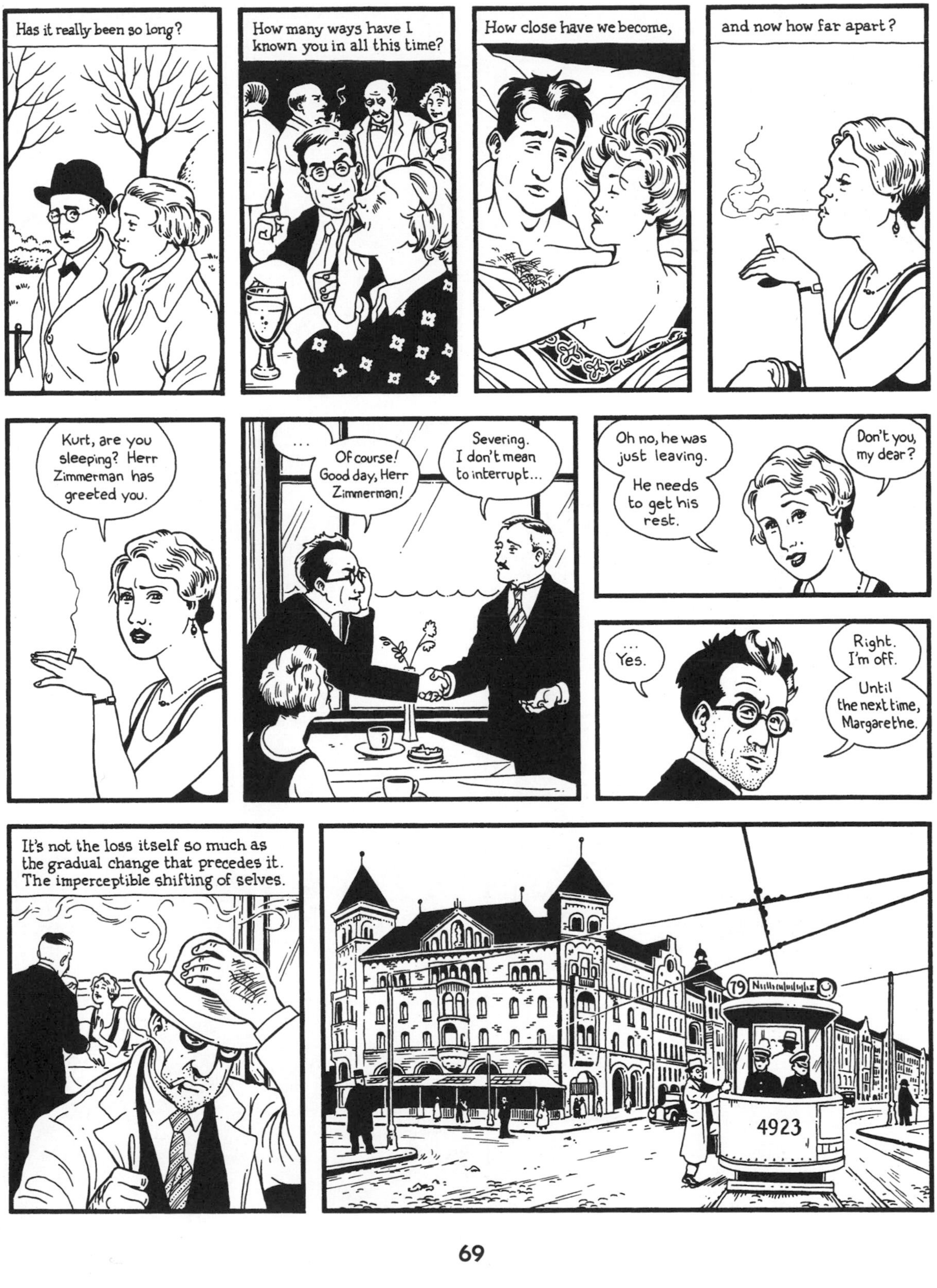
Has it really been so long?
How many ways have I known you in all this time?
How close have we become,
and now how far apart?
Kurt, are you sleeping? Herr Zimmerman has greeted you.
...
Of course! Good day, Herr Zimmerman!
Severing. I don't mean to interrupt...
Oh no, he was just leaving.
He needs to get his rest.
Don't you, my dear?
... Yes.
Right. I'm off.
Until the next time, Margarethe.
It's not the loss itself so much as the gradual change that precedes it. The imperceptible shifting of selves.
79
4923

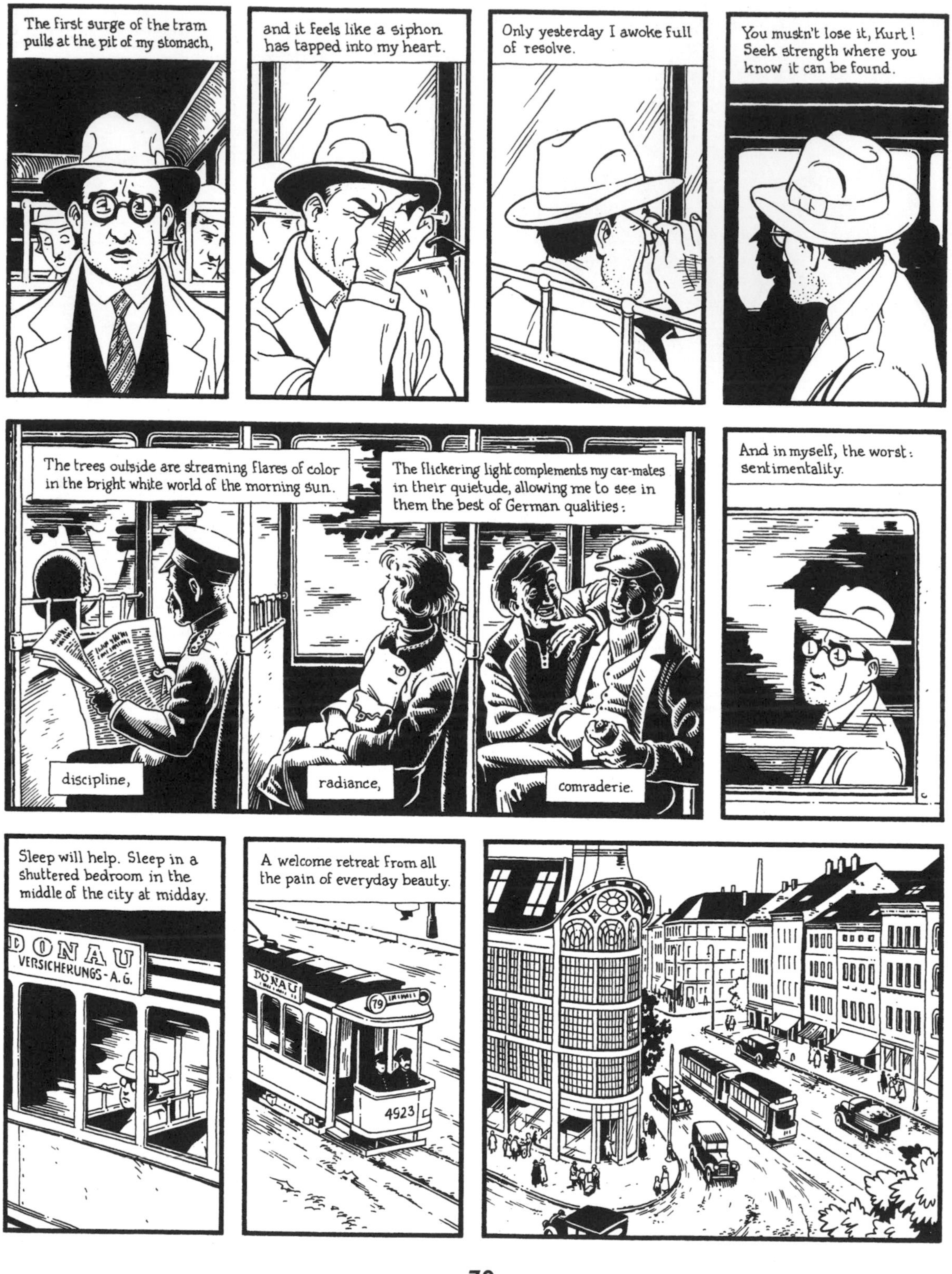
The first surge of the tram pulls at the pit of my stomach,
and it feels like a siphon has tapped into my heart.
Only yesterday I awoke full of resolve.
You mustn't lose it, Kurt! Seek strength where you know it can be found.
The trees outside are streaming flares of color in the bright white world of the morning sun.
The flickering light complements my car-mates in their quietude, allowing me to see in them the best of German qualities:
discipline,
radiance,
comraderie.
And in myself, the worst: sentimentality.
Sleep will help. Sleep in a shuttered bedroom in the middle of the city at midday.
DONAU
VERSICHERUNGS - A. G.
A welcome retreat from all the pain of everyday beauty.
DONAU
79
4523

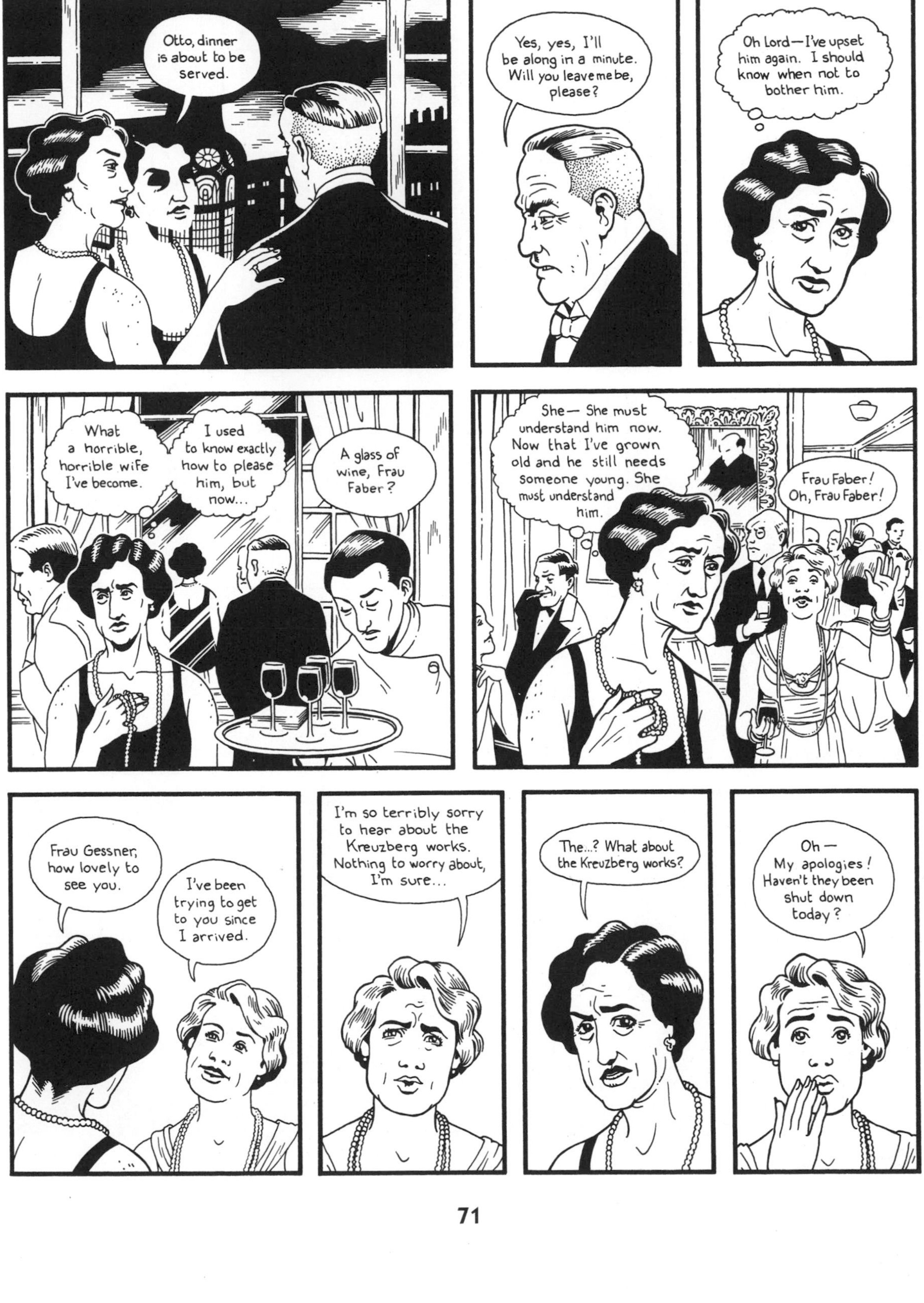

Otto, dinner is about to be served.
Yes, yes, I'll be along in a minute. Will you leave me be, please?
Oh Lord—I've upset him again. I should know when not to bother him.
What a horrible, horrible wife I've become.
I used to know exactly how to please him, but now...
A glass of wine, Frau Faber?
She— She must understand him now. Now that I've grown old and he still needs someone young. She must understand him.
Frau Faber! Oh, Frau Faber!
Frau Gessner, how lovely to see you.
I've been trying to get to you since I arrived.
I'm so terribly sorry to hear about the Kreuzberg works. Nothing to worry about, I'm sure...
The...? What about the Kreuzberg works?
Oh— My apologies! Haven't they been shut down today?

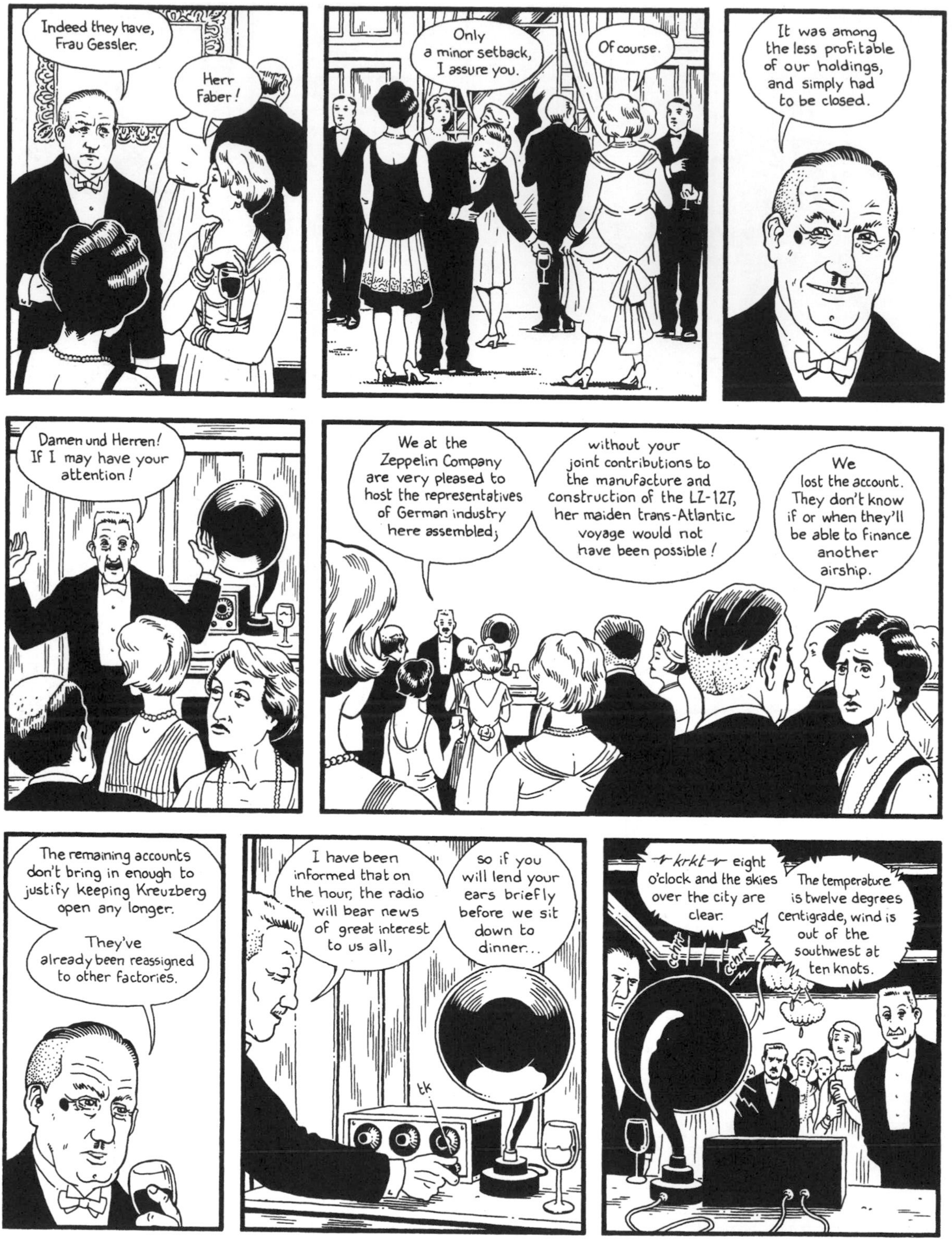
Indeed they have, Frau Gessler.
Herr Faber!
Only a minor setback, I assure you.
Of course.
It was among the less profitable of our holdings, and simply had to be closed.
Damen und Herren! If I may have your attention!
We at the Zeppelin Company are very pleased to host the representatives of German industry here assembled;
without your joint contributions to the manufacture and construction of the LZ-127, her maiden trans-Atlantic voyage would not have been possible!
We lost the account. They don't know if or when they'll be able to finance another airship.
The remaining accounts don't bring in enough to justify keeping Kreuzberg open any longer.
They've already been reassigned to other factories.
I have been informed that on the hour, the radio will bear news of great interest to us all,
so if you will lend your ears briefly before we sit down to dinner...
tk
krkt eight o'clock and the skies over the city are clear.
The temperature is twelve degrees centigrade, wind is out of the southwest at ten knots.
cchrr
cchrr

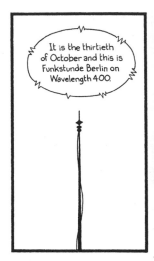

It is the thirtieth of October and this is Funkstunde Berlin on Wavelength 400.

The airship *Graf Zeppelin*, LZ-127, left the United States today to begin the return leg of the first transoceanic passenger flight in history.

Captain Hugo Eckener and his crew caused quite a stir in America, receiving a ticker tape parade in New York City and a flood of requests for return passage.

Out of all of them, Captain Eckener selected twenty passengers, each of whom has paid 3,000 American dollars, or 12,000 Reichsmarks, for the privilege of travelling aboard the great dirigible.

The *Graf Zeppelin* will fly close to 7,000 kilometers at a speed of sixty kilometers per hour,

and is scheduled to reach its hangar at Friedrichshafen on the First of November.

We at Funkstunde Berlin would like to wish Captain Eckener and crew a swift and untroubled journey home.

In their honor we now present a live transmission of the Leipzig Radio Symphony Orchestra, performing "On the Beautiful Blue Danube," by Johann Strauss.

Hurrah! 12,000 Marks!

Hurrah for Captain Eckener!

And y'can't even smoke!

If y'did— BOOM!

BOOM!

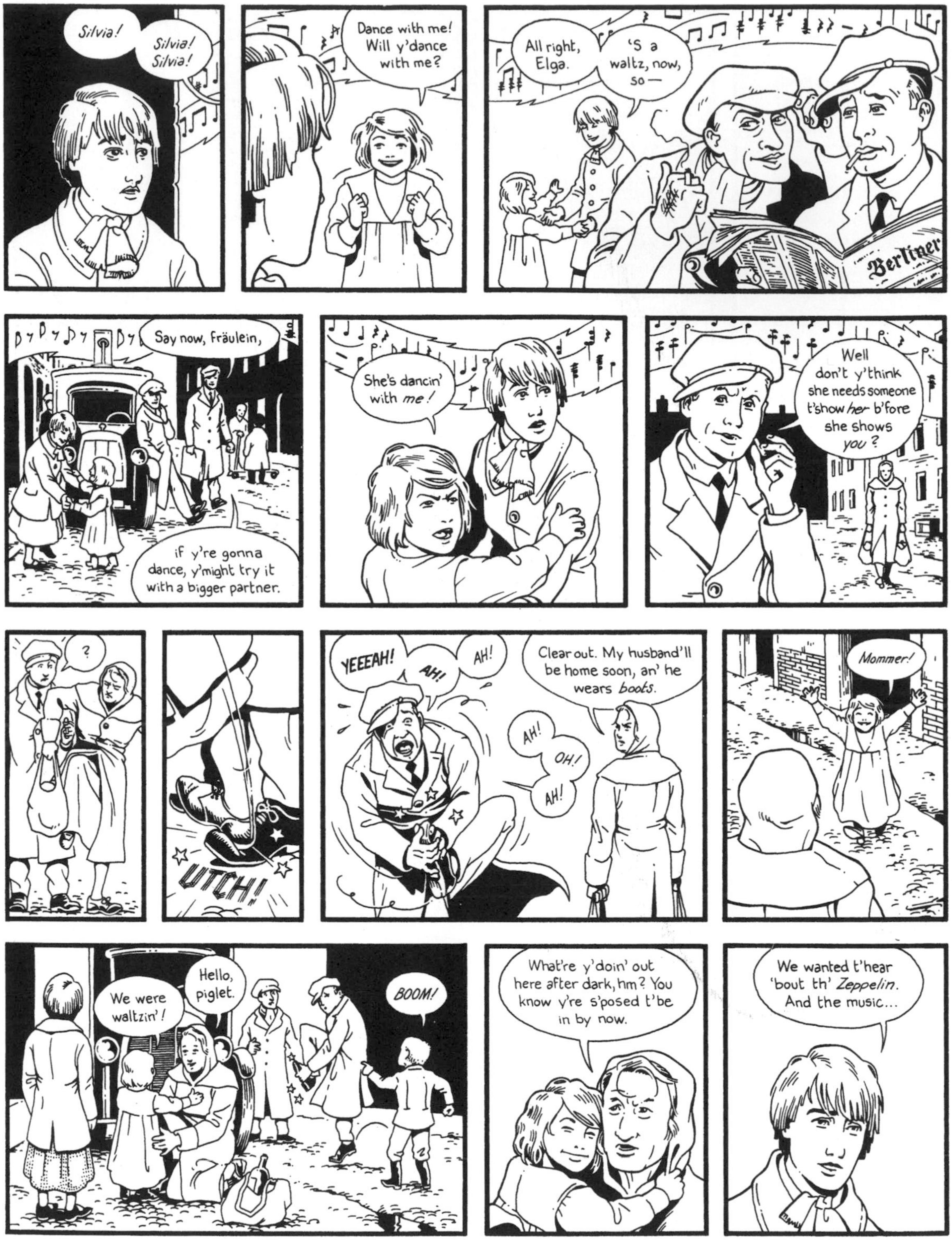

Silvia!
Silvia! Silvia!
Dance with me! Will y'dance with me?
All right, Elga.
'S a waltz, now, so—
Berliner
Say now, fräulein,
if y're gonna dance, y'might try it with a bigger partner.
She's dancin' with *me*!
Well don't y'think she needs someone t'show *her* b'fore she shows *you*?
?
UTCH!
YEEEAH!
AH!
AH!
Clear out. My husband'll be home soon, an' he wears *boots*.
AH!
OH!
AH!
Mommer!
We were waltzin'!
Hello, piglet.
BOOM!
What're y'doin' out here after dark, hm? You know y're s'posed t'be in by now.
We wanted t'hear 'bout th' *Zeppelin*. And the music...

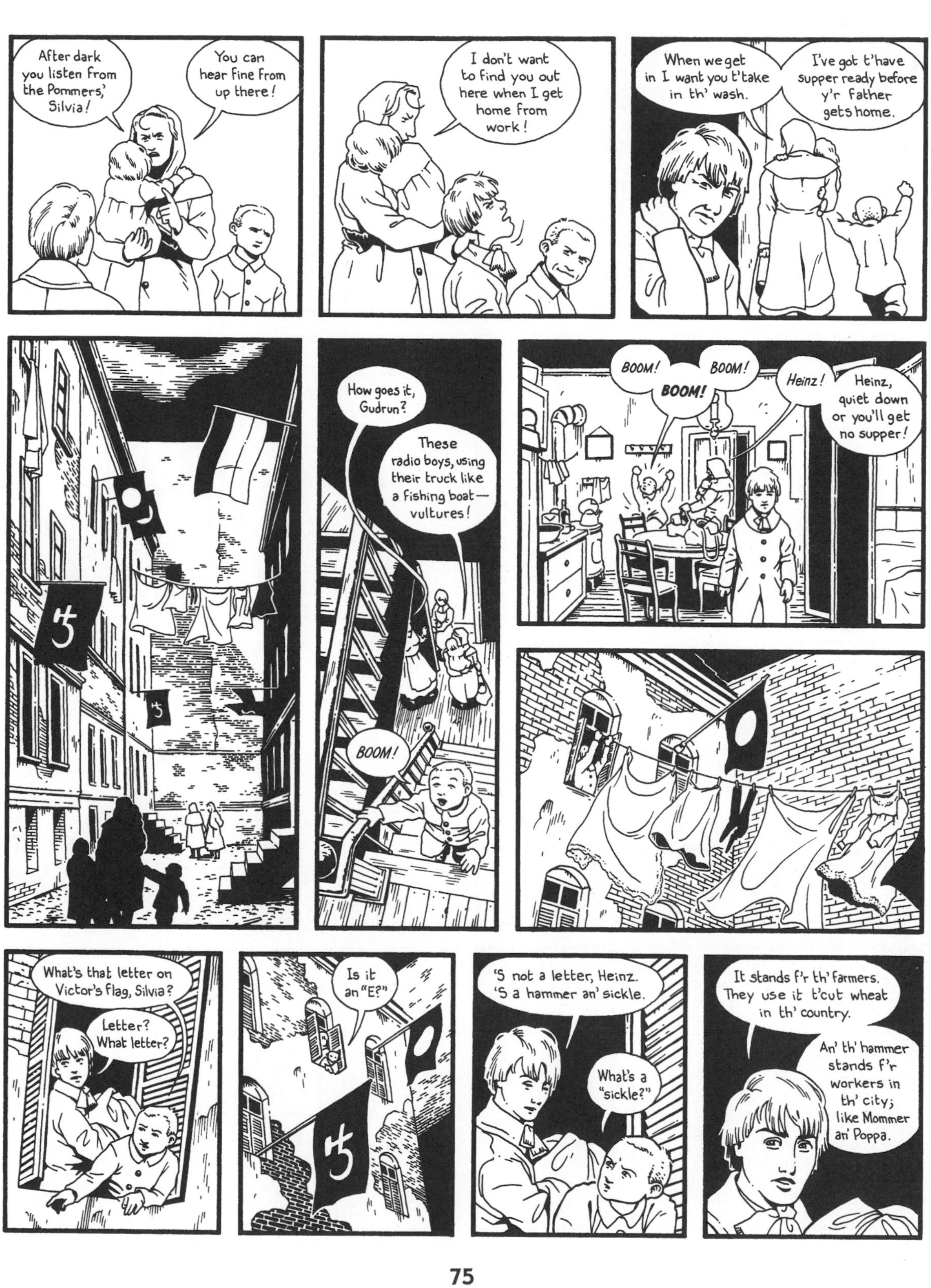
After dark you listen from the Pommers,' Silvia!
You can hear fine from up there!
I don't want to find you out here when I get home from work!
When we get in I want you t'take in th' wash.
I've got t'have supper ready before y'r father gets home.
How goes it, Gudrun?
These radio boys, using their truck like a fishing boat— vultures!
BOOM!
BOOM!
BOOM!
BOOM!
Heinz!
Heinz, quiet down or you'll get no supper!
What's that letter on Victor's flag, Silvia?
Letter? What letter?
Is it an "E?"
'S not a letter, Heinz. 'S a hammer an' sickle.
What's a "sickle?"
It stands f'r th' farmers. They use it t'cut wheat in th' country.
An' th' hammer stands f'r workers in th' city; like Mommer an' Poppa.

D'ya use a hammer when y're makin' the Zeppelin, Mommer?

No...

Why not?

We use looms, Heinzie. We make the cloth that covers it an' holds all th' gas inside.

You make its clothes?

That's right, Heinz, Mommer makes the Zeppelin's clothes. Now why don't you help me fold *our* clothes?

Poppa's home! Poppa's home!

Hello, little Elga!

Poppa!

—so's rare I need t'use a hammer, Heinz, but I use a wrench reg'larly.

What's got ya thinkin' 'bout hammers, anyway?

He was askin' about th' flags.

Well I hope y'didn't go fillin' his head with any a that Red rot!

Like was in that paper y'r mother brought home th' other day.

'D ya burn that like I told ya to, Gudrun?

I burned it, Poppa.

That flag's a lie, Heinz. Th' Reds say they're f'r th' workers, but they're really f'r th' Jews, un'erstand?

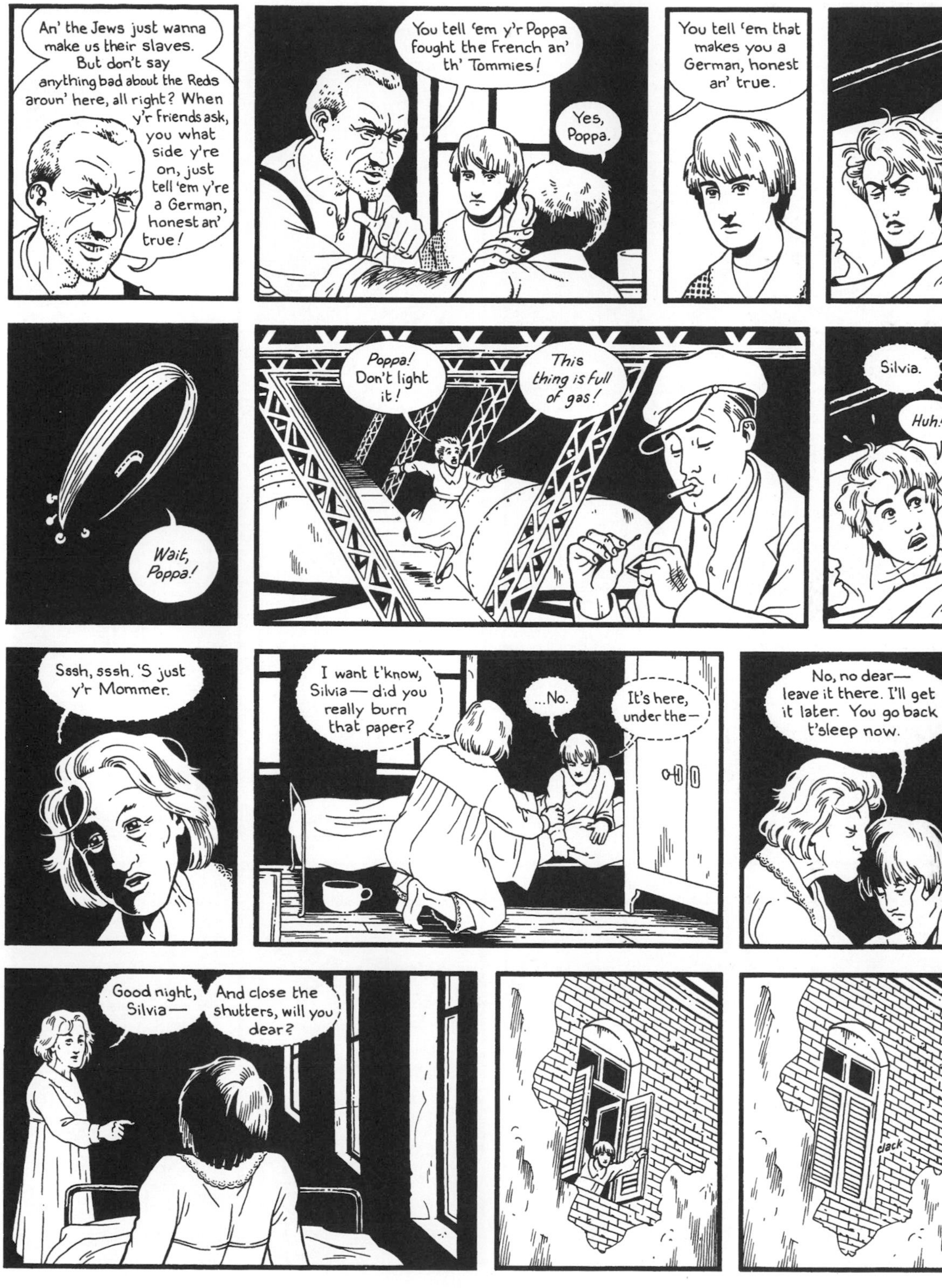

An' the Jews just wanna make us their slaves. But don't say anything bad about the Reds aroun' here, all right? When y'r friends ask, you what side y're on, just tell 'em y're a German, honest an' true!
You tell 'em y'r Poppa fought the French an' th' Tommies!
Yes, Poppa.
You tell 'em that makes you a German, honest an' true.
Wait, Poppa!
Poppa! Don't light it!
This thing is full of gas!
Silvia.
Huh!
Sssh, sssh. 'S just y'r Mommer.
I want t'know, Silvia— did you really burn that paper?
...No.
It's here, under the—
No, no dear— leave it there. I'll get it later. You go back t'sleep now.
Good night, Silvia—
And close the shutters, will you dear?
clack

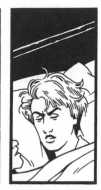

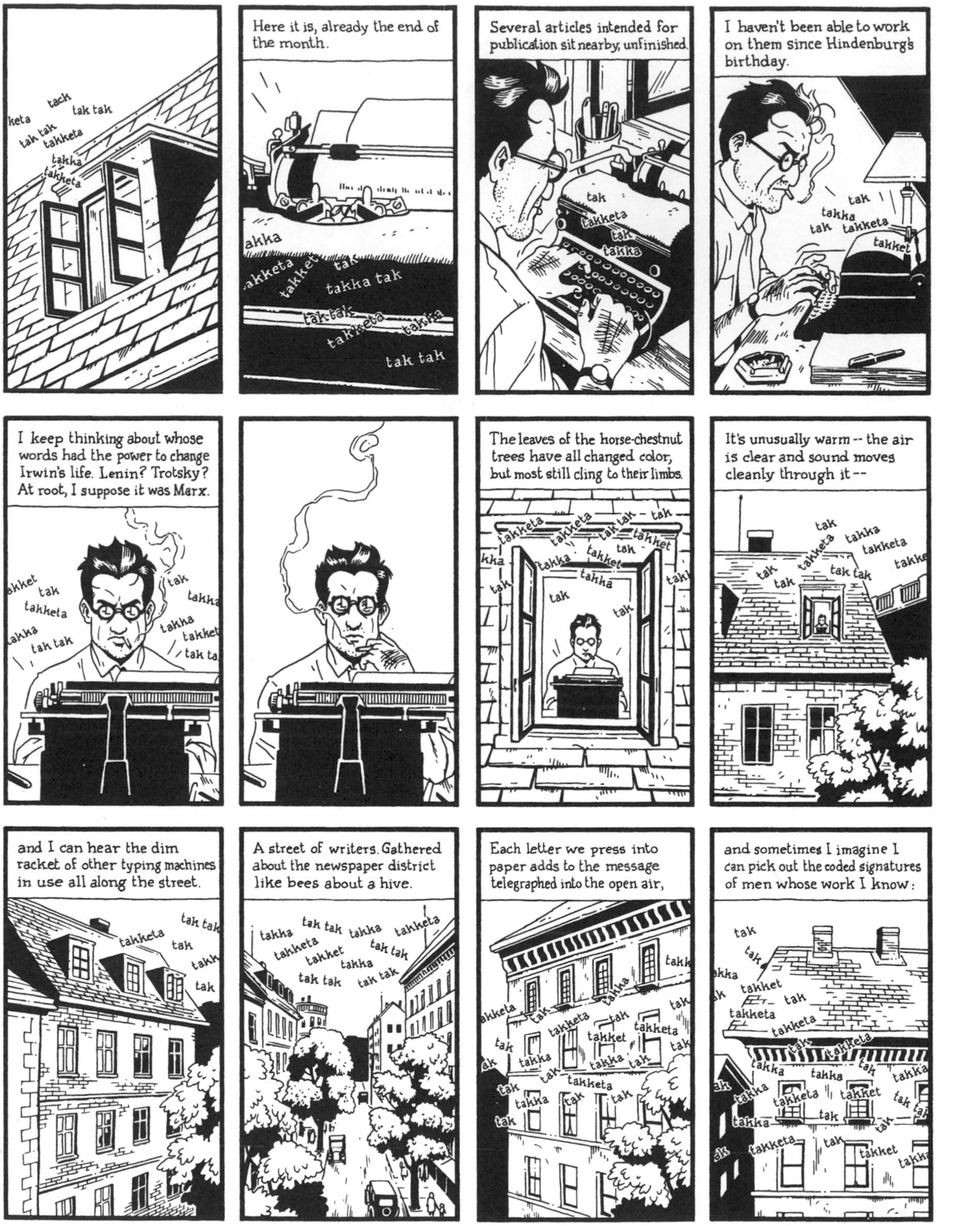
keta tack tak tak tak tak takketa takka takketa
Here it is, already the end of the month.
akka takketa takket tak takka tak tak tak takketa takka tak tak
Several articles intended for publication sit nearby, unfinished.
tak takketa tak takka
I haven't been able to work on them since Hindenburg's birthday.
tak takka tak takketa takket
I keep thinking about whose words had the power to change Irwin's life. Lenin? Trotsky? At root, I suppose it was Marx.
akket tak takketa akka tak tak tak takka takka takket tak ta
The leaves of the horse-chestnut trees have all changed color, but most still cling to their limbs.
It's unusually warm -- the air is clear and sound moves cleanly through it --
and I can hear the dim racket of other typing machines in use all along the street.
takketa tak tak tak takk tak
A street of writers. Gathered about the newspaper district like bees about a hive.
takka tak tak takka takketa takketa takket tak tak takka tak tak tak tak
Each letter we press into paper adds to the message telegraphed into the open air,
and sometimes I imagine I can pick out the coded signatures of men whose work I know:

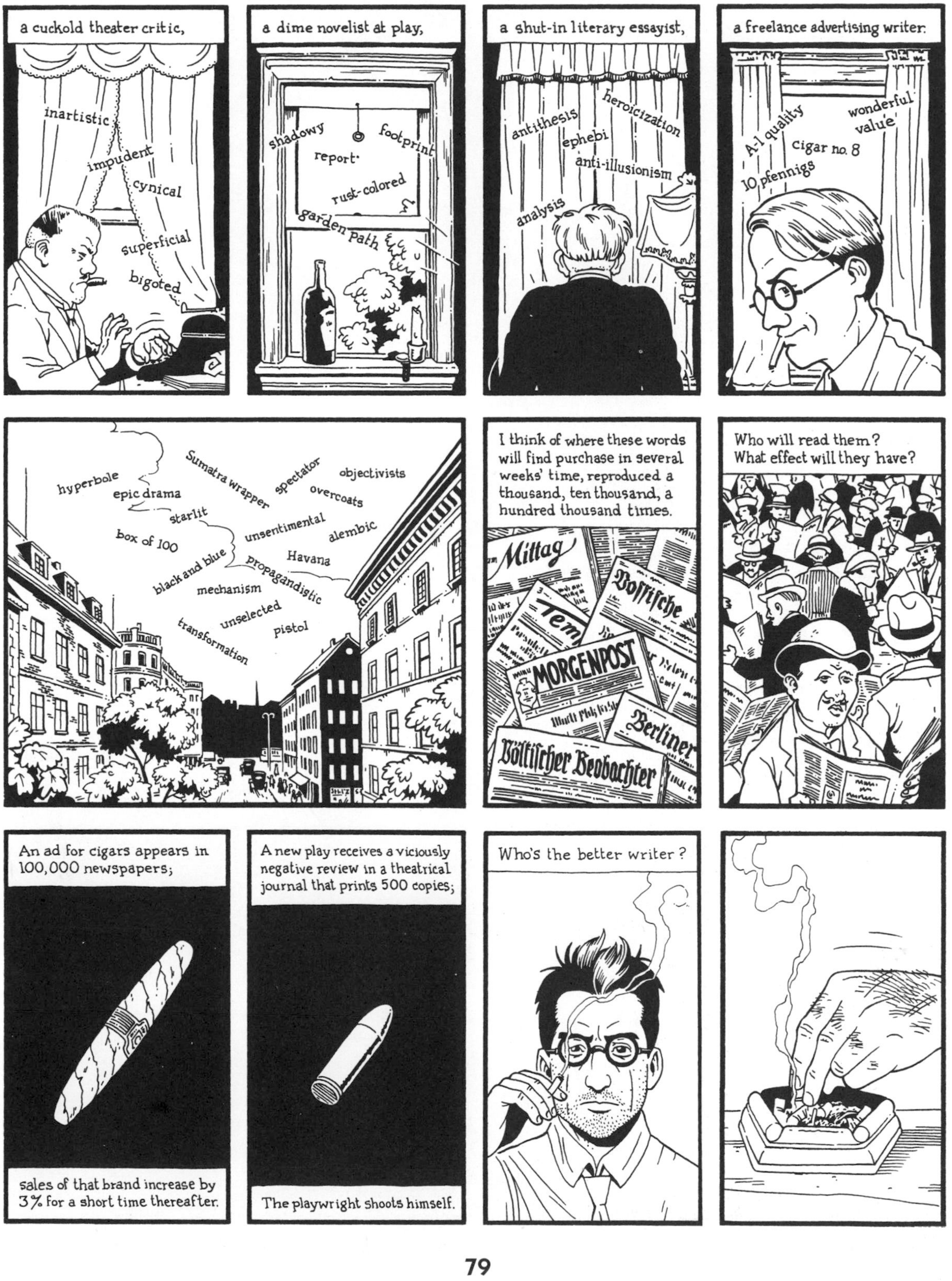

a cuckold theater critic,
inartistic
impudent
cynical
superficial
bigoted
a dime novelist at play,
shadowy
footprint
report
rust-colored
garden path
a shut-in literary essayist,
antithesis
heroicization
ephebi
anti-illusionism
analysis
a freelance advertising writer.
A-1 quality
wonderful value
cigar no. 8
10 pfennigs
hyperbole
epic drama
Sumatra wrapper
spectator
objectivists
overcoats
starlit
unsentimental
alembic
box of 100
Havana
black and blue
propagandistic
mechanism
unselected
pistol
transformation
I think of where these words will find purchase in several weeks' time, reproduced a thousand, ten thousand, a hundred thousand times.
Mittag
Vossische
MORGENPOST
Berliner
Völkischer Beobachter
Who will read them? What effect will they have?
An ad for cigars appears in 100,000 newspapers;
sales of that brand increase by 3% for a short time thereafter.
A new play receives a viciously negative review in a theatrical journal that prints 500 copies;
The playwright shoots himself.
Who's the better writer?

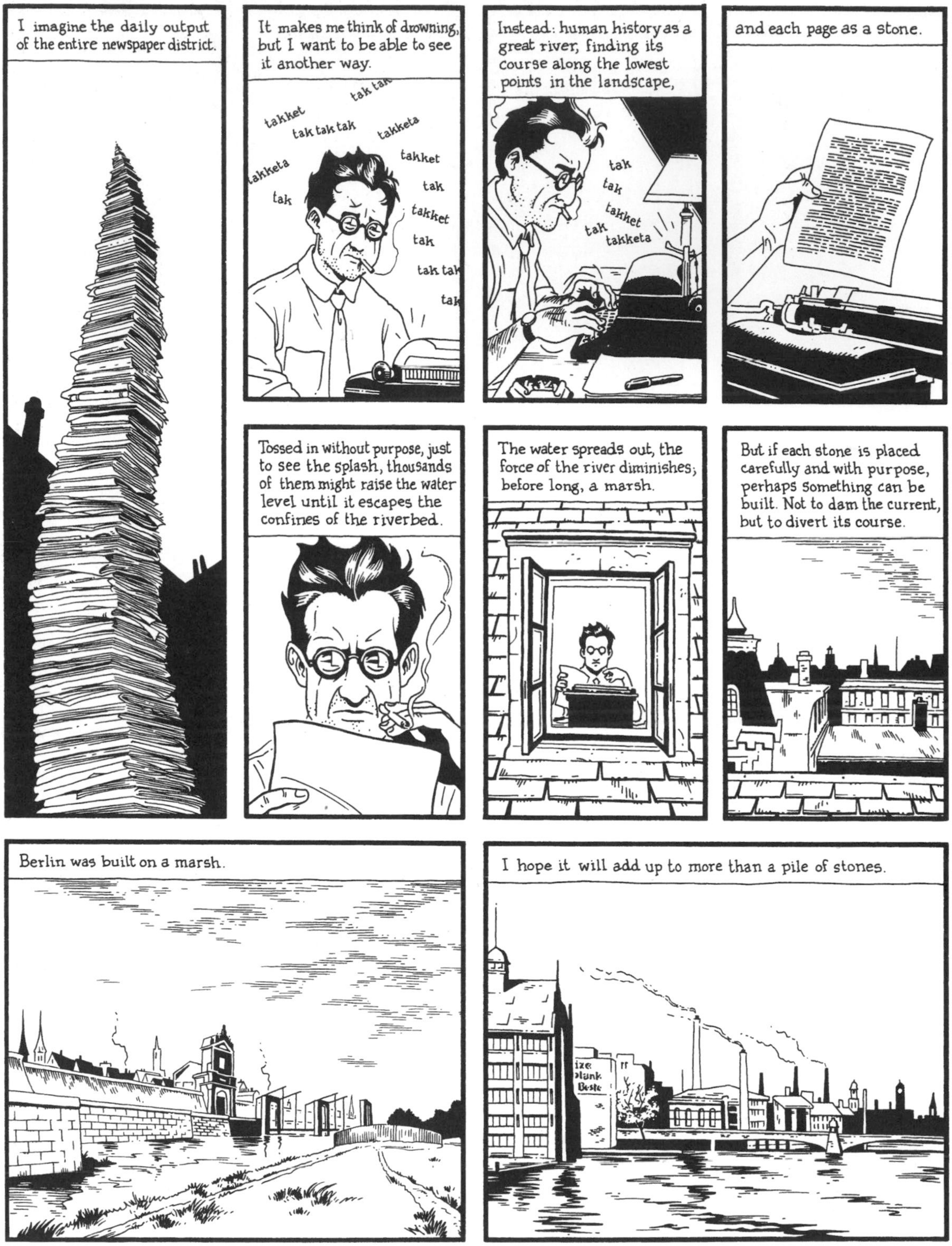
I imagine the daily output of the entire newspaper district.
It makes me think of drowning, but I want to be able to see it another way.
takket tak tak tak tak tak takketa takket takketa tak tak takket tak tak tak tak
Instead: human history as a great river, finding its course along the lowest points in the landscape,
tak tak takket tak takketa
and each page as a stone.
Tossed in without purpose, just to see the splash, thousands of them might raise the water level until it escapes the confines of the riverbed.
The water spreads out, the force of the river diminishes; before long, a marsh.
But if each stone is placed carefully and with purpose, perhaps something can be built. Not to dam the current, but to divert its course.
Berlin was built on a marsh.
I hope it will add up to more than a pile of stones.

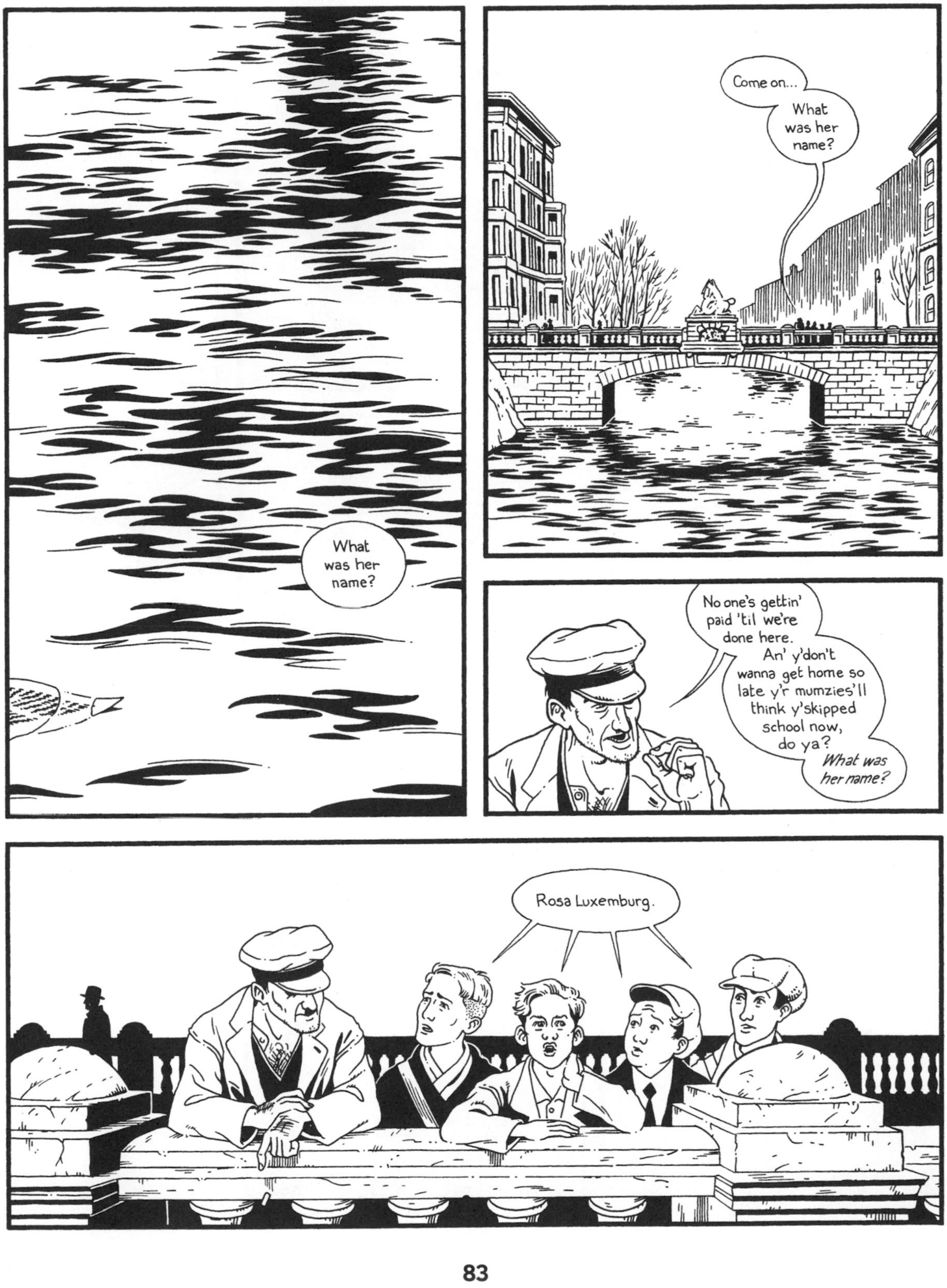
What was her name?
Come on... What was her name?
No one's gettin' paid 'til we're done here.
An' y'don't wanna get home so late y'r mumzies'll think y'skipped school now, do ya?
What was her name?
Rosa Luxemburg.

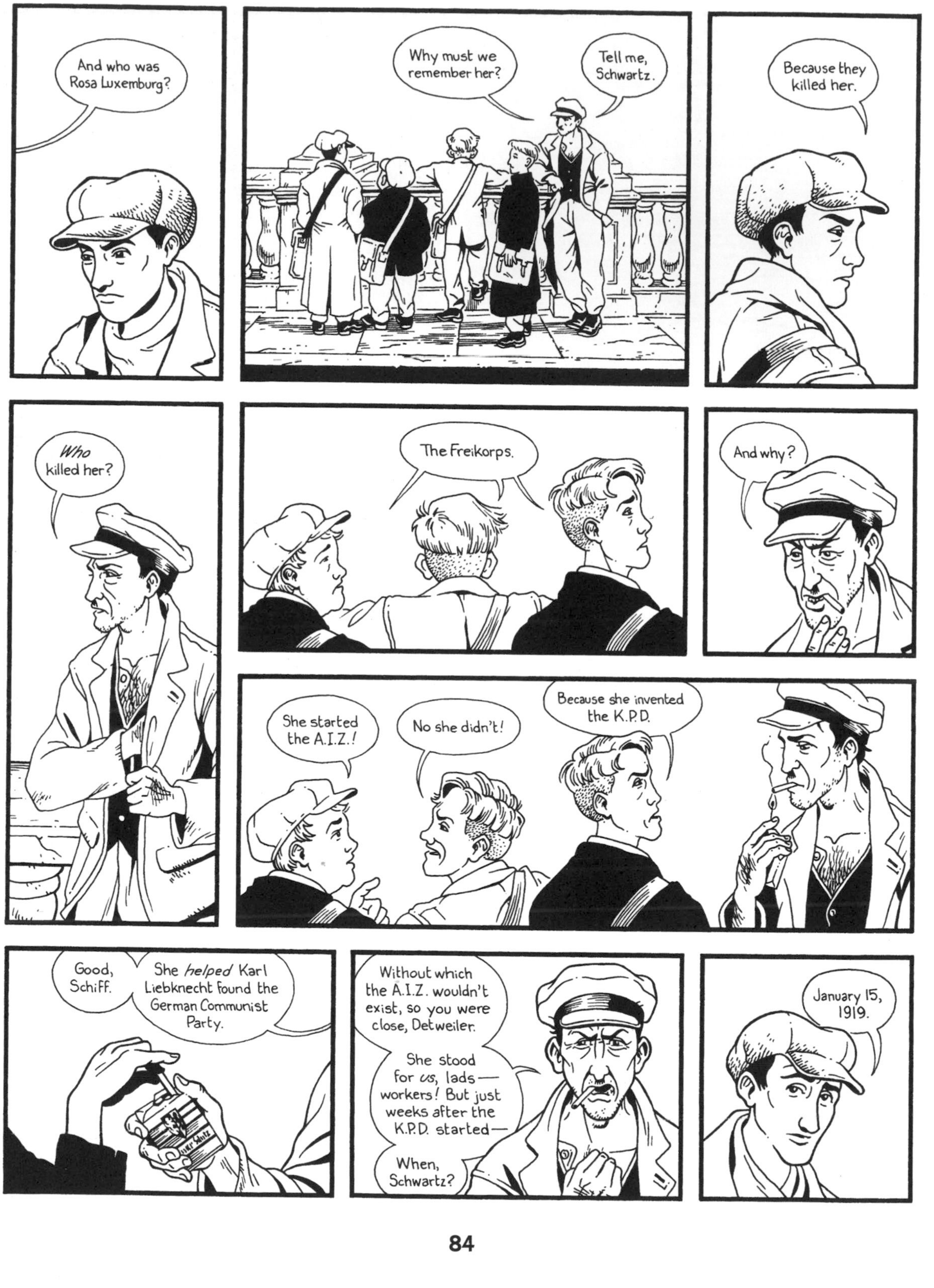

And who was Rosa Luxemburg?
Why must we remember her?
Tell me, Schwartz.
Because they killed her.
Who killed her?
The Freikorps.
And why?
She started the A.I.Z.!
No she didn't!
Because she invented the K.P.D.
Good, Schiff.
She *helped* Karl Liebknecht found the German Communist Party.
Without which the A.I.Z. wouldn't exist, so you were close, Detweiler.
She stood for *us*, lads— workers! But just weeks after the K.P.D. started—
When, Schwartz?
January 15, 1919.

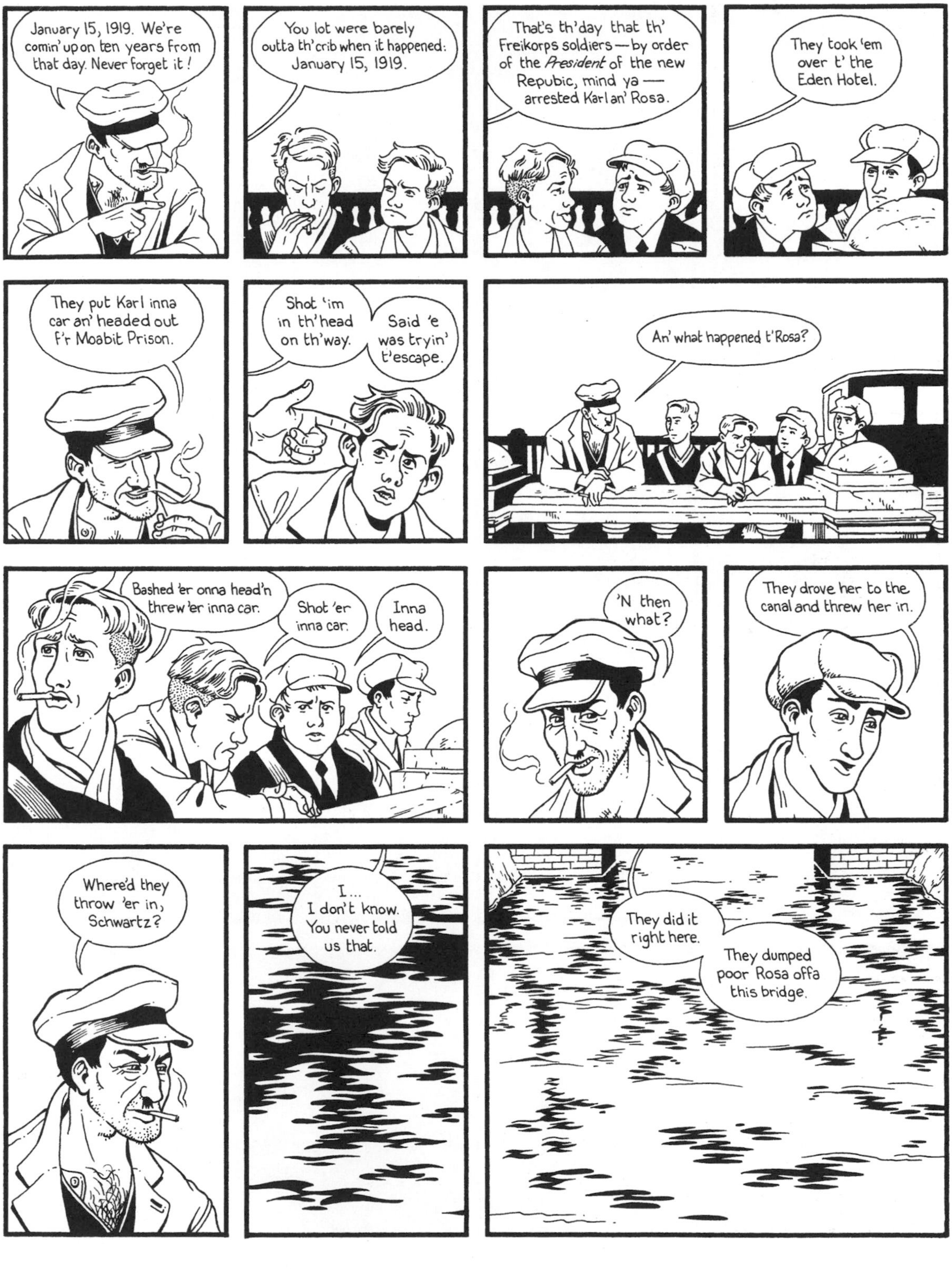
January 15, 1919. We're comin' up on ten years from that day. Never forget it!
You lot were barely outta th' crib when it happened: January 15, 1919.
That's th'day that th' Freikorps soldiers — by order of the *President* of the new Repubic, mind ya — arrested Karl an' Rosa.
They took 'em over t' the Eden Hotel.
They put Karl inna car an' headed out f'r Moabit Prison.
Shot 'im in th'head on th'way.
Said 'e was tryin' t'escape.
An' what happened t'Rosa?
Bashed 'er onna head'n threw 'er inna car.
Shot 'er inna car.
Inna head.
'N then what?
They drove her to the canal and threw her in.
Where'd they throw 'er in, Schwartz?
I... I don't know. You never told us that.
They did it right here.
They dumped poor Rosa offa this bridge.

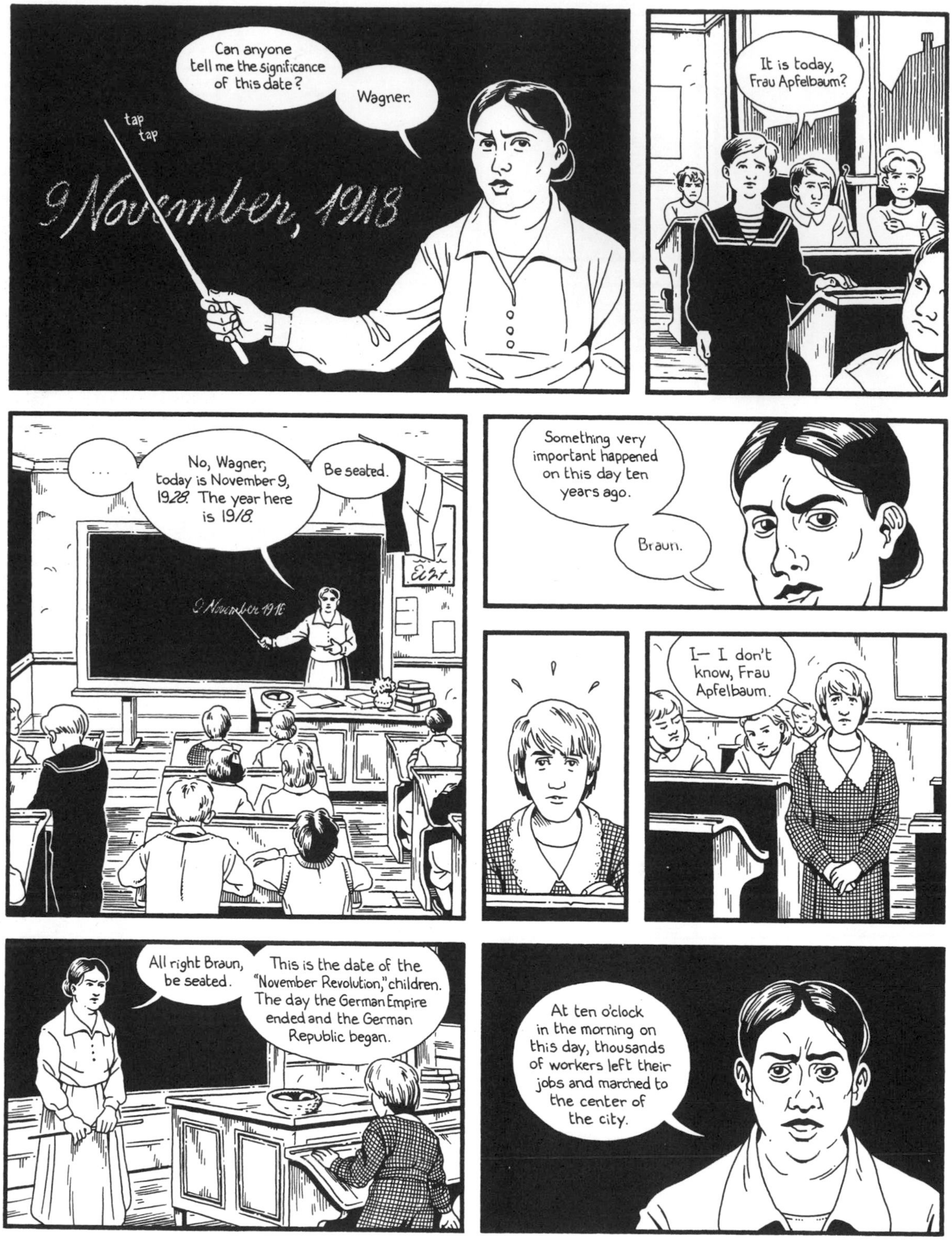

Can anyone tell me the significance of this date?
Wagner.
tap tap
9 November, 1918
It is today, Frau Apfelbaum?
...
No, Wagner, today is November 9, 1928. The year here is 1918.
Be seated.
Something very important happened on this day ten years ago.
Braun.
I— I don't know, Frau Apfelbaum.
All right Braun, be seated.
This is the date of the "November Revolution," children. The day the German Empire ended and the German Republic began.
At ten o'clock in the morning on this day, thousands of workers left their jobs and marched to the center of the city.

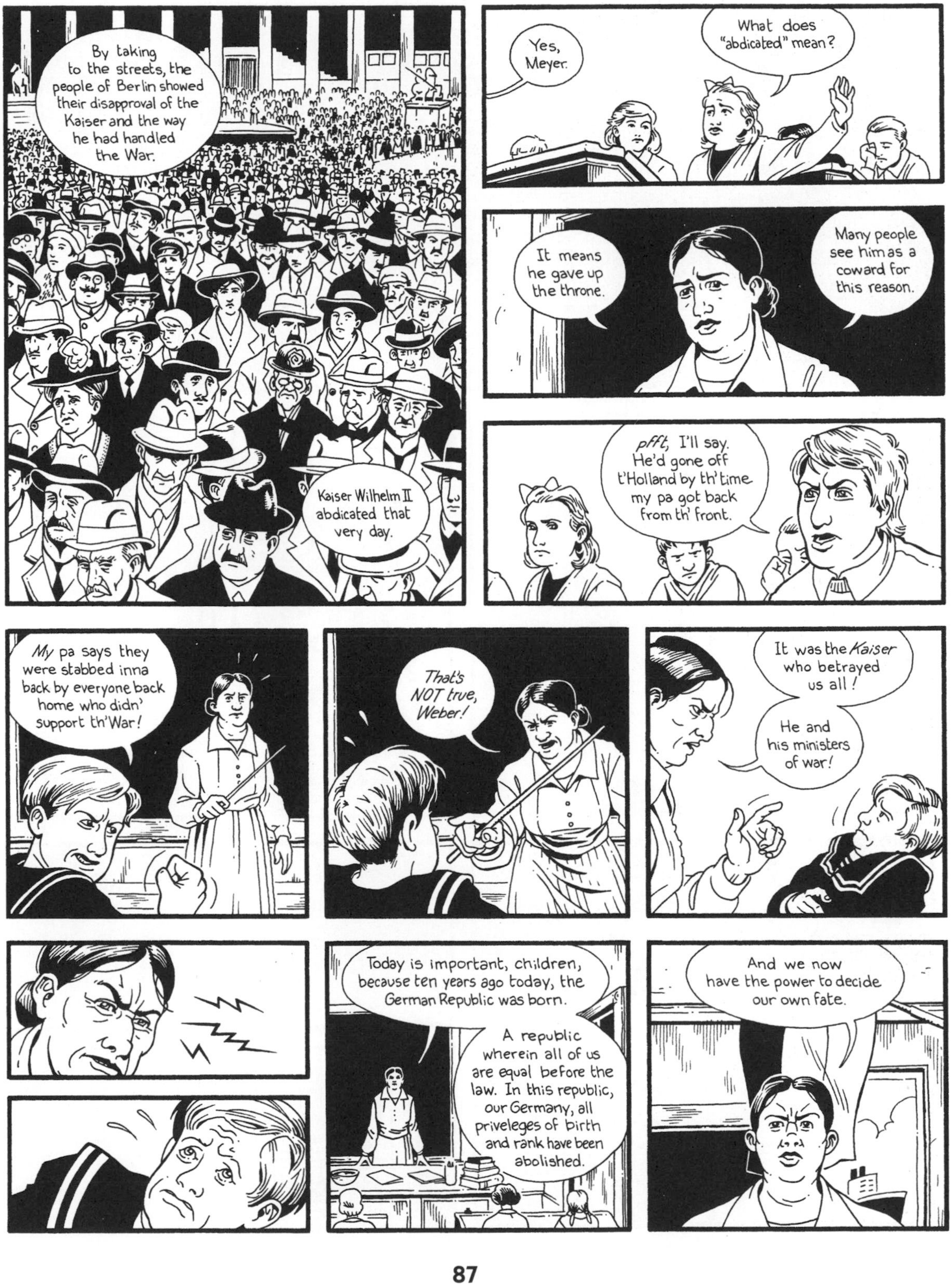

By taking to the streets, the people of Berlin showed their disapproval of the Kaiser and the way he had handled the War.
Kaiser Wilhelm II abdicated that very day.
Yes, Meyer.
What does "abdicated" mean?
It means he gave up the throne.
Many people see him as a coward for this reason.
pfft, I'll say. He'd gone off t'Holland by th' time my pa got back from th' front.
My pa says they were stabbed inna back by everyone back home who didn' support th' War!
That's NOT true, Weber!
It was the Kaiser who betrayed us all!
He and his ministers of war!
Today is important, children, because ten years ago today, the German Republic was born.
A republic wherein all of us are equal before the law. In this republic, our Germany, all priveleges of birth and rank have been abolished.
And we now have the power to decide our own fate.

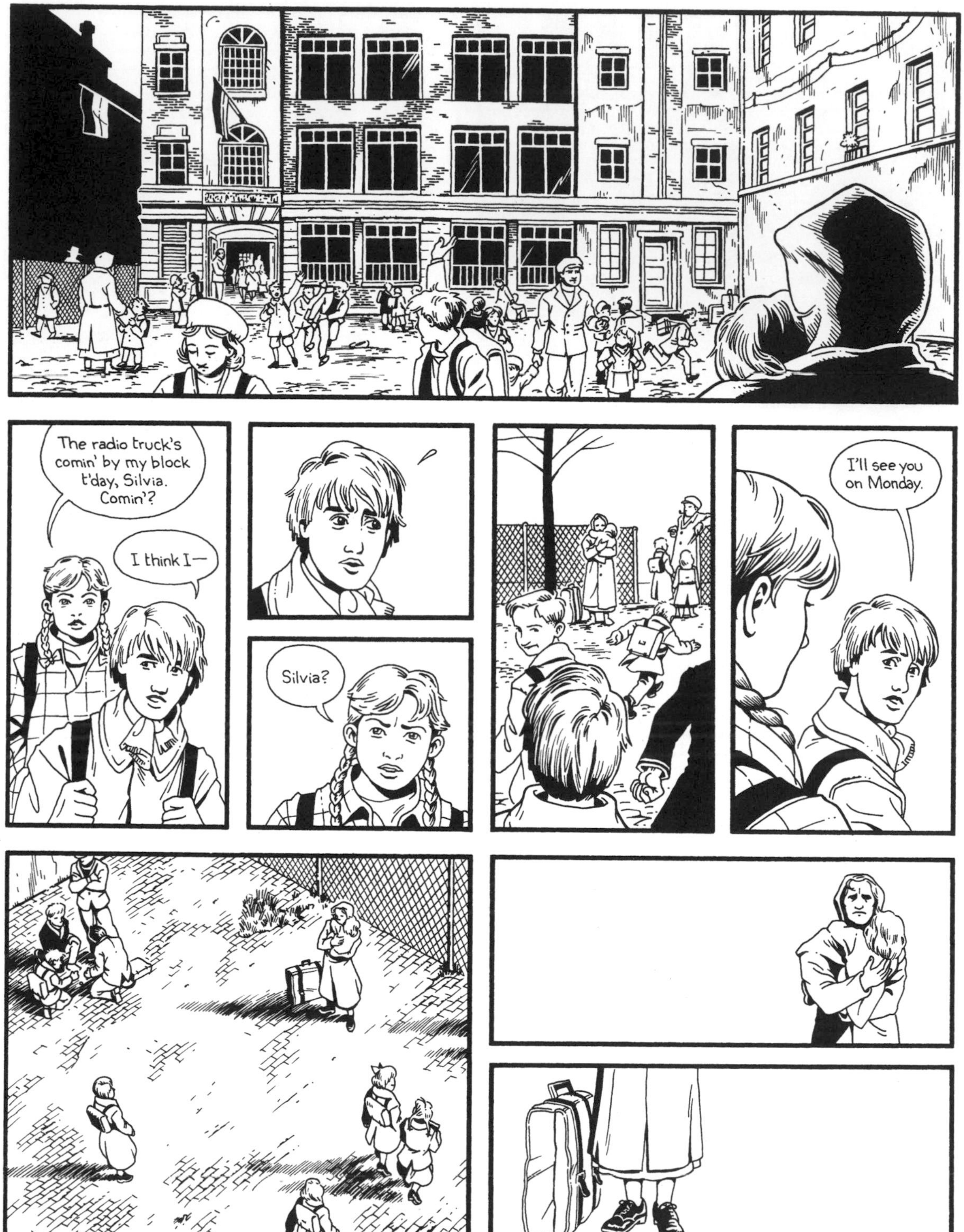

The radio truck's comin' by my block t'day, Silvia. Comin'?
I think I—
Silvia?
I'll see you on Monday.

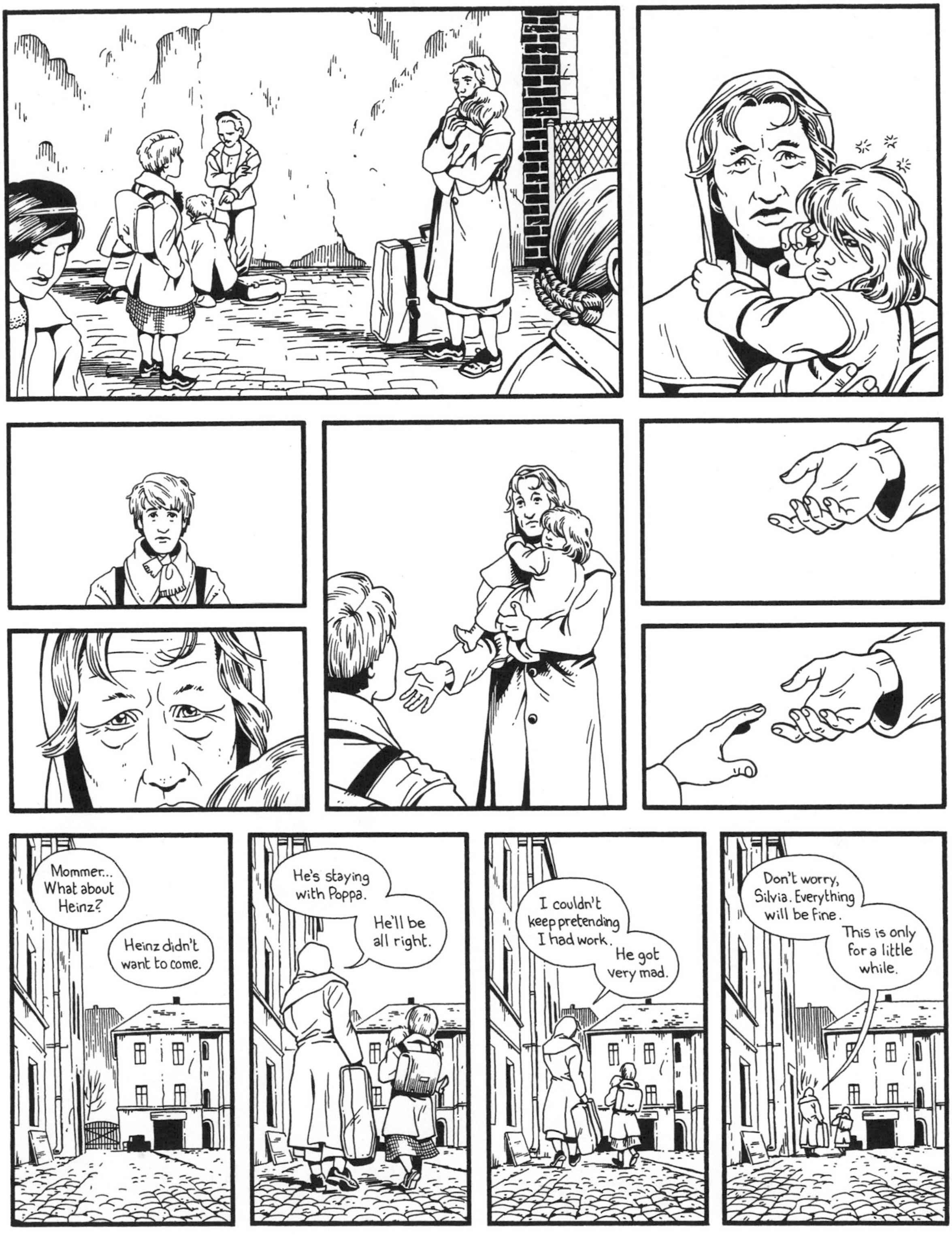
Mommer... What about Heinz?
Heinz didn't want to come.
He's staying with Poppa.
He'll be all right.
I couldn't keep pretending I had work.
He got very mad.
Don't worry, Silvia. Everything will be fine.
This is only for a little while.

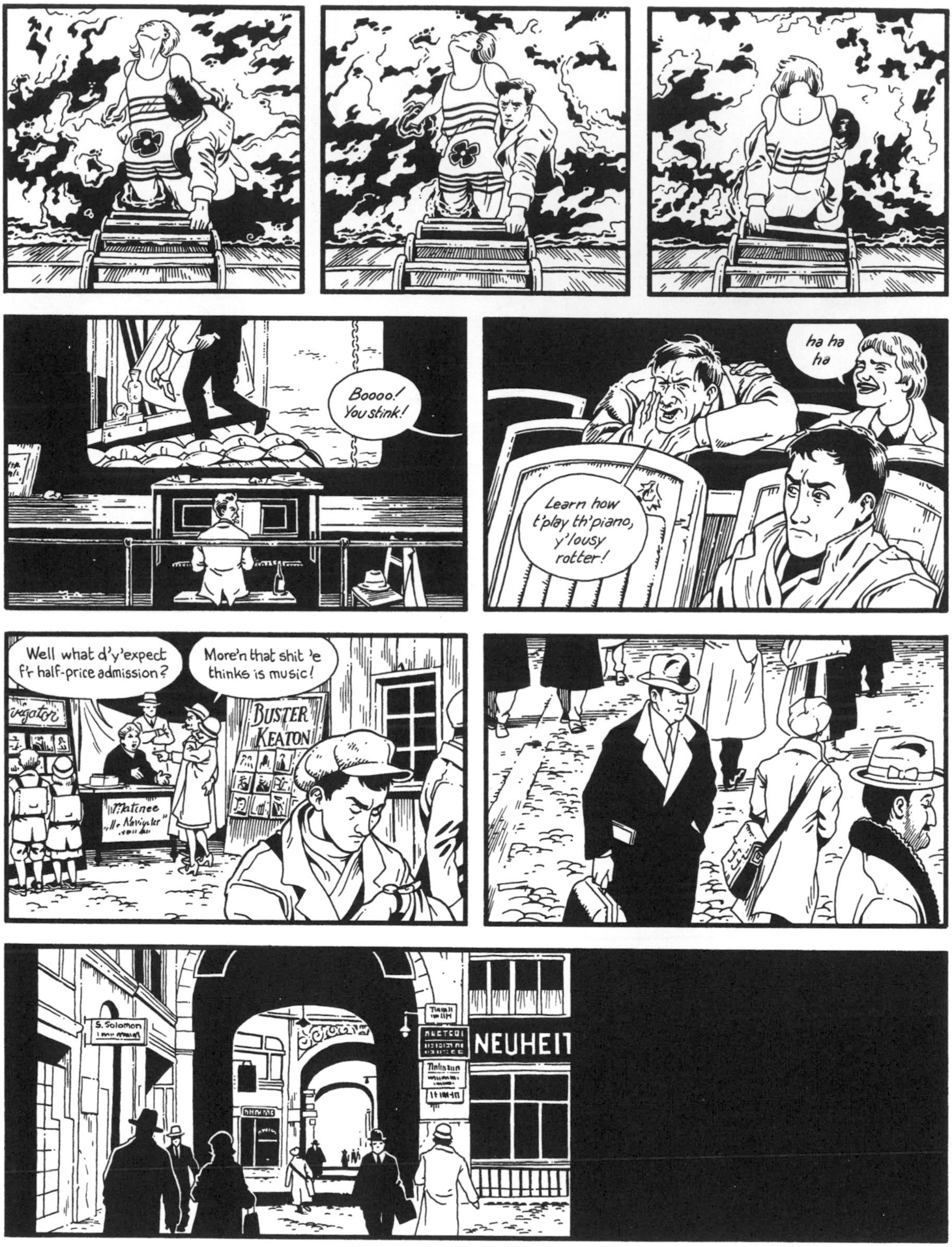

Boooo! You stink!
Learn how t'play th'piano, y'lousy rotter!
ha ha ha
Well what d'y'expect f'r half-price admission?
More'n that shit 'e thinks is music!
BUSTER KEATON
Matinee
S. Solomon
NEUHEIT

And what did they teach you in school today, David?

More about Charlemagne.

This is how he spends his days?

God *weeps* over one who might have studied the Torah but neglected to do so!

Tateh, we're German now. David must go to a German school and learn the same things as all the other German children.

And not as other Jews? Born here he may have been, but no home has he who knows not the Five Books of Moses!

A *kaporeh* on these "Emperors!"

More important is the word of —

ENOUGH!

You are German now as well, Abraham, like it or not!

It's Germany that allowed us to bring you from Breslau! It's Germany that feeds us and clothes us!

Feh!

To Germany, to Austria, to France—What good are these places when the further west we move, the further we get from ourselves?

You're excused, David. Go up and study.

Your own parents, Berthold...

They don't even go to temple!

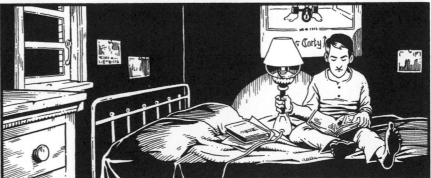

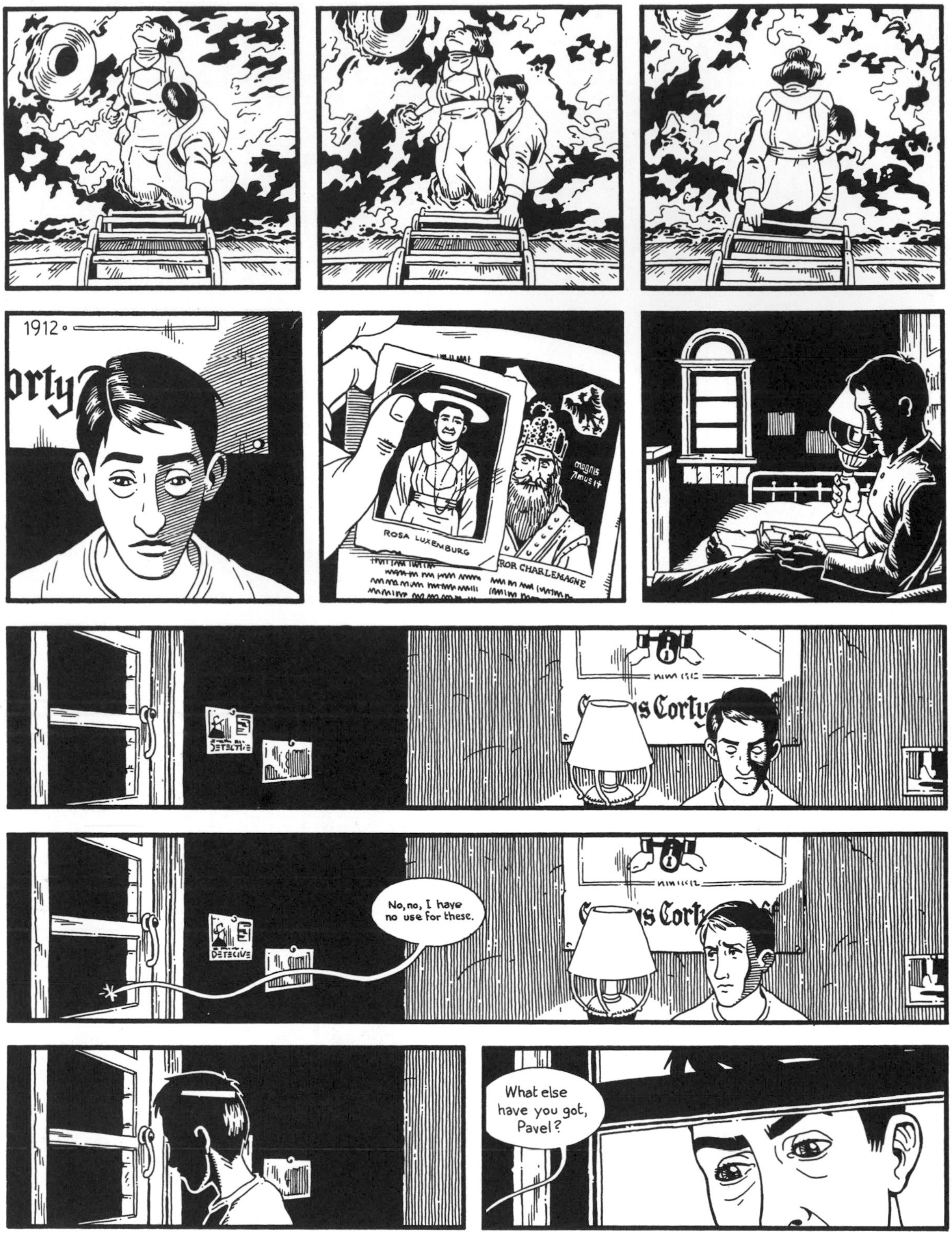
1912
ROSA LUXEMBURG
ROR CHARLEMAGNE
DETECTIVE
No, no, I have no use for these.
What else have you got, Pavel?

Ah, a little scuffed, but...

Tearing down old buildings in Wedding, they are — All kinds of things left in the rubble.

Excellent. Did you find anything else worth keeping?

One other thing only, this trip. In what was left of the old post office.

Ha ha! The seal of the Imperial Post! I can't believe it!

Would you look at that! A fine price this'll fetch from any closet Kaiser-lover!

Little need I see them having to hide such love, these Germans.

Yes, well... Pavel, the tools are useless, but I'll take the rest. Fifteen marks for the lot.

Fifteen! Don't do me any favors, eh, Herr Schwartz?

Twenty is all I'll allow, and only because I'm feeling so generous.

I should be that rich! Seventeen is all you'll get from me.

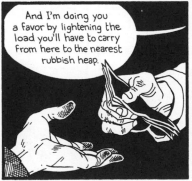

And I'm doing you a favor by lightening the load you'll have to carry from here to the nearest rubbish heap.

You remain in debt to me, Herr Schwartz!

Next week, I'll collect with interest!

Seventeen marks—
Fish cooked in garlic sauce...
New leather soles, a book...
What book?
Fish cooked in garlic sauce!
Fresh off th'... Fresh...
Where're y'from?
Are y'listenin' t'me?
BOY! I ASKED YA A QUESTION!
I CAN'T HEAR YOU— SHELLING'S TOO LOUD!
There—It's stopped now, hasn't it?
It's f'r you t'decide— I can hardly tell th' difference anymore.
Y'll get used to it soon enough.
I'd ask you y'r name, but I tend t' think it's bad luck.
M-Müller...

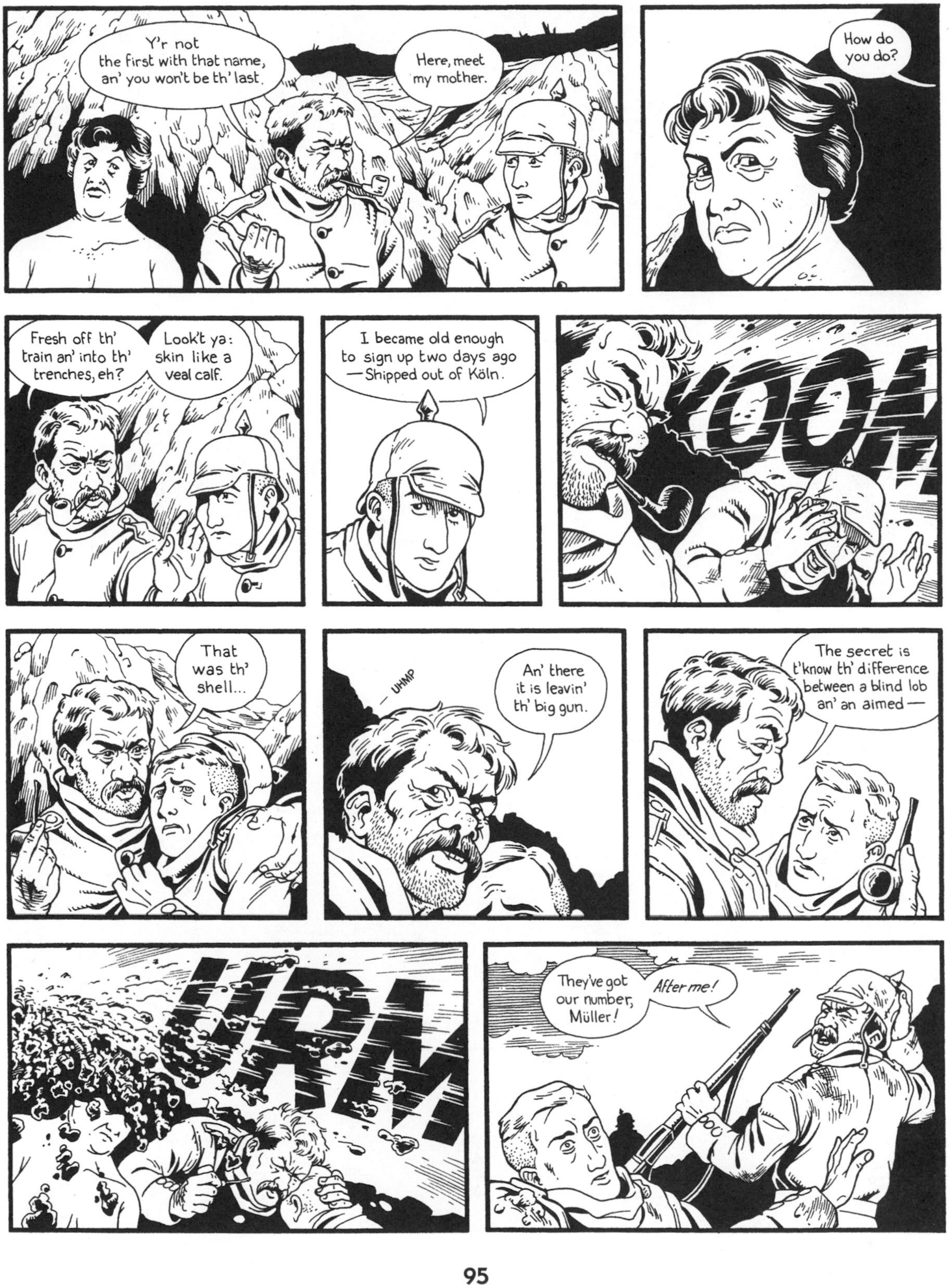

Y'r not the first with that name, an' you won't be th' last.
Here, meet my mother.
How do you do?
Fresh off th' train an' into th' trenches, eh?
Look't ya: skin like a veal calf.
I became old enough to sign up two days ago —Shipped out of Köln.
VOOM
That was th' shell...
UHMP
An' there it is leavin' th' big gun.
The secret is t'know th' difference between a blind lob an' an aimed —
URM
They've got our number, Müller!
After me!

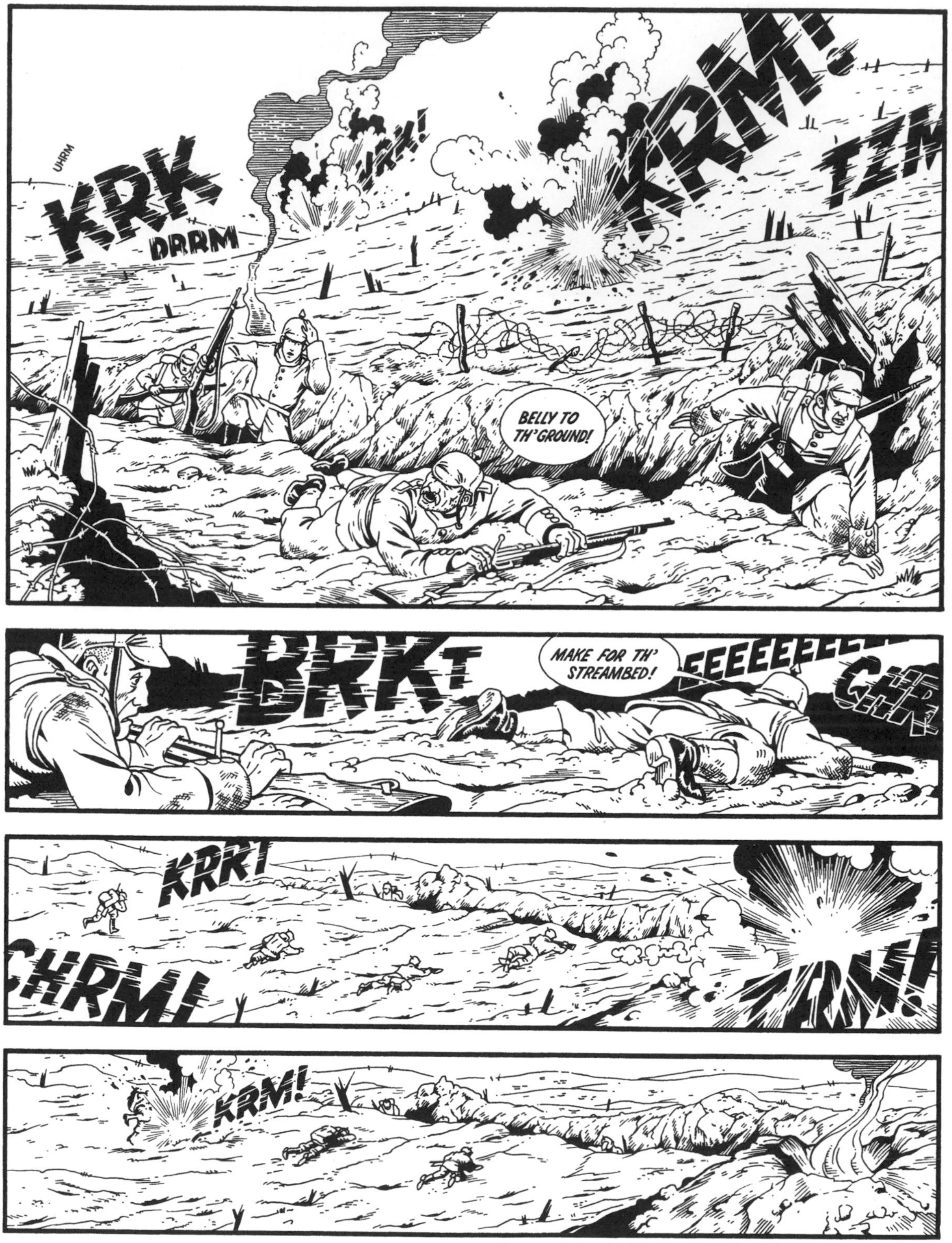
UHRM
KRK
DRRM
KRM!
TZM
BELLY TO TH' GROUND!
BRKT
MAKE FOR TH' STREAMBED!
CHRM!
KRM!

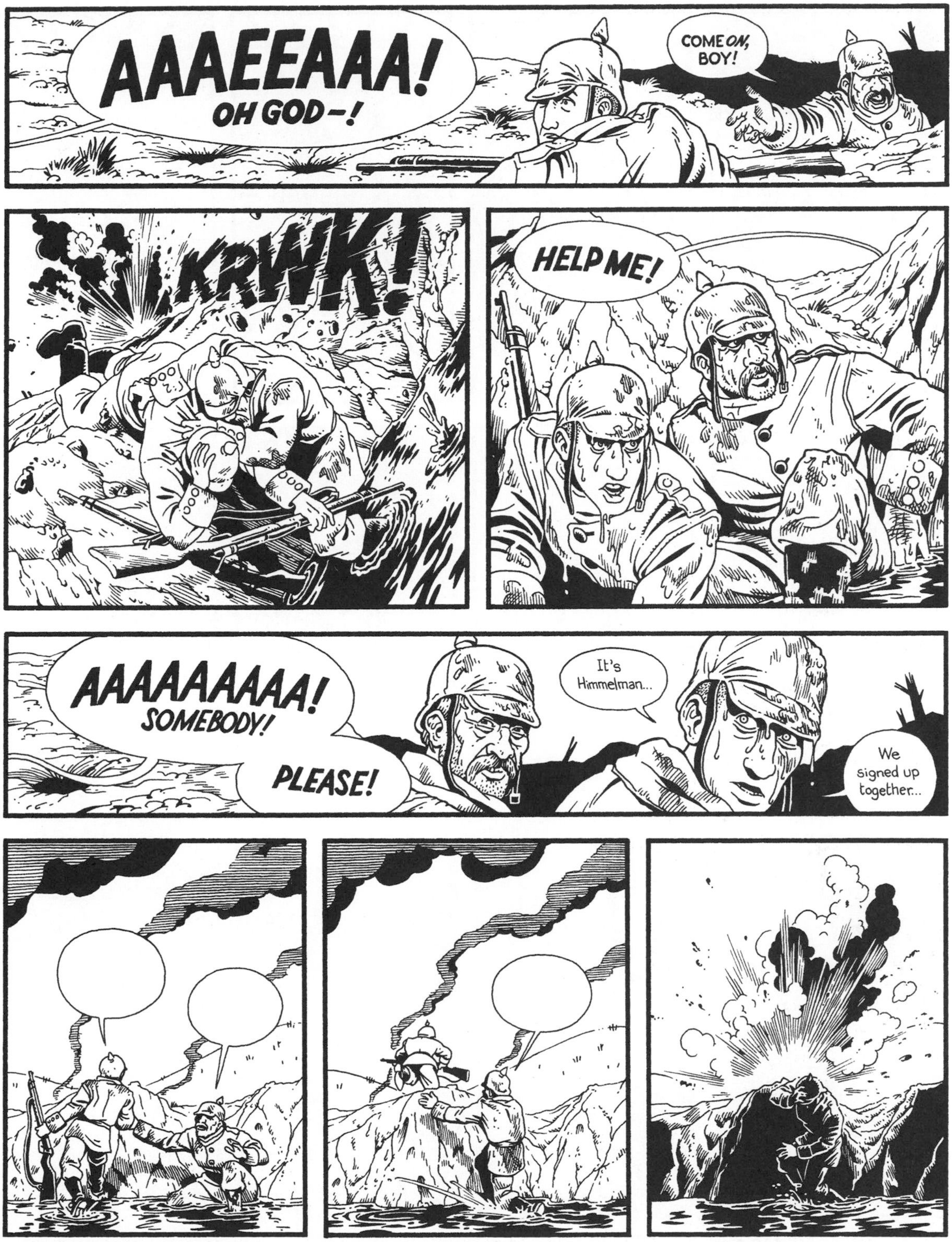
AAAEEAAA!
OH GOD–!
COME ON, BOY!
KRWK!
HELP ME!
AAAAAAAAA!
SOMEBODY!
PLEASE!
It's Himmelman...
We signed up together...

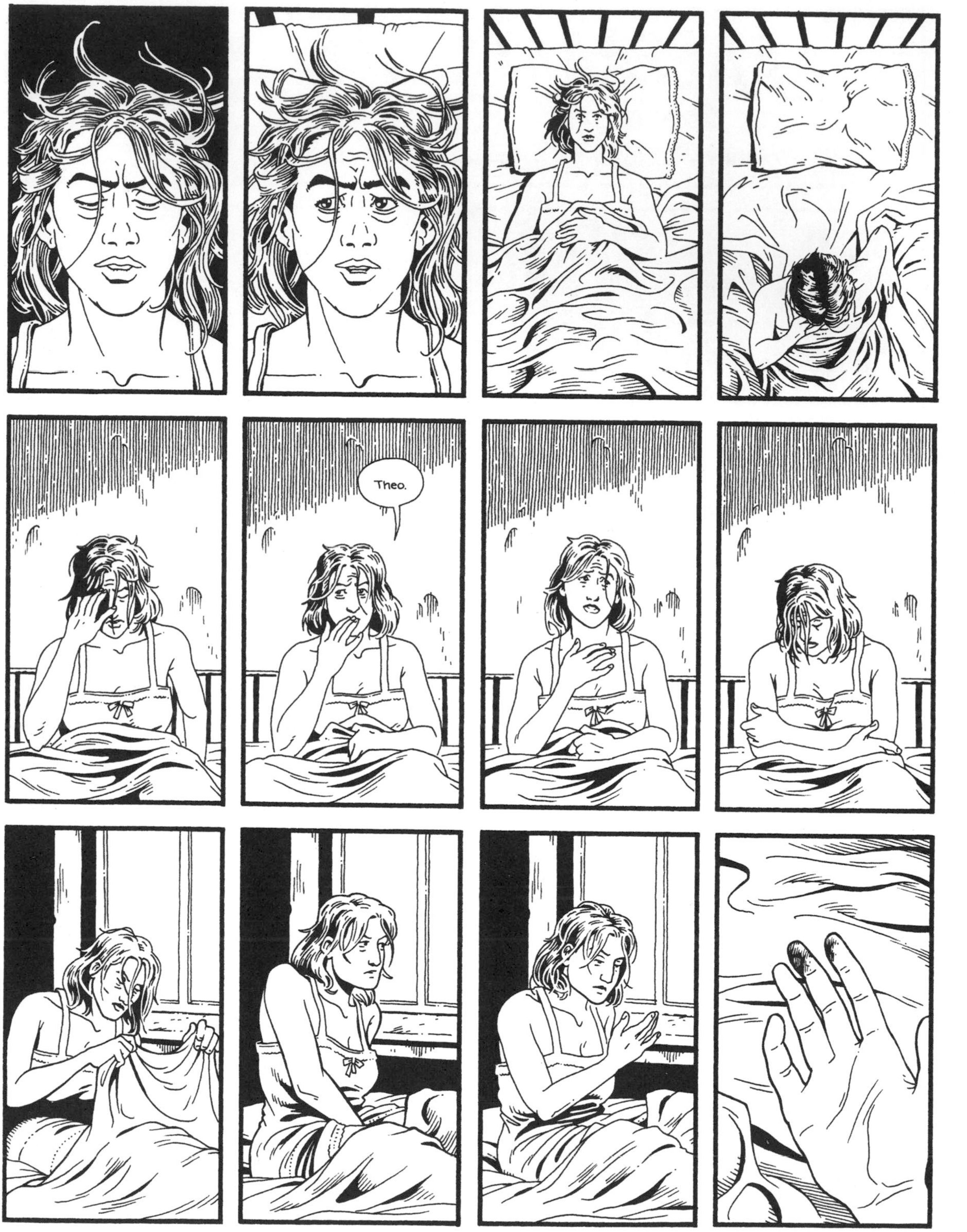
Theo.

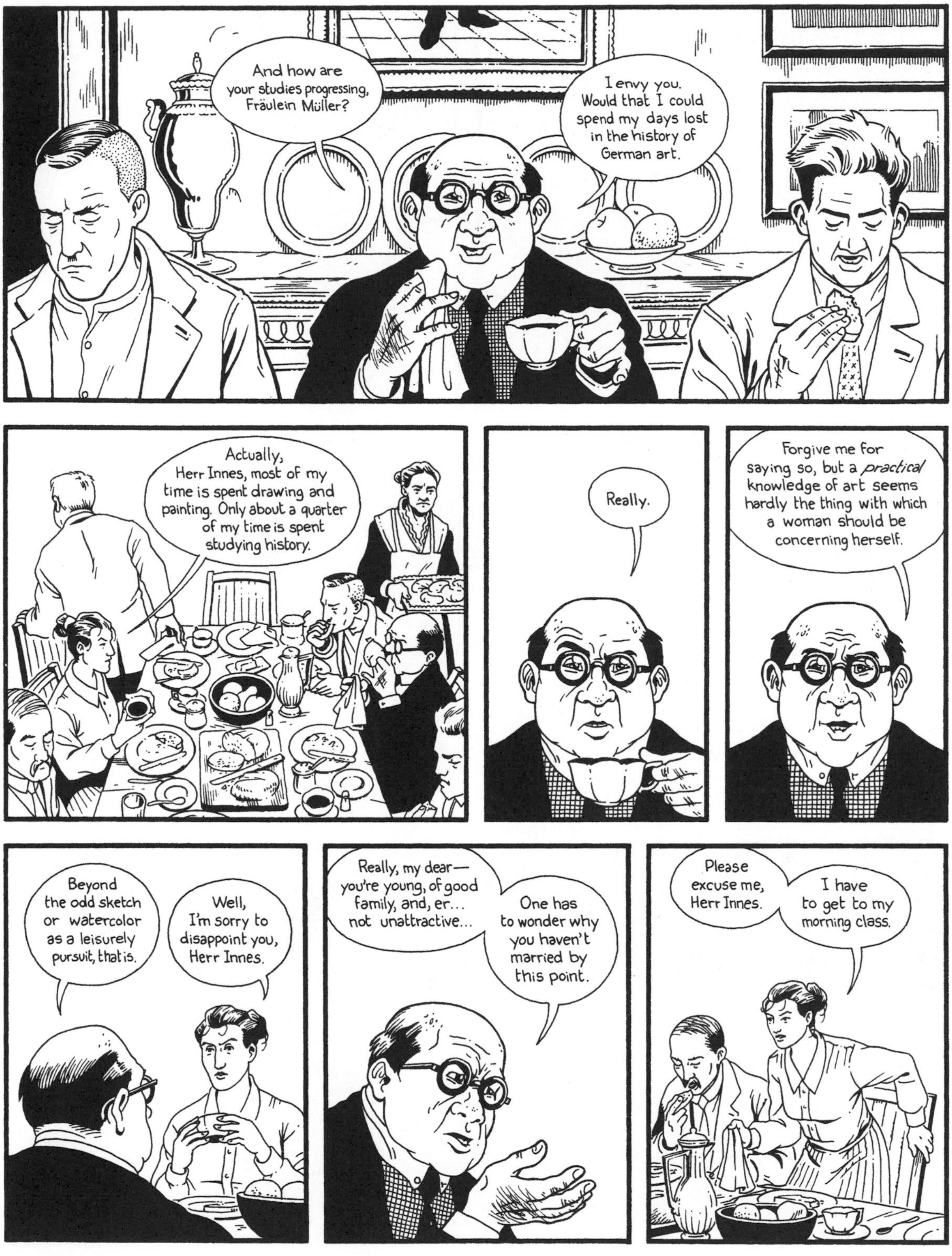
And how are your studies progressing, Fräulein Müller?
I envy you. Would that I could spend my days lost in the history of German art.
Actually, Herr Innes, most of my time is spent drawing and painting. Only about a quarter of my time is spent studying history.
Really.
Forgive me for saying so, but a *practical* knowledge of art seems hardly the thing with which a woman should be concerning herself.
Beyond the odd sketch or watercolor as a leisurely pursuit, that is.
Well, I'm sorry to disappoint you, Herr Innes.
Really, my dear— you're young, of good family, and, er... not unattractive...
One has to wonder why you haven't married by this point.
Please excuse me, Herr Innes.
I have to get to my morning class.

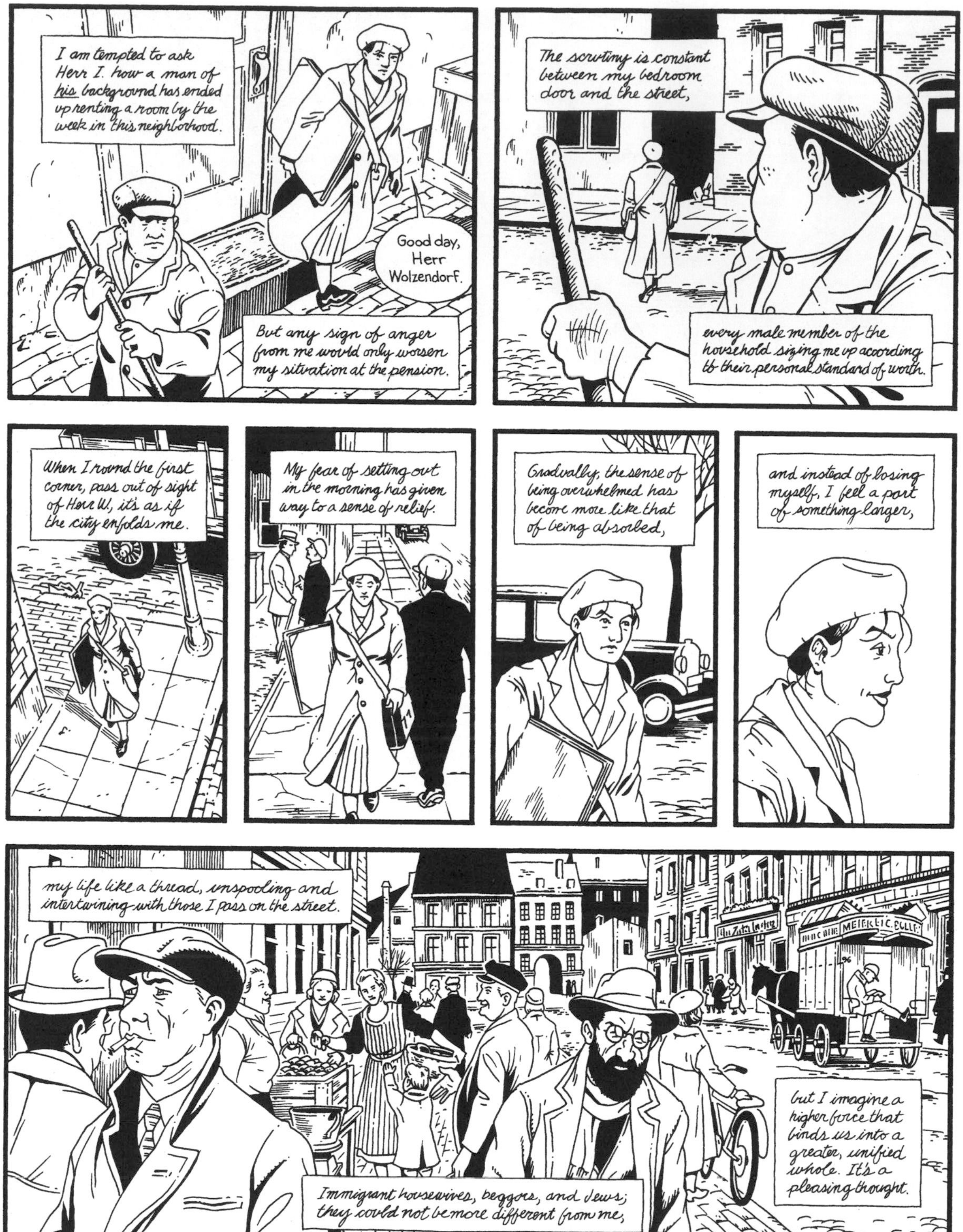
I am tempted to ask Herr I. how a man of his background has ended up renting a room by the week in this neighborhood.
Good day, Herr Wolzendorf.
But any sign of anger from me would only worsen my situation at the pension.
The scrutiny is constant between my bedroom door and the street,
every male member of the household sizing me up according to their personal standard of worth.
When I round the first corner, pass out of sight of Herr W, it's as if the city enfolds me.
My fear of setting out in the morning has given way to a sense of relief.
Gradually, the sense of being overwhelmed has become more like that of being absorbed,
and instead of losing myself, I feel a part of something larger,
my life like a thread, unspooling and intertwining with those I pass on the street.
Immigrant housewives, beggars, and Jews; they could not be more different from me,
but I imagine a higher force that binds us into a greater, unified whole. It's a pleasing thought.

"Horizontal" derives from the word "horizon."

Here, we have a horizontal dividing the drawing surface into two halves, which we'll call sky and ground; a horizon line.

As the horizontal, mm, defines the extent of our vision in the world, so the horizon *line* defines the extent of the draughtsman's vision in his *representation* of the world on the page.

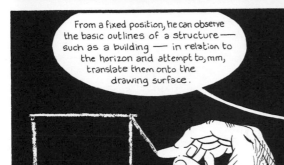

From a fixed position, he can observe the basic outlines of a structure — such as a building — in relation to the horizon and attempt to, mm, translate them onto the drawing surface.

Through such, mm, observation, Renaissance artists and architects discovered a set of scientific laws which govern the two-dimensional depiction of three-dimensional objects.

The foremost of these states that the parallel horizontal edges of a plane not directly facing the observer — the top and bottom edges of the right side of the building, in this case—

when drawn out to intersect the horizon line, meet at a single point.

The point towards which objects begin to vanish. Or, "vanishing point."

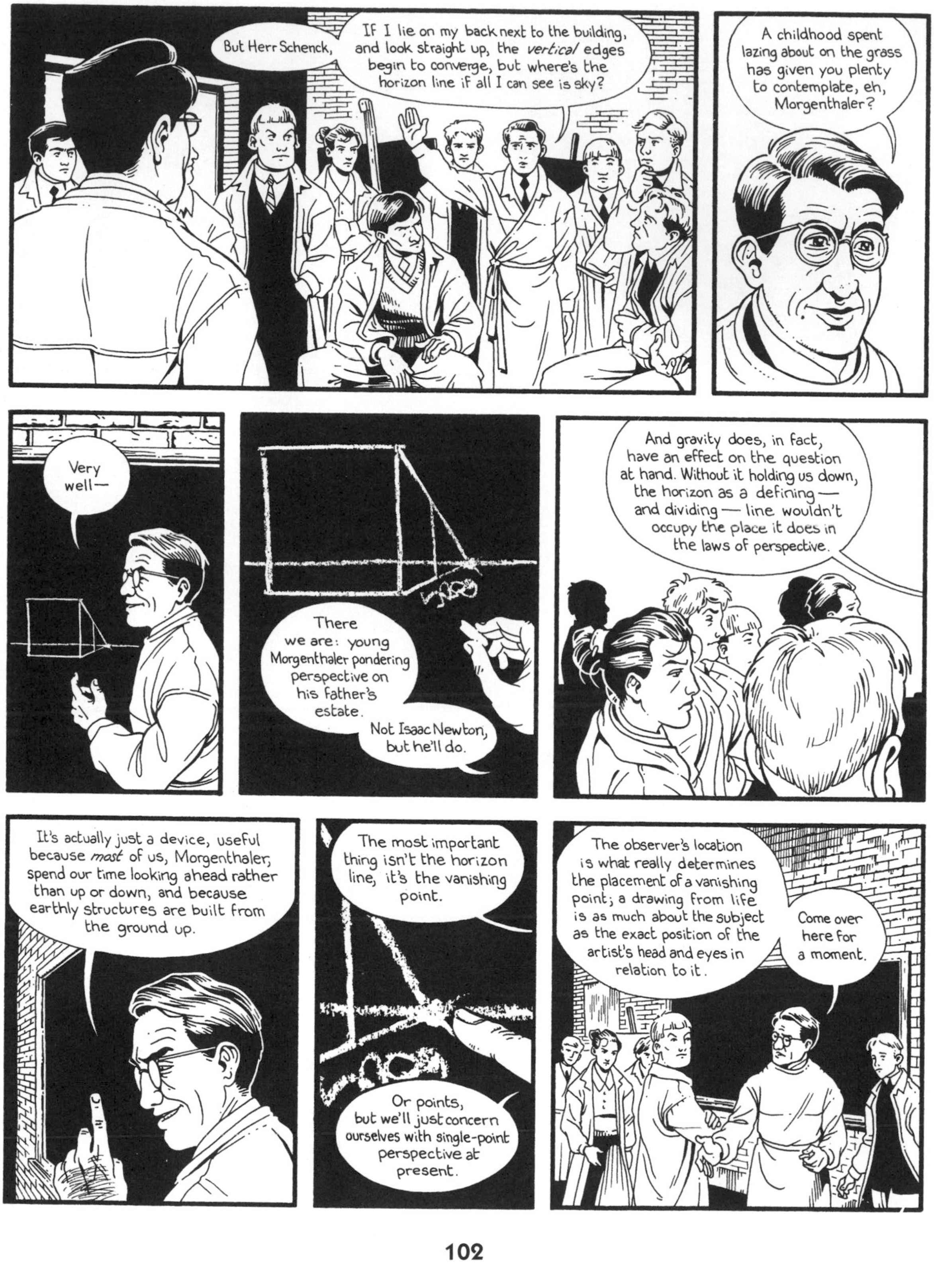
But Herr Schenck,
If I lie on my back next to the building, and look straight up, the *vertical* edges begin to converge, but where's the horizon line if all I can see is sky?
A childhood spent lazing about on the grass has given you plenty to contemplate, eh, Morgenthaler?
Very well—
There we are: young Morgenthaler pondering perspective on his father's estate.
Not Isaac Newton, but he'll do.
And gravity does, in fact, have an effect on the question at hand. Without it holding us down, the horizon as a defining — and dividing — line wouldn't occupy the place it does in the laws of perspective.
It's actually just a device, useful because *most* of us, Morgenthaler, spend our time looking ahead rather than up or down, and because earthly structures are built from the ground up.
The most important thing isn't the horizon line, it's the vanishing point.
Or points, but we'll just concern ourselves with single-point perspective at present.
The observer's location is what really determines the placement of a vanishing point; a drawing from life is as much about the subject as the exact position of the artist's head and eyes in relation to it.
Come over here for a moment.

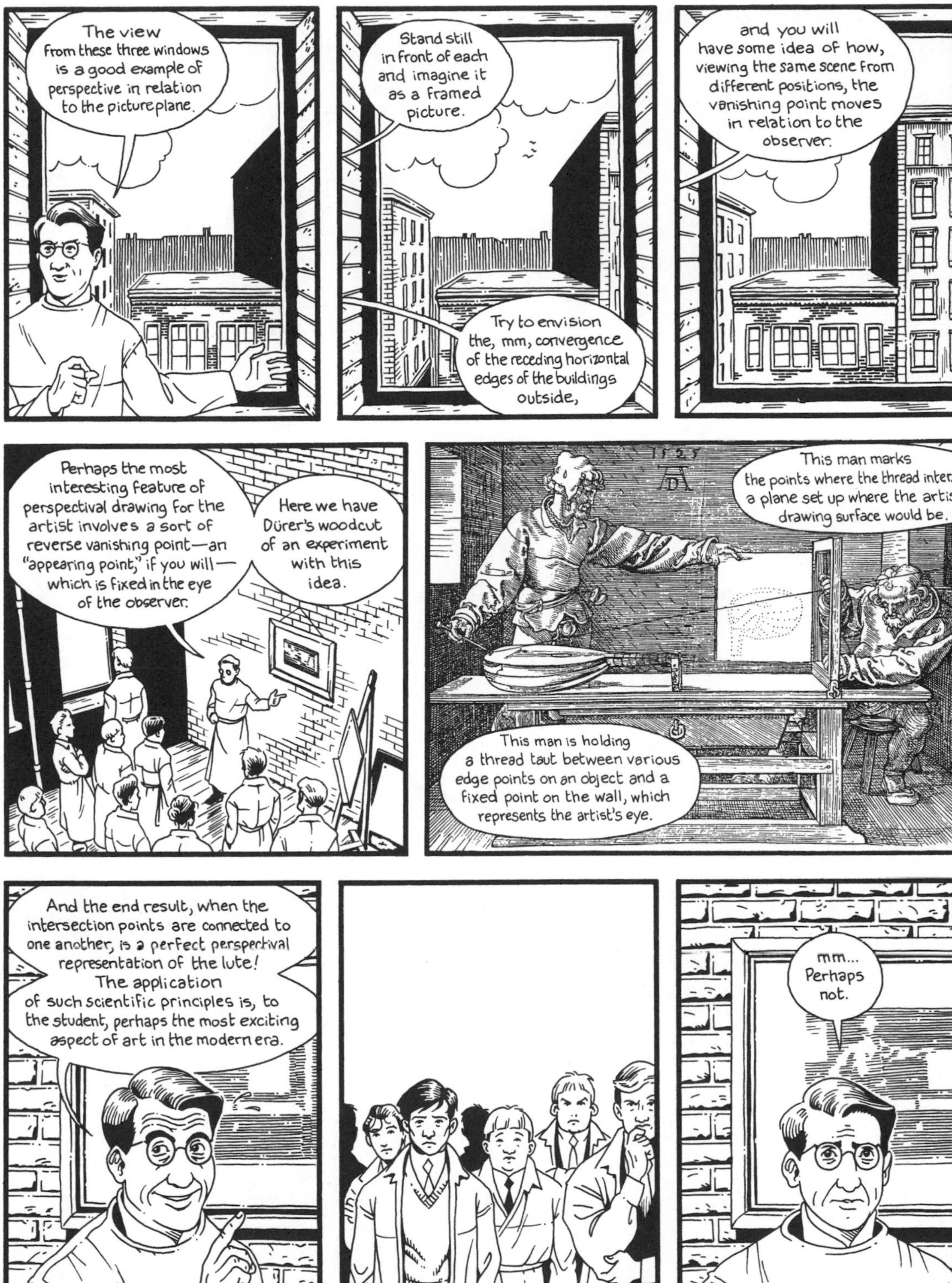
The view from these three windows is a good example of perspective in relation to the pictureplane.
Stand still in front of each and imagine it as a framed picture.
Try to envision the, mm, convergence of the receding horizontal edges of the buildings outside,
and you will have some idea of how, viewing the same scene from different positions, the vanishing point moves in relation to the observer.
Perhaps the most interesting feature of perspectival drawing for the artist involves a sort of reverse vanishing point—an "appearing point," if you will—which is fixed in the eye of the observer.
Here we have Dürer's woodcut of an experiment with this idea.
This man marks the points where the thread intersects a plane set up where the artist's drawing surface would be.
This man is holding a thread taut between various edge points on an object and a fixed point on the wall, which represents the artist's eye.
And the end result, when the intersection points are connected to one another, is a perfect perspectival representation of the lute! The application of such scientific principles is, to the student, perhaps the most exciting aspect of art in the modern era.
mm... Perhaps not.

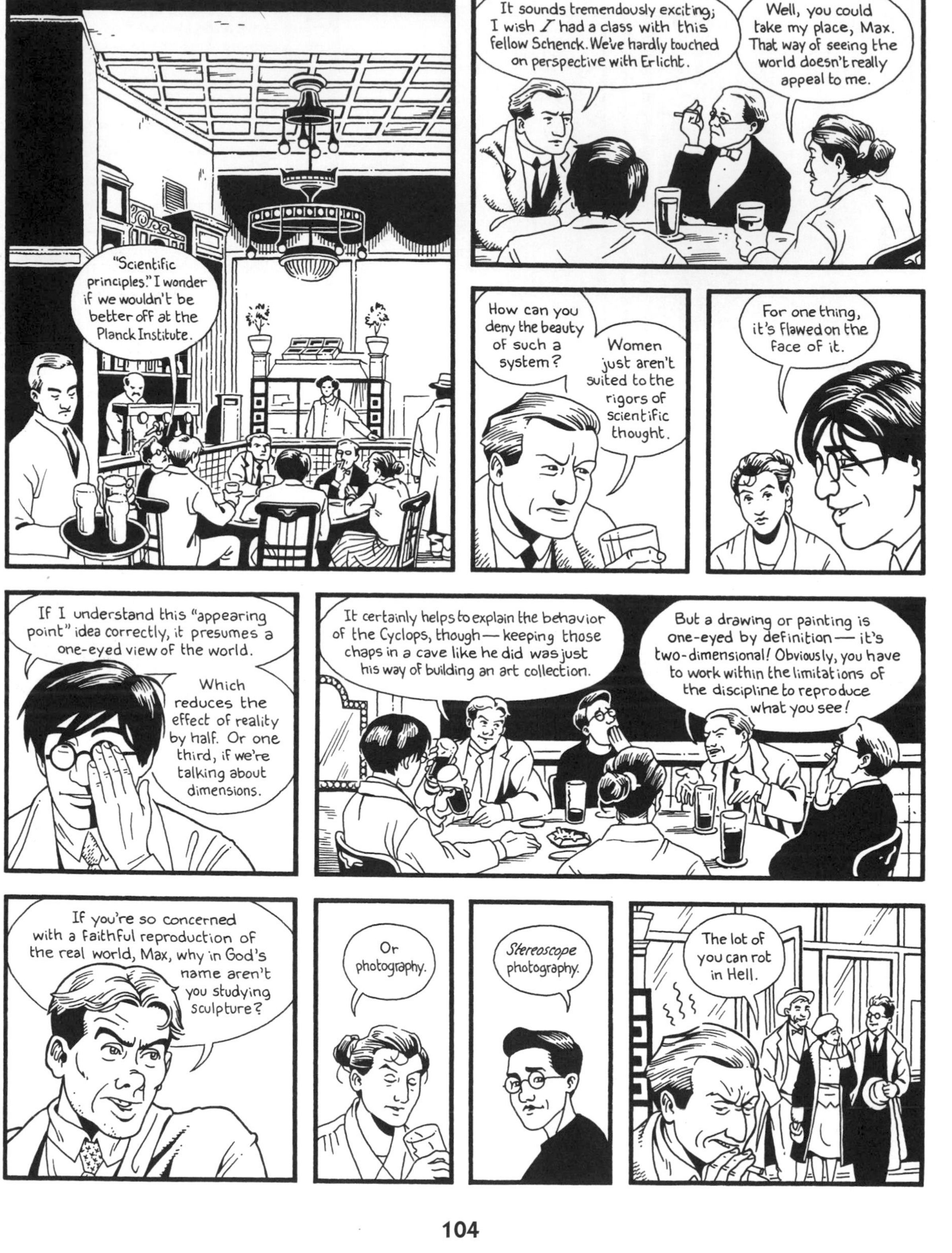
"Scientific principles." I wonder if we wouldn't be better off at the Planck Institute.
It sounds tremendously exciting; I wish *I* had a class with this fellow Schenck. We've hardly touched on perspective with Erlicht.
Well, you could take my place, Max. That way of seeing the world doesn't really appeal to me.
How can you deny the beauty of such a system?
Women just aren't suited to the rigors of scientific thought.
For one thing, it's flawed on the face of it.
If I understand this "appearing point" idea correctly, it presumes a one-eyed view of the world.
Which reduces the effect of reality by half. Or one third, if we're talking about dimensions.
It certainly helps to explain the behavior of the Cyclops, though — keeping those chaps in a cave like he did was just his way of building an art collection.
But a drawing or painting is one-eyed by definition — it's two-dimensional! Obviously, you have to work within the limitations of the discipline to reproduce what you see!
If you're so concerned with a faithful reproduction of the real world, Max, why in God's name aren't you studying sculpture?
Or photography.
Stereoscope photography.
The lot of you can rot in Hell.

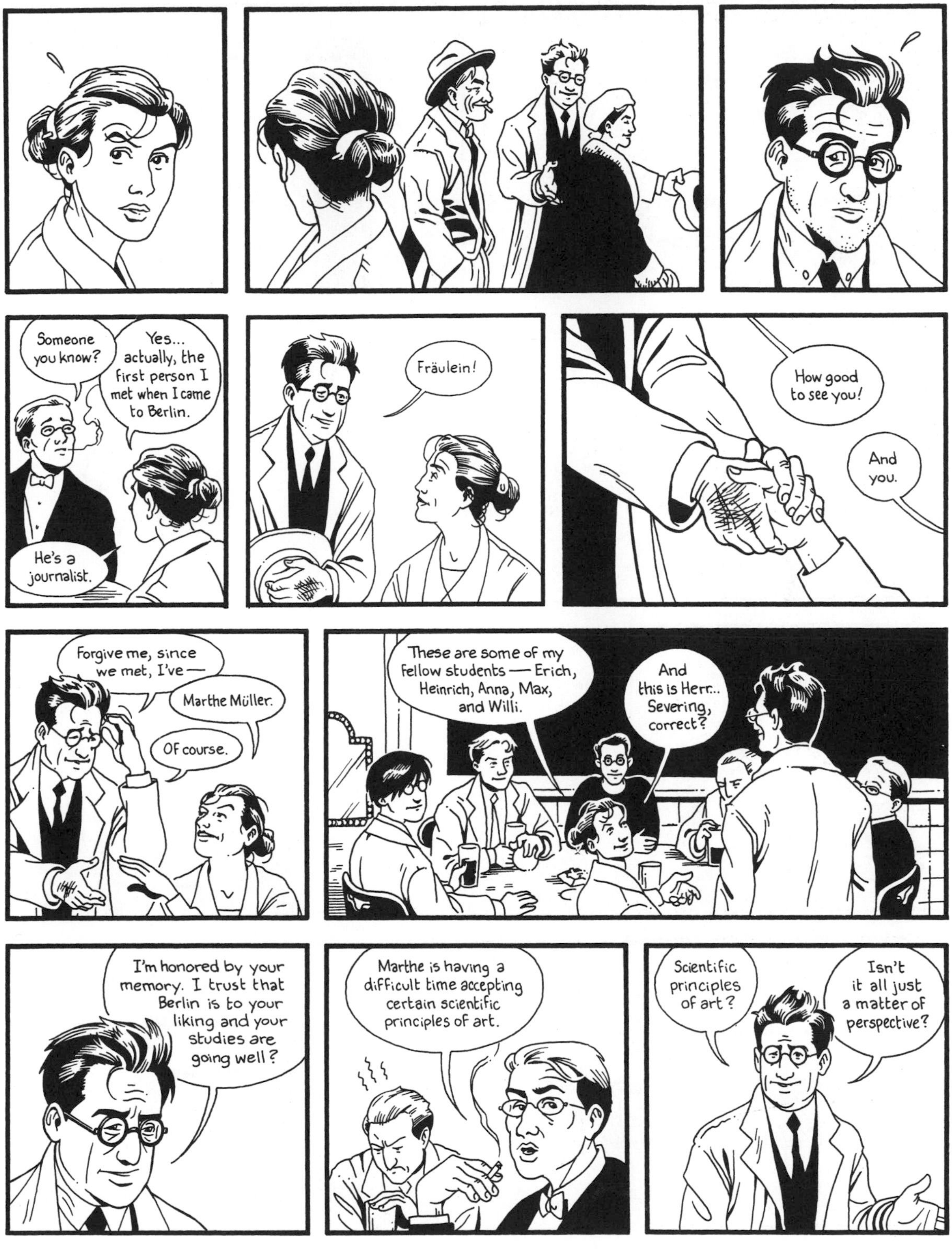
Someone you know?
Yes... actually, the first person I met when I came to Berlin.
He's a journalist.
Fräulein!
How good to see you!
And you.
Forgive me, since we met, I've —
Marthe Müller.
Of course.
These are some of my fellow students — Erich, Heinrich, Anna, Max, and Willi.
And this is Herr.. Severing, correct?
I'm honored by your memory. I trust that Berlin is to your liking and your studies are going well?
Marthe is having a difficult time accepting certain scientific principles of art.
Scientific principles of art?
Isn't it all just a matter of perspective?

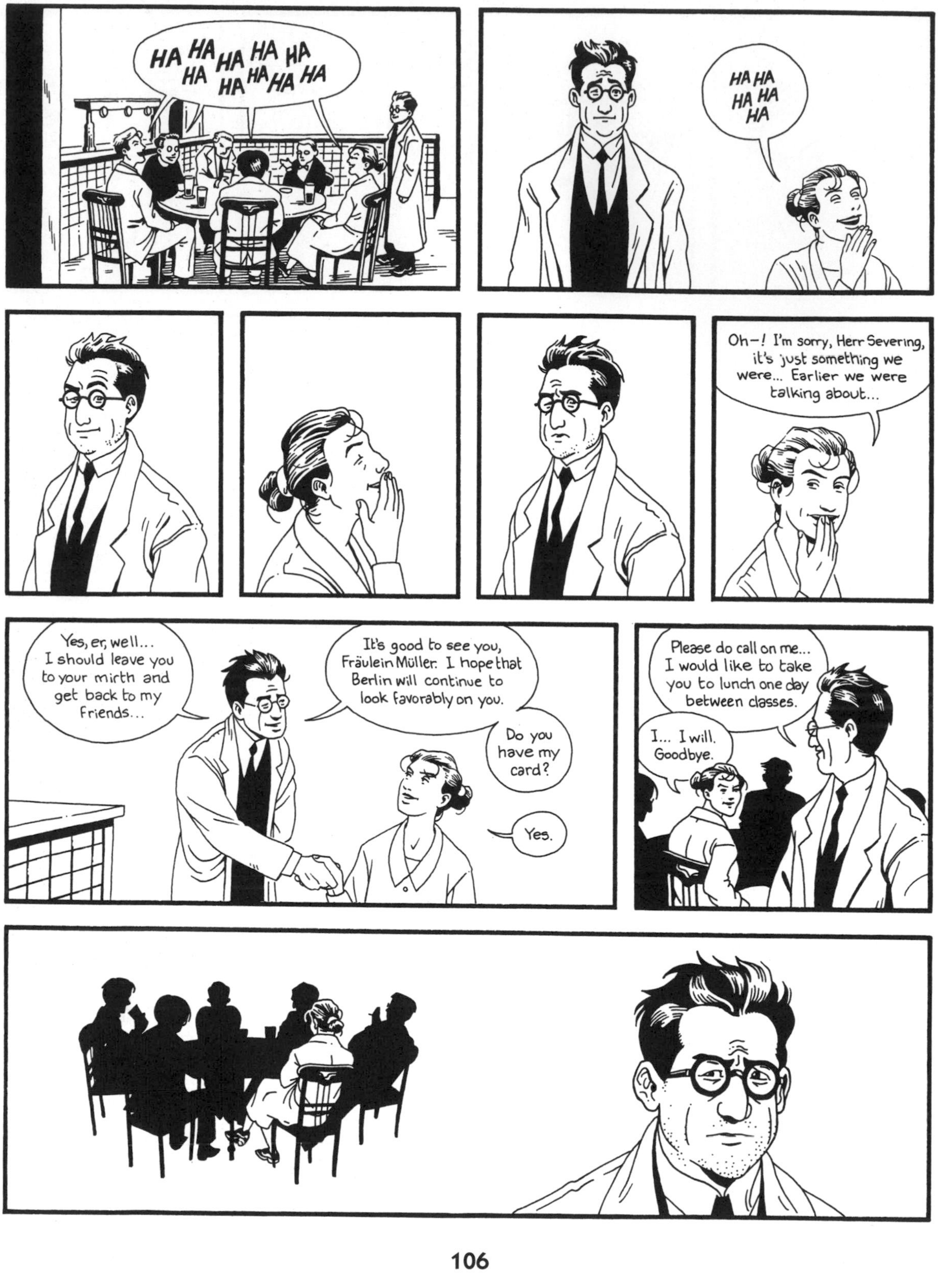
HA HA HA HA HA HA HA HA HA HA HA
HA HA HA HA HA
Oh—! I'm sorry, Herr Severing, it's just something we were... Earlier we were talking about...
Yes, er, well... I should leave you to your mirth and get back to my friends...
It's good to see you, Fräulein Müller. I hope that Berlin will continue to look favorably on you.
Do you have my card?
Yes.
Please do call on me... I would like to take you to lunch one day between classes.
I... I will. Goodbye.

I can remember that it's Christmas Day.

That journalist Herr Severing is there, for some reason, sitting on the couch between Aunt Hilde and Uncle Tomas, and I think I'm sitting on the floor — I'm lower than them.

I recall most clearly his right sock, it's garter against the white skin of his ankle, the pattern of the carpet pooled up at his feet.

The more aware I become of the voices and clinking of glassware around us, the more muffled they get.

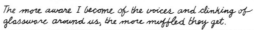

The house is filled with family. Everyone is there, laughing and singing.

Except Theo.

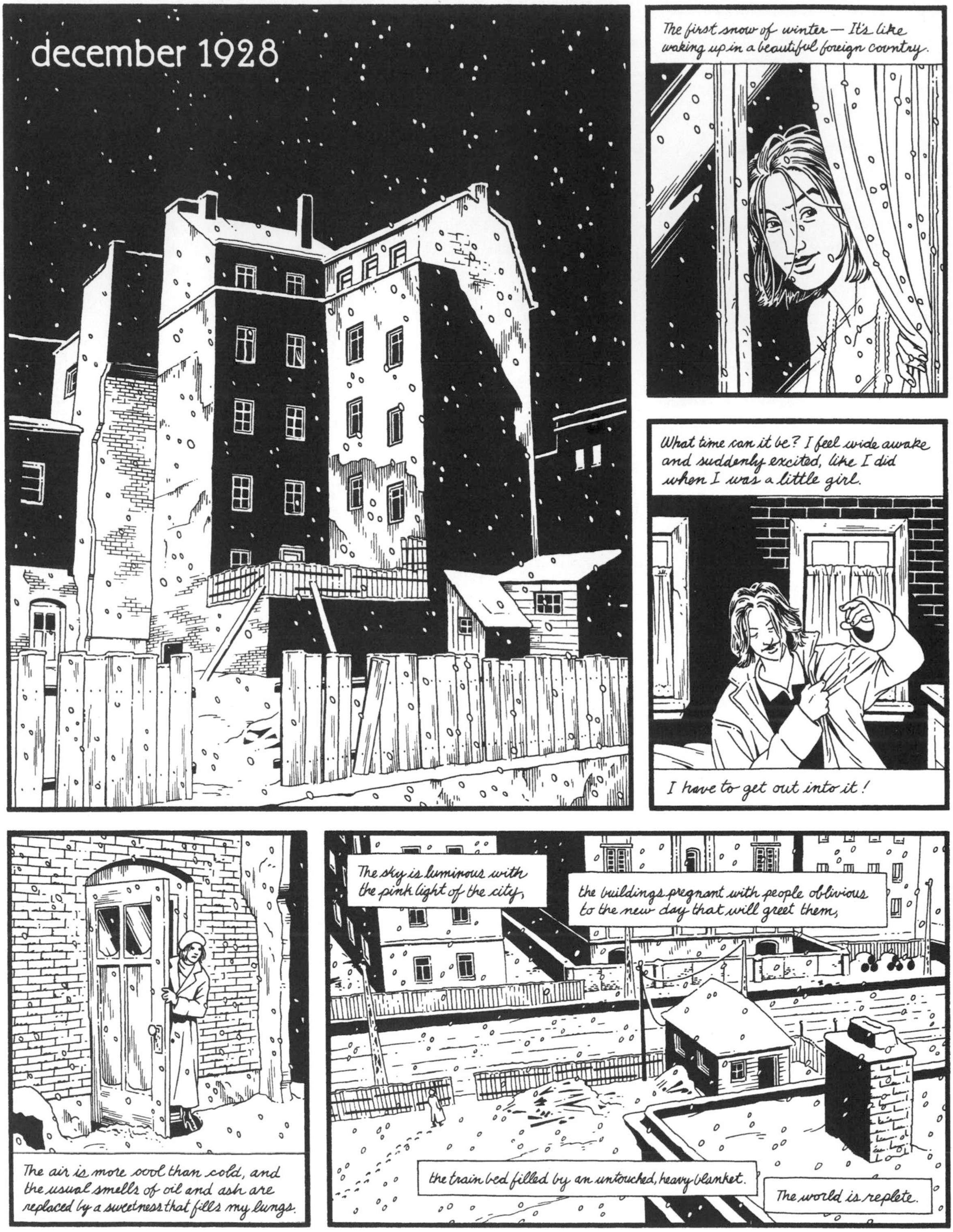
december 1928
The first snow of winter — It's like waking up in a beautiful foreign country.
What time can it be? I feel wide awake and suddenly excited, like I did when I was a little girl.
I have to get out into it!
The air is more cool than cold, and the usual smells of oil and ash are replaced by a sweetness that fills my lungs.
The sky is luminous with the pink light of the city,
the buildings pregnant with people oblivious to the new day that will greet them,
the train bed filled by an untouched, heavy blanket.
The world is replete.

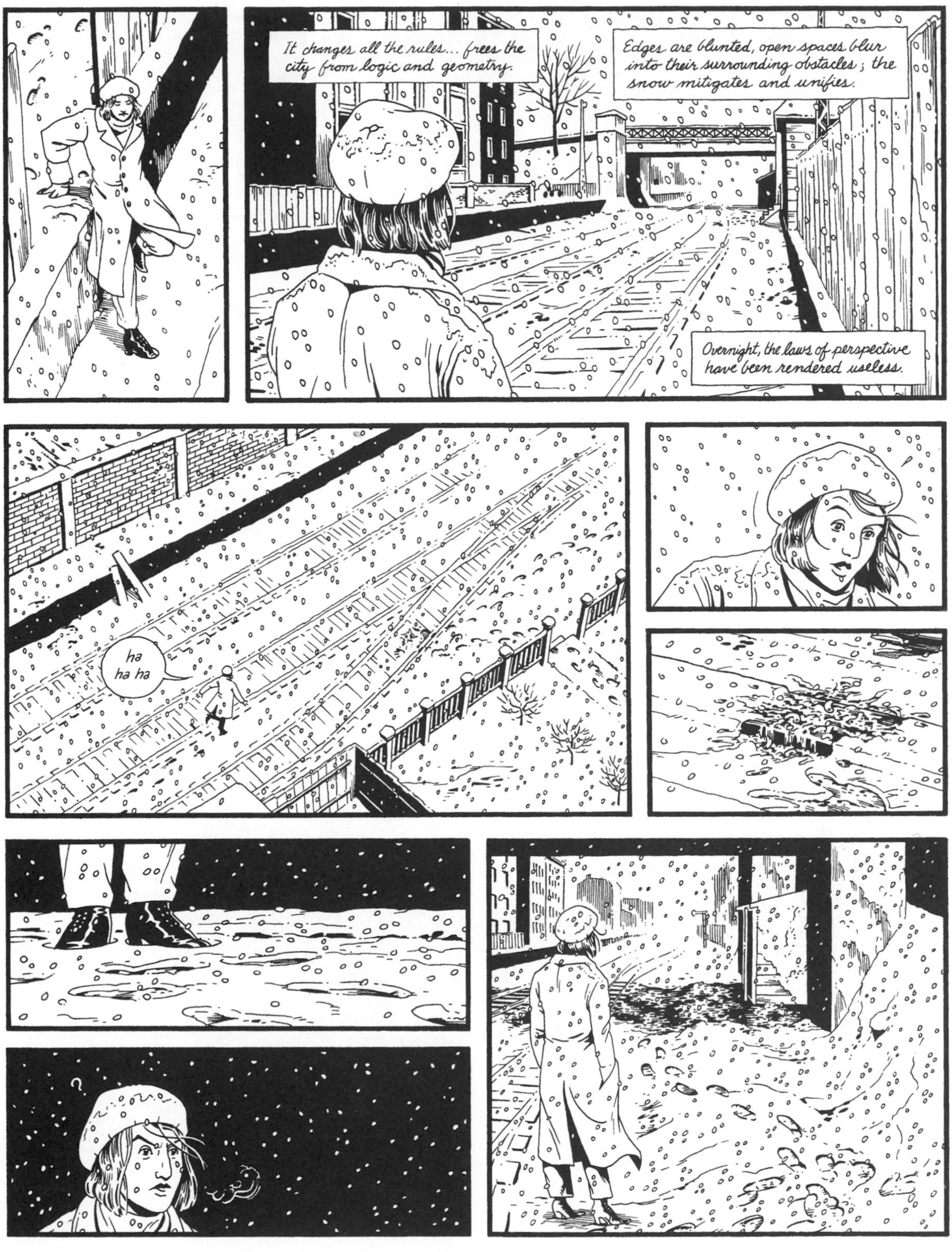
It changes all the rules... frees the city from logic and geometry.
Edges are blunted, open spaces blur into their surrounding obstacles; the snow mitigates and unifies.
Overnight, the laws of perspective have been rendered useless.
ha ha ha
?

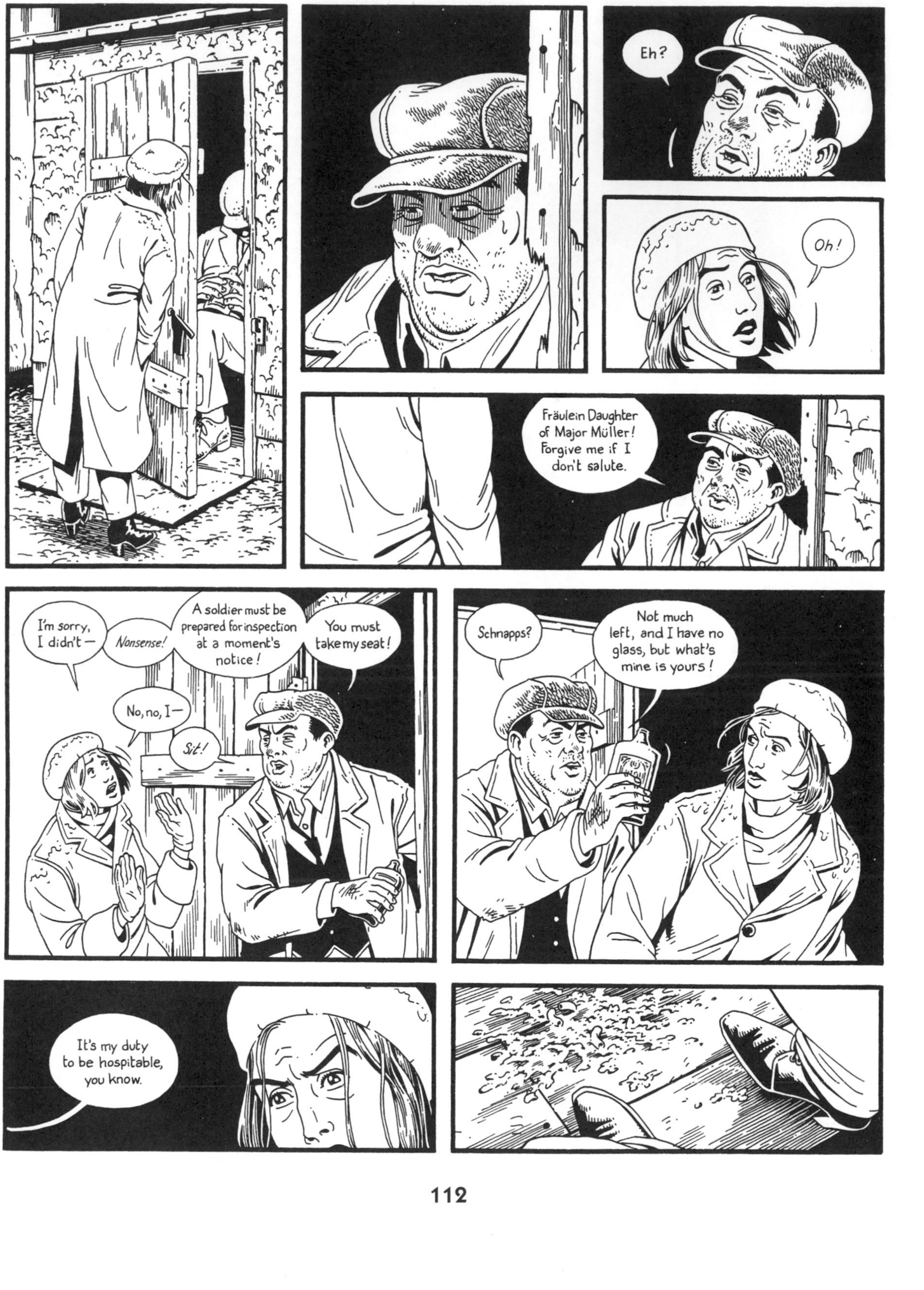
Eh?
Oh!
Fräulein Daughter of Major Müller! Forgive me if I don't salute.
I'm sorry, I didn't —
Nonsense!
A soldier must be prepared for inspection at a moment's notice!
You must take my seat!
No, no, I—
Sit!
Schnapps?
Not much left, and I have no glass, but what's mine is yours!
It's my duty to be hospitable, you know.

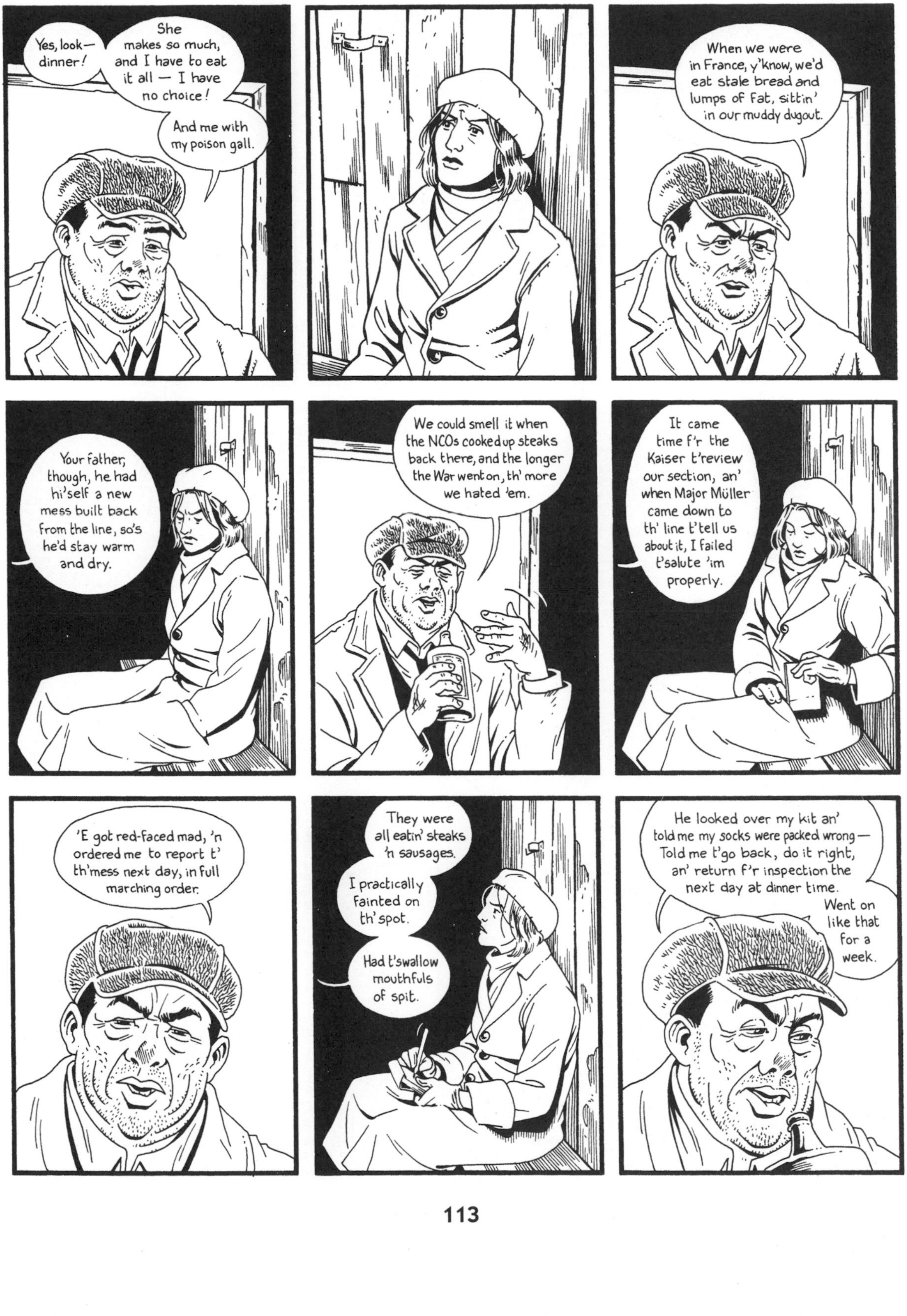
Yes, look— dinner!
She makes so much, and I have to eat it all — I have no choice!
And me with my poison gall.
When we were in France, y'know, we'd eat stale bread and lumps of fat, sittin' in our muddy dugout.
Your father, though, he had hi'self a new mess built back from the line, so's he'd stay warm and dry.
We could smell it when the NCOs cooked up steaks back there, and the longer the War went on, th' more we hated 'em.
It came time f'r the Kaiser t'review our section, an' when Major Müller came down to th' line t'tell us about it, I failed t'salute 'im properly.
'E got red-faced mad, 'n ordered me to report t' th'mess next day, in full marching order.
They were all eatin' steaks 'n sausages.
I practically fainted on th' spot.
Had t'swallow mouthfuls of spit.
He looked over my kit an' told me my socks were packed wrong— Told me t'go back, do it right, an' return f'r inspection the next day at dinner time.
Went on like that for a week.

ch ch ch
ch ch ch CH CH CH CH CH CH
What're y'doin'?
CHCHCHCH CH CH CH CH

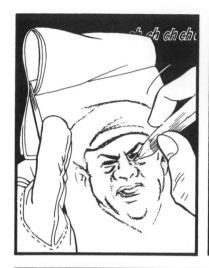

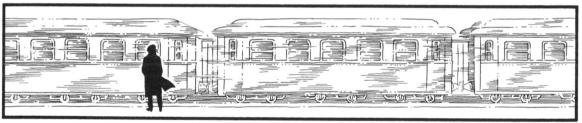

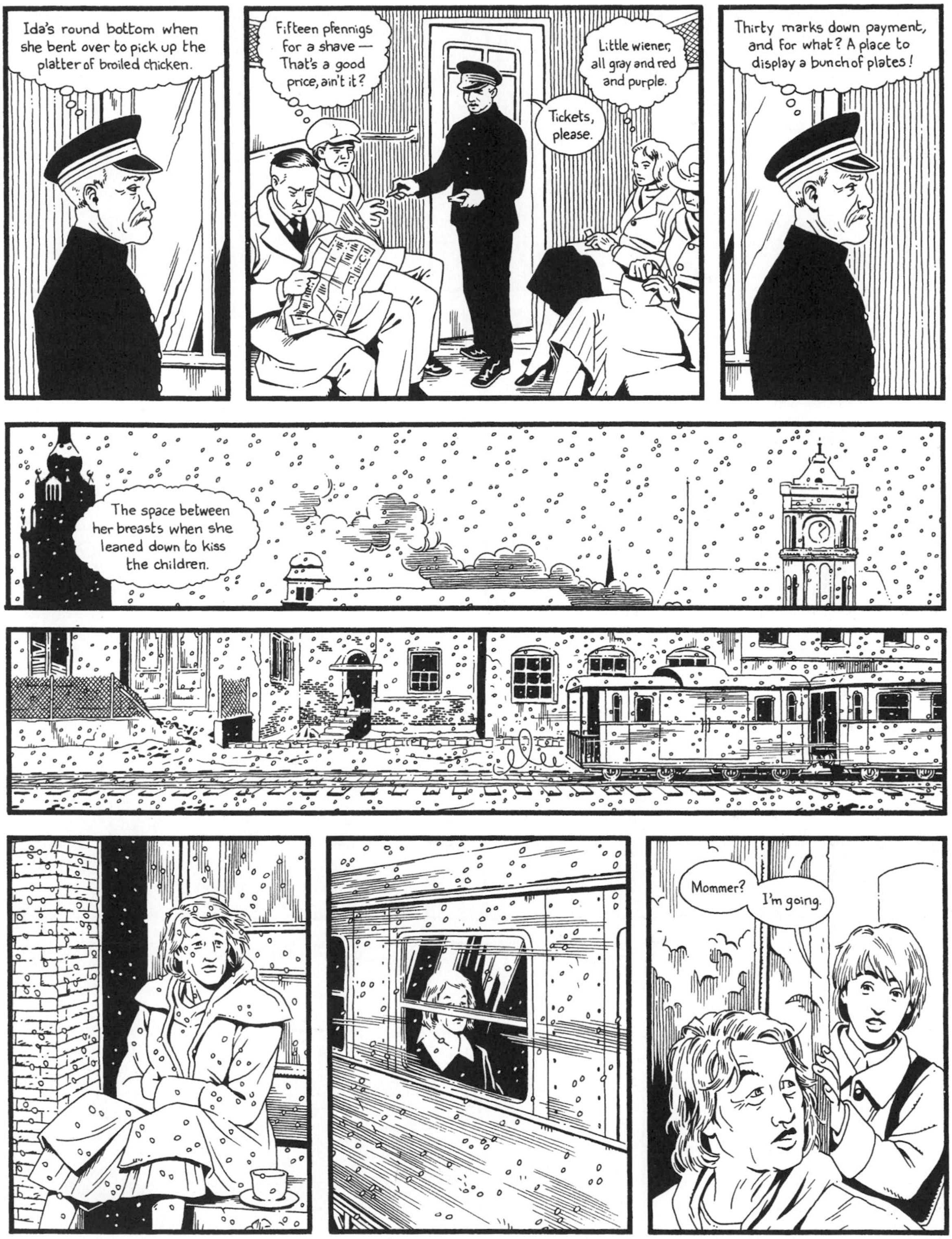
Ida's round bottom when she bent over to pick up the platter of broiled chicken.
Fifteen pfennigs for a shave — That's a good price, ain't it?
Little wiener, all gray and red and purple.
Tickets, please.
Thirty marks down payment, and for what? A place to display a bunch of plates!
The space between her breasts when she leaned down to kiss the children.
Mommer?
I'm going.

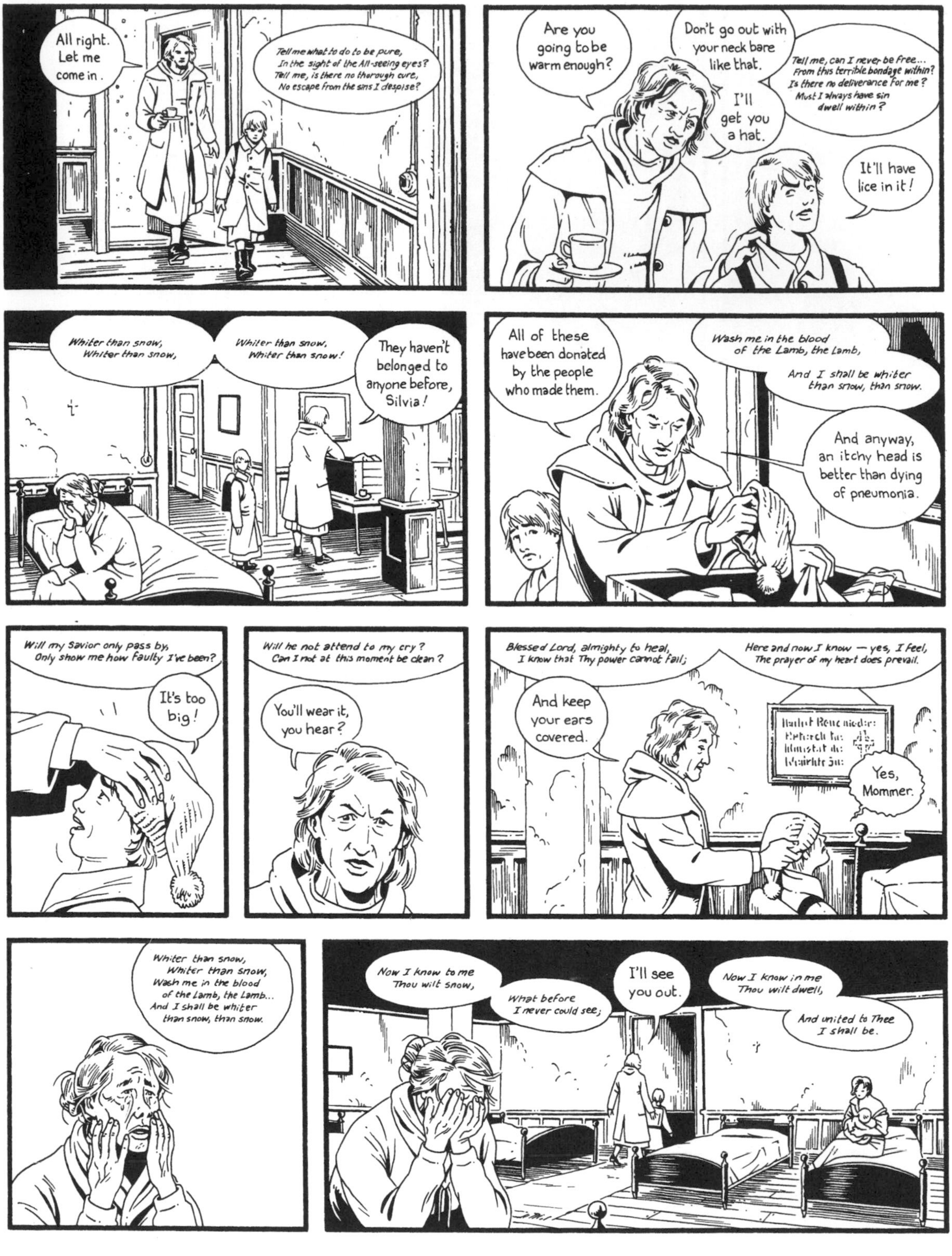
All right. Let me come in.
Tell me what to do to be pure, In the sight of the All-seeing eyes? Tell me, is there no thorough cure, No escape from the sins I despise?
Are you going to be warm enough?
Don't go out with your neck bare like that.
I'll get you a hat.
Tell me, can I never be free... From this terrible bondage within? Is there no deliverance for me? Must I always have sin dwell within?
It'll have lice in it!
Whiter than snow, Whiter than snow,
Whiter than snow, Whiter than snow!
They haven't belonged to anyone before, Silvia!
All of these have been donated by the people who made them.
Wash me in the blood of the Lamb, the Lamb, And I shall be whiter than snow, than snow.
And anyway, an itchy head is better than dying of pneumonia.
Will my Savior only pass by, Only show me how faulty I've been?
It's too big!
Will he not attend to my cry? Can I not at this moment be clean?
You'll wear it, you hear?
Blessed Lord, almighty to heal, I know that Thy power cannot fail;
Here and now I know — yes, I feel, The prayer of my heart does prevail.
And keep your ears covered.
Yes, Mommer.
Whiter than snow, Whiter than snow, Wash me in the blood of the Lamb, the Lamb... And I shall be whiter than snow, than snow.
Now I know to me Thou wilt snow,
What before I never could see;
I'll see you out.
Now I know in me Thou wilt dwell,
And united to Thee I shall be.

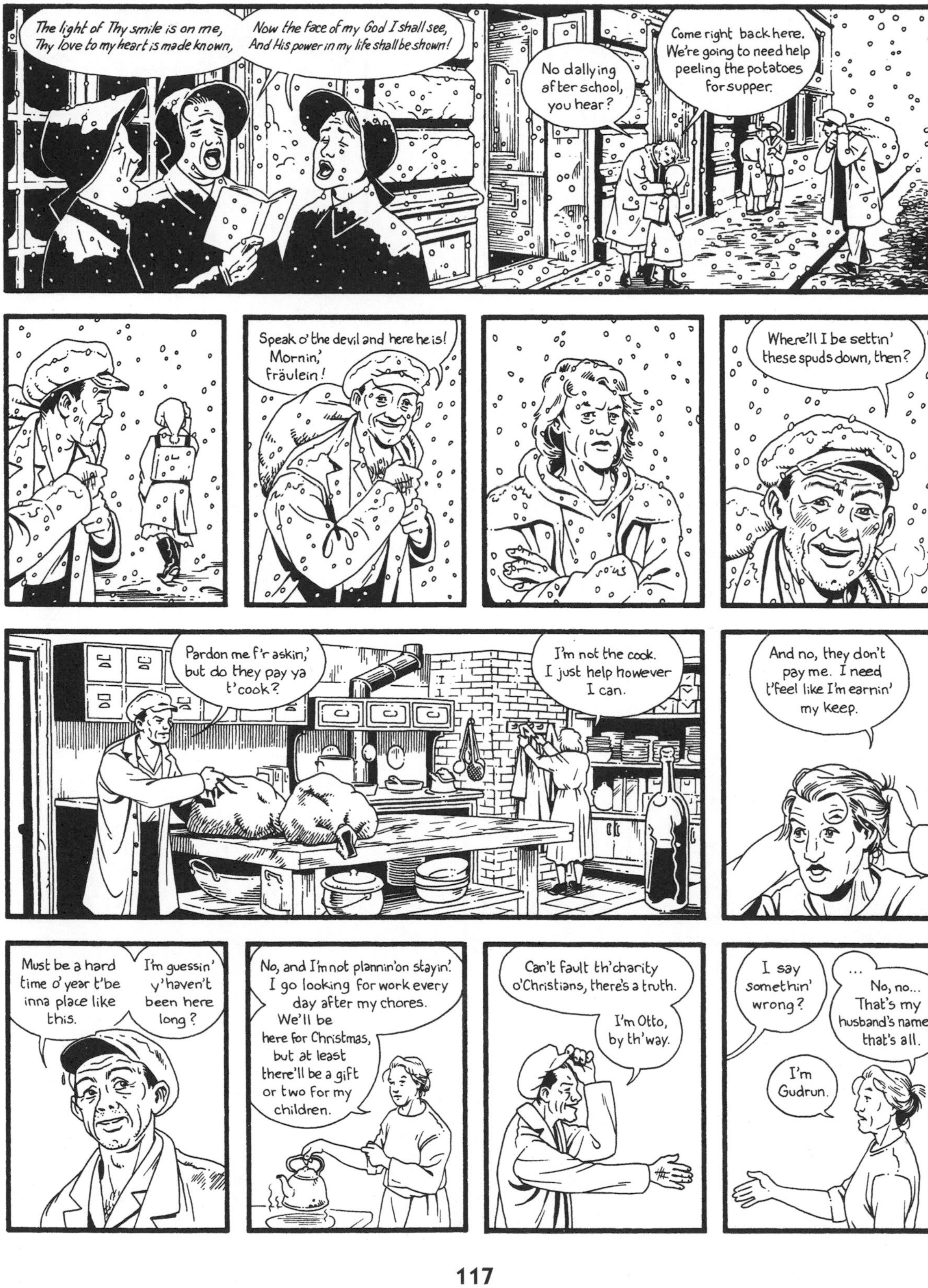
The light of Thy smile is on me,
Thy love to my heart is made known,
Now the face of my God I shall see,
And His power in my life shall be shown!
No dallying after school, you hear?
Come right back here. We're going to need help peeling the potatoes for supper.
Speak o' the devil and here he is! Mornin,' fräulein!
Where'll I be settin' these spuds down, then?
Pardon me f'r askin,' but do they pay ya t'cook?
I'm not the cook. I just help however I can.
And no, they don't pay me. I need t'feel like I'm earnin' my keep.
Must be a hard time o' year t'be inna place like this.
I'm guessin' y'haven't been here long?
No, and I'm not plannin'on stayin'. I go looking for work every day after my chores.
We'll be here for Christmas, but at least there'll be a gift or two for my children.
Can't fault th'charity o'Christians, there's a truth.
I'm Otto, by th'way.
I say somethin' wrong?
... No, no... That's my husband's name, that's all.
I'm Gudrun.

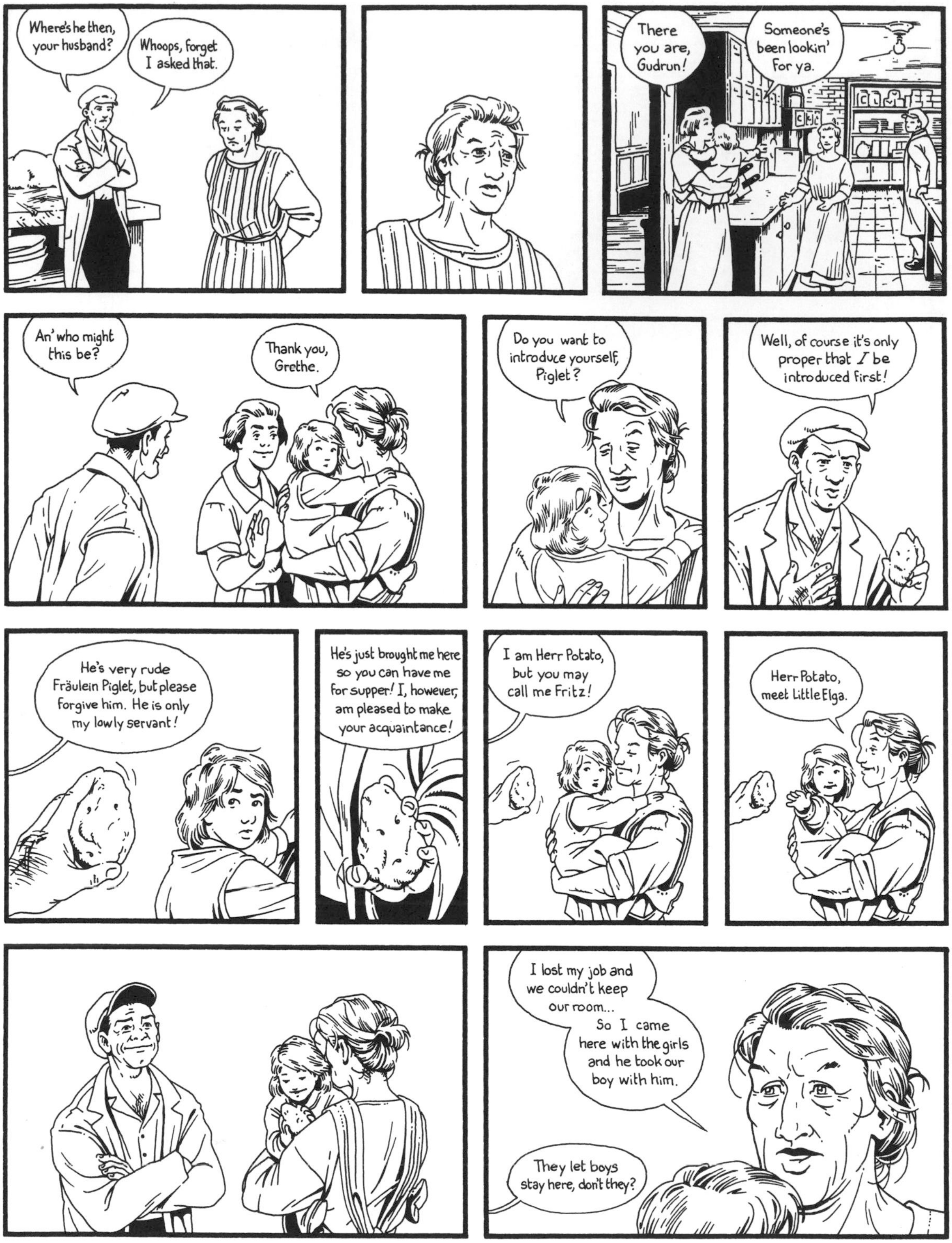
Where's he then, your husband?
Whoops, forget I asked that.
There you are, Gudrun!
Someone's been lookin' for ya.
An' who might this be?
Thank you, Grethe.
Do you want to introduce yourself, Piglet?
Well, of course it's only proper that I be introduced first!
He's very rude Fräulein Piglet, but please forgive him. He is only my lowly servant!
He's just brought me here so you can have me for supper! I, however, am pleased to make your acquaintance!
I am Herr Potato, but you may call me Fritz!
Herr Potato, meet Little Elga.
I lost my job and we couldn't keep our room...
So I came here with the girls and he took our boy with him.
They let boys stay here, don't they?

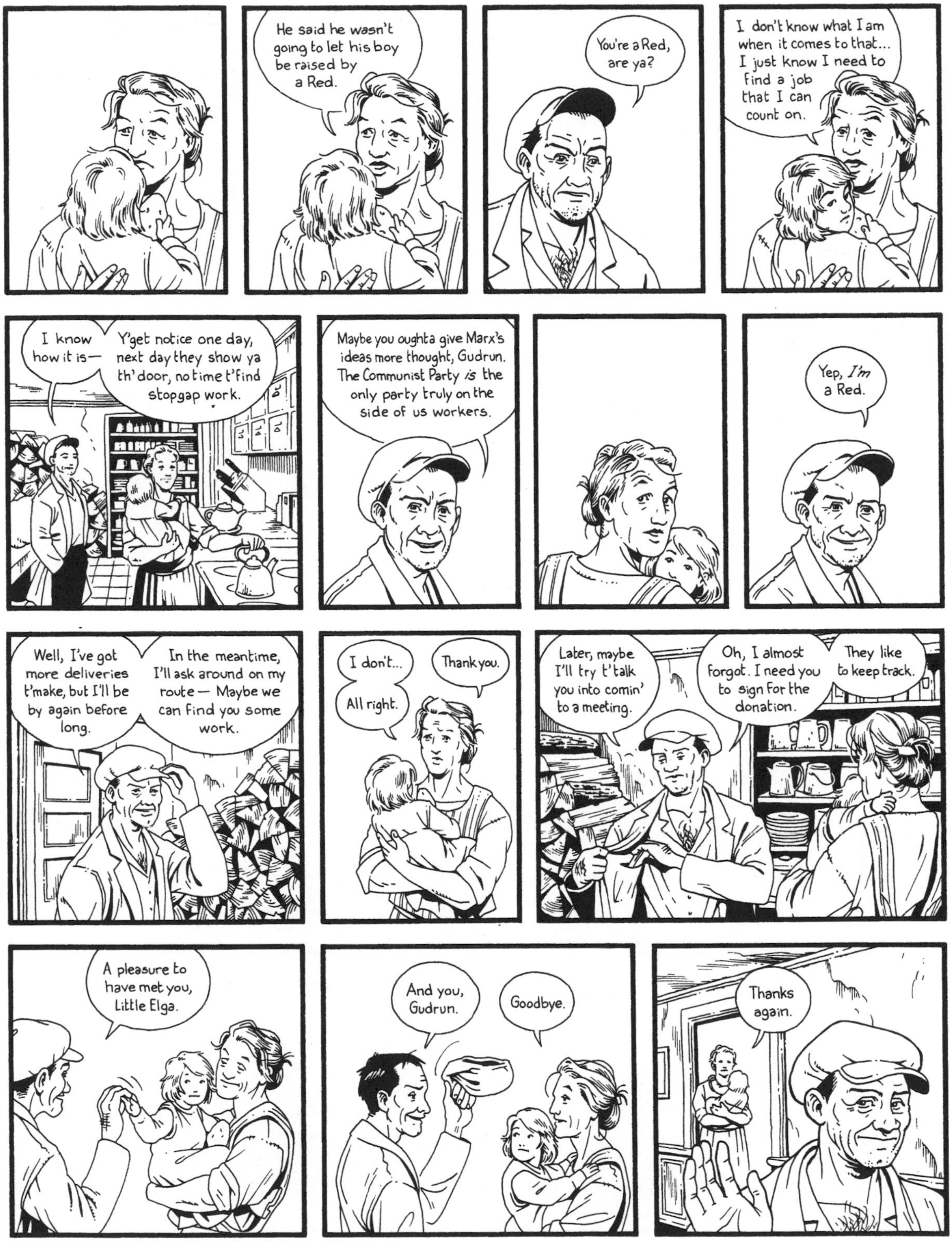
He said he wasn't going to let his boy be raised by a Red.
You're a Red, are ya?
I don't know what I am when it comes to that... I just know I need to find a job that I can count on.
I know how it is—
Y'get notice one day, next day they show ya th' door, no time t'find stopgap work.
Maybe you oughta give Marx's ideas more thought, Gudrun. The Communist Party *is* the only party truly on the side of us workers.
Yep, *I'm* a Red.
Well, I've got more deliveries t'make, but I'll be by again before long.
In the meantime, I'll ask around on my route — Maybe we can find you some work.
I don't...
Thank you.
All right.
Later, maybe I'll try t' talk you into comin' to a meeting.
Oh, I almost forgot. I need you to sign for the donation.
They like to keep track.
A pleasure to have met you, Little Elga.
And you, Gudrun.
Goodbye.
Thanks again.

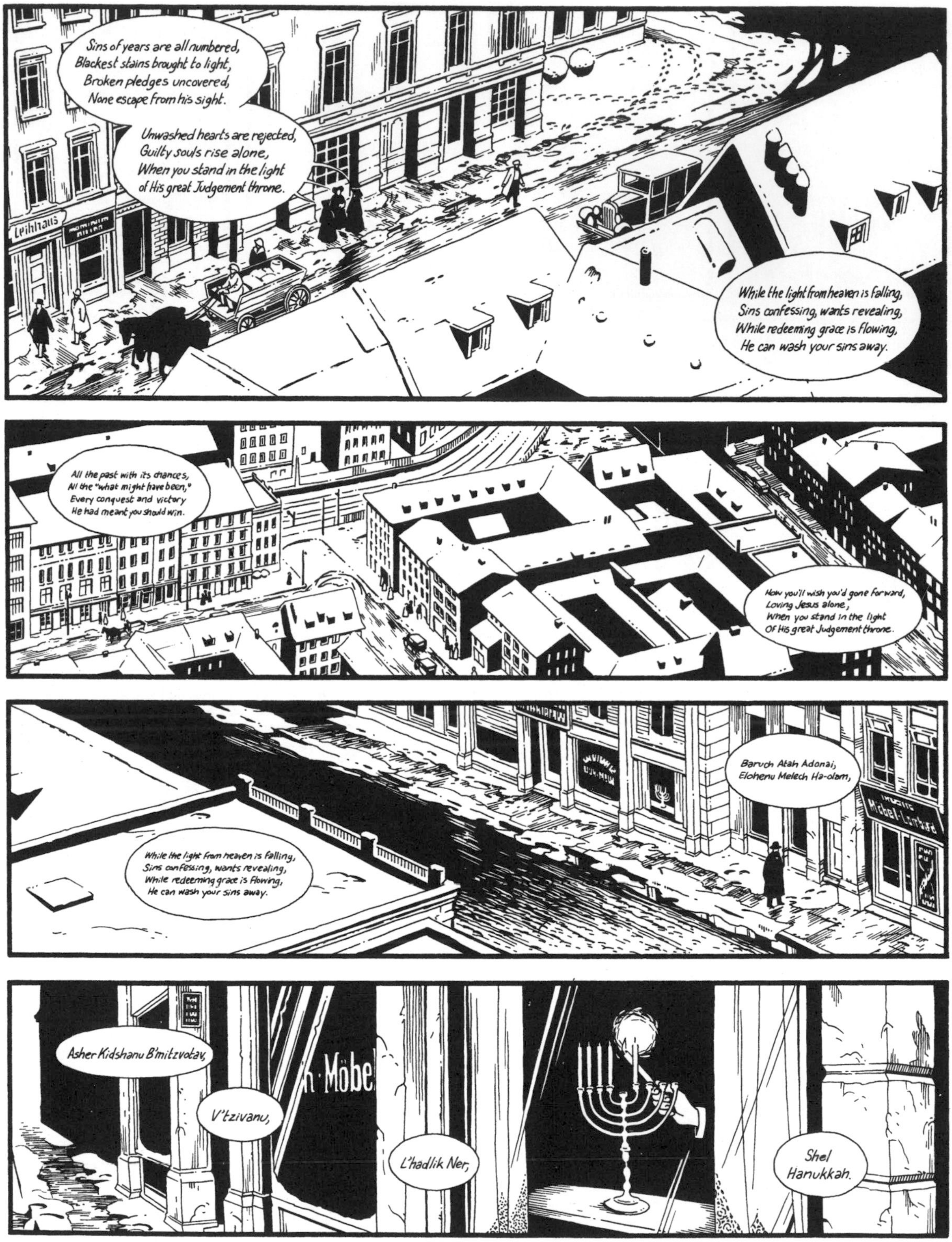
Sins of years are all numbered,
Blackest stains brought to light,
Broken pledges uncovered,
None escape from his sight.
Unwashed hearts are rejected,
Guilty souls rise alone,
When you stand in the light
of His great Judgement throne.
Leihhaus
While the light from heaven is falling,
Sins confessing, wants revealing,
While redeeming grace is flowing,
He can wash your sins away.
All the past with its chances,
All the "what might have been,"
Every conquest and victory
He had meant you should win.
How you'll wish you'd gone forward,
Loving Jesus alone,
When you stand in the light
Of His great Judgement throne.
Baruch Atah Adonai,
Elohenu Melech Ha-olam,
Möbel-Lombard
While the light from heaven is falling,
Sins confessing, wants revealing,
While redeeming grace is flowing,
He can wash your sins away.
Asher Kidshanu B'mitzvotav,
h·Möbel
V'tzivanu,
L'hadlik Ner,
Shel
Hanukkah.

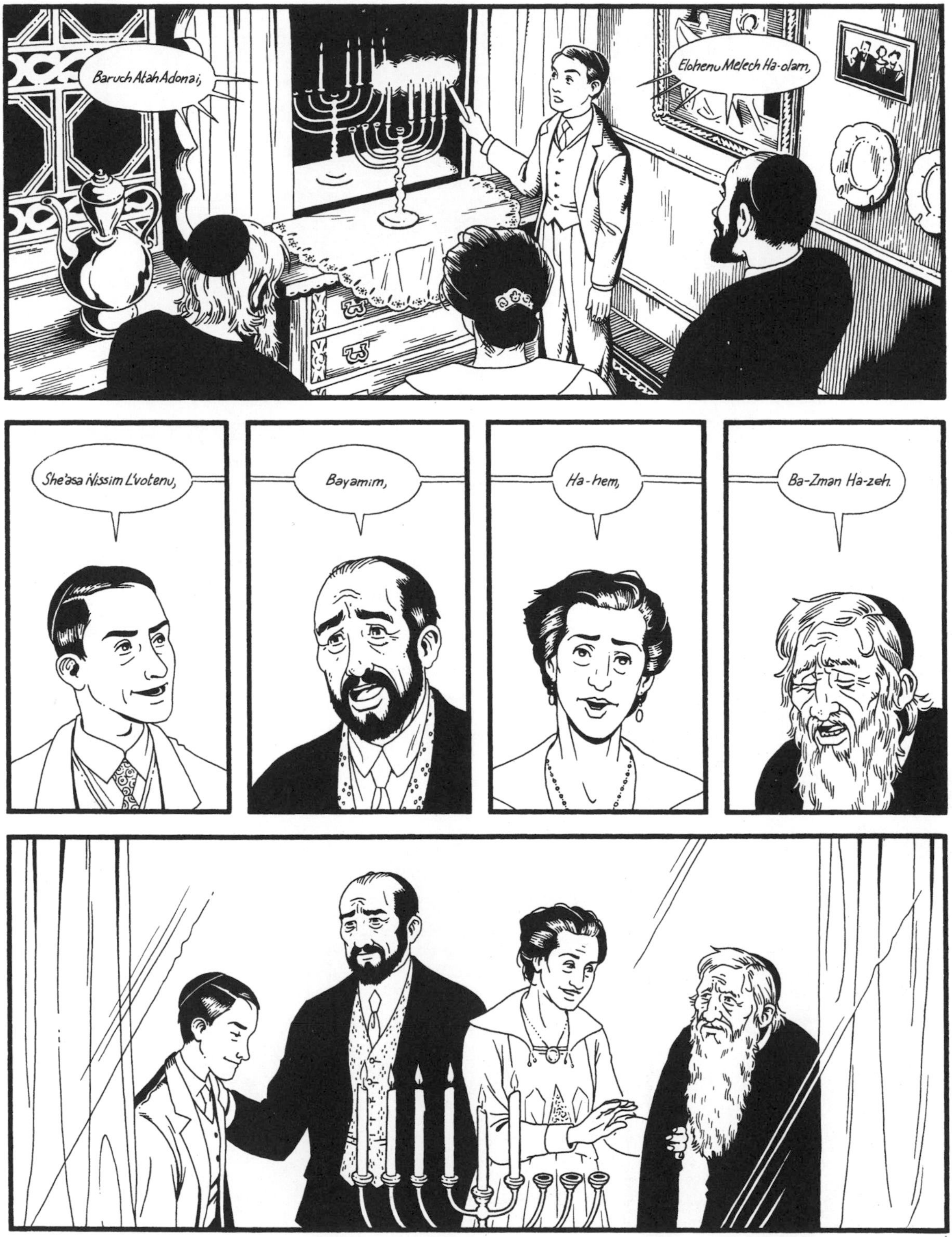
Baruch Atah Adonai,
Elohenu Melech Ha-olam,
She'asa Nissim L'votenu,
Bayamim,
Ha-hem,
Ba-Zman Ha-zeh.

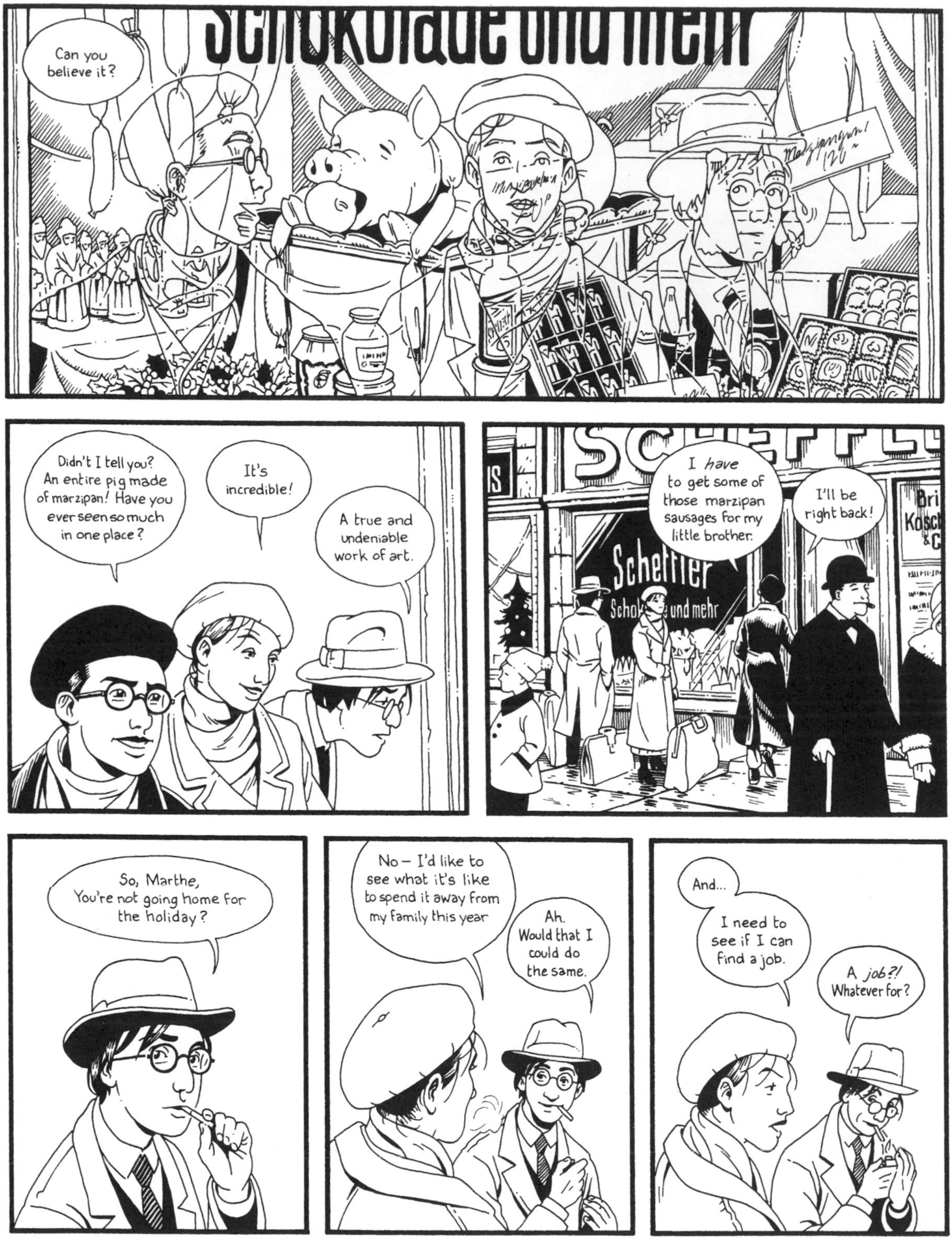
Schokolade und mehr
Can you believe it?
Didn't I tell you? An entire pig made of marzipan! Have you ever seen so much in one place?
It's incredible!
A true and undeniable work of art.
I *have* to get some of those marzipan sausages for my little brother.
I'll be right back!
Scheffler Schokolade und mehr
So, Marthe, You're not going home for the holiday?
No – I'd like to see what it's like to spend it away from my family this year
Ah. Would that I could do the same.
And...
I need to see if I can find a job.
A *job?!* Whatever for?

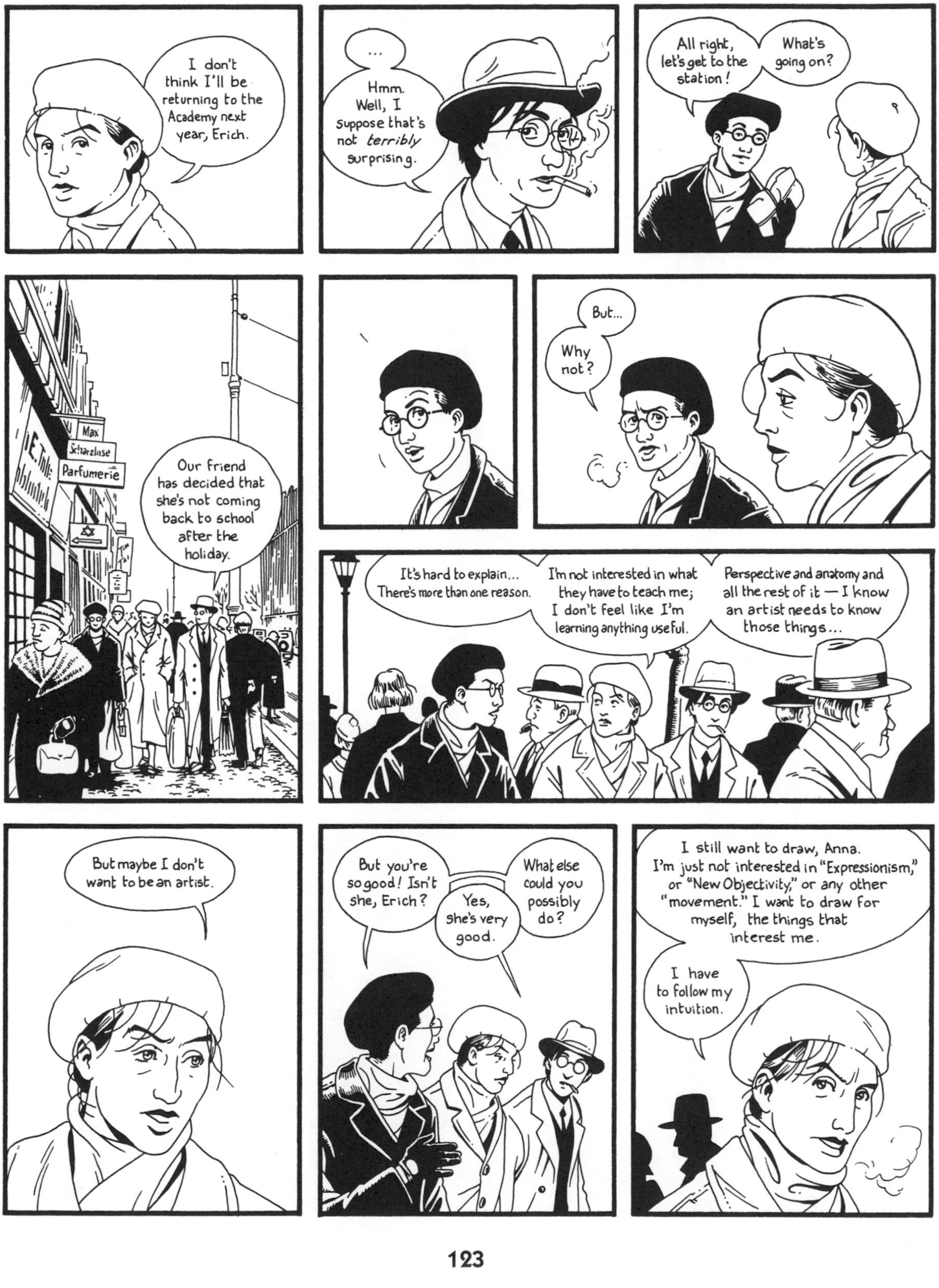
I don't think I'll be returning to the Academy next year, Erich.
...
Hmm. Well, I suppose that's not *terribly* surprising.
All right, let's get to the station!
What's going on?
Max Scharzluse Parfumerie
Our friend has decided that she's not coming back to school after the holiday.
But...
Why not?
It's hard to explain... There's more than one reason.
I'm not interested in what they have to teach me; I don't feel like I'm learning anything useful.
Perspective and anatomy and all the rest of it — I know an artist needs to know those things...
But maybe I don't want to be an artist.
But you're so good! Isn't she, Erich?
Yes, she's very good.
What else could you possibly do?
I still want to draw, Anna. I'm just not interested in "Expressionism," or "New Objectivity," or any other "movement." I want to draw for myself, the things that interest me.
I have to follow my intuition.

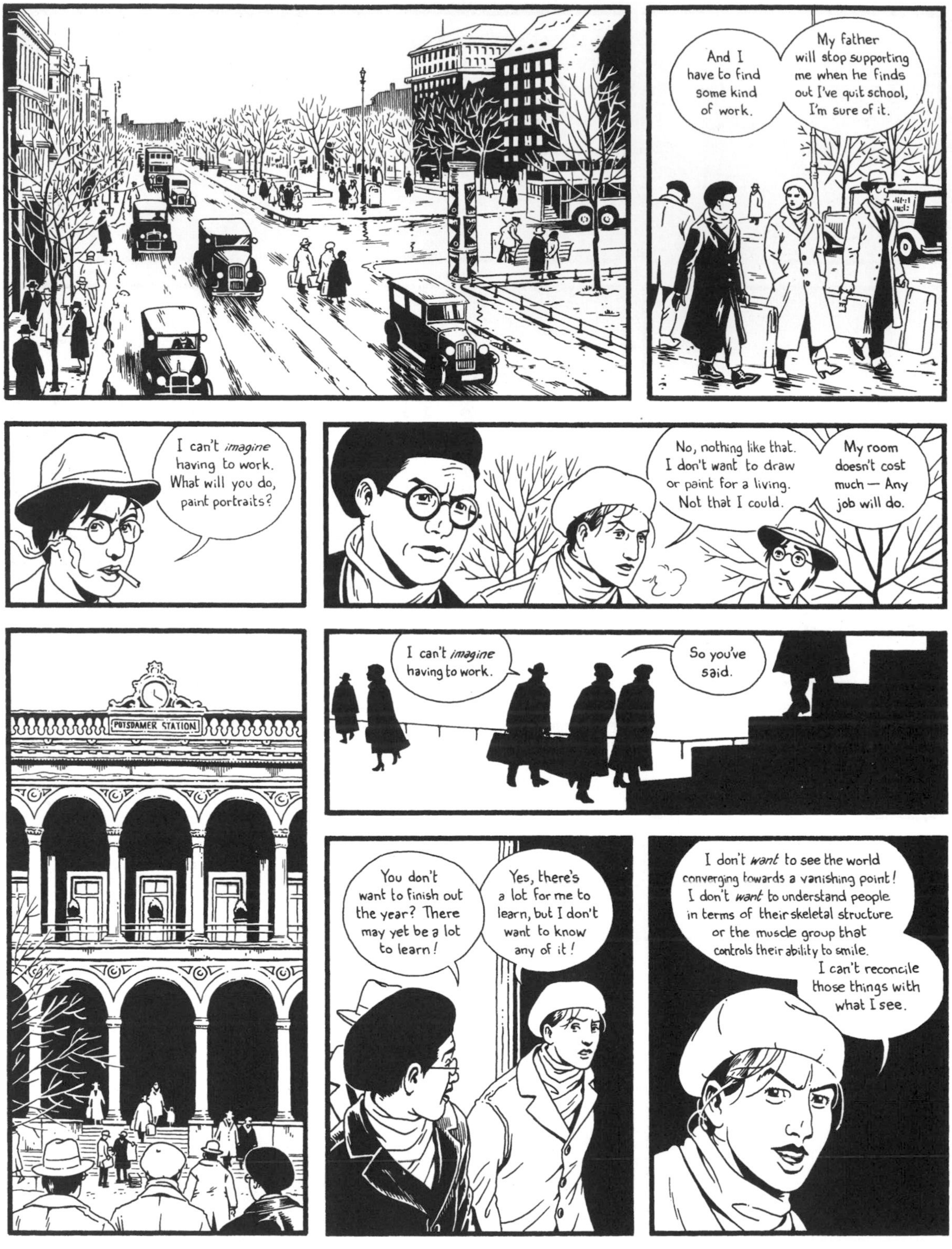
My father will stop supporting me when he finds out I've quit school, I'm sure of it.
And I have to find some kind of work.
I can't *imagine* having to work. What will you do, paint portraits?
No, nothing like that. I don't want to draw or paint for a living. Not that I could.
My room doesn't cost much — Any job will do.
POTSDAMER STATION
I can't *imagine* having to work.
So you've said.
You don't want to finish out the year? There may yet be a lot to learn!
Yes, there's a lot for me to learn, but I don't want to know any of it!
I don't *want* to see the world converging towards a vanishing point! I don't *want* to understand people in terms of their skeletal structure or the muscle group that controls their ability to smile.
I can't reconcile those things with what I see.

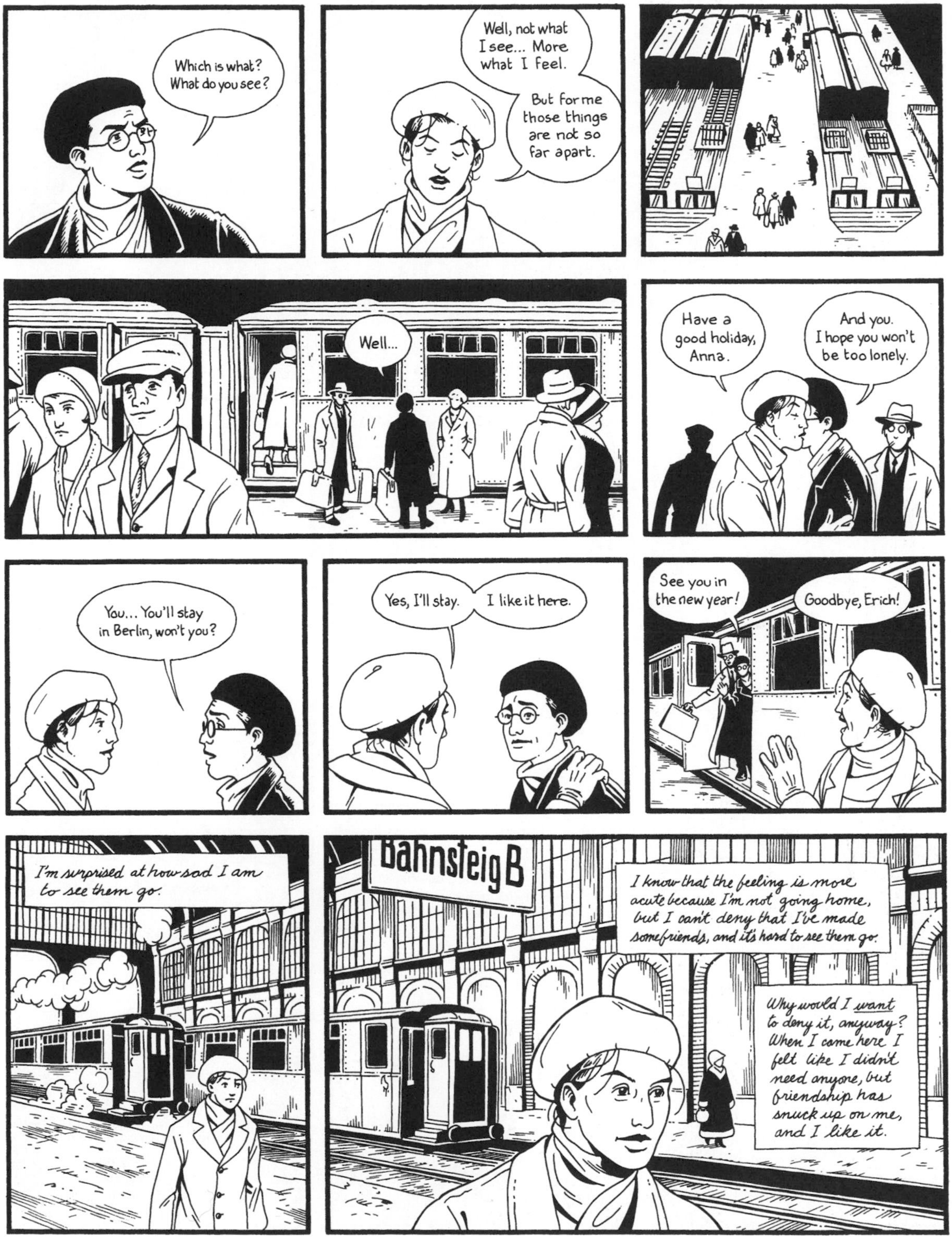
Which is what? What do you see?
Well, not what I see... More what I feel.
But for me those things are not so far apart.
Well...
Have a good holiday, Anna.
And you. I hope you won't be too lonely.
You... You'll stay in Berlin, won't you?
Yes, I'll stay.
I like it here.
See you in the new year!
Goodbye, Erich!
I'm surprised at how sad I am to see them go.
Bahnsteig B
I know that the feeling is more acute because I'm not going home, but I can't deny that I've made some friends, and it's hard to see them go.
Why would I want to deny it, anyway? When I came here I felt like I didn't need anyone, but friendship has snuck up on me, and I like it.

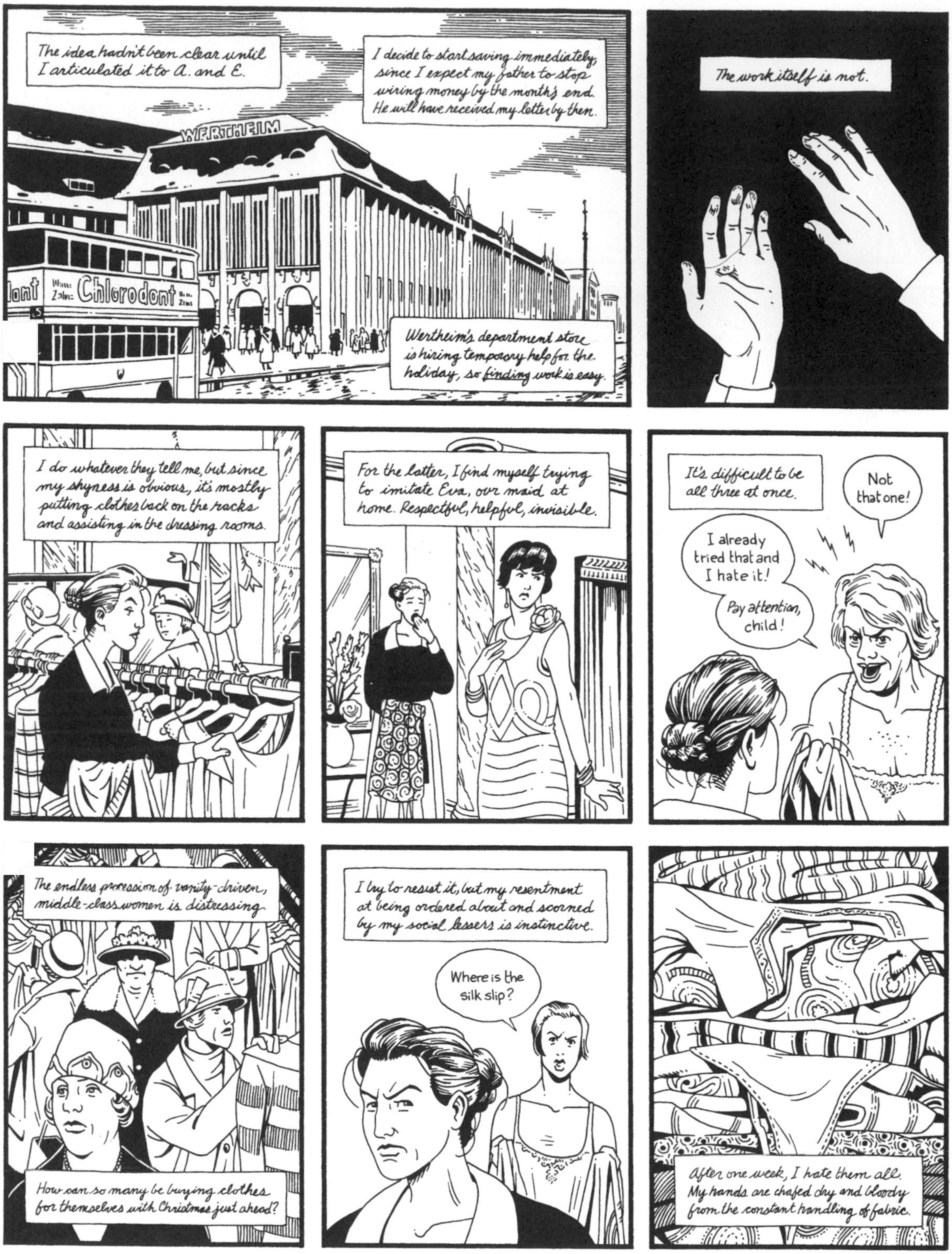

The idea hadn't been clear until I articulated it to A. and E.
I decide to start saving immediately, since I expect my father to stop wiring money by the month's end. He will have received my letter by then.
WERTHEIM
Chlorodont
Wertheim's department store is hiring temporary help for the holiday, so finding work is easy.
The work itself is not.
I do whatever they tell me, but since my shyness is obvious, it's mostly putting clothes back on the racks and assisting in the dressing rooms.
For the latter, I find myself trying to imitate Eva, our maid at home. Respectful, helpful, invisible.
It's difficult to be all three at once.
Not that one!
I already tried that and I hate it!
Pay attention, child!
The endless procession of vanity-driven, middle-class women is distressing.
How can so many be buying clothes for themselves with Christmas just ahead?
I try to resist it, but my resentment at being ordered about and scorned by my social lessers is instinctive.
Where is the silk slip?
After one week, I hate them all. My hands are chafed dry and bloody from the constant handling of fabric.

By Christmas Eve I feel disheartened beyond repair. How can I hope to make a living in this world?

At ten o'clock I pick up my pay and vow never to return to the store.

I'm lonely.

This is my life.

Where am I going?

Silent night, holy night...

KURT SEVERING
FREISINGER S. 9
SW 12 BERLIN

rap rap rap

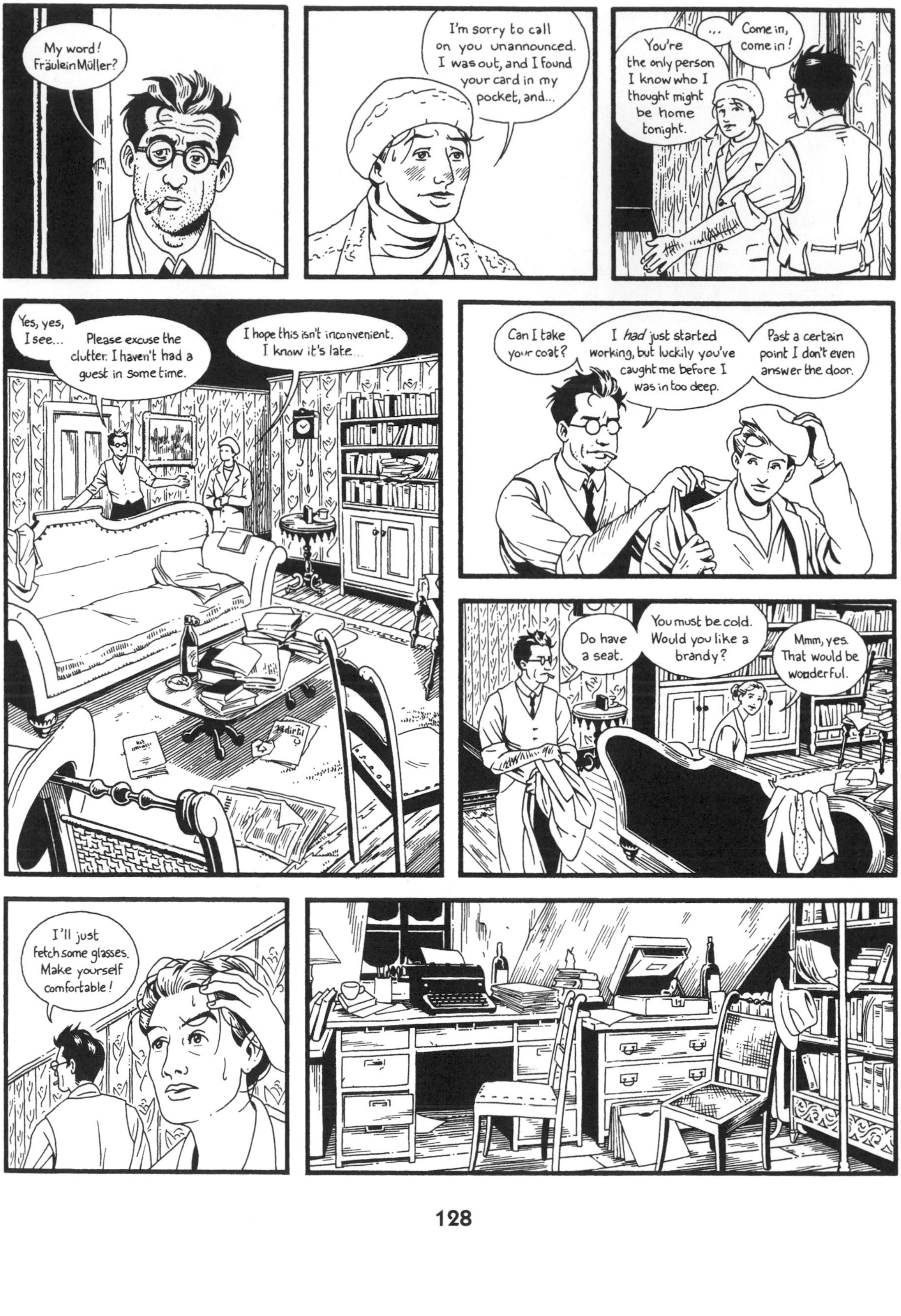
My word! Fräulein Müller?
I'm sorry to call on you unannounced. I was out, and I found your card in my pocket, and...
You're the only person I know who I thought might be home tonight.
...
Come in, come in!
Yes, yes, I see...
Please excuse the clutter. I haven't had a guest in some time.
I hope this isn't inconvenient. I know it's late...
Can I take your coat?
I *had* just started working, but luckily you've caught me before I was in too deep.
Past a certain point I don't even answer the door.
Do have a seat.
You must be cold. Would you like a brandy?
Mmm, yes. That would be wonderful.
I'll just fetch some glasses. Make yourself comfortable!

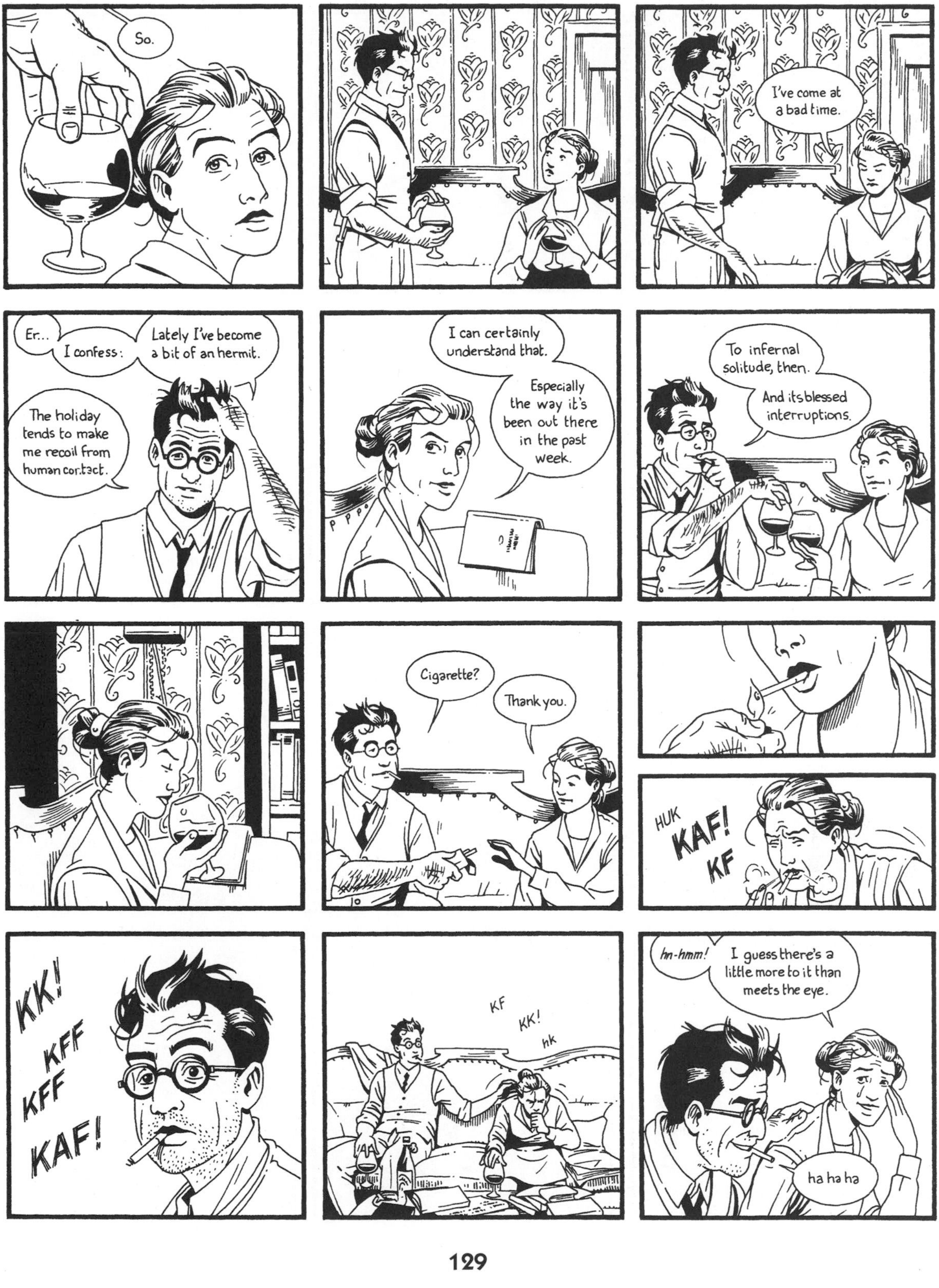
So.
I've come at a bad time.
Er...
I confess:
Lately I've become a bit of an hermit.
The holiday tends to make me recoil from human contact.
I can certainly understand that.
Especially the way it's been out there in the past week.
To infernal solitude, then.
And its blessed interruptions.
Cigarette?
Thank you.
HUK
KAF!
KF
KK!
KFF
KFF
KAF!
KF
KK!
hk
hn-hmm!
I guess there's a little more to it than meets the eye.
ha ha ha

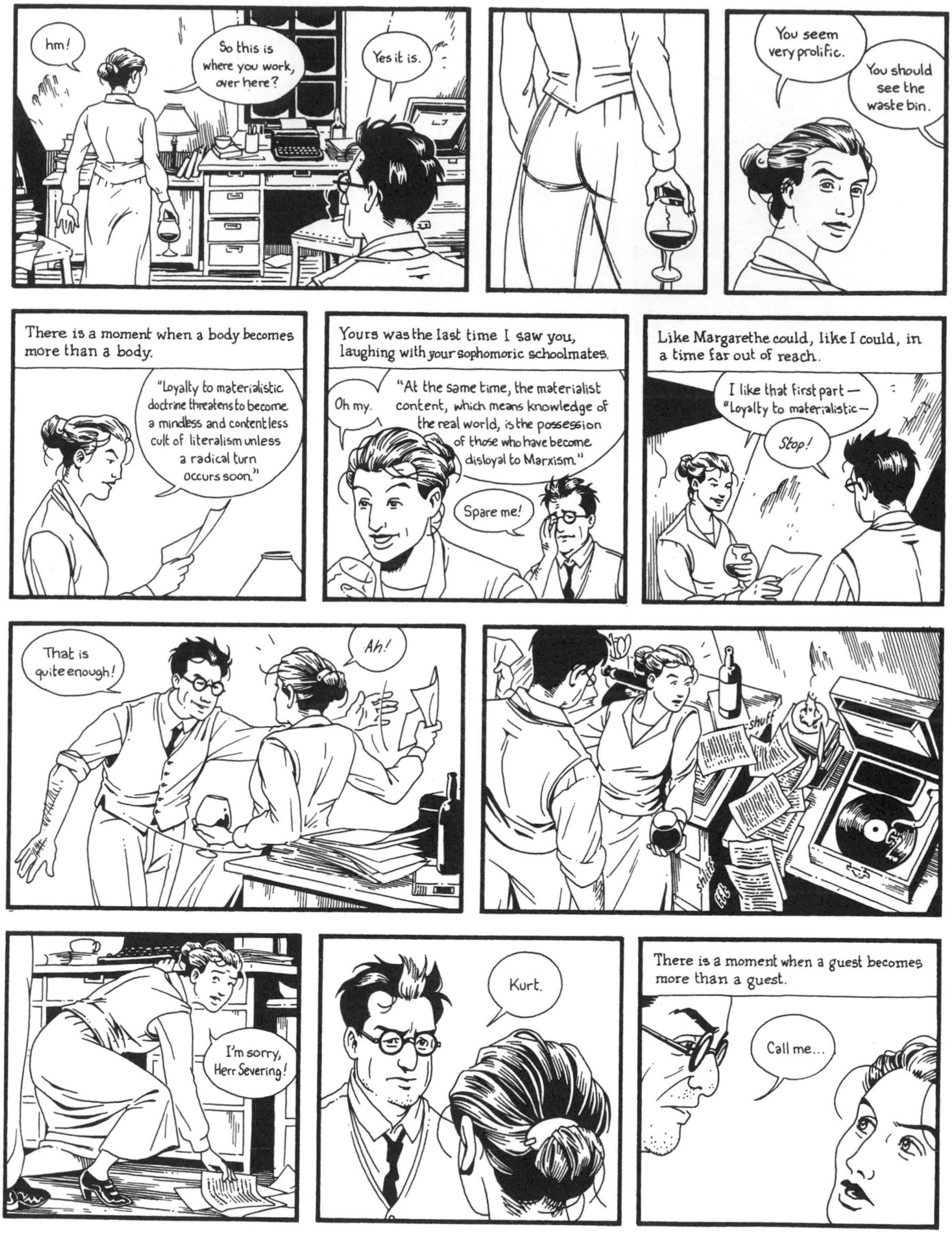
hm!
So this is where you work, over here?
Yes it is.
You seem very prolific.
You should see the waste bin.
There is a moment when a body becomes more than a body.
"Loyalty to materialistic doctrine threatens to become a mindless and contentless cult of literalism unless a radical turn occurs soon."
Yours was the last time I saw you, laughing with your sophomoric schoolmates.
Oh my.
"At the same time, the materialist content, which means knowledge of the real world, is the possession of those who have become disloyal to Marxism."
Spare me!
Like Margarethe could, like I could, in a time far out of reach.
I like that first part — "Loyalty to materialistic—
Stop!
That is quite enough!
Ah!
shuff
shuff
I'm sorry, Herr Severing!
Kurt.
There is a moment when a guest becomes more than a guest.
Call me...

The brandy in my belly teases me out of gravity's grasp,

and with my eyes closed I can feel our heads in mutual orbit.

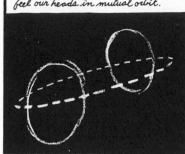

A watering-hole in a stubblefield.

Bricks flaking away like buttercrust and falling with the snow.

It's beautiful and senseless. There's no need for any explanation.

All of the rules we know so well and abide by so carefully become completely meaningless.

We'll become children again.

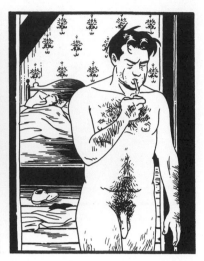

Good morning.

Happy Christmas.

6

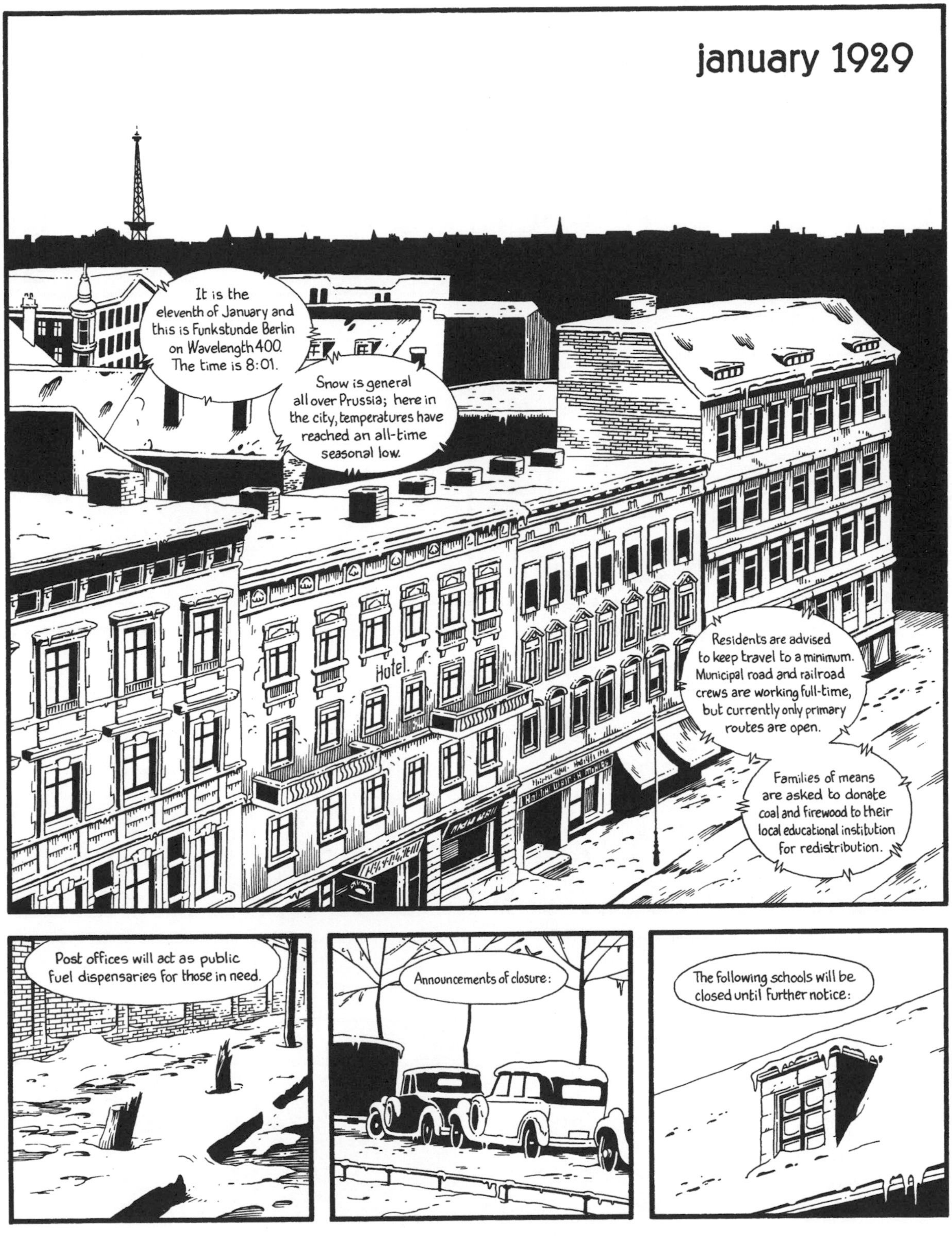
january 1929
It is the eleventh of January and this is Funkstunde Berlin on Wavelength 400. The time is 8:01.
Snow is general all over Prussia; here in the city, temperatures have reached an all-time seasonal low.
Hotel.
Residents are advised to keep travel to a minimum. Municipal road and railroad crews are working full-time, but currently only primary routes are open.
Families of means are asked to donate coal and firewood to their local educational institution for redistribution.
Post offices will act as public fuel dispensaries for those in need.
Announcements of closure:
The following schools will be closed until further notice:

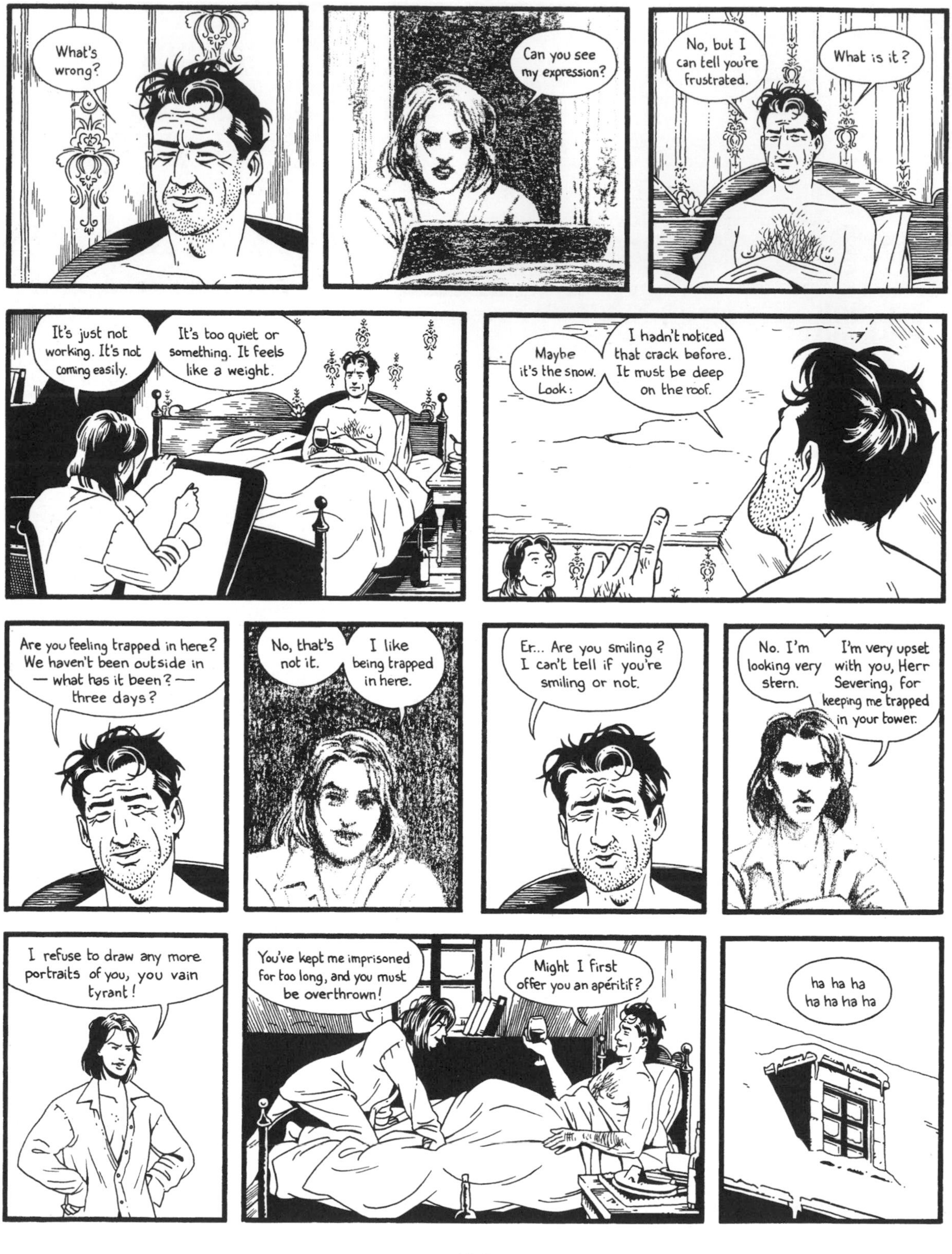
What's wrong?
Can you see my expression?
No, but I can tell you're frustrated.
What is it?
It's just not working. It's not coming easily.
It's too quiet or something. It feels like a weight.
Maybe it's the snow. Look:
I hadn't noticed that crack before. It must be deep on the roof.
Are you feeling trapped in here? We haven't been outside in — what has it been? — three days?
No, that's not it.
I like being trapped in here.
Er... Are you smiling? I can't tell if you're smiling or not.
No. I'm looking very stern.
I'm very upset with you, Herr Severing, for keeping me trapped in your tower.
I refuse to draw any more portraits of you, you vain tyrant!
You've kept me imprisoned for too long, and you must be overthrown!
Might I first offer you an apéritif?
ha ha ha
ha ha ha ha

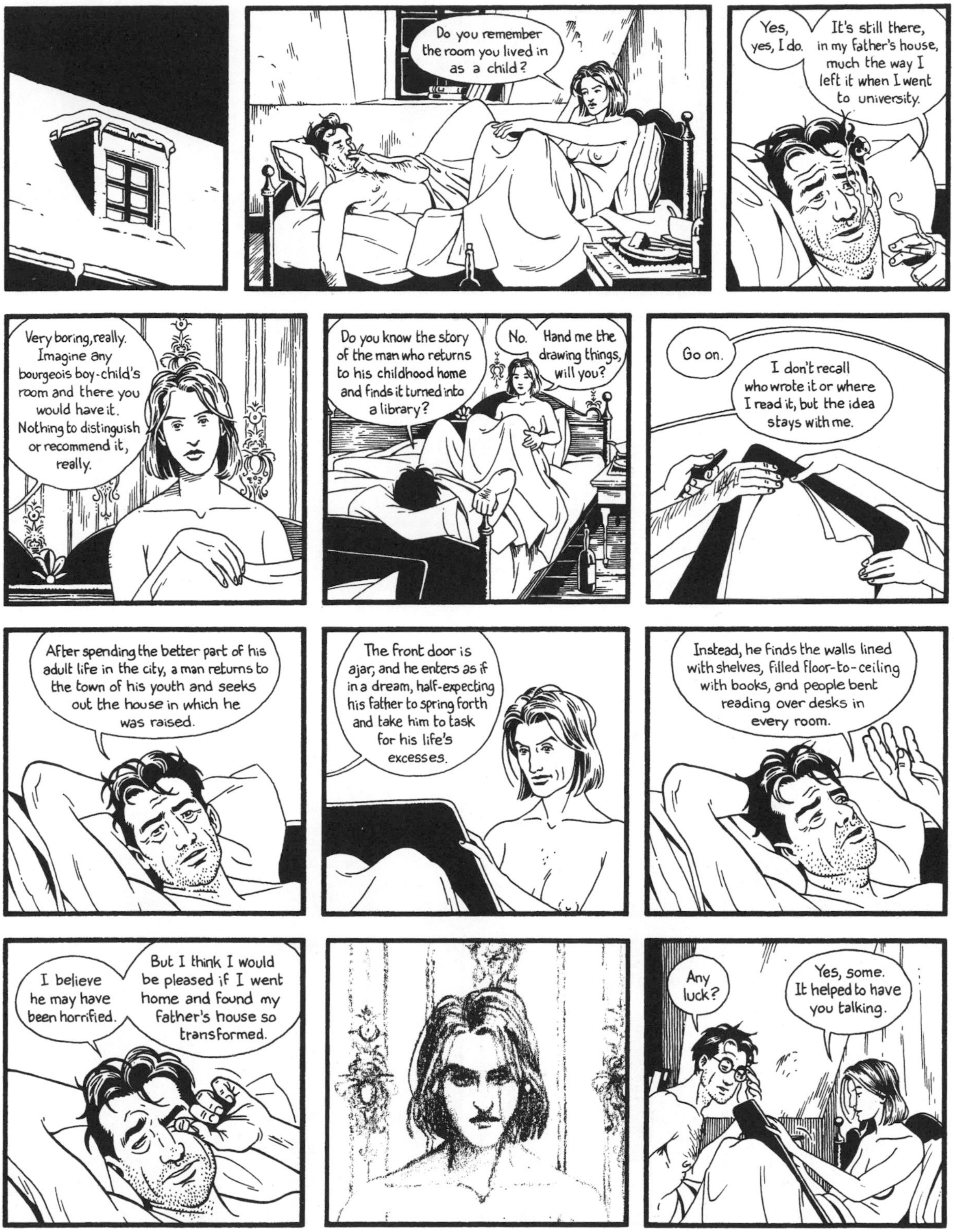

Do you remember the room you lived in as a child?
Yes, yes, I do.
It's still there, in my father's house, much the way I left it when I went to university.
Very boring, really. Imagine any bourgeois boy-child's room and there you would have it. Nothing to distinguish or recommend it, really.
Do you know the story of the man who returns to his childhood home and finds it turned into a library?
No.
Hand me the drawing things, will you?
Go on.
I don't recall who wrote it or where I read it, but the idea stays with me.
After spending the better part of his adult life in the city, a man returns to the town of his youth and seeks out the house in which he was raised.
The front door is ajar, and he enters as if in a dream, half-expecting his father to spring forth and take him to task for his life's excesses.
Instead, he finds the walls lined with shelves, filled floor-to-ceiling with books, and people bent reading over desks in every room.
I believe he may have been horrified.
But I think I would be pleased if I went home and found my father's house so transformed.
Any luck?
Yes, some. It helped to have you talking.

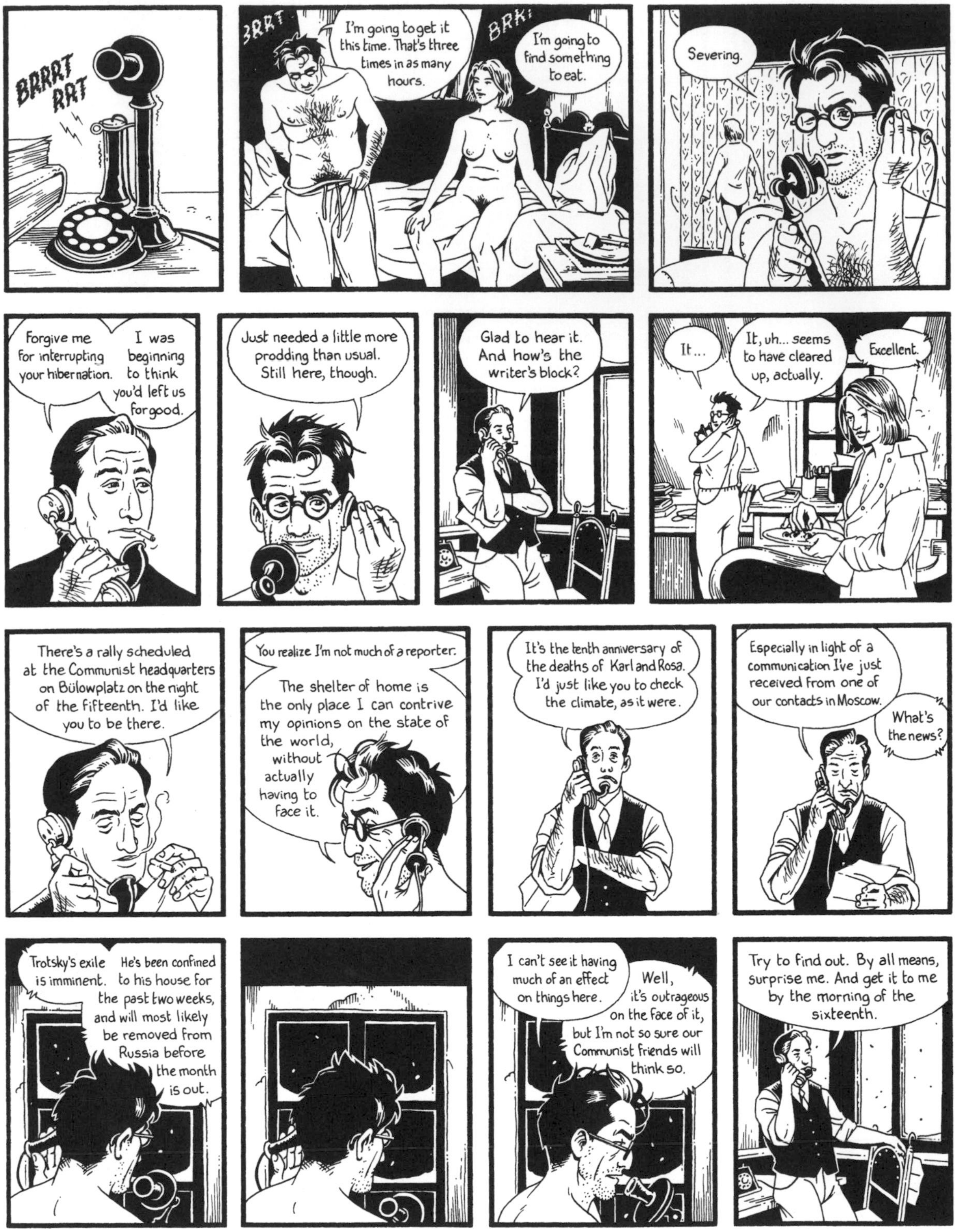
BRRRT RRT
BRRT
I'm going to get it this time. That's three times in as many hours.
BRK
I'm going to find something to eat.
Severing.
Forgive me for interrupting your hibernation.
I was beginning to think you'd left us for good.
Just needed a little more prodding than usual. Still here, though.
Glad to hear it. And how's the writer's block?
It...
It, uh... seems to have cleared up, actually.
Excellent.
There's a rally scheduled at the Communist headquarters on Bülowplatz on the night of the fifteenth. I'd like you to be there.
You realize I'm not much of a reporter.
The shelter of home is the only place I can contrive my opinions on the state of the world, without actually having to face it.
It's the tenth anniversary of the deaths of Karl and Rosa. I'd just like you to check the climate, as it were.
Especially in light of a communication I've just received from one of our contacts in Moscow.
What's the news?
Trotsky's exile is imminent.
He's been confined to his house for the past two weeks, and will most likely be removed from Russia before the month is out.
I can't see it having much of an effect on things here.
Well, it's outrageous on the face of it, but I'm not so sure our Communist friends will think so.
Try to find out. By all means, surprise me. And get it to me by the morning of the sixteenth.

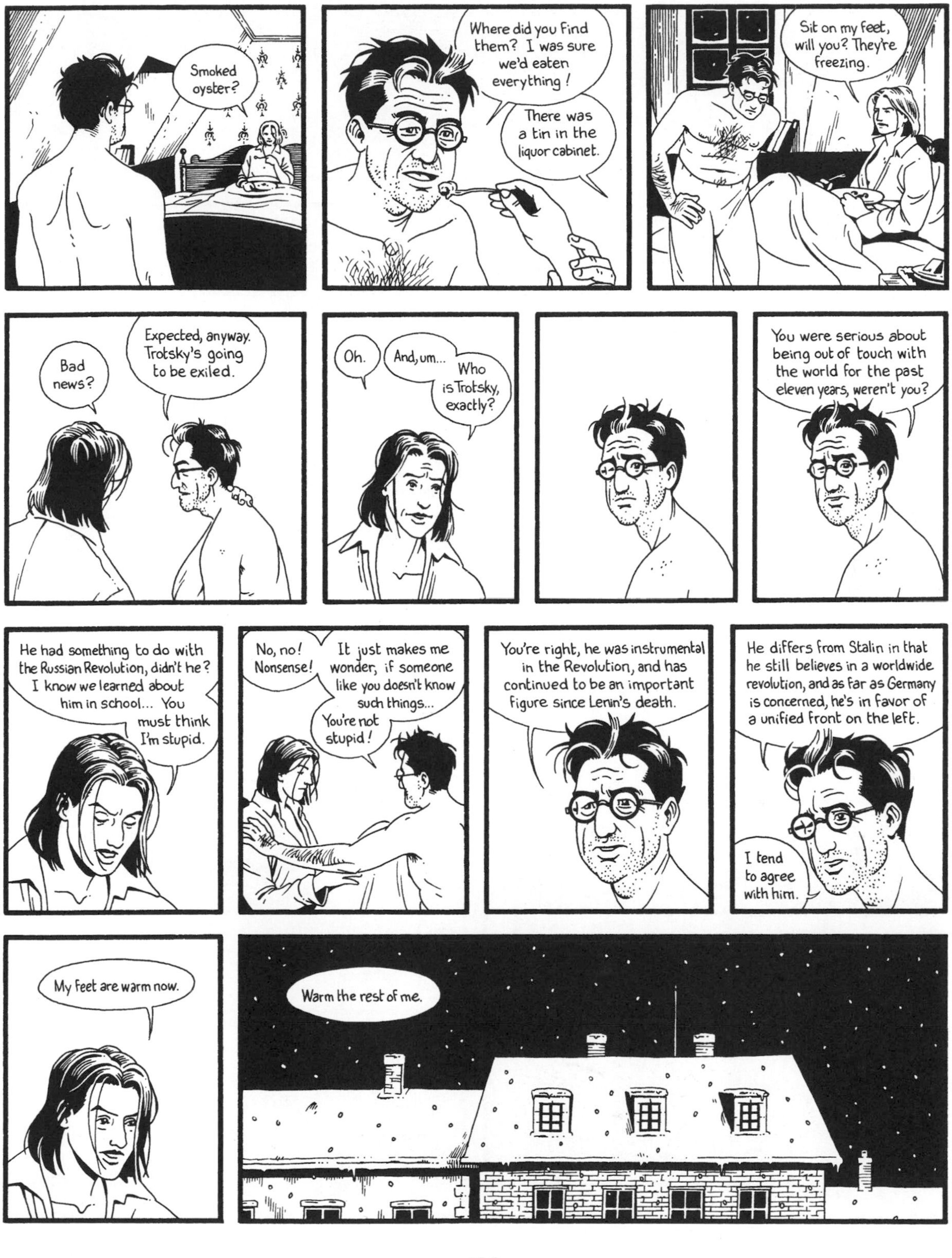

Smoked oyster?
Where did you find them? I was sure we'd eaten everything!
There was a tin in the liquor cabinet.
Sit on my feet, will you? They're freezing.
Bad news?
Expected, anyway. Trotsky's going to be exiled.
Oh.
And, um... Who is Trotsky, exactly?
You were serious about being out of touch with the world for the past eleven years, weren't you?
He had something to do with the Russian Revolution, didn't he? I know we learned about him in school... You must think I'm stupid.
No, no! Nonsense!
It just makes me wonder, if someone like you doesn't know such things...
You're not stupid!
You're right, he was instrumental in the Revolution, and has continued to be an important figure since Lenin's death.
He differs from Stalin in that he still believes in a worldwide revolution, and as far as Germany is concerned, he's in favor of a unified front on the left.
I tend to agree with him.
My feet are warm now.
Warm the rest of me.

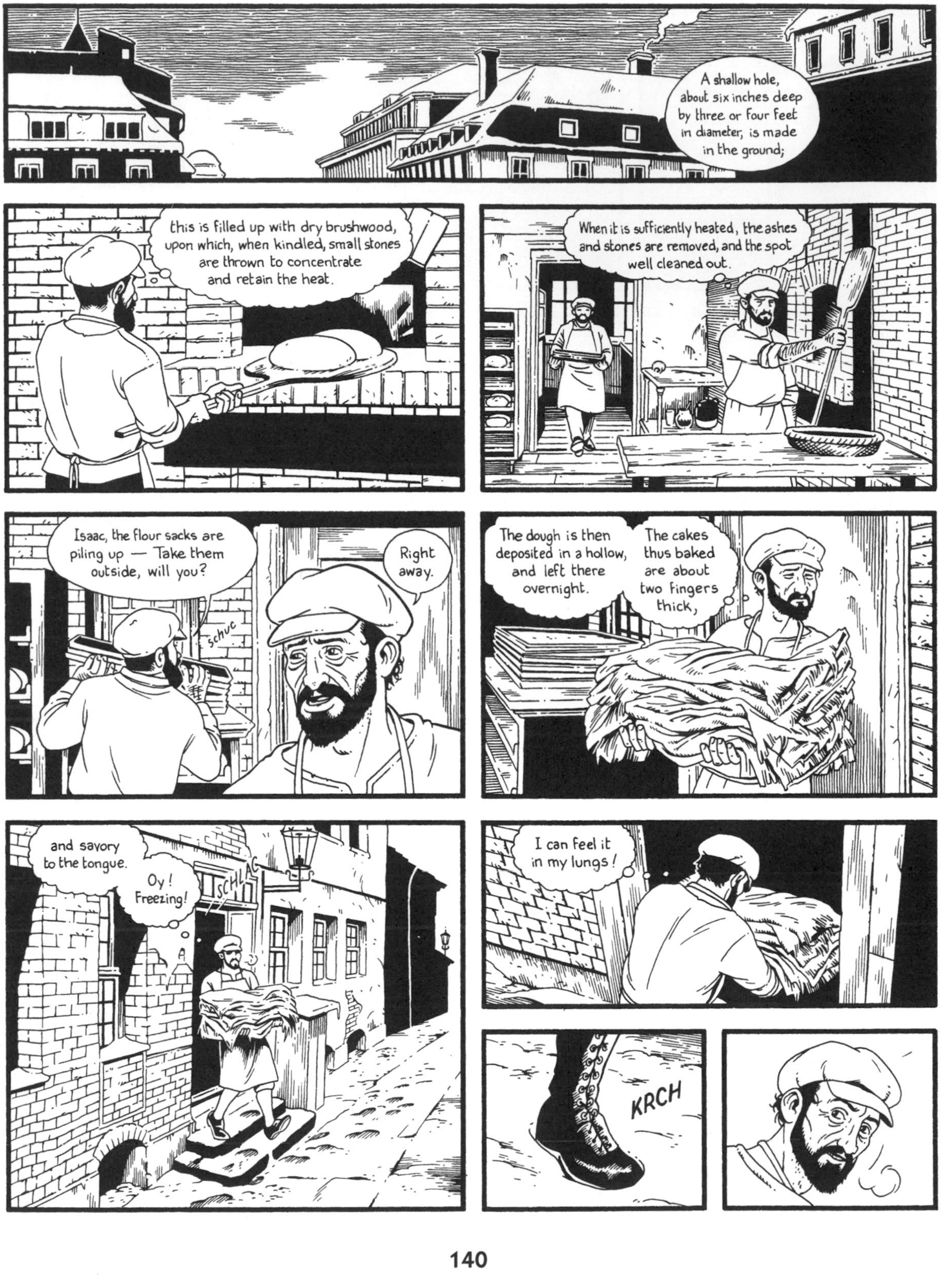
A shallow hole, about six inches deep by three or four feet in diameter, is made in the ground;
this is filled up with dry brushwood, upon which, when kindled, small stones are thrown to concentrate and retain the heat.
When it is sufficiently heated, the ashes and stones are removed, and the spot well cleaned out.
Isaac, the flour sacks are piling up — Take them outside, will you?
schuc
Right away.
The dough is then deposited in a hollow, and left there overnight.
The cakes thus baked are about two fingers thick,
and savory to the tongue.
Oy! Freezing!
SCHLAC
I can feel it in my lungs!
KRCH

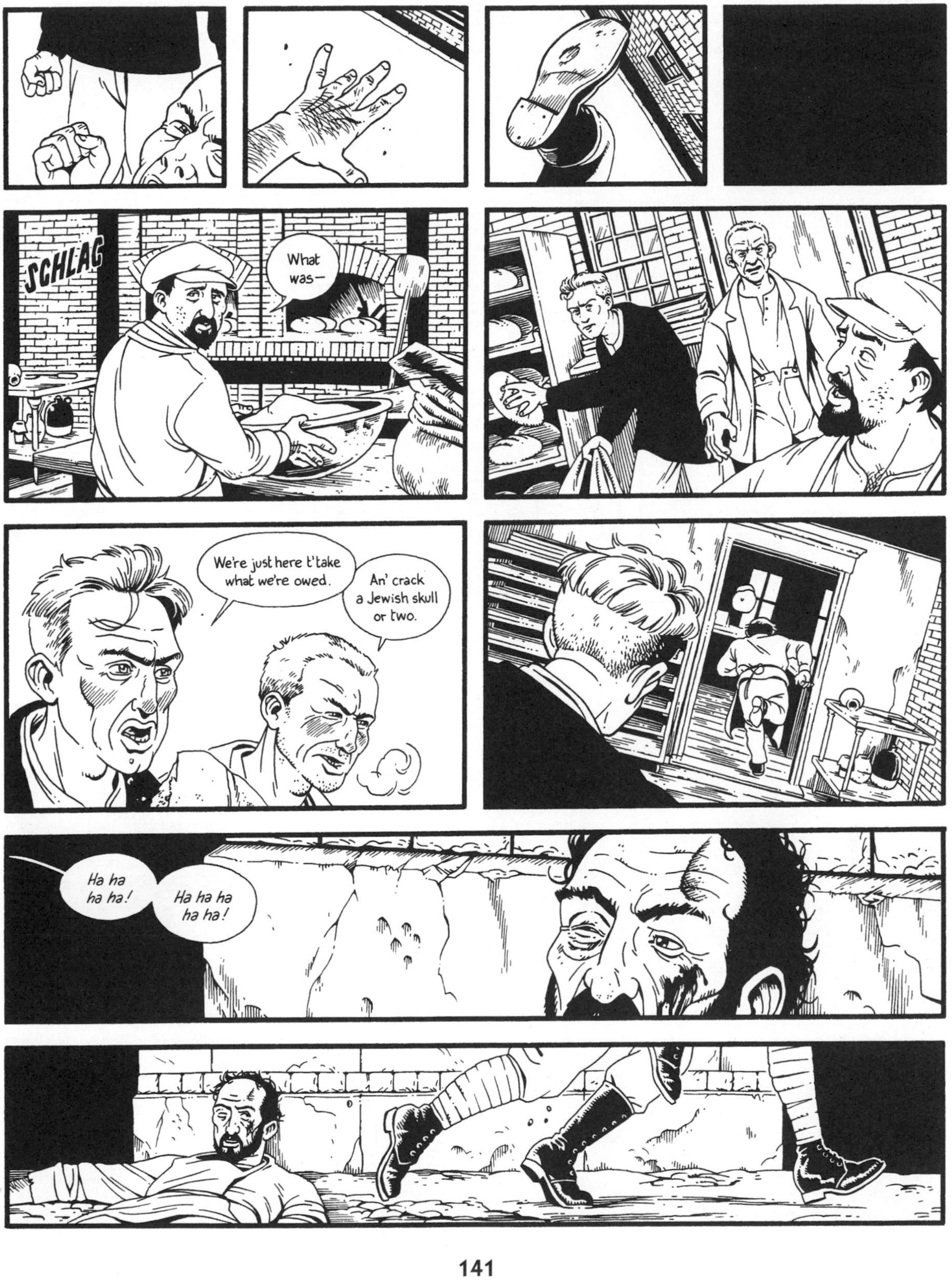
SCHLAG
What was—
We're just here t'take what we're owed.
An' crack a Jewish skull or two.
Ha ha ha ha!
Ha ha ha ha ha!

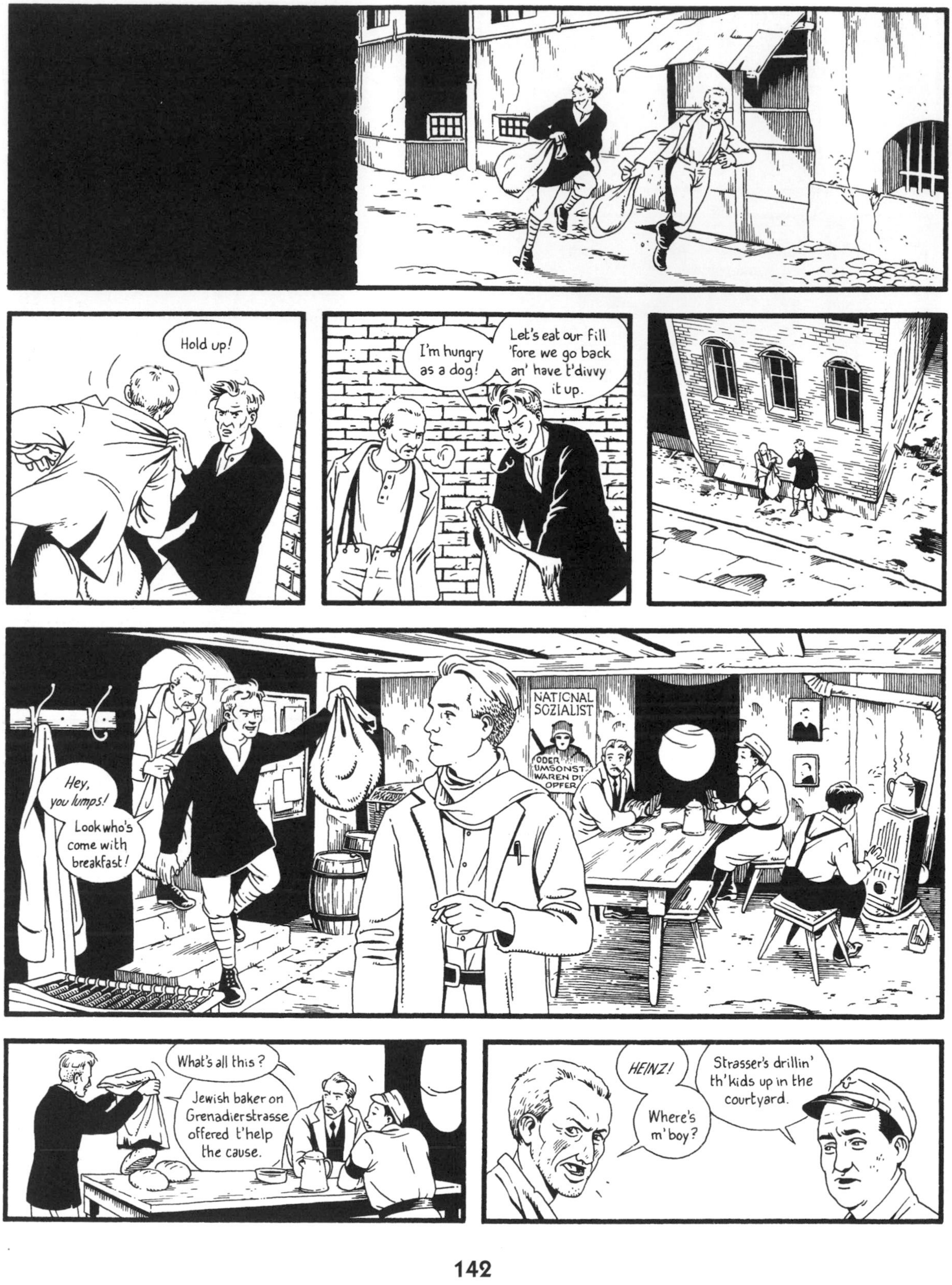
Hold up!
I'm hungry as a dog!
Let's eat our fill 'fore we go back an' have t'divvy it up.
NATIONAL SOZIALIST
ODER UMSONST WAREN DIE OPFER
Hey, you lumps!
Look who's come with breakfast!
What's all this?
Jewish baker on Grenadierstrasse offered t'help the cause.
HEINZ!
Where's m'boy?
Strasser's drillin' th'kids up in the courtyard.

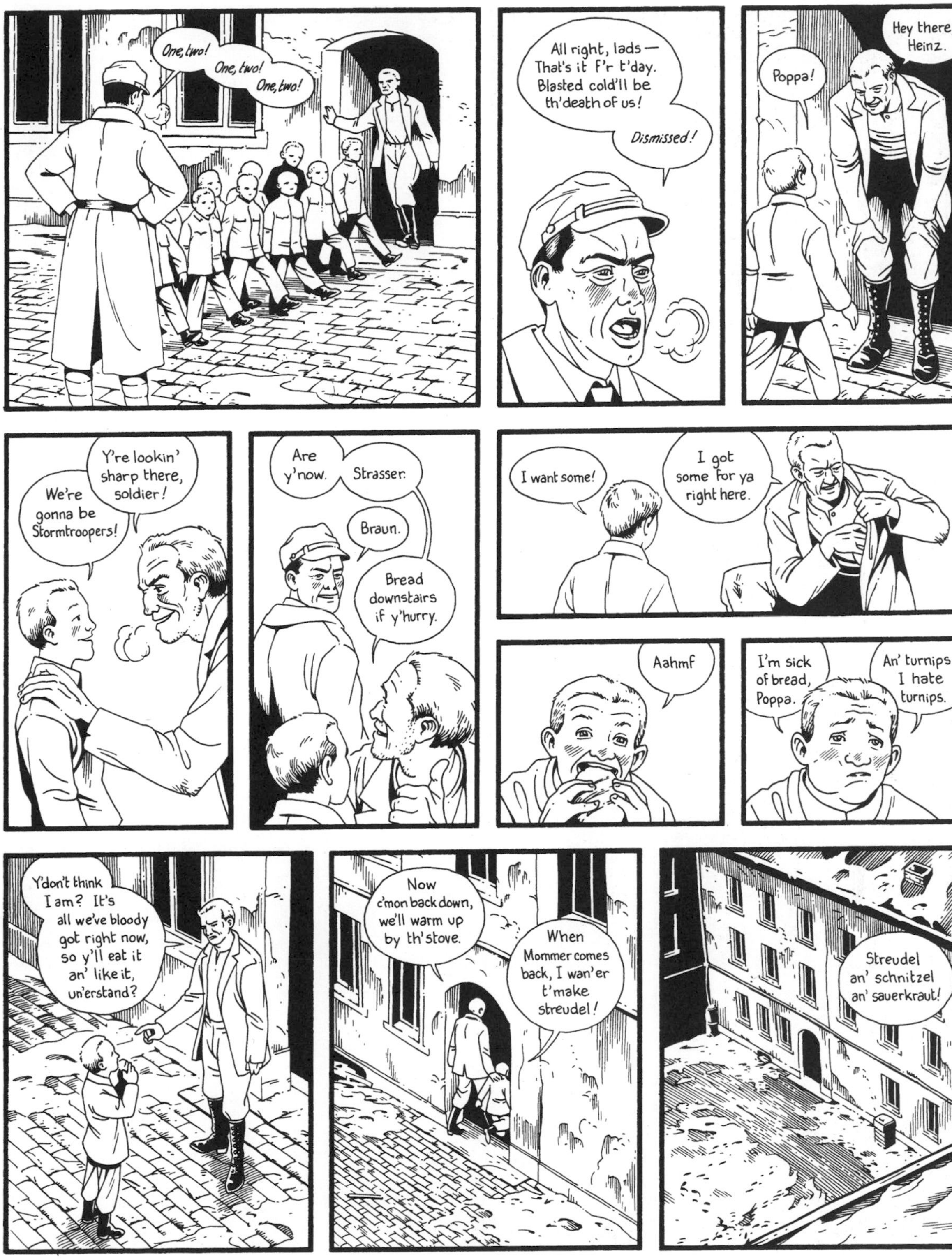
One, two!
One, two!
One, two!
All right, lads — That's it f'r t'day. Blasted cold'll be th'death of us!
Dismissed!
Hey there, Heinz.
Poppa!
Y're lookin' sharp there, soldier!
We're gonna be Stormtroopers!
Are y'now.
Strasser.
Braun.
Bread downstairs if y'hurry.
I want some!
I got some for ya right here.
Aahmf
I'm sick of bread, Poppa.
An' turnips. I hate turnips.
Y'don't think I am? It's all we've bloody got right now, so y'll eat it an' like it, un'erstand?
Now c'mon back down, we'll warm up by th'stove.
When Mommer comes back, I wan'er t'make streudel!
Streudel an' schnitzel an' sauerkraut!

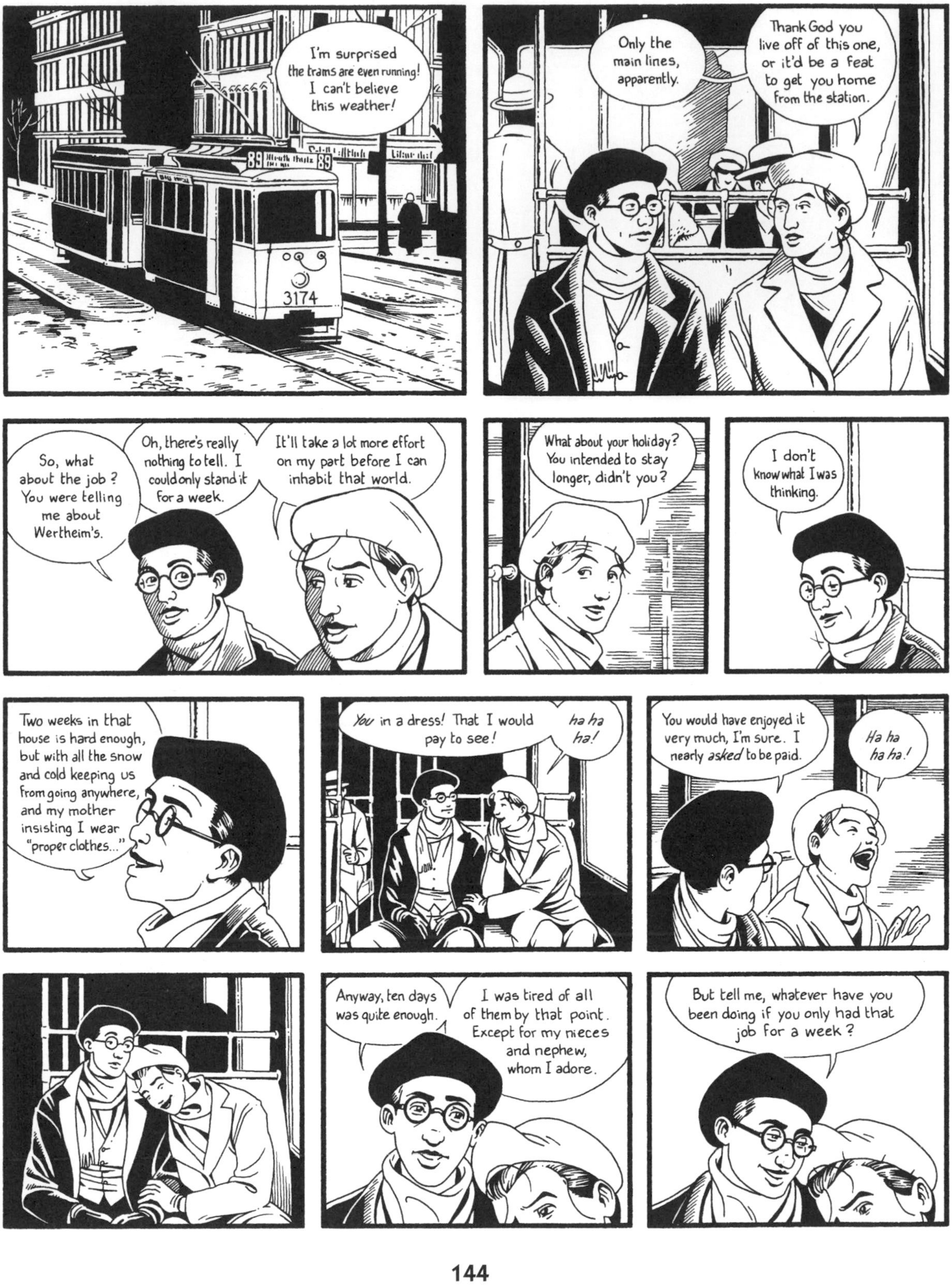
I'm surprised the trams are even running! I can't believe this weather!
89
3174
Only the main lines, apparently.
Thank God you live off of this one, or it'd be a feat to get you home from the station.
So, what about the job? You were telling me about Wertheim's.
Oh, there's really nothing to tell. I could only stand it for a week.
It'll take a lot more effort on my part before I can inhabit that world.
What about your holiday? You intended to stay longer, didn't you?
I don't know what I was thinking.
Two weeks in that house is hard enough, but with all the snow and cold keeping us from going anywhere, and my mother insisting I wear "proper clothes..."
You in a dress! That I would pay to see!
ha ha ha!
You would have enjoyed it very much, I'm sure. I nearly *asked* to be paid.
Ha ha ha ha!
Anyway, ten days was quite enough.
I was tired of all of them by that point. Except for my nieces and nephew, whom I adore.
But tell me, whatever have you been doing if you only had that job for a week?

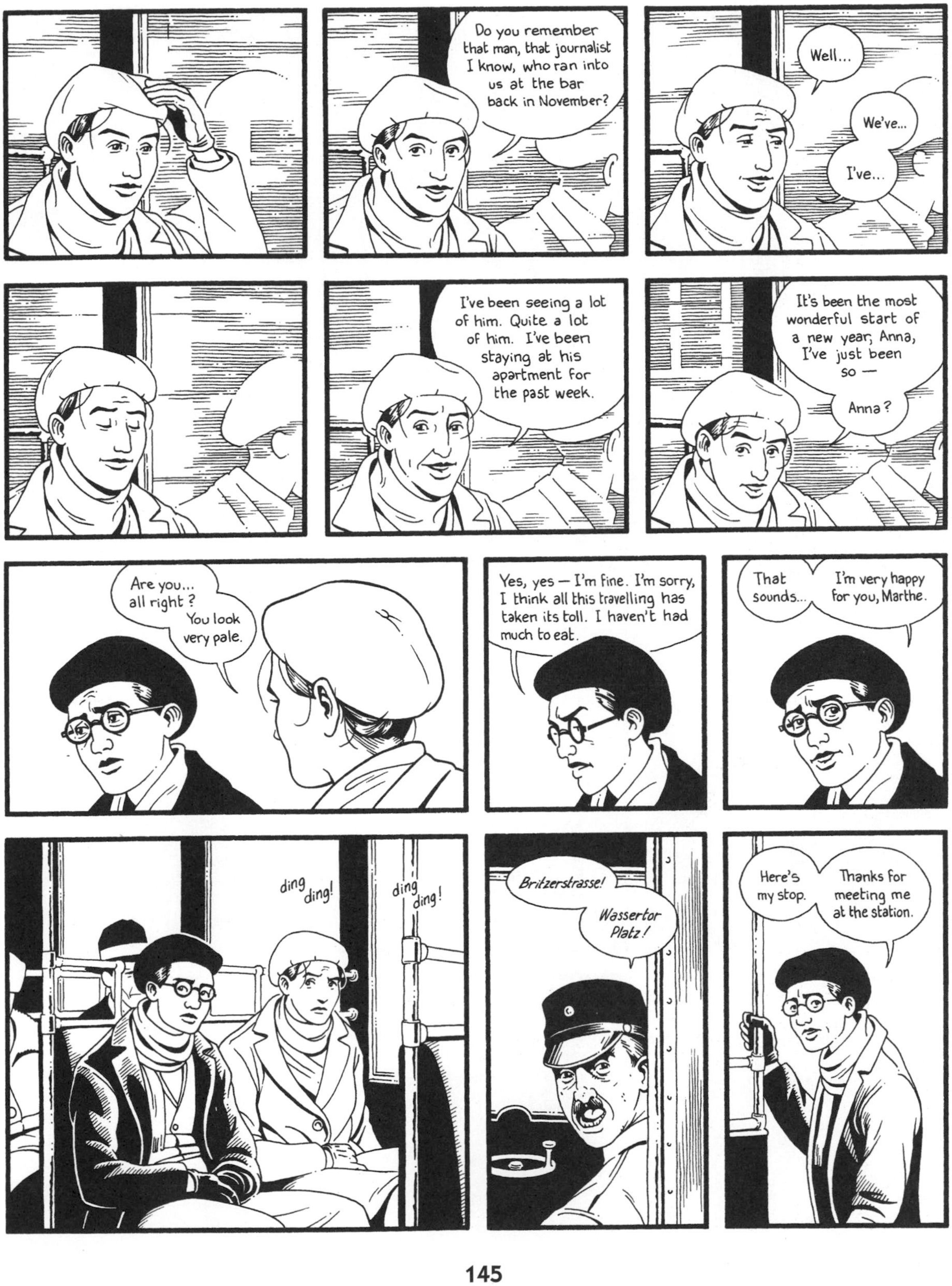

Do you remember that man, that journalist I know, who ran into us at the bar back in November?
Well...
We've...
I've...
I've been seeing a lot of him. Quite a lot of him. I've been staying at his apartment for the past week.
It's been the most wonderful start of a new year, Anna, I've just been so —
Anna?
Are you... all right?
You look very pale.
Yes, yes — I'm fine. I'm sorry, I think all this travelling has taken its toll. I haven't had much to eat.
That sounds...
I'm very happy for you, Marthe.
ding ding!
ding ding!
Britzerstrasse!
Wassertor Platz!
Here's my stop.
Thanks for meeting me at the station.

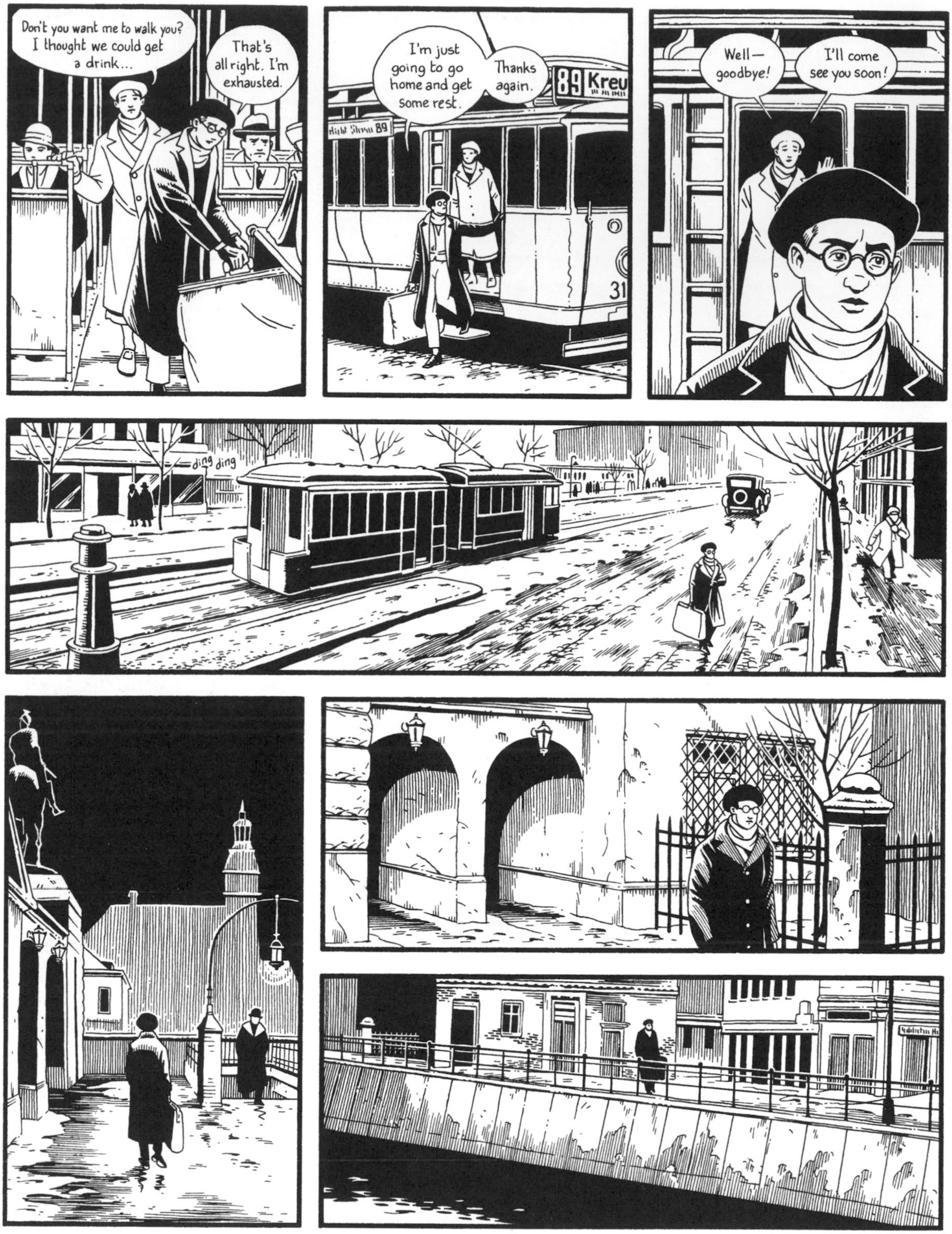
Don't you want me to walk you? I thought we could get a drink...
That's all right. I'm exhausted.
I'm just going to go home and get some rest.
Thanks again.
89 Kreu
Well— goodbye!
I'll come see you soon!
ding ding

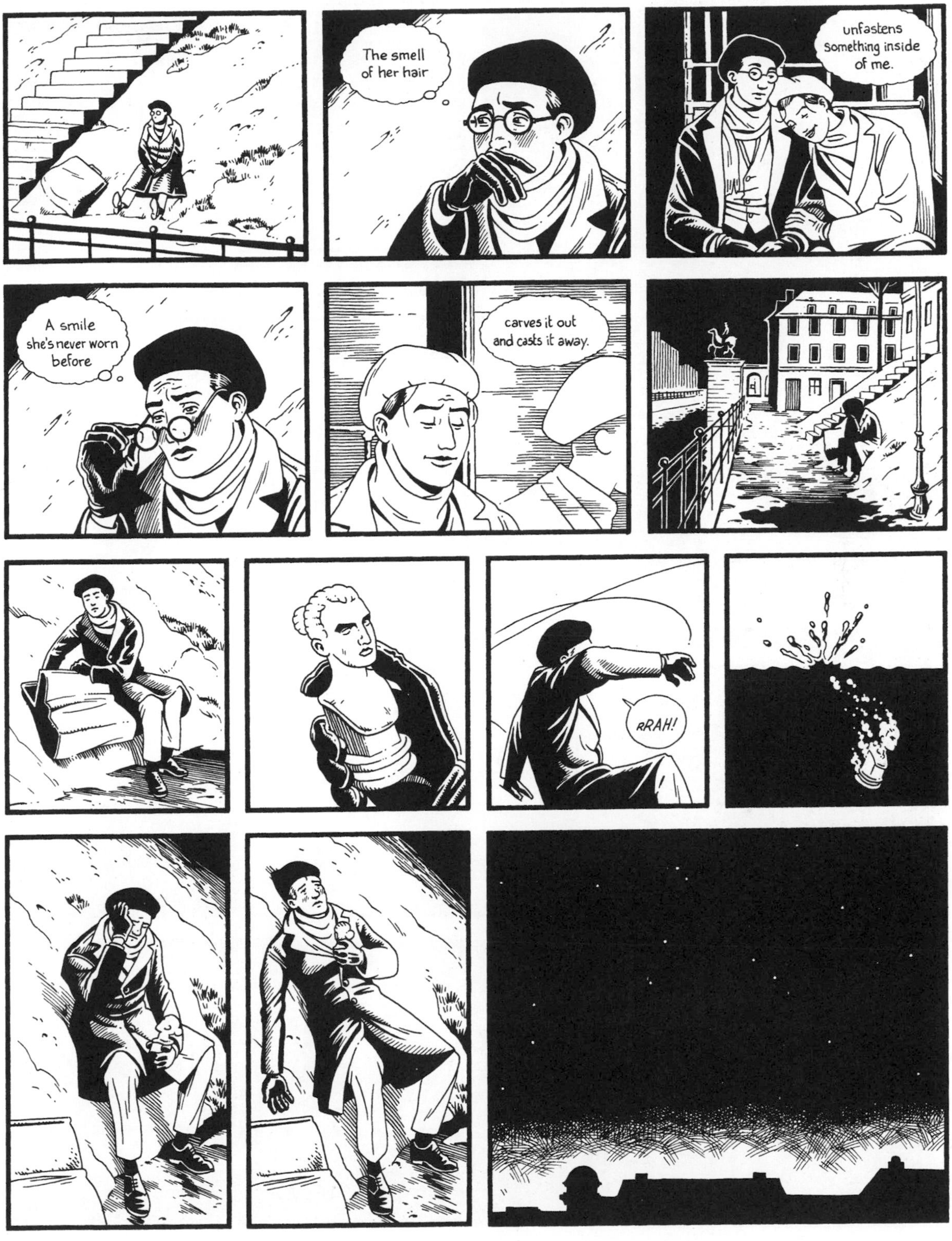

The smell of her hair
unfastens something inside of me.
A smile she's never worn before
carves it out and casts it away.
rRAH!

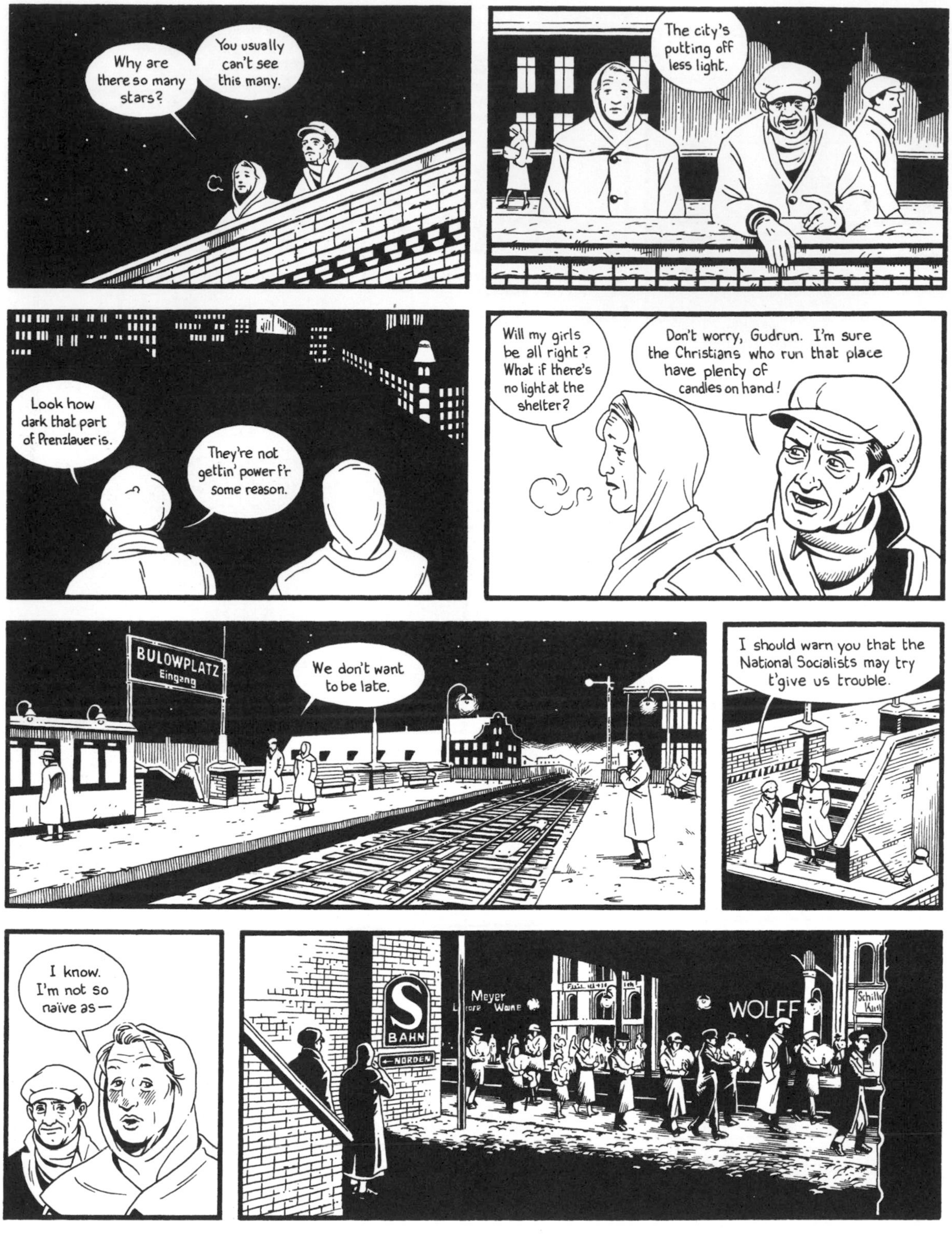
Why are there so many stars?
You usually can't see this many.
The city's putting off less light.
Look how dark that part of Prenzlauer is.
They're not gettin' power f'r some reason.
Will my girls be all right? What if there's no light at the shelter?
Don't worry, Gudrun. I'm sure the Christians who run that place have plenty of candles on hand!
BULOWPLATZ
Eingang
We don't want to be late.
I should warn you that the National Socialists may try t'give us trouble.
I know. I'm not so naïve as—
S
BAHN
←NORDEN
Meyer
WOLFF

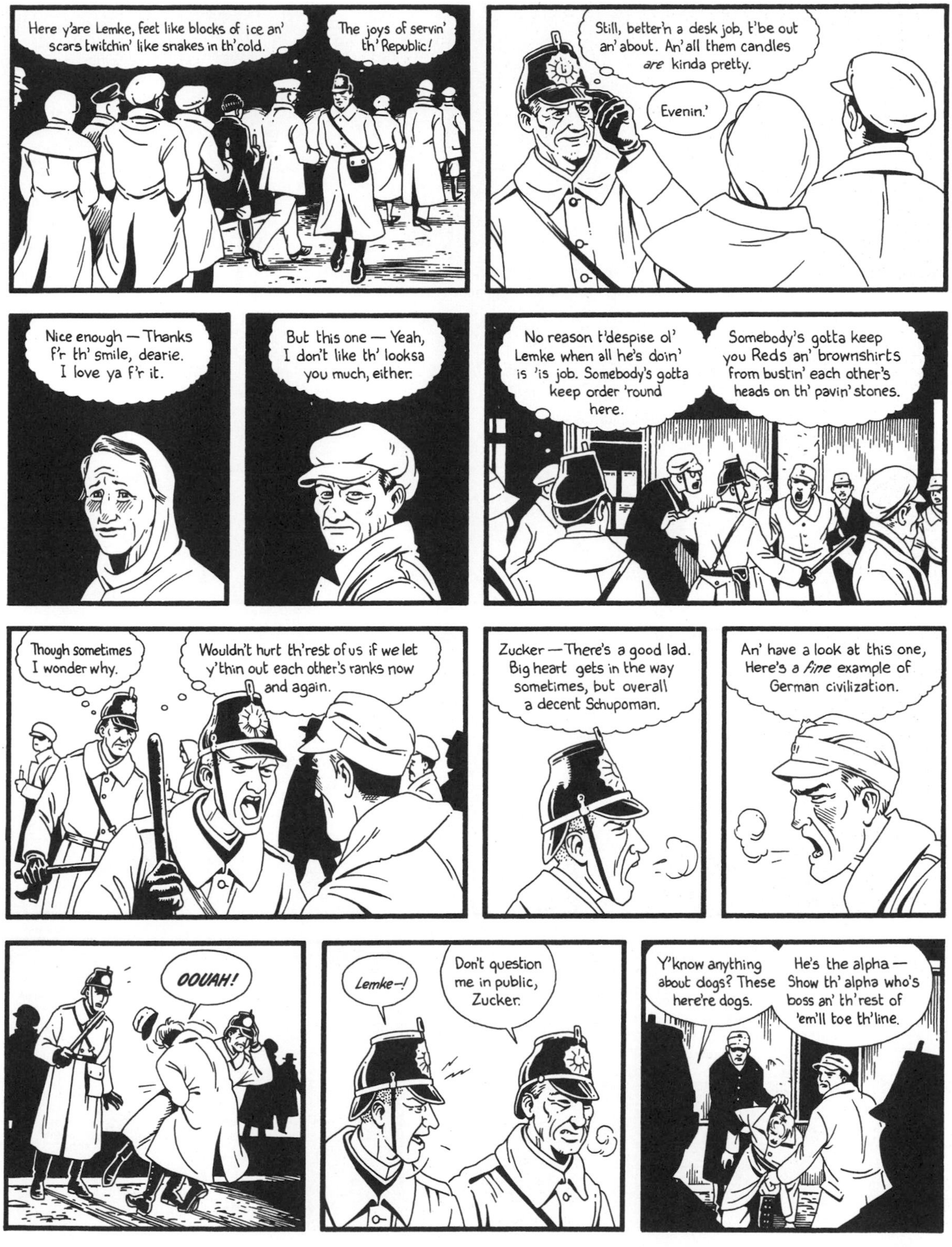
Here y'are Lemke, feet like blocks of ice an' scars twitchin' like snakes in th'cold.
The joys of servin' th' Republic!
Still, better'n a desk job, t'be out an' about. An' all them candles *are* kinda pretty.
Evenin.'
Nice enough — Thanks f'r th' smile, dearie. I love ya f'r it.
But this one — Yeah, I don't like th' looksa you much, either.
No reason t'despise ol' Lemke when all he's doin' is 'is job. Somebody's gotta keep order 'round here.
Somebody's gotta keep you Reds an' brownshirts from bustin' each other's heads on th' pavin' stones.
Though sometimes I wonder why.
Wouldn't hurt th'rest of us if we let y'thin out each other's ranks now and again.
Zucker — There's a good lad. Big heart gets in the way sometimes, but overall a decent Schupoman.
An' have a look at this one, Here's a *fine* example of German civilization.
OOUAH!
Lemke—!
Don't question me in public, Zucker.
Y'know anything about dogs? These here're dogs.
He's the alpha — Show th' alpha who's boss an' th'rest of 'em'll toe th'line.

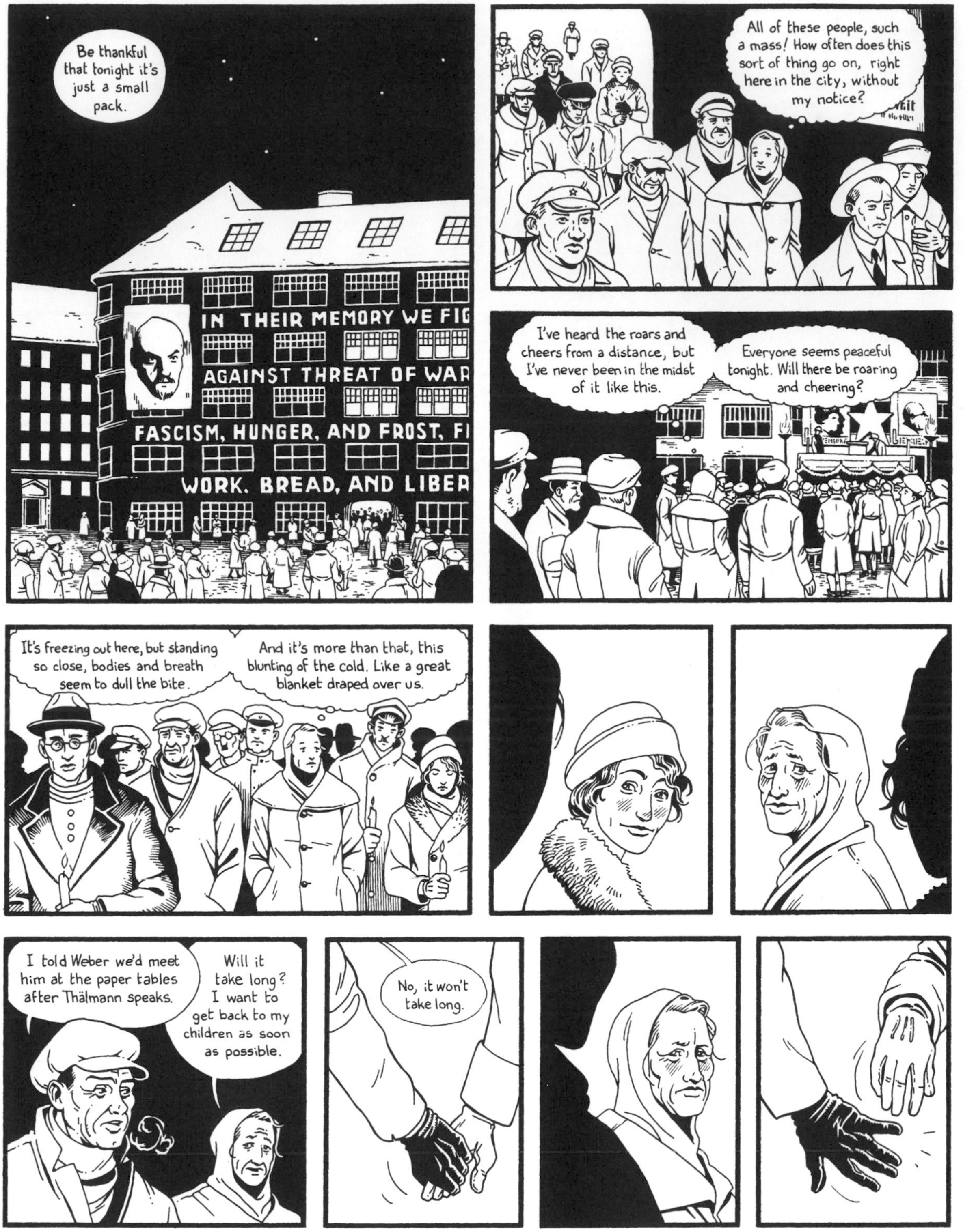
Be thankful that tonight it's just a small pack.
IN THEIR MEMORY WE FIG
AGAINST THREAT OF WAR
FASCISM, HUNGER, AND FROST, FI
WORK. BREAD, AND LIBER
All of these people, such a mass! How often does this sort of thing go on, right here in the city, without my notice?
I've heard the roars and cheers from a distance, but I've never been in the midst of it like this.
Everyone seems peaceful tonight. Will there be roaring and cheering?
It's freezing out here, but standing so close, bodies and breath seem to dull the bite.
And it's more than that, this blunting of the cold. Like a great blanket draped over us.
I told Weber we'd meet him at the paper tables after Thälmann speaks.
Will it take long? I want to get back to my children as soon as possible.
No, it won't take long.

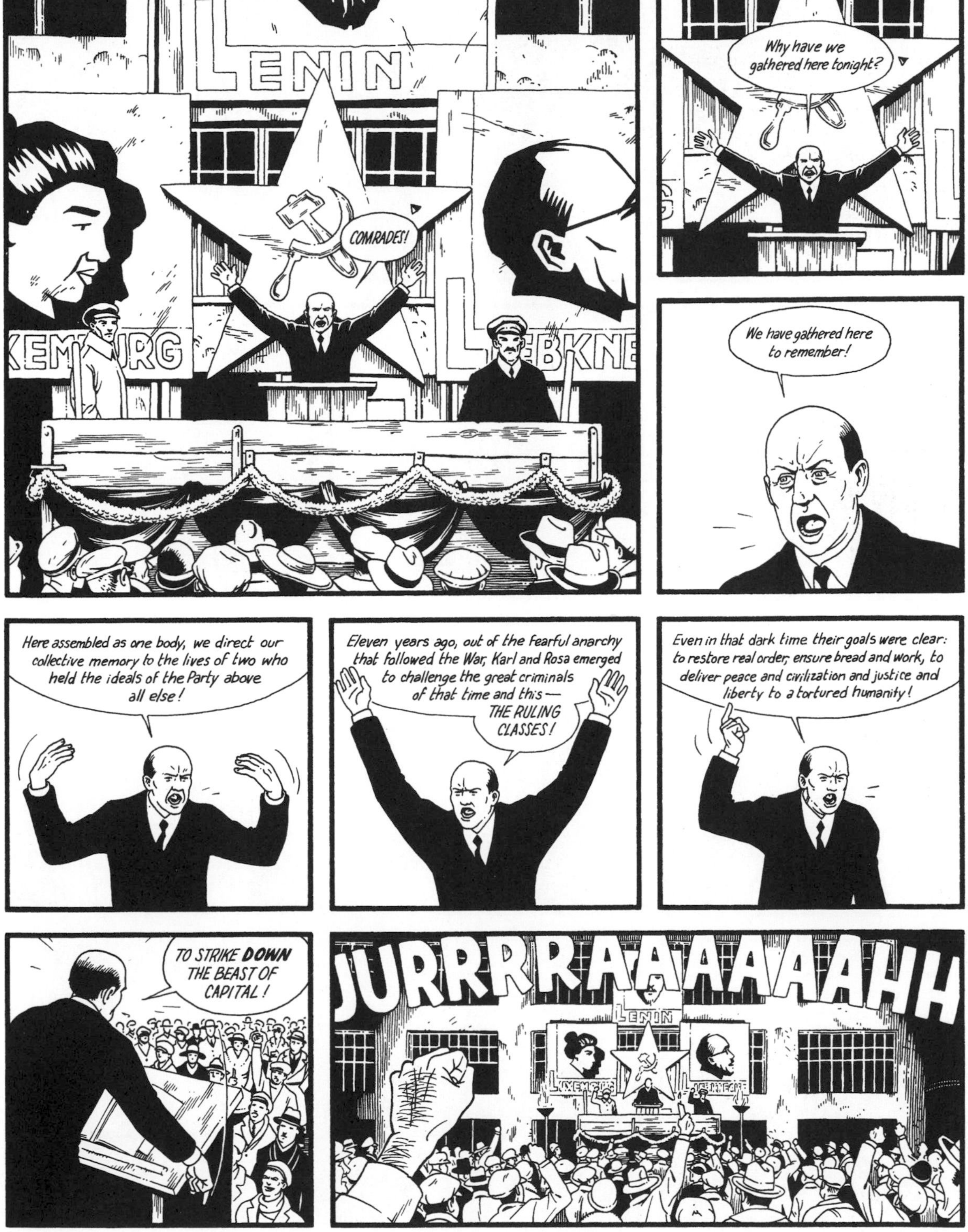
LENIN
COMRADES!
Why have we gathered here tonight?
We have gathered here to remember!
Here assembled as one body, we direct our collective memory to the lives of two who held the ideals of the Party above all else!
Eleven years ago, out of the fearful anarchy that followed the War, Karl and Rosa emerged to challenge the great criminals of that time and this—
THE RULING CLASSES!
Even in that dark time their goals were clear: to restore real order, ensure bread and work, to deliver peace and civilization and justice and liberty to a tortured humanity!
TO STRIKE **DOWN** THE BEAST OF CAPITAL!
JURRRRAAAAAAAHH
LENIN

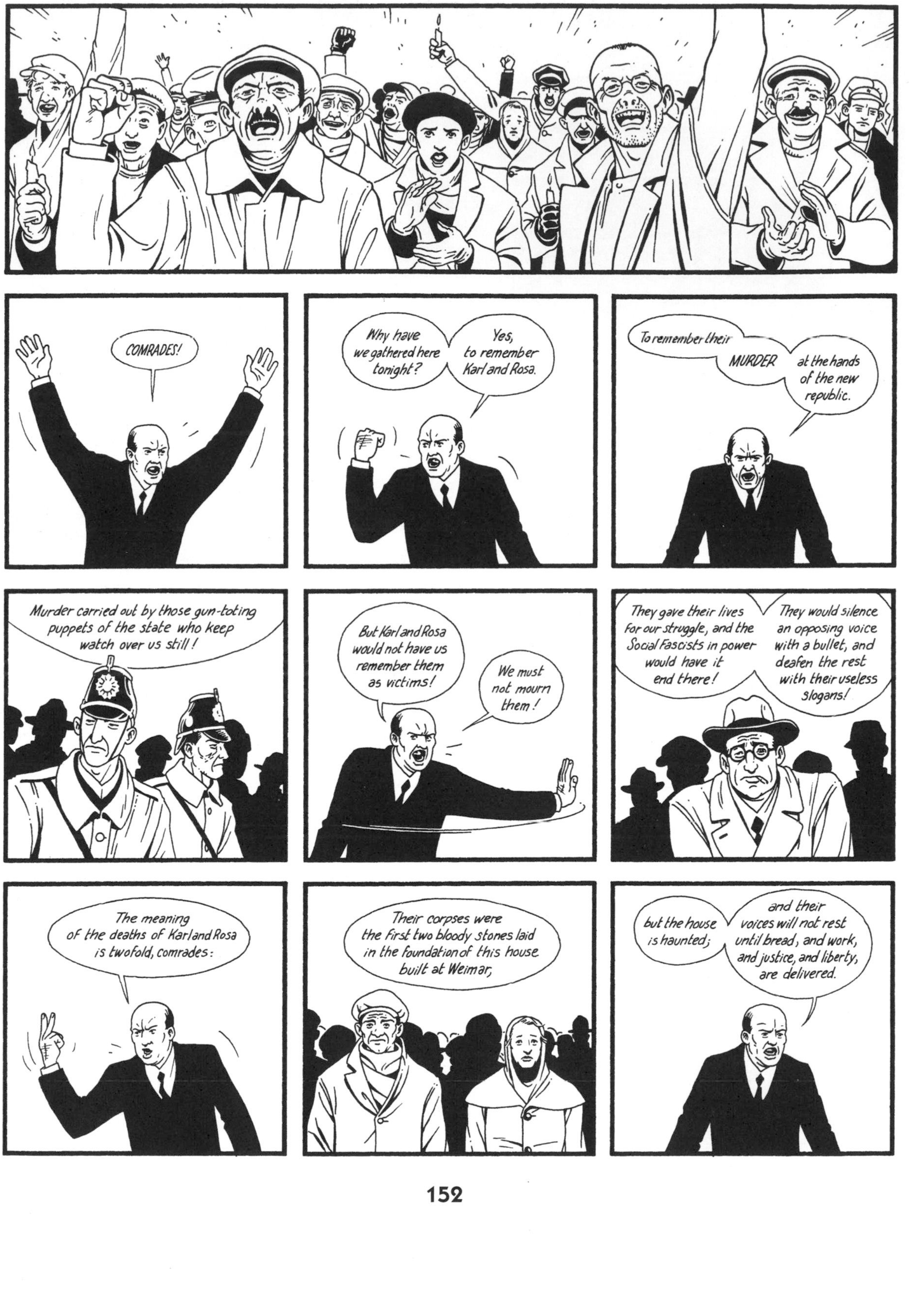
COMRADES!
Why have we gathered here tonight?
Yes, to remember Karl and Rosa.
To remember their MURDER at the hands of the new republic.
Murder carried out by those gun-toting puppets of the state who keep watch over us still!
But Karl and Rosa would not have us remember them as victims!
We must not mourn them!
They gave their lives for our struggle, and the Social Fascists in power would have it end there!
They would silence an opposing voice with a bullet, and deafen the rest with their useless slogans!
The meaning of the deaths of Karl and Rosa is twofold, comrades:
Their corpses were the first two bloody stones laid in the foundation of this house built at Weimar,
but the house is haunted;
and their voices will not rest until bread, and work, and justice, and liberty, are delivered.

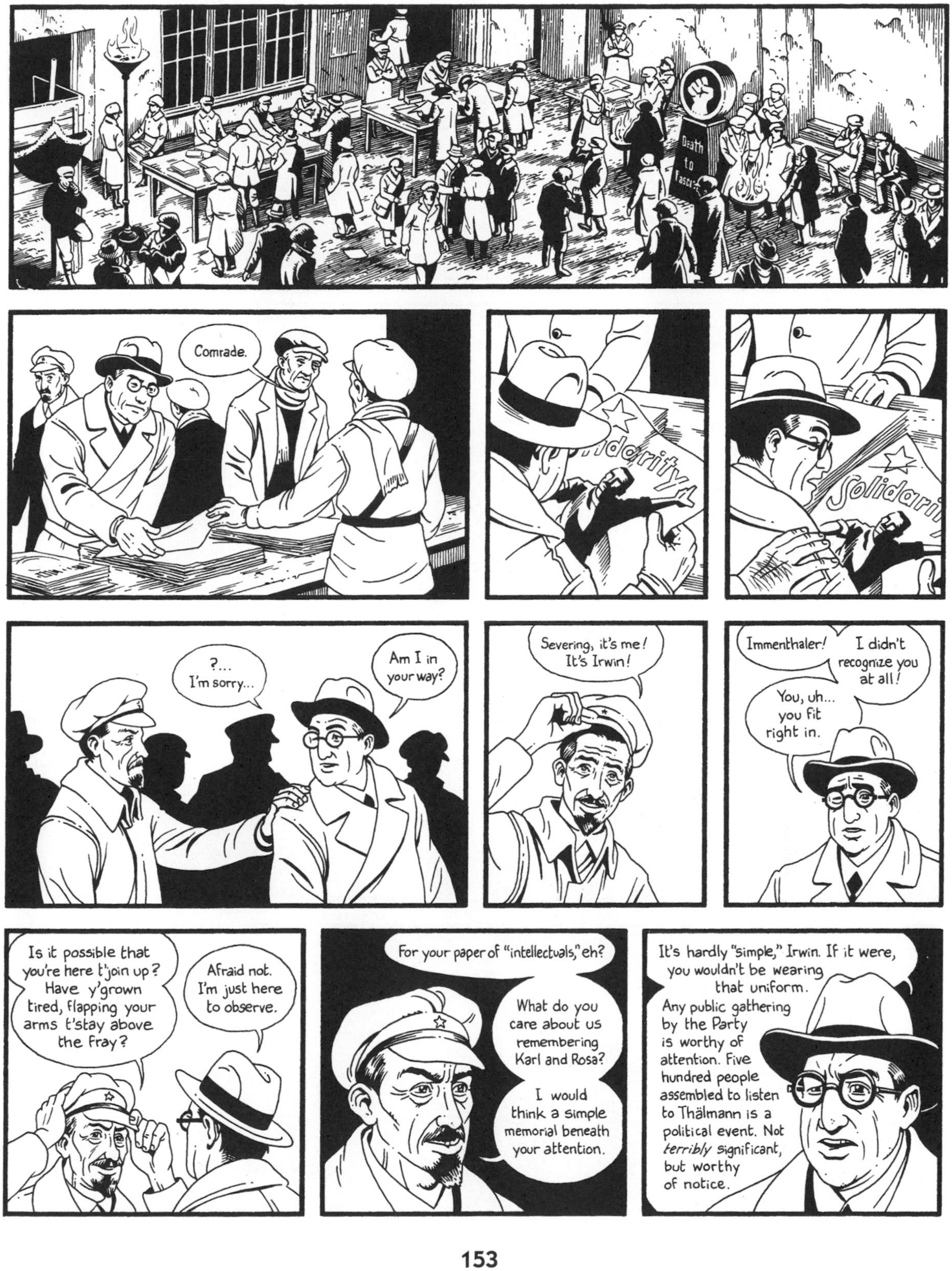
Death to Fascis
Comrade.
olidarity
Solidari
?... I'm sorry...
Am I in your way?
Severing, it's me! It's Irwin!
Immenthaler!
I didn't recognize you at all!
You, uh... you fit right in.
Is it possible that you're here t'join up? Have y'grown tired, flapping your arms t'stay above the fray?
Afraid not. I'm just here to observe.
For your paper of "intellectuals," eh?
What do you care about us remembering Karl and Rosa?
I would think a simple memorial beneath your attention.
It's hardly "simple," Irwin. If it were, you wouldn't be wearing that uniform.
Any public gathering by the Party is worthy of attention. Five hundred people assembled to listen to Thälmann is a political event. Not *terribly* significant, but worthy of notice.

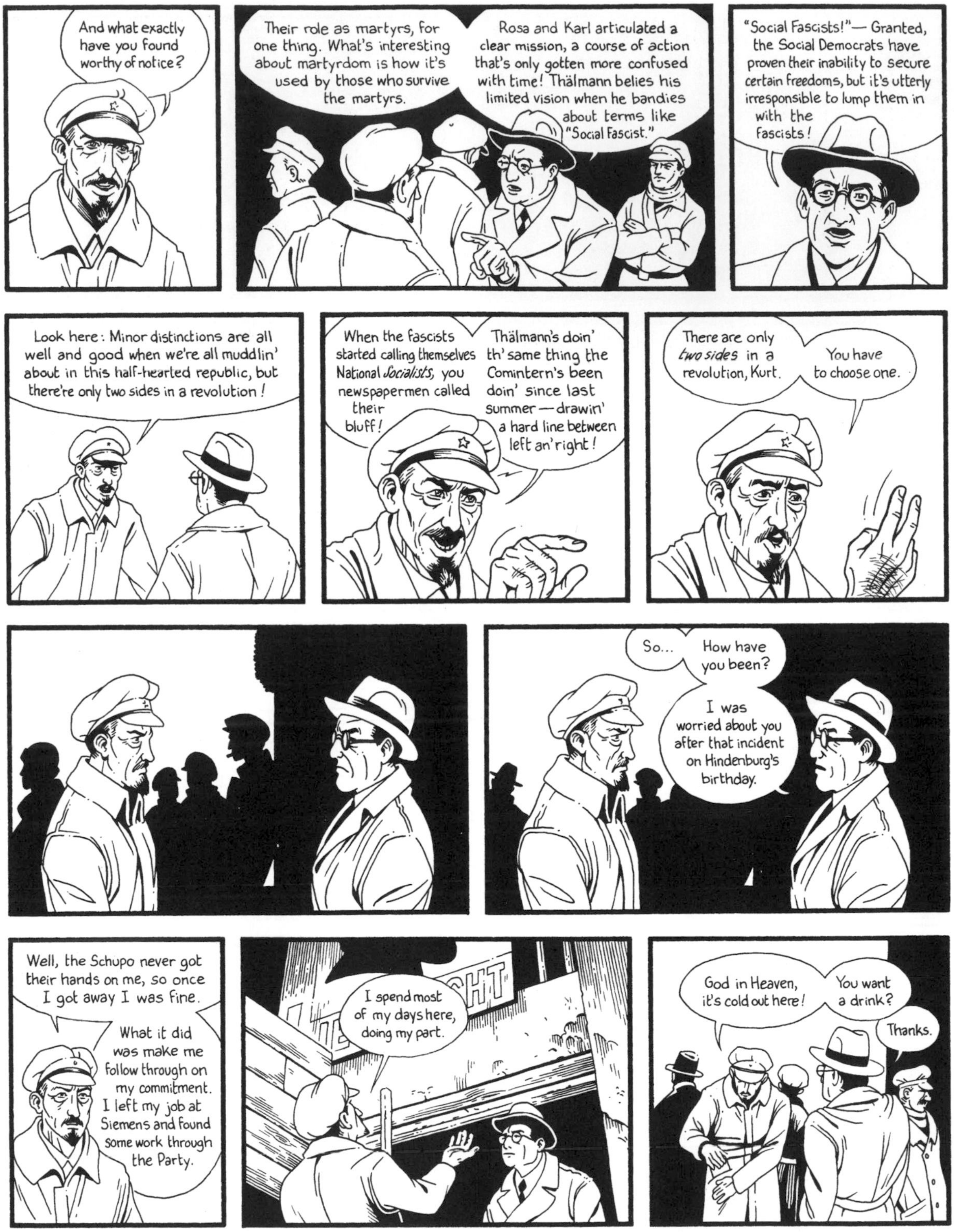
And what exactly have you found worthy of notice?
Their role as martyrs, for one thing. What's interesting about martyrdom is how it's used by those who survive the martyrs.
Rosa and Karl articulated a clear mission, a course of action that's only gotten more confused with time! Thälmann belies his limited vision when he bandies about terms like "Social Fascist."
"Social Fascists!"— Granted, the Social Democrats have proven their inability to secure certain freedoms, but it's utterly irresponsible to lump them in with the Fascists!
Look here: Minor distinctions are all well and good when we're all muddlin' about in this half-hearted republic, but there're only two sides in a revolution!
When the fascists started calling themselves National *Socialists,* you newspapermen called their bluff!
Thälmann's doin' th' same thing the Comintern's been doin' since last summer — drawin' a hard line between left an' right!
There are only *two sides* in a revolution, Kurt.
You have to choose one.
So...
How have you been?
I was worried about you after that incident on Hindenburg's birthday.
Well, the Schupo never got their hands on me, so once I got away I was fine.
What it did was make me follow through on my commitment. I left my job at Siemens and found some work through the Party.
I spend most of my days here, doing my part.
God in Heaven, it's cold out here!
You want a drink?
Thanks.

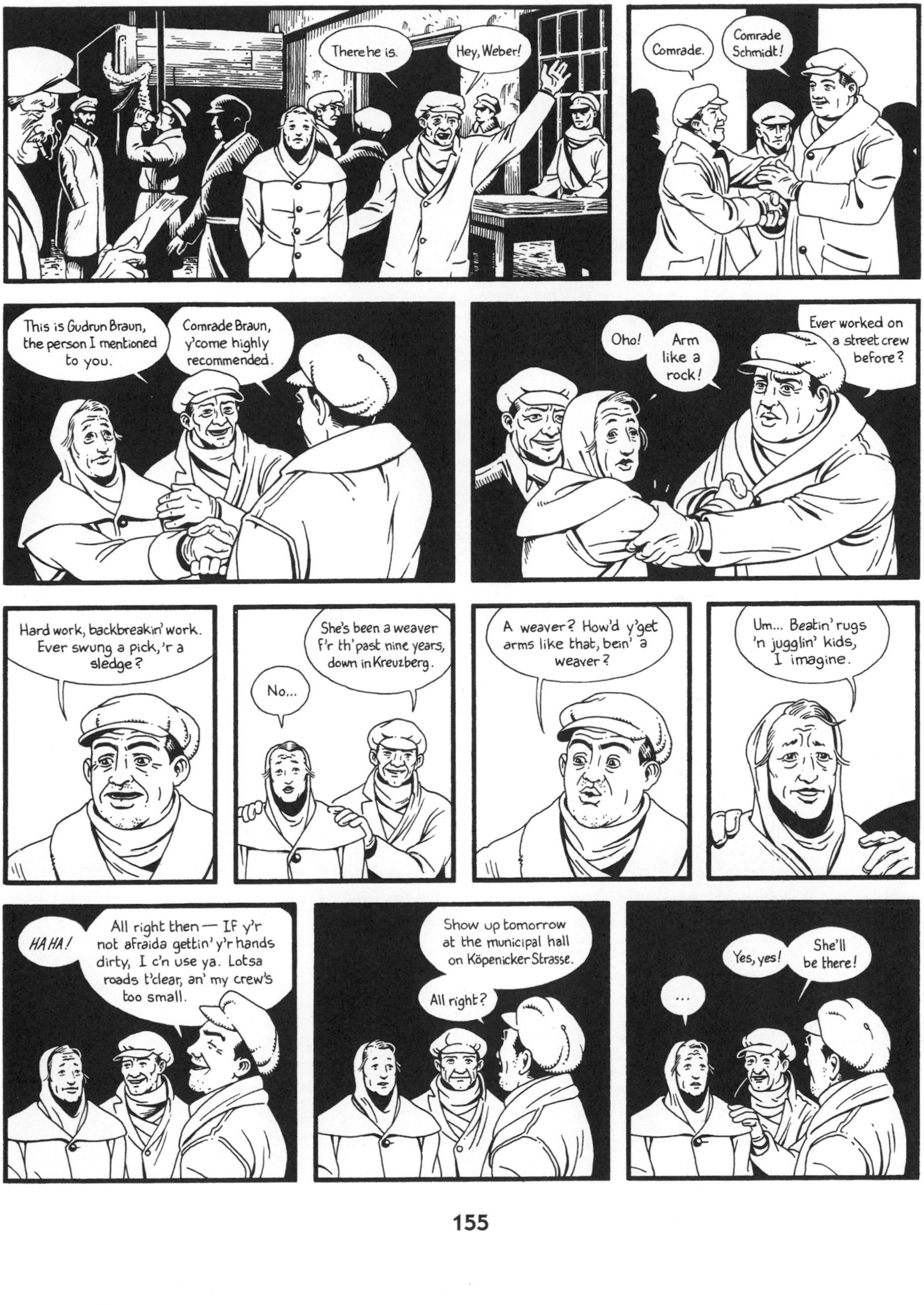
There he is.
Hey, Weber!
Comrade.
Comrade Schmidt!
This is Gudrun Braun, the person I mentioned to you.
Comrade Braun, y'come highly recommended.
Oho!
Arm like a rock!
Ever worked on a street crew before?
Hard work, backbreakin' work. Ever swung a pick, 'r a sledge?
No...
She's been a weaver f'r th' past nine years, down in Kreuzberg.
A weaver? How'd y'get arms like that, bein' a weaver?
Um... Beatin' rugs 'n jugglin' kids, I imagine.
HA HA!
All right then — If y'r not afraida gettin' y'r hands dirty, I c'n use ya. Lotsa roads t'clear, an' my crew's too small.
Show up tomorrow at the municipal hall on Köpenicker Strasse.
All right?
...
Yes, yes!
She'll be there!

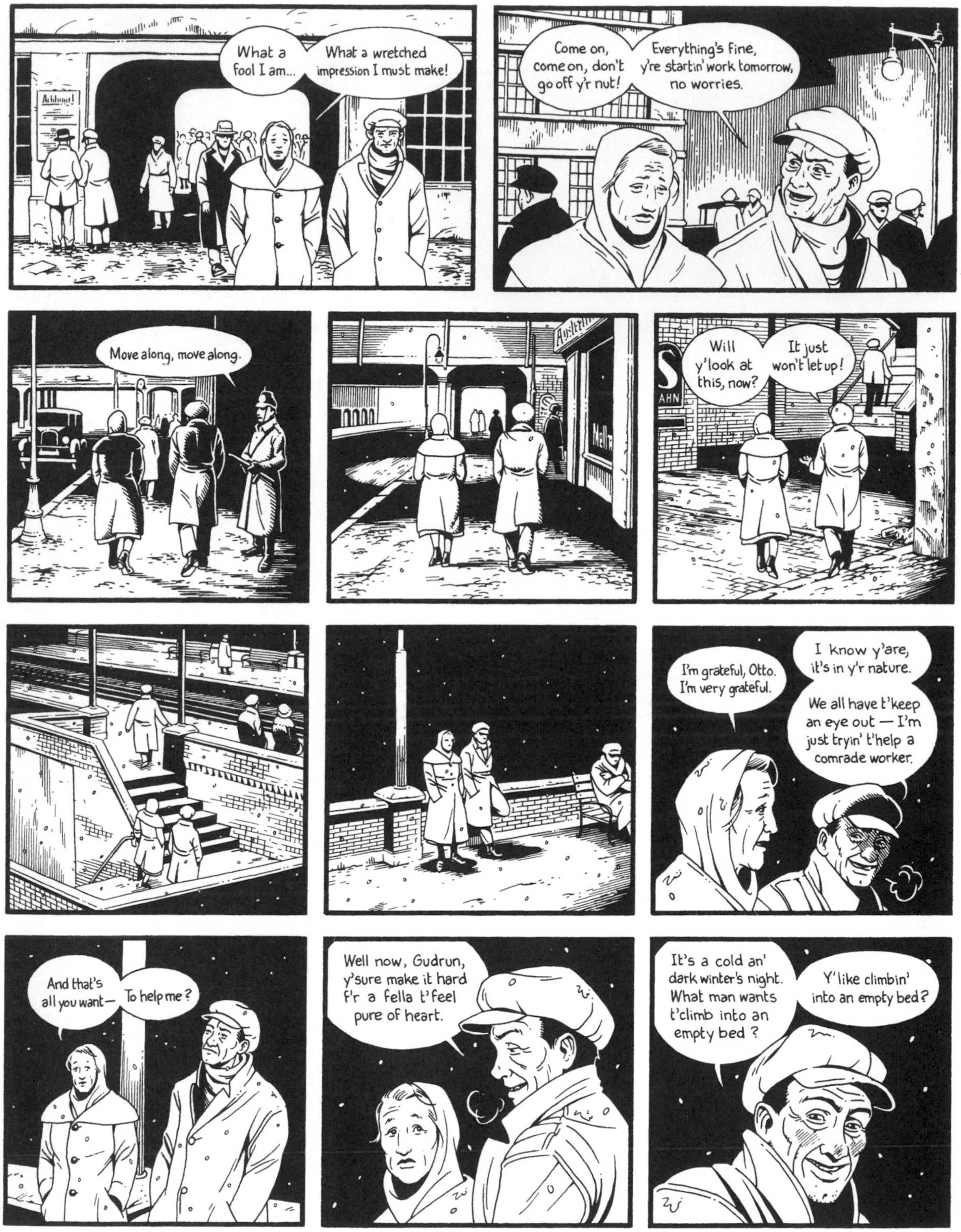
What a fool I am...
What a wretched impression I must make!
Achtung!
Come on, come on, don't go off y'r nut!
Everything's fine, y're startin' work tomorrow, no worries.
Move along, move along.
Will y'look at this, now?
It just won't let up!
I'm grateful, Otto. I'm very grateful.
I know y'are, it's in y'r nature.
We all have t'keep an eye out — I'm just tryin' t'help a comrade worker.
And that's all you want—
To help me?
Well now, Gudrun, y'sure make it hard f'r a fella t'feel pure of heart.
It's a cold an' dark winter's night. What man wants t'climb into an empty bed?
Y'like climbin' into an empty bed?

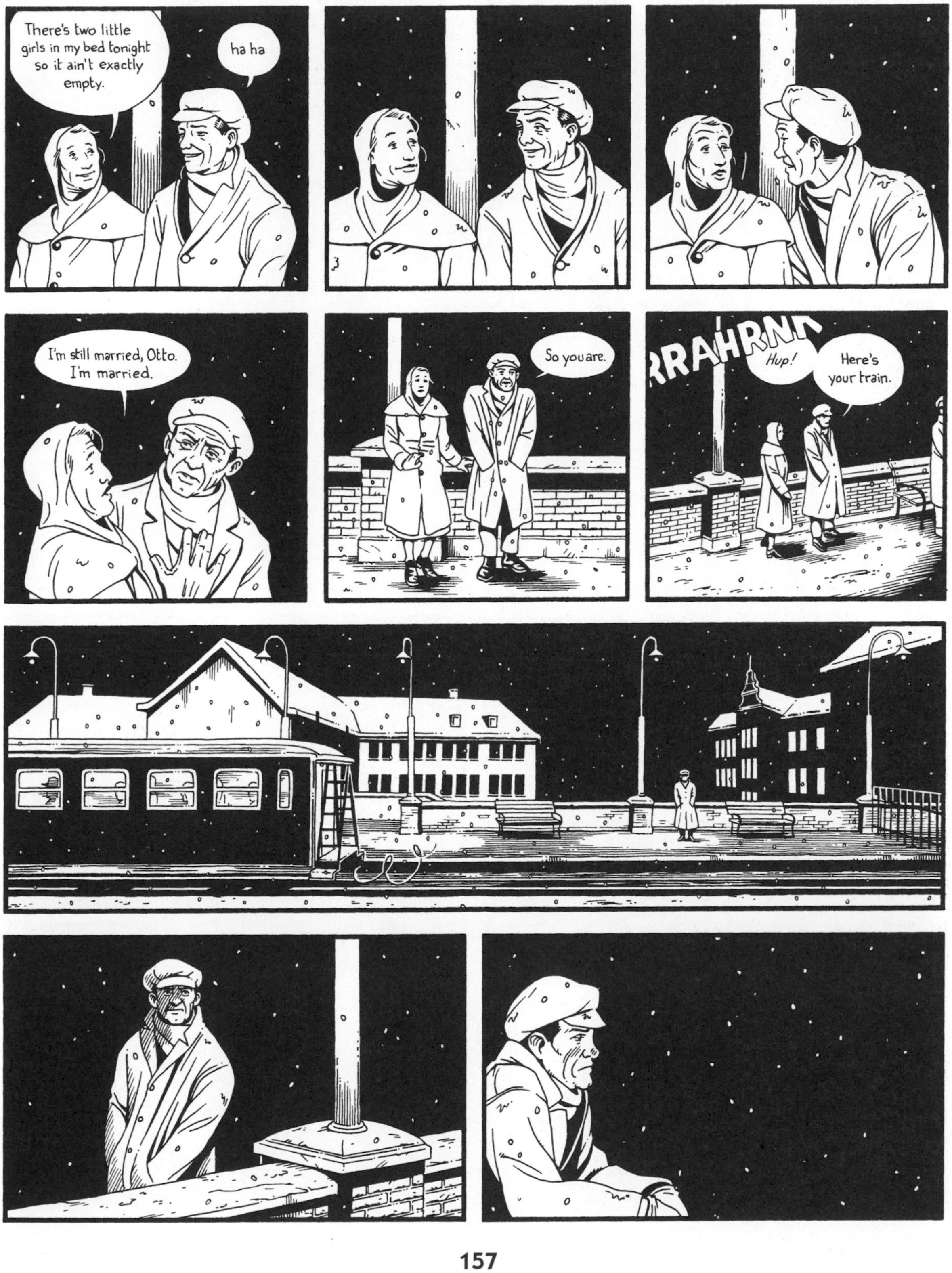
There's two little girls in my bed tonight so it ain't exactly empty.
ha ha
I'm still married, Otto. I'm married.
So you are.
RRAHRNN
Hup!
Here's your train.

RESTAURANT

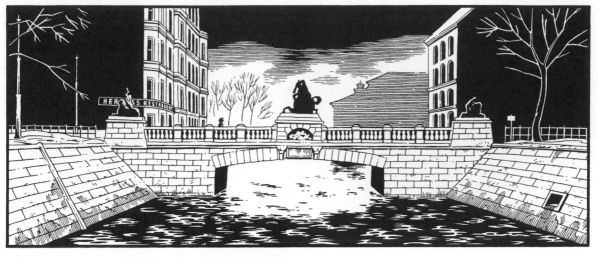

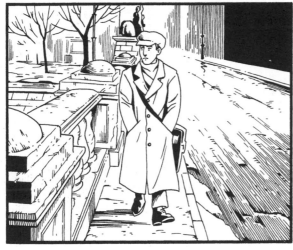

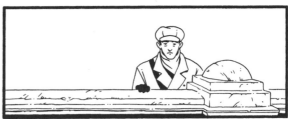

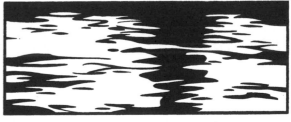

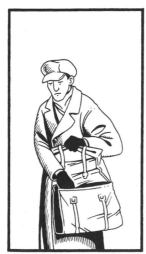

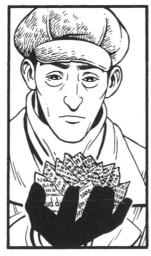

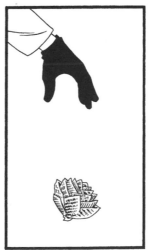

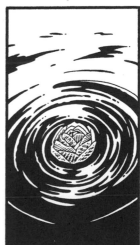

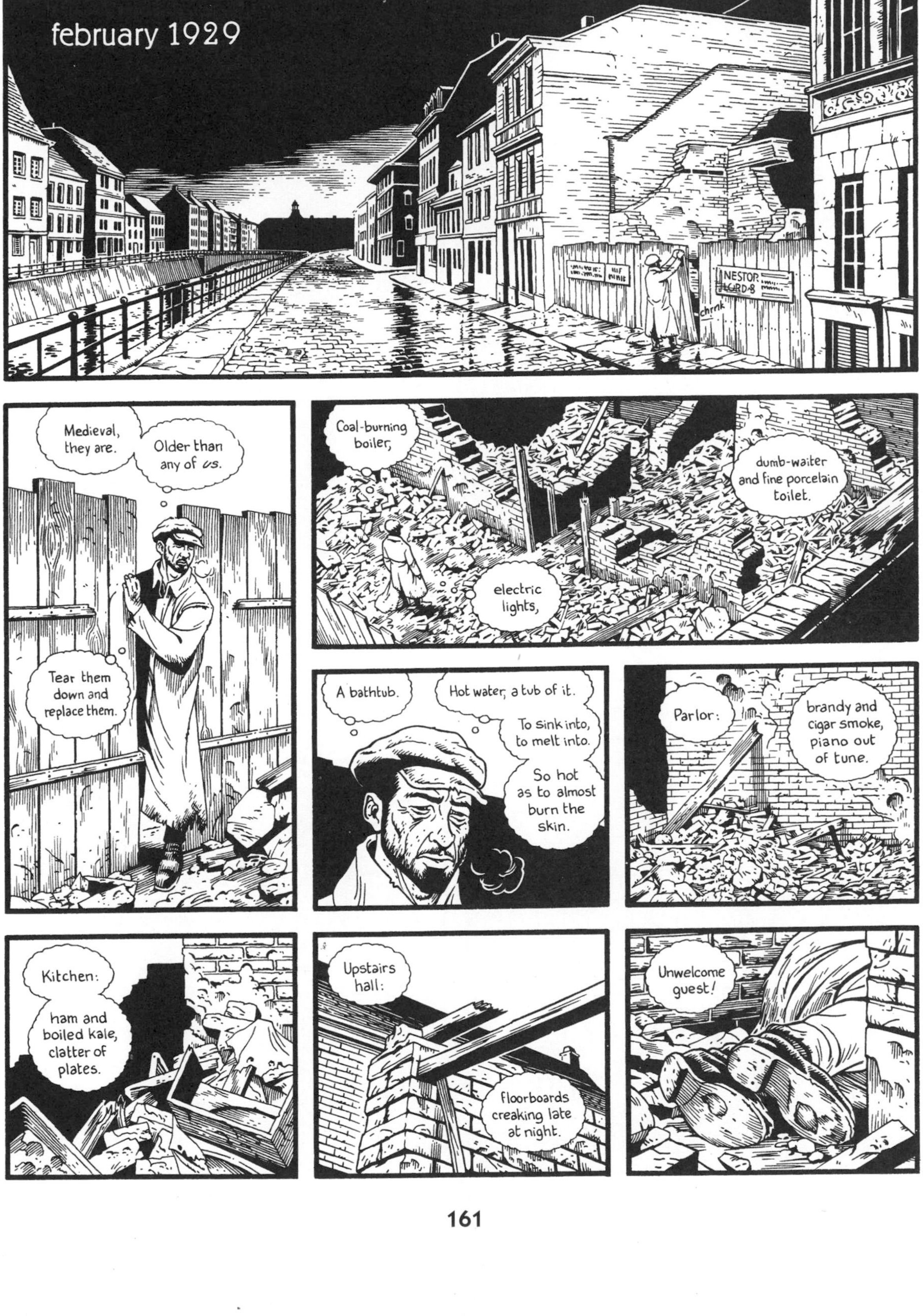
february 1929
NESTOR LORD &
chrnk
Medieval, they are.
Older than any of us.
Tear them down and replace them.
Coal-burning boiler,
electric lights,
dumb-waiter and fine porcelain toilet.
A bathtub.
Hot water, a tub of it.
To sink into, to melt into.
So hot as to almost burn the skin.
Parlor:
brandy and cigar smoke, piano out of tune.
Kitchen:
ham and boiled kale, clatter of plates.
Upstairs hall:
floorboards creaking late at night.
Unwelcome guest!

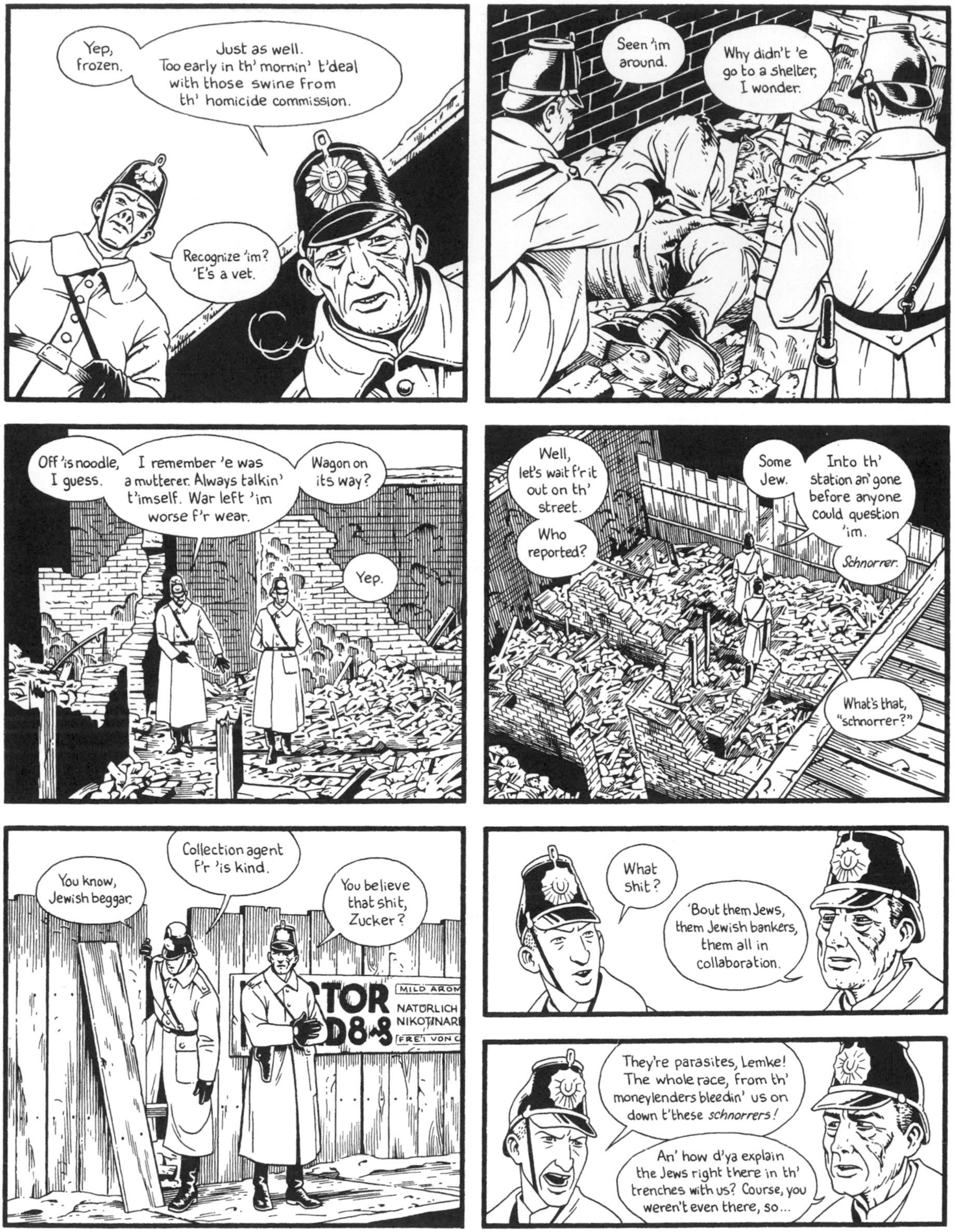
Yep, frozen.
Just as well. Too early in th' mornin' t'deal with those swine from th' homicide commission.
Recognize 'im? 'E's a vet.
Seen 'im around.
Why didn't 'e go to a shelter, I wonder.
Off 'is noodle, I guess.
I remember 'e was a mutterer. Always talkin' t'imself. War left 'im worse f'r wear.
Wagon on its way?
Yep.
Well, let's wait f'r it out on th' street.
Who reported?
Some Jew.
Into th' station an' gone before anyone could question 'im.
Schnorrer.
What's that, "schnorrer?"
You know, Jewish beggar.
Collection agent f'r 'is kind.
You believe that shit, Zucker?
MILD AROM
NATÜRLICH
NIKOTINAR
FREI VON C
What shit?
'Bout them Jews, them Jewish bankers, them all in collaboration.
They're parasites, Lemke! The whole race, from th' moneylenders bleedin' us on down t'these *schnorrers*!
An' how d'ya explain the Jews right there in th' trenches with us? Course, you weren't even there, so...

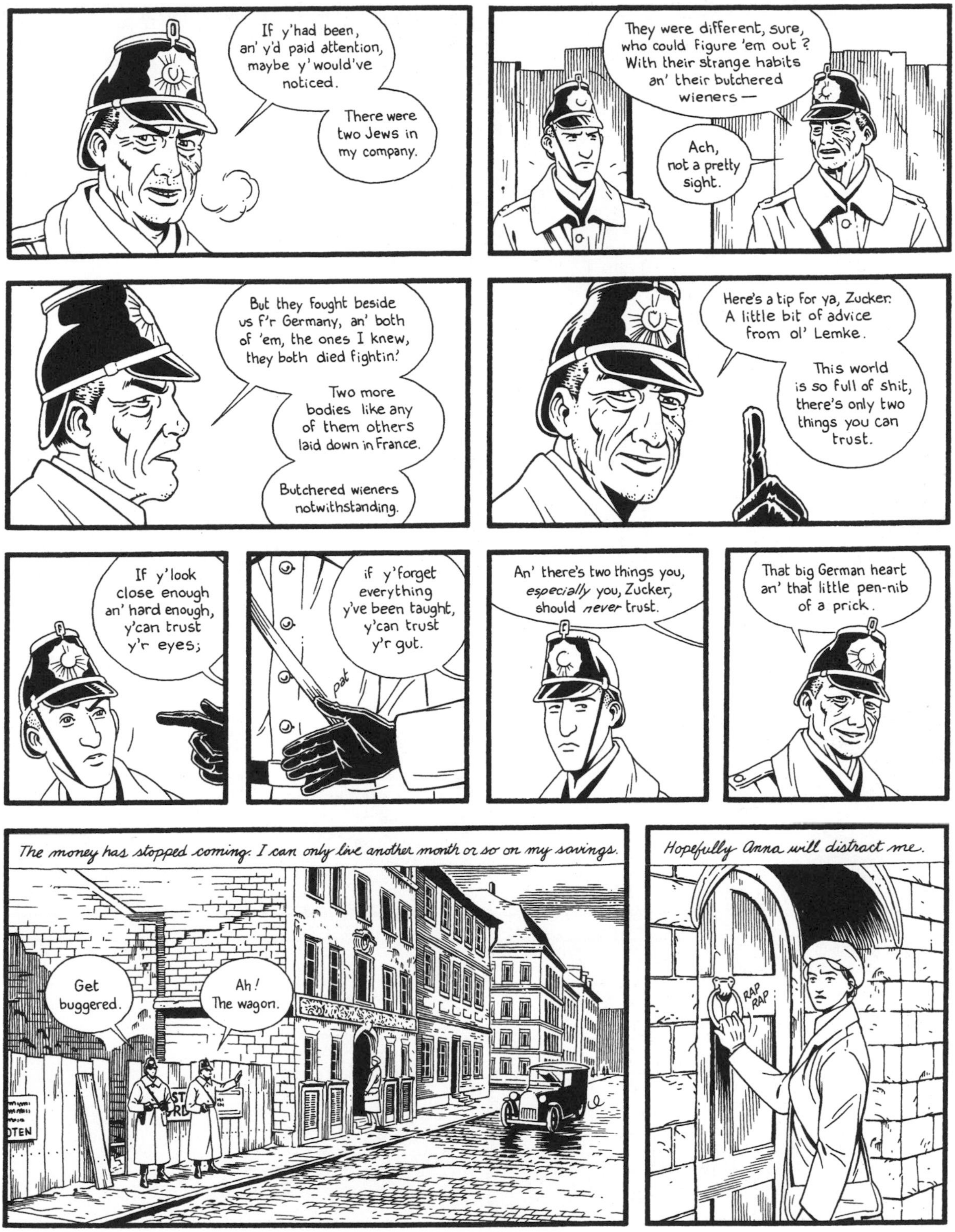
If y'had been, an' y'd paid attention, maybe y'would've noticed.
There were two Jews in my company.
They were different, sure, who could figure 'em out? With their strange habits an' their butchered wieners —
Ach, not a pretty sight.
But they fought beside us f'r Germany, an' both of 'em, the ones I knew, they both died fightin.'
Two more bodies like any of them others laid down in France.
Butchered wieners notwithstanding.
Here's a tip for ya, Zucker. A little bit of advice from ol' Lemke.
This world is so full of shit, there's only two things you can trust.
If y'look close enough an' hard enough, y'can trust y'r eyes;
if y'forget everything y've been taught, y'can trust y'r gut.
pat
An' there's two things you, *especially* you, Zucker, should *never* trust.
That big German heart an' that little pen-nib of a prick.
The money has stopped coming. I can only live another month or so on my savings.
Get buggered.
Ah! The wagon.
Hopefully Anna will distract me.
RAP RAP

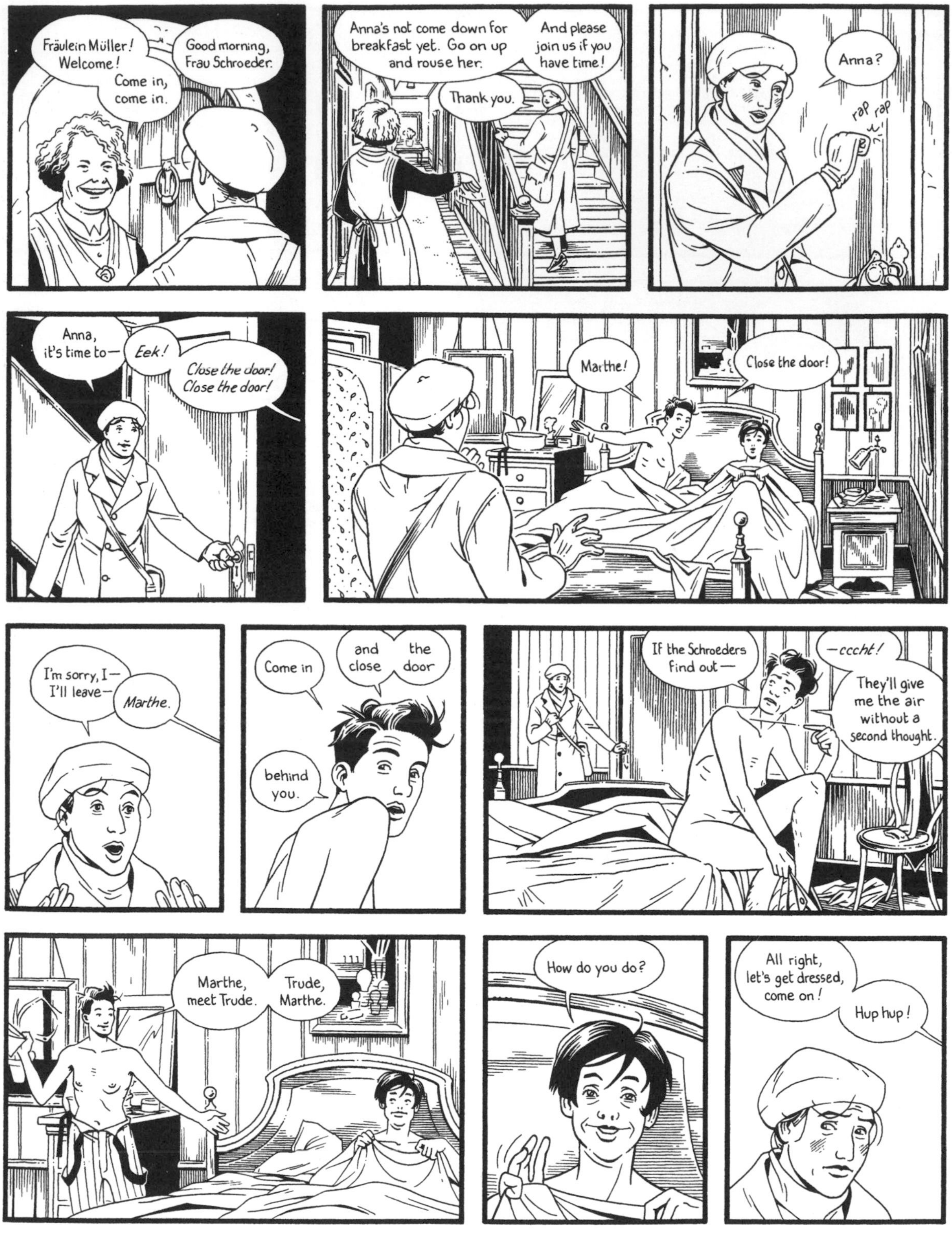
Fräulein Müller! Welcome!
Good morning, Frau Schroeder.
Come in, come in.
Anna's not come down for breakfast yet. Go on up and rouse her.
And please join us if you have time!
Thank you.
Anna?
rap rap
Anna, it's time to—
Eek!
Close the door! Close the door!
Marthe!
Close the door!
I'm sorry, I— I'll leave—
Marthe.
Come in
and close
the door
behind you.
If the Schroeders find out—
—ccchť!
They'll give me the air without a second thought.
Marthe, meet Trude.
Trude, Marthe.
How do you do?
All right, let's get dressed, come on!
Hup hup!

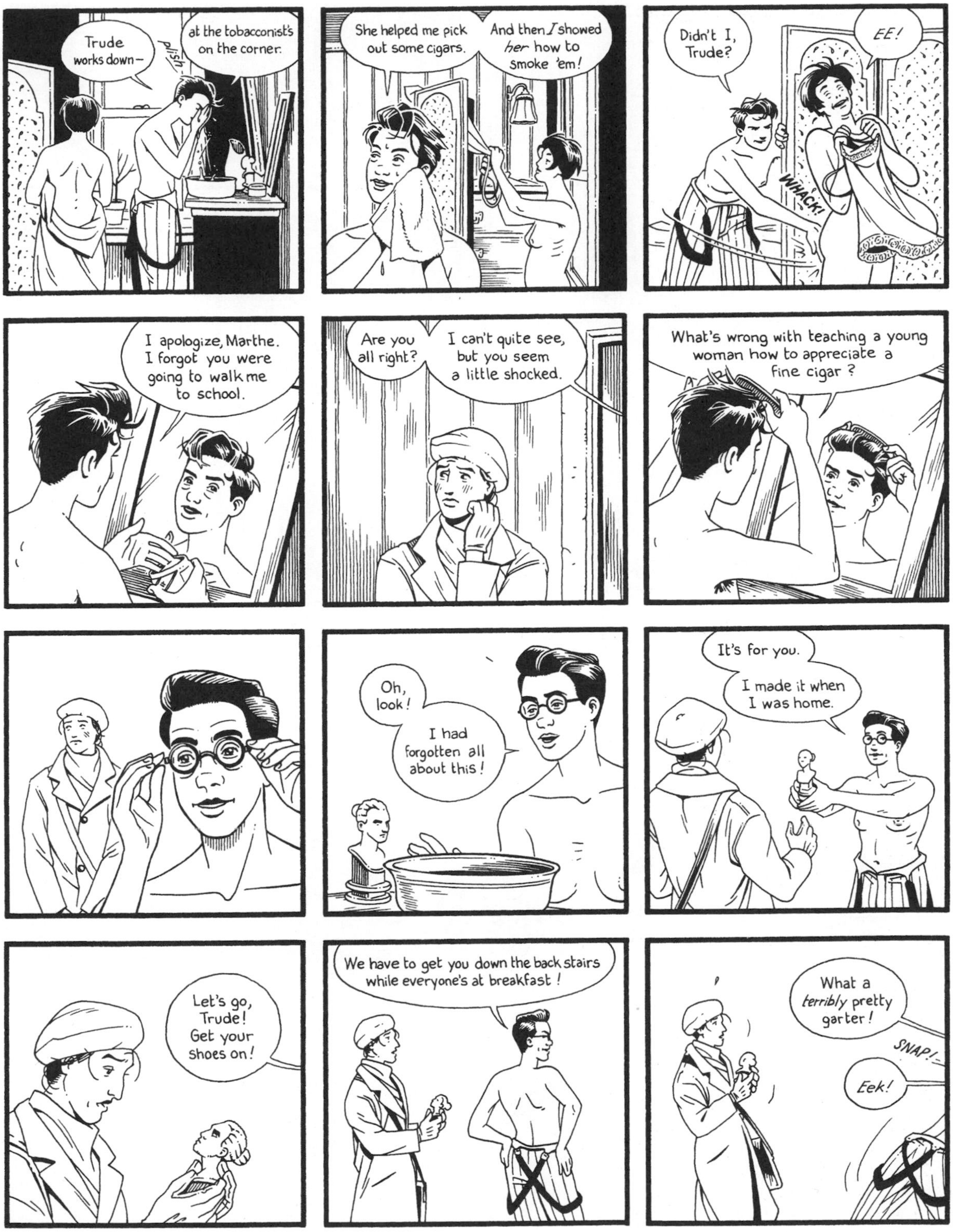

Trude works down —
plish
at the tobacconist's on the corner.
She helped me pick out some cigars.
And then *I* showed *her* how to smoke 'em!
Didn't I, Trude?
EE!
WHACK!
I apologize, Marthe. I forgot you were going to walk me to school.
Are you all right?
I can't quite see, but you seem a little shocked.
What's wrong with teaching a young woman how to appreciate a fine cigar?
Oh, look!
I had forgotten all about this!
It's for you.
I made it when I was home.
Let's go, Trude! Get your shoes on!
We have to get you down the back stairs while everyone's at breakfast!
What a *terribly* pretty garter!
SNAP!
Eek!

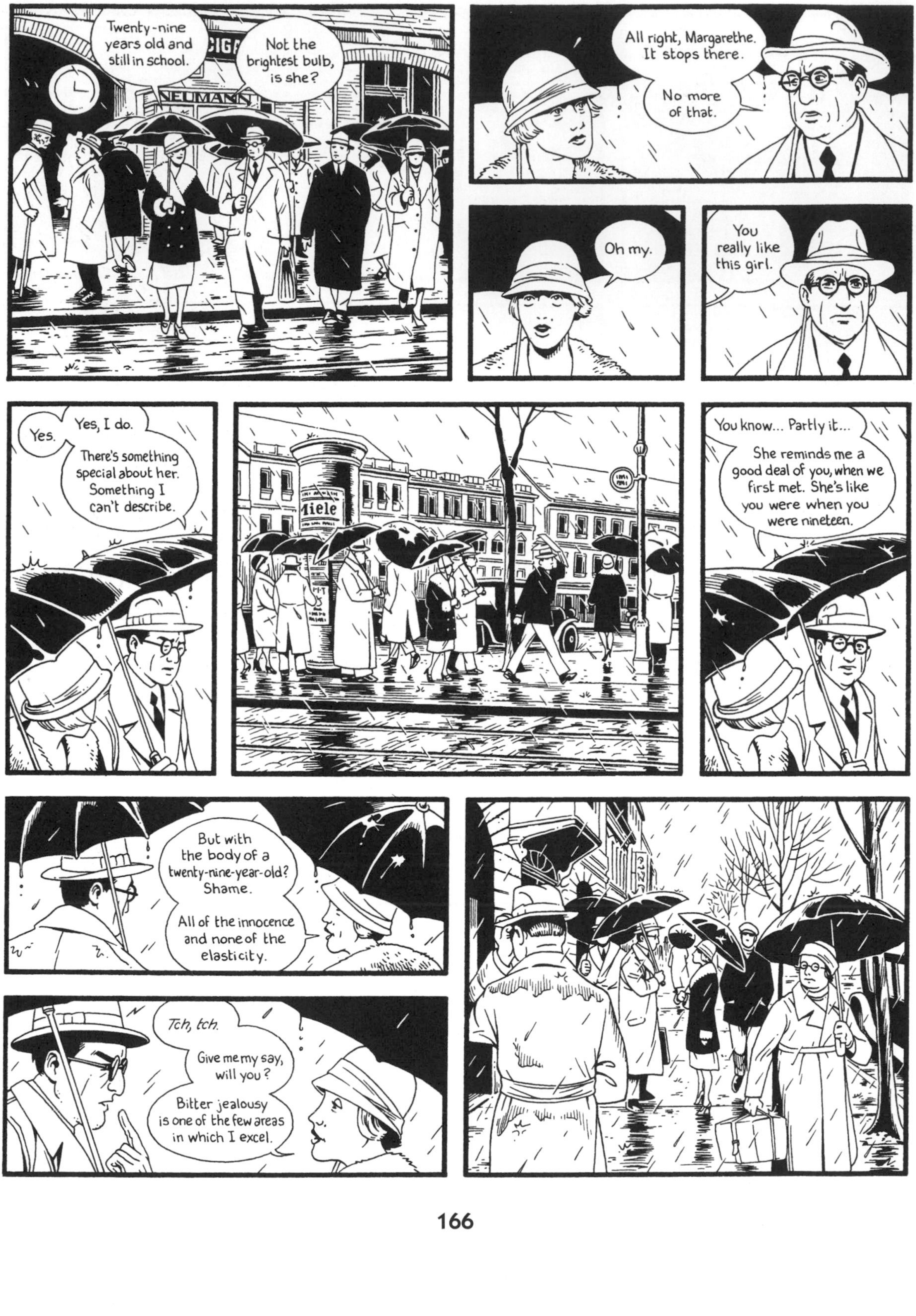
Twenty-nine years old and still in school.
Not the brightest bulb, is she?
CIGA
NEUMANN
All right, Margarethe. It stops there.
No more of that.
Oh my.
You really like this girl.
Yes.
Yes, I do.
There's something special about her. Something I can't describe.
Miele
You know... Partly it...
She reminds me a good deal of you, when we first met. She's like you were when you were nineteen.
But with the body of a twenty-nine-year-old? Shame.
All of the innocence and none of the elasticity.
Tch, tch.
Give me my say, will you?
Bitter jealousy is one of the few areas in which I excel.

You must tell me one thing, darling.

What's that?

And then I will leave you.

Do you love her?

That's entirely unfair. Do I ask you that every time that you bed a bellboy?

Well, that answers my question.

Look...

Ssh.

That's all I wanted to know.

I'll ring you soon.

Die Weltbühne

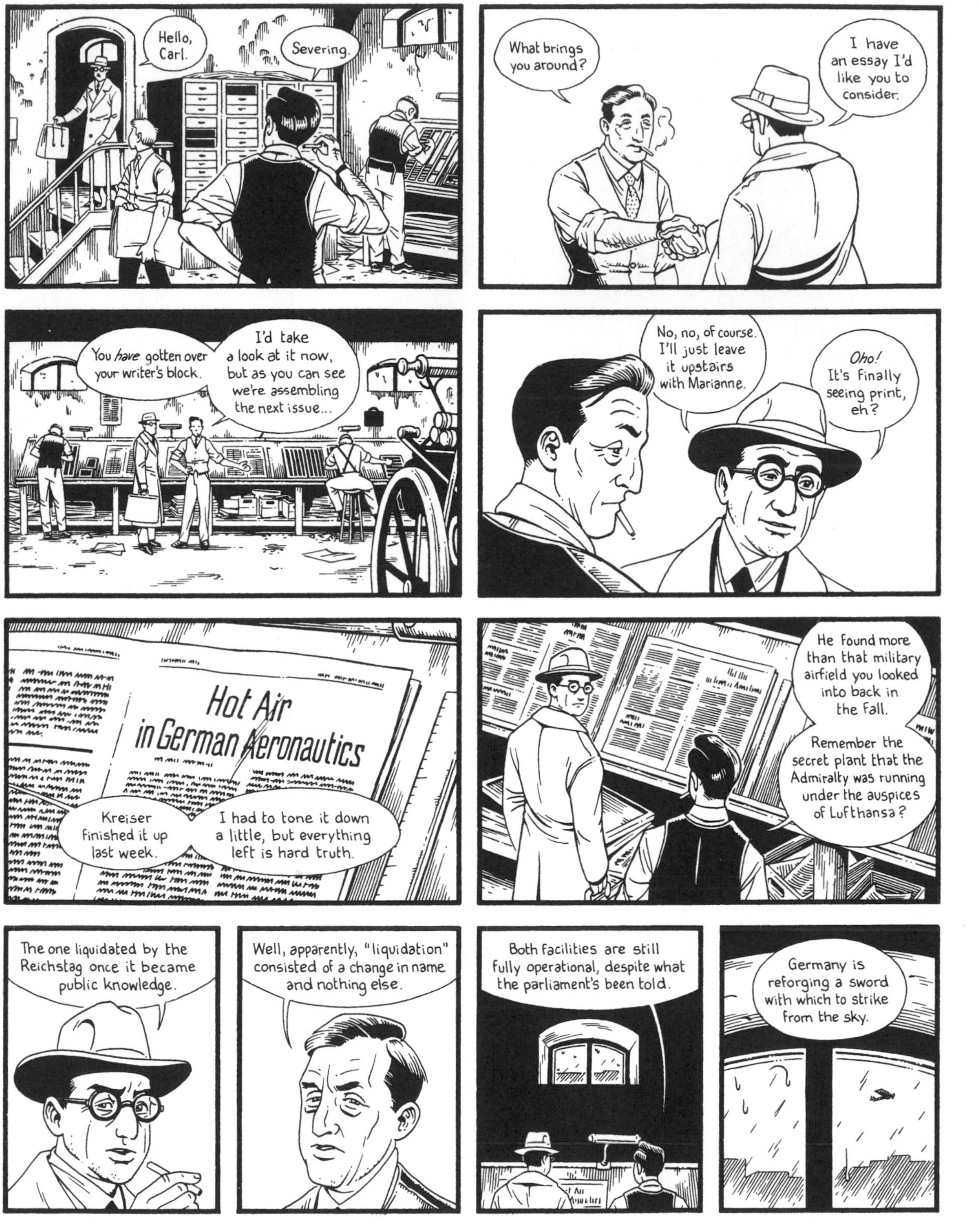
Hello, Carl.
Severing.
What brings you around?
I have an essay I'd like you to consider.
You *have* gotten over your writer's block.
I'd take a look at it now, but as you can see we're assembling the next issue...
No, no, of course. I'll just leave it upstairs with Marianne.
Oho! It's finally seeing print, eh?
Hot Air in German Aeronautics
Kreiser finished it up last week.
I had to tone it down a little, but everything left is hard truth.
He found more than that military airfield you looked into back in the Fall.
Remember the secret plant that the Admiralty was running under the auspices of Lufthansa?
The one liquidated by the Reichstag once it became public knowledge.
Well, apparently, "liquidation" consisted of a change in name and nothing else.
Both facilities are still fully operational, despite what the parliament's been told.
Germany is reforging a sword with which to strike from the sky.

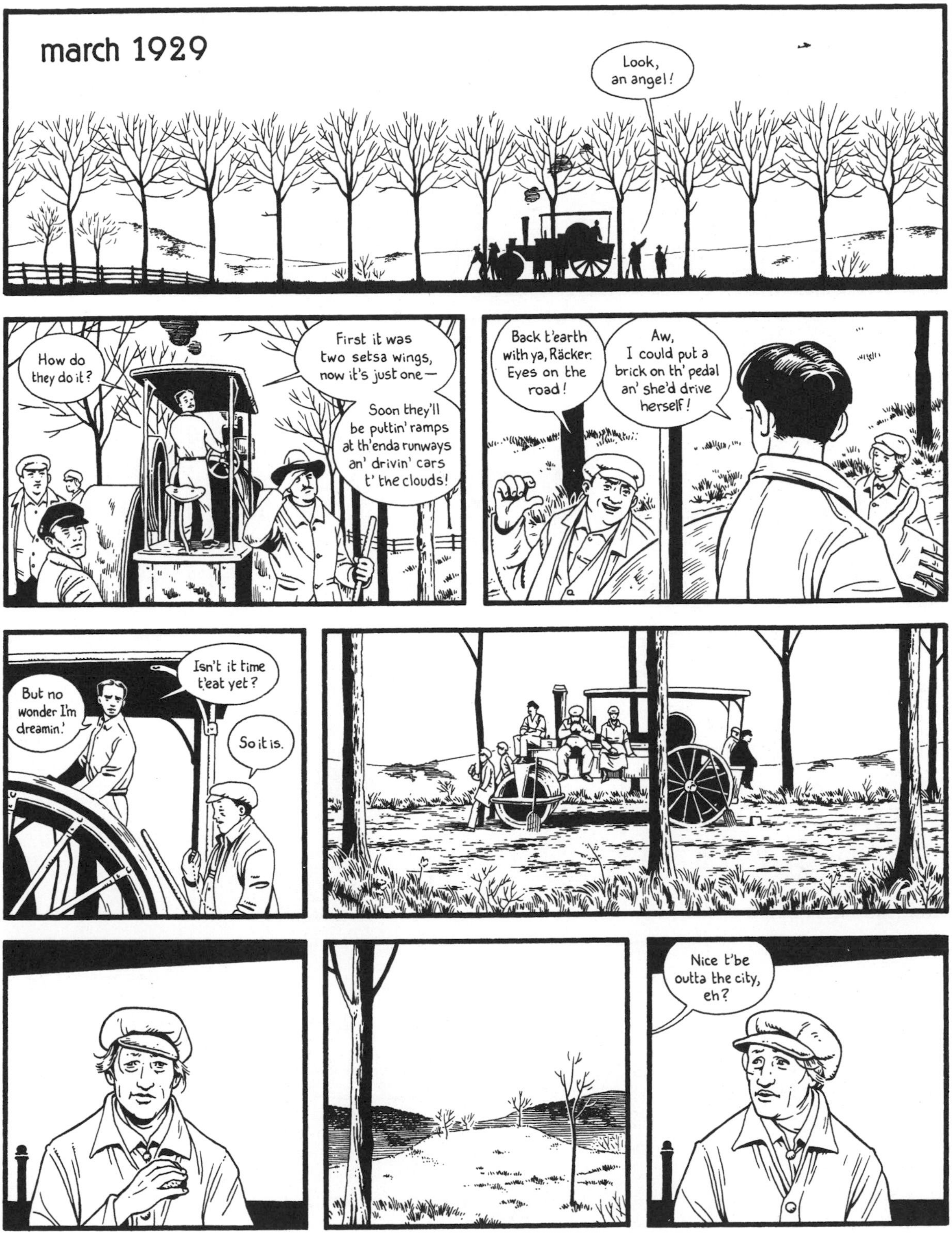
march 1929
Look, an angel!
How do they do it?
First it was two setsa wings, now it's just one —
Soon they'll be puttin' ramps at th'enda runways an' drivin' cars t' the clouds!
Back t'earth with ya, Räcker. Eyes on the road!
Aw, I could put a brick on th' pedal an' she'd drive herself!
But no wonder I'm dreamin'.
Isn't it time t'eat yet?
So it is.
Nice t'be outta the city, eh?

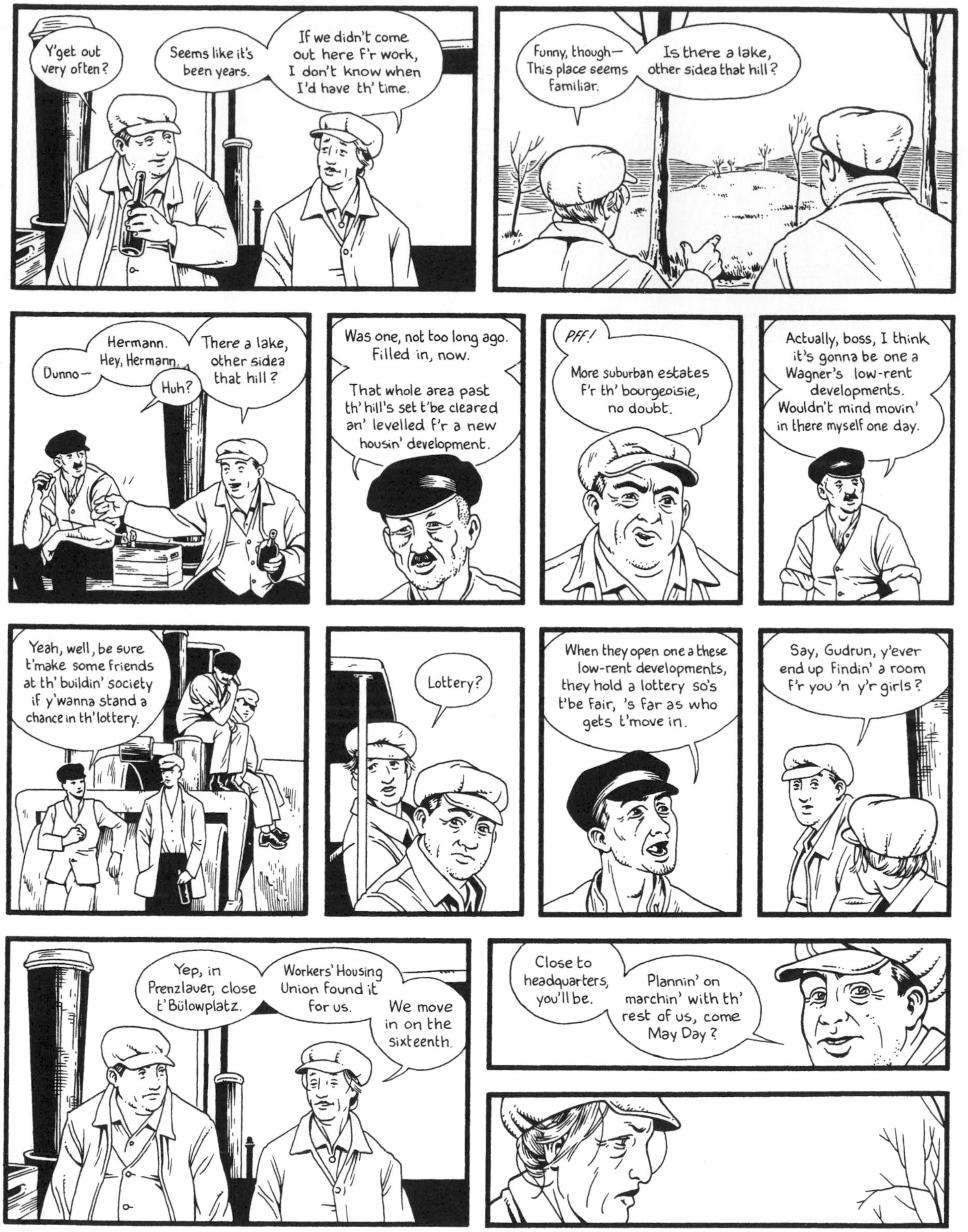
Y'get out very often?
Seems like it's been years.
If we didn't come out here f'r work, I don't know when I'd have th' time.
Funny, though— This place seems familiar.
Is there a lake, other sidea that hill?
Dunno—
Hermann. Hey, Hermann.
Huh?
There a lake, other sidea that hill?
Was one, not too long ago. Filled in, now.
That whole area past th' hill's set t'be cleared an' levelled f'r a new housin' development.
Pff!
More suburban estates f'r th' bourgeoisie, no doubt.
Actually, boss, I think it's gonna be one a Wagner's low-rent developments. Wouldn't mind movin' in there myself one day.
Yeah, well, be sure t'make some friends at th' buildin' society if y'wanna stand a chance in th'lottery.
Lottery?
When they open one a these low-rent developments, they hold a lottery so's t'be fair, 's far as who gets t'move in.
Say, Gudrun, y'ever end up findin' a room f'r you 'n y'r girls?
Yep, in Prenzlauer, close t'Bülowplatz.
Workers' Housing Union found it for us.
We move in on the sixteenth.
Close to headquarters, you'll be.
Plannin' on marchin' with th' rest of us, come May Day?

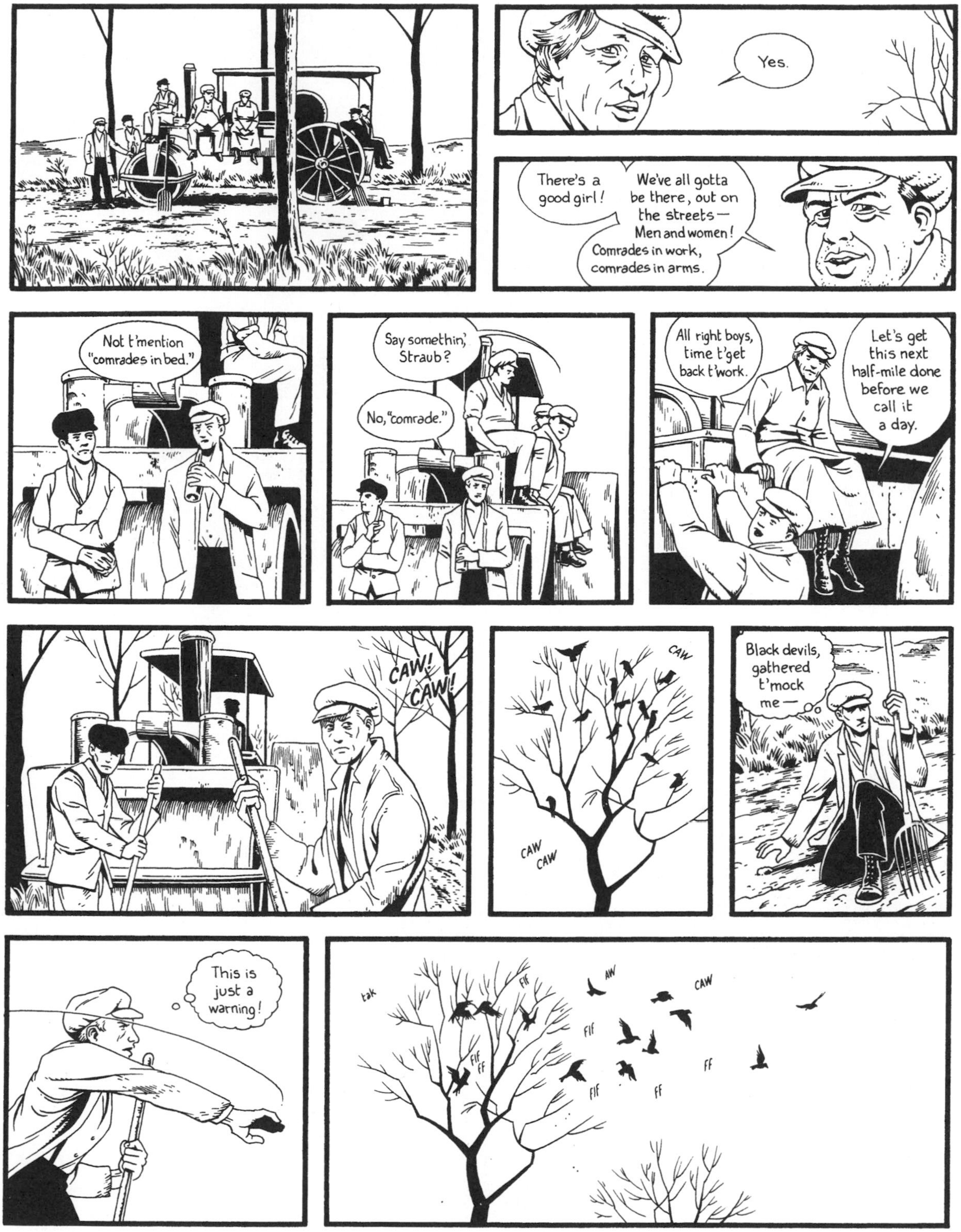

Yes.
There's a good girl!
We've all gotta be there, out on the streets — Men and women! Comrades in work, comrades in arms.
Not t'mention "comrades in bed."
Say somethin', Straub?
No, "comrade."
All right boys, time t'get back t'work.
Let's get this next half-mile done before we call it a day.
CAW! CAW!
CAW
CAW CAW
Black devils, gathered t'mock me —
This is just a warning!
tak
AW
CAW
FIF
FF

DOWN WITH THE REPUBLIC!

SOLIDARITY WITH RUSSIA!

Hold it!

HOLD IT! STOP!

DOWN WITH THE PUPPETS OF THE STATE!

ENK! ENK!! ENK!

AHOOGA!!

I ORDER YOU TO STOP!

FOR THE WORKERS!

rRAH!

ughk!

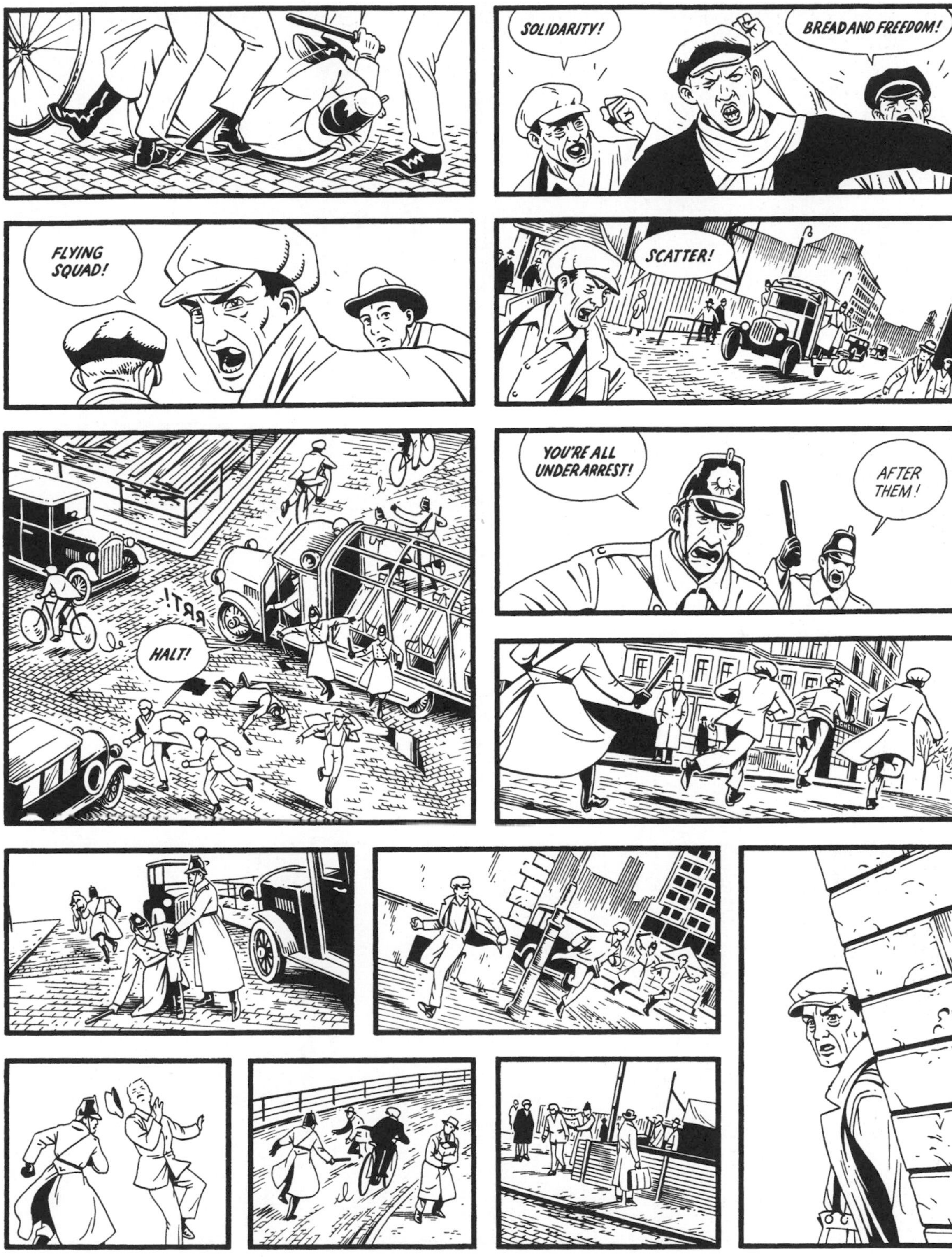
SOLIDARITY!
BREAD AND FREEDOM!
FLYING SQUAD!
SCATTER!
RRT!
HALT!
YOU'RE ALL UNDER ARREST!
AFTER THEM!

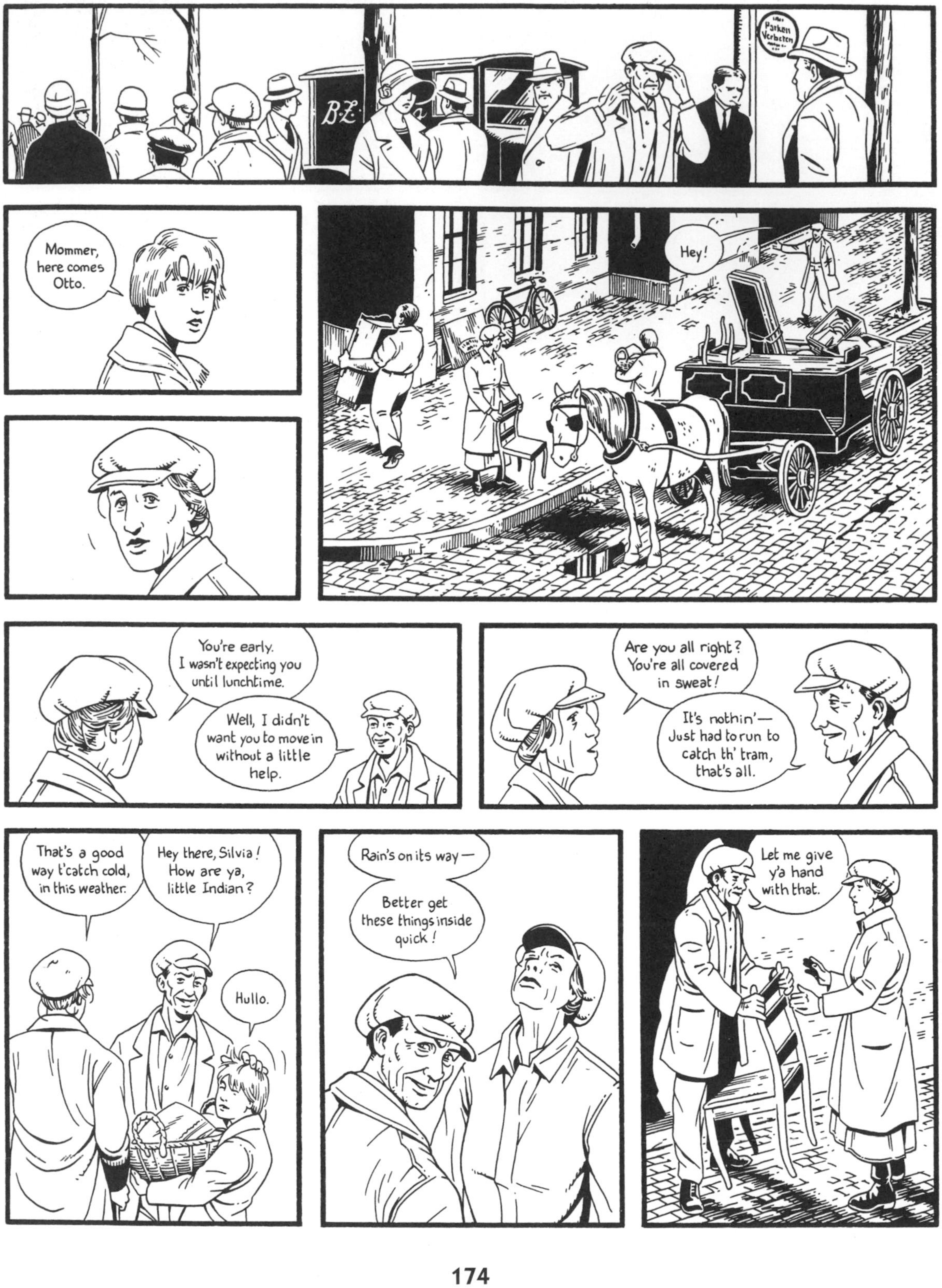
Parken Verboten
Mommer, here comes Otto.
Hey!
You're early. I wasn't expecting you until lunchtime.
Well, I didn't want you to move in without a little help.
Are you all right? You're all covered in sweat!
It's nothin'— Just had to run to catch th' tram, that's all.
That's a good way t'catch cold, in this weather.
Hey there, Silvia! How are ya, little Indian?
Hullo.
Rain's on its way—
Better get these things inside quick!
Let me give y'a hand with that.

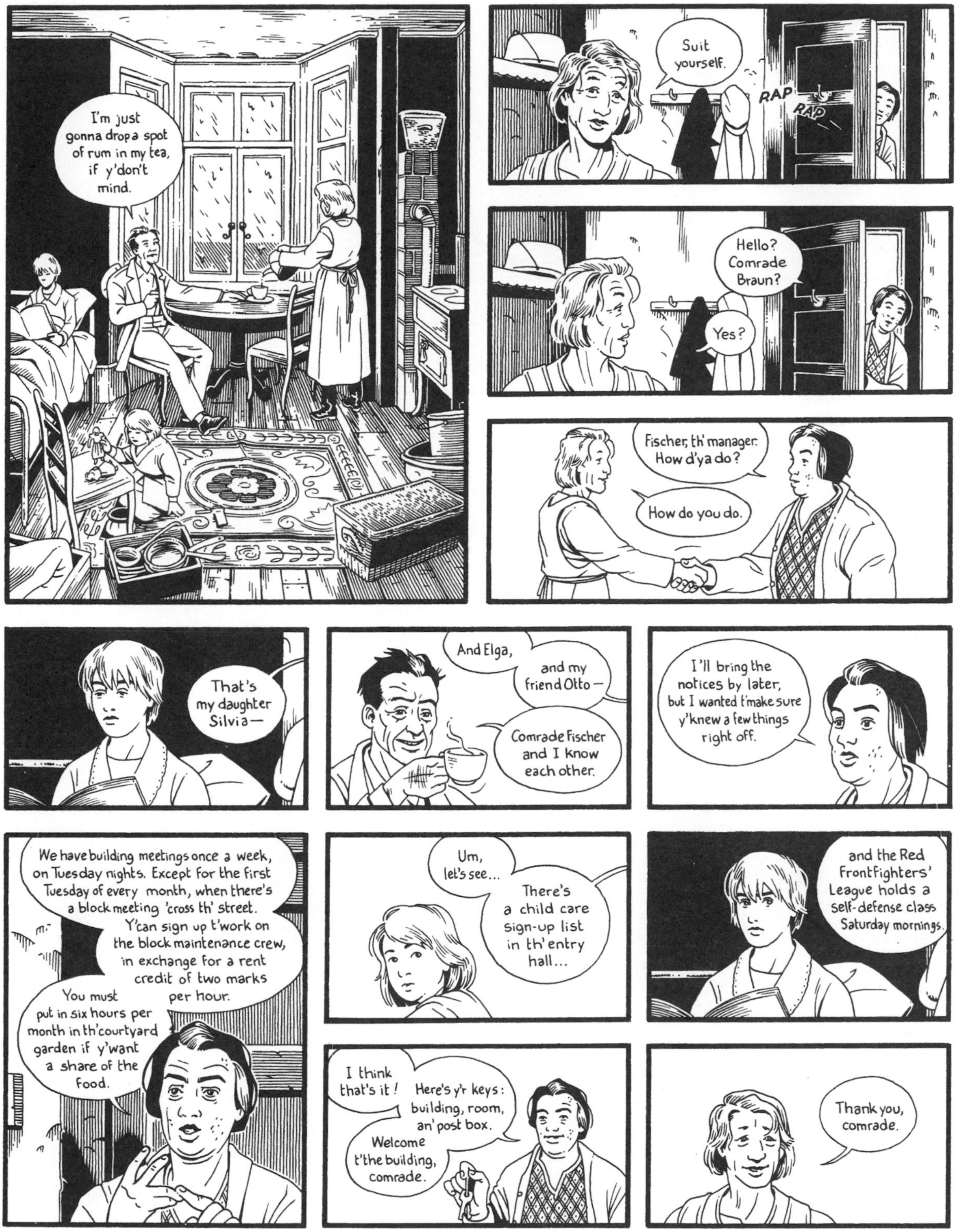
I'm just gonna drop a spot of rum in my tea, if y'don't mind.
Suit yourself.
RAP RAP
Hello? Comrade Braun?
Yes?
Fischer, th' manager. How d'ya do?
How do you do.
That's my daughter Silvia—
And Elga,
and my friend Otto—
Comrade Fischer and I know each other.
I'll bring the notices by later, but I wanted t'make sure y'knew a few things right off.
We have building meetings once a week, on Tuesday nights. Except for the first Tuesday of every month, when there's a block meeting 'cross th' street.
Y'can sign up t'work on the block maintenance crew, in exchange for a rent credit of two marks per hour.
You must put in six hours per month in th'courtyard garden if y'want a share of the food.
Um, let's see...
There's a child care sign-up list in th' entry hall...
and the Red Frontfighters' League holds a self-defense class Saturday mornings.
I think that's it!
Here's y'r keys: building, room, an' post box.
Welcome t'the building, comrade.
Thank you, comrade.

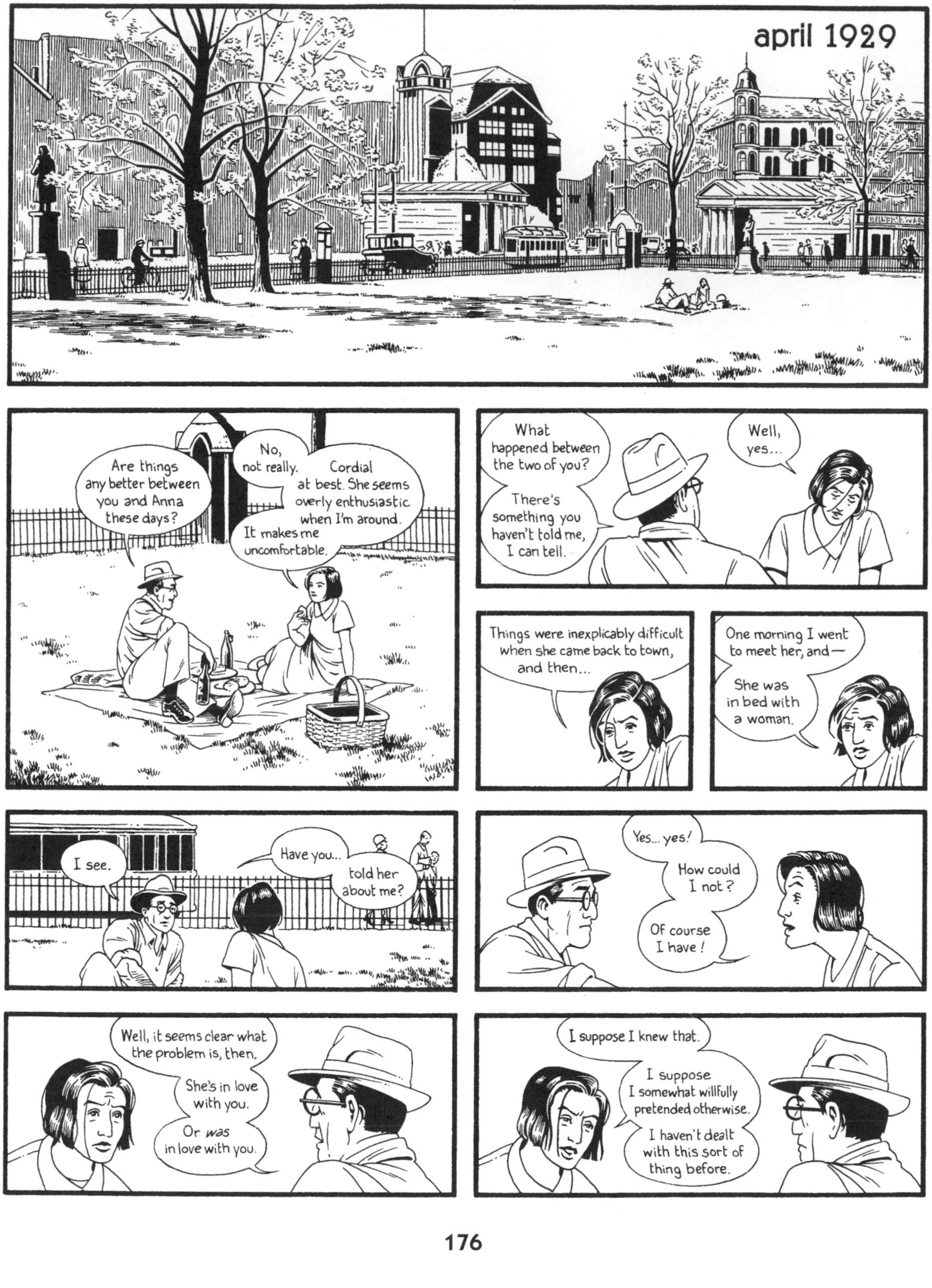
april 1929
Are things any better between you and Anna these days?
No, not really.
Cordial at best. She seems overly enthusiastic when I'm around.
It makes me uncomfortable.
What happened between the two of you?
There's something you haven't told me, I can tell.
Well, yes...
Things were inexplicably difficult when she came back to town, and then...
One morning I went to meet her, and—
She was in bed with a woman.
I see.
Have you...
told her about me?
Yes... yes!
How could I not?
Of course I have!
Well, it seems clear what the problem is, then.
She's in love with you.
Or *was* in love with you.
I suppose I knew that.
I suppose I somewhat willfully pretended otherwise.
I haven't dealt with this sort of thing before.

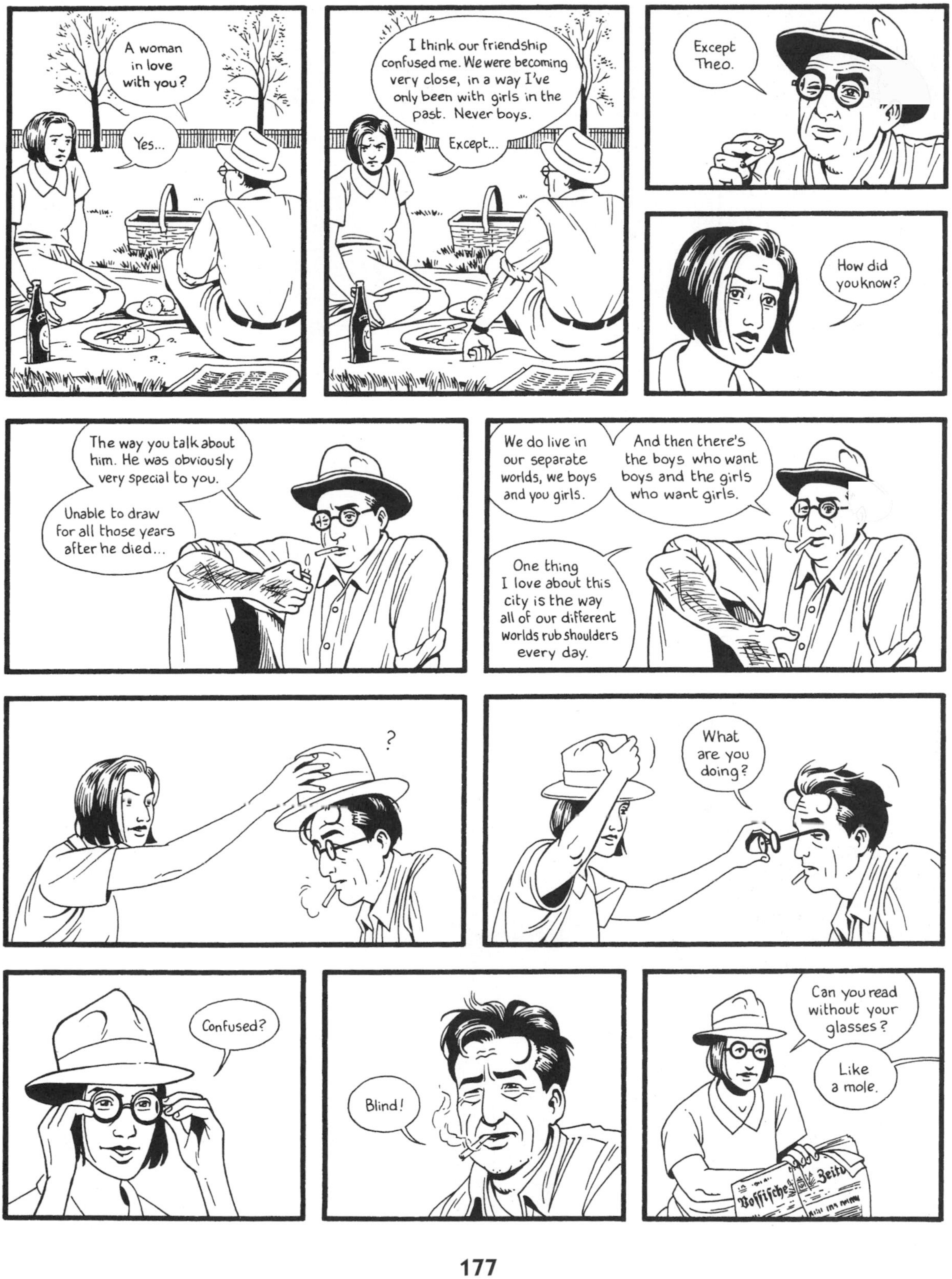
A woman in love with you?
Yes...
I think our friendship confused me. We were becoming very close, in a way I've only been with girls in the past. Never boys.
Except...
Except Theo.
How did you know?
The way you talk about him. He was obviously very special to you.
Unable to draw for all those years after he died...
We do live in our separate worlds, we boys and you girls.
And then there's the boys who want boys and the girls who want girls.
One thing I love about this city is the way all of our different worlds rub shoulders every day.
?
What are you doing?
Confused?
Blind!
Can you read without your glasses?
Like a mole.

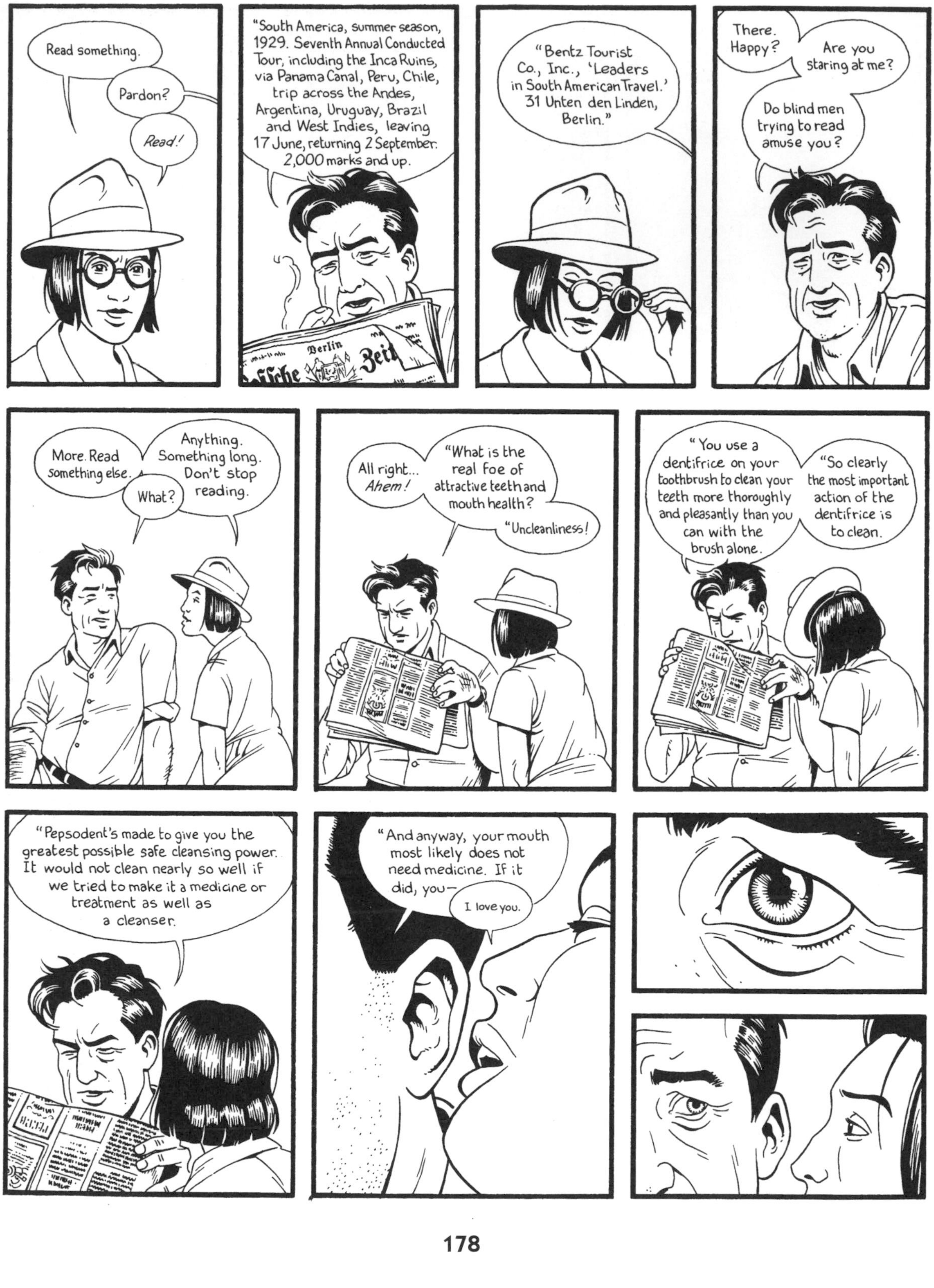

Read something.
Pardon?
Read!
"South America, summer season, 1929. Seventh Annual Conducted Tour, including the Inca Ruins, via Panama Canal, Peru, Chile, trip across the Andes, Argentina, Uruguay, Brazil and West Indies, leaving 17 June, returning 2 September. 2,000 marks and up.
"Bentz Tourist Co., Inc., 'Leaders in South American Travel.' 31 Unten den Linden, Berlin."
There. Happy?
Are you staring at me?
Do blind men trying to read amuse you?
More. Read something else.
What?
Anything. Something long. Don't stop reading.
All right... Ahem!
"What is the real foe of attractive teeth and mouth health?
"Uncleanliness!
"You use a dentifrice on your toothbrush to clean your teeth more thoroughly and pleasantly than you can with the brush alone.
"So clearly the most important action of the dentifrice is to clean.
"Pepsodent's made to give you the greatest possible safe cleansing power. It would not clean nearly so well if we tried to make it a medicine or treatment as well as a cleanser.
"And anyway, your mouth most likely does not need medicine. If it did, you—
I love you.

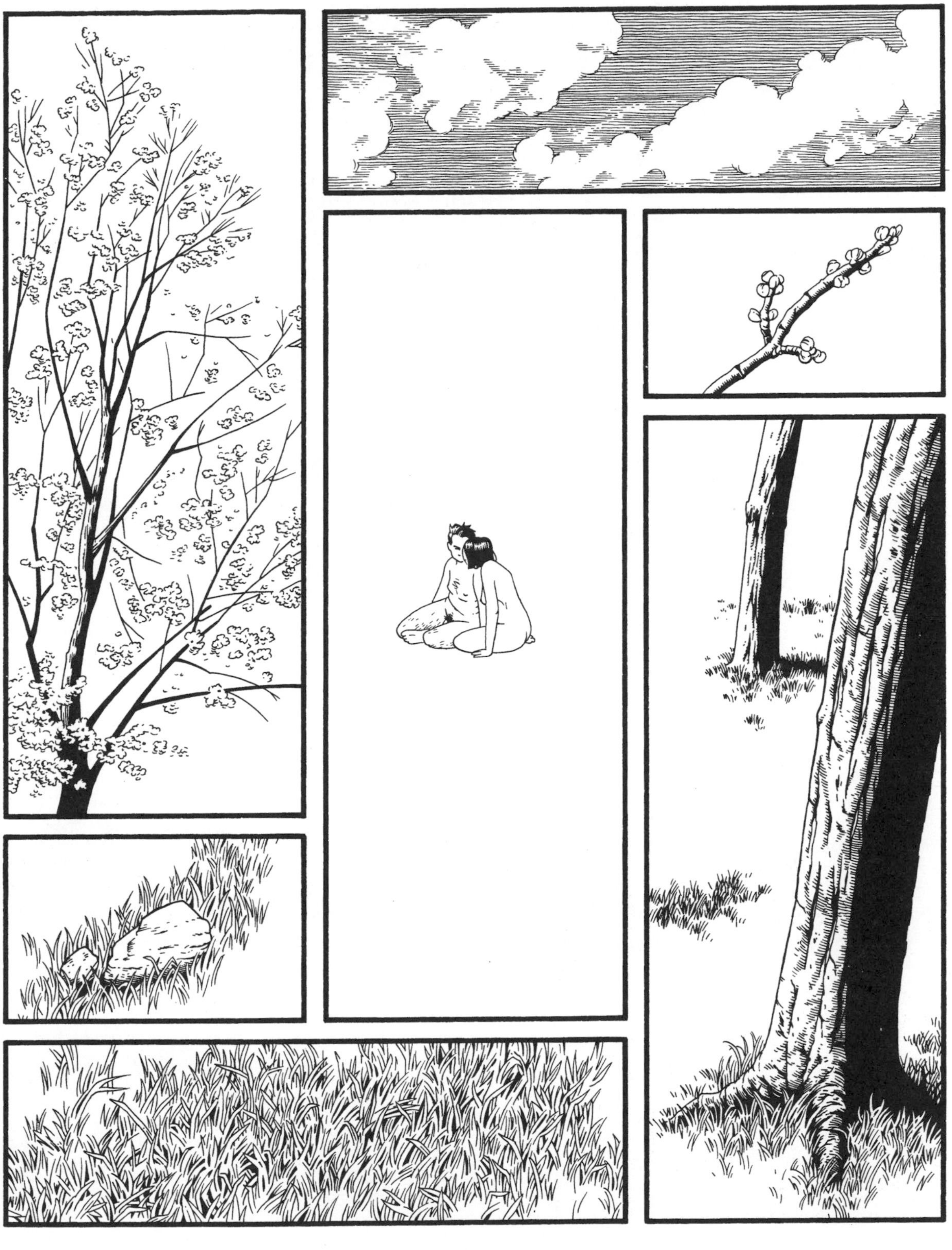

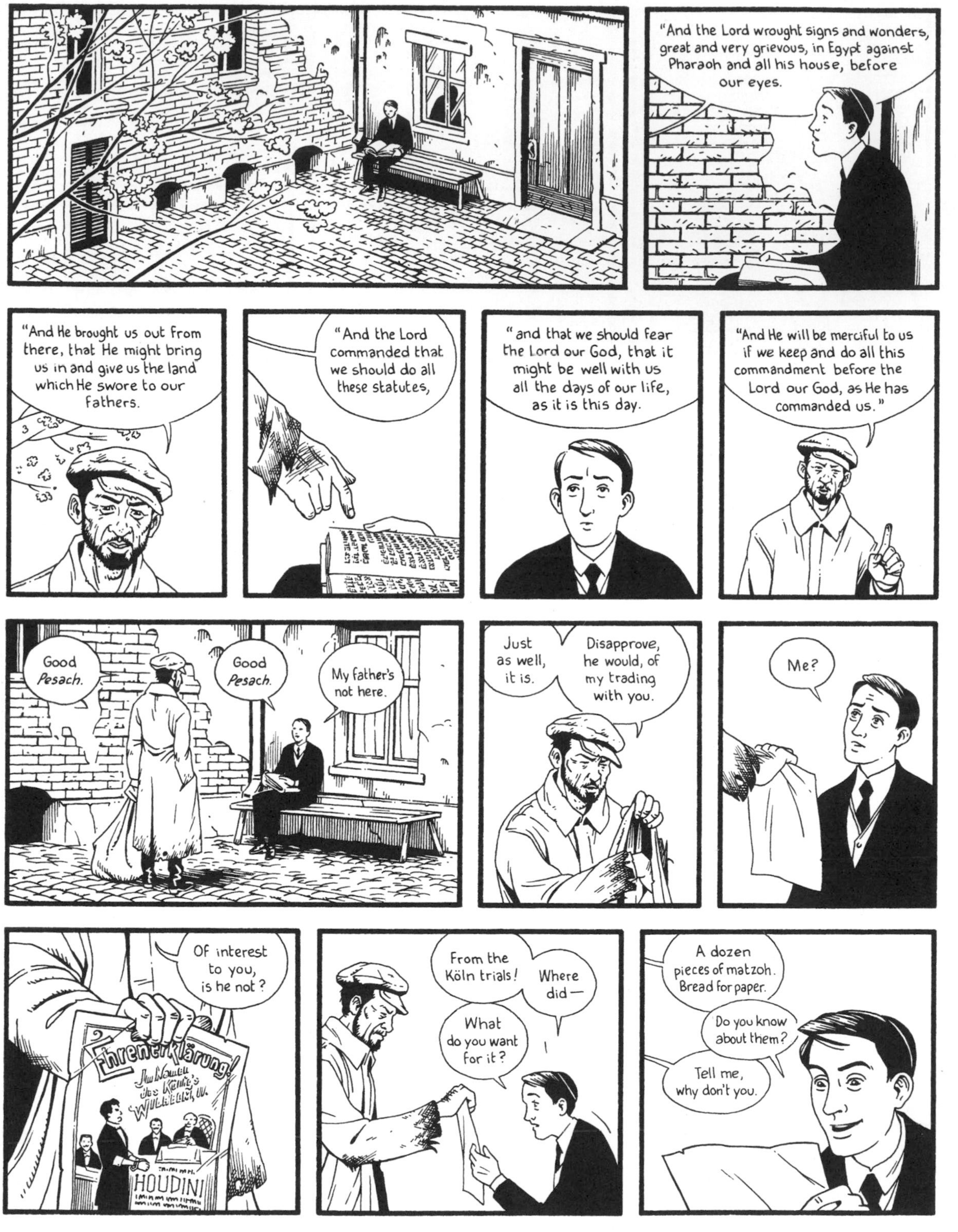
"And the Lord wrought signs and wonders, great and very grievous, in Egypt against Pharaoh and all his house, before our eyes.
"And He brought us out from there, that He might bring us in and give us the land which He swore to our fathers.
"And the Lord commanded that we should do all these statutes,
"and that we should fear the Lord our God, that it might be well with us all the days of our life, as it is this day.
"And He will be merciful to us if we keep and do all this commandment before the Lord our God, as He has commanded us."
Good Pesach.
Good Pesach.
My father's not here.
Just as well, it is.
Disapprove, he would, of my trading with you.
Me?
Of interest to you, is he not?
Ehrenerklärung!
HOUDINI
From the Köln trials!
Where did—
What do you want for it?
A dozen pieces of matzoh. Bread for paper.
Do you know about them?
Tell me, why don't you.

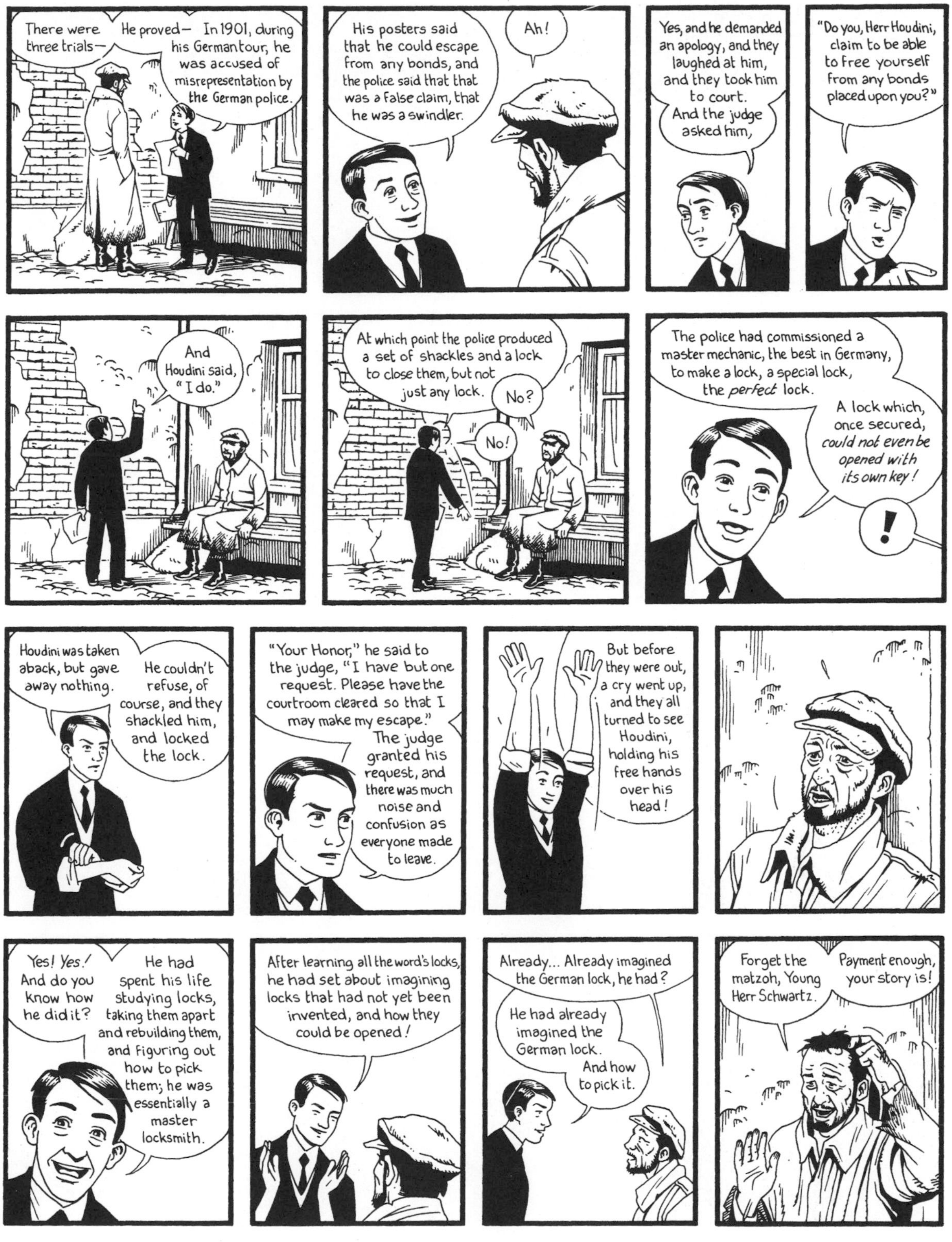
There were three trials—
He proved—
In 1901, during his German tour, he was accused of misrepresentation by the German police.
His posters said that he could escape from any bonds, and the police said that that was a false claim, that he was a swindler.
Ah!
Yes, and he demanded an apology, and they laughed at him, and they took him to court.
And the judge asked him,
"Do you, Herr Houdini, claim to be able to free yourself from any bonds placed upon you?"
And Houdini said, "I do."
At which point the police produced a set of shackles and a lock to close them, but not just any lock.
No?
No!
The police had commissioned a master mechanic, the best in Germany, to make a lock, a special lock, the perfect lock.
A lock which, once secured, could not even be opened with its own key!
!
Houdini was taken aback, but gave away nothing.
He couldn't refuse, of course, and they shackled him, and locked the lock.
"Your Honor," he said to the judge, "I have but one request. Please have the courtroom cleared so that I may make my escape."
The judge granted his request, and there was much noise and confusion as everyone made to leave.
But before they were out, a cry went up, and they all turned to see Houdini, holding his free hands over his head!
Yes! Yes! And do you know how he did it?
He had spent his life studying locks, taking them apart and rebuilding them, and figuring out how to pick them; he was essentially a master locksmith.
After learning all the word's locks, he had set about imagining locks that had not yet been invented, and how they could be opened!
Already... Already imagined the German lock, he had?
He had already imagined the German lock.
And how to pick it.
Forget the matzoh, Young Herr Schwartz.
Payment enough, your story is!

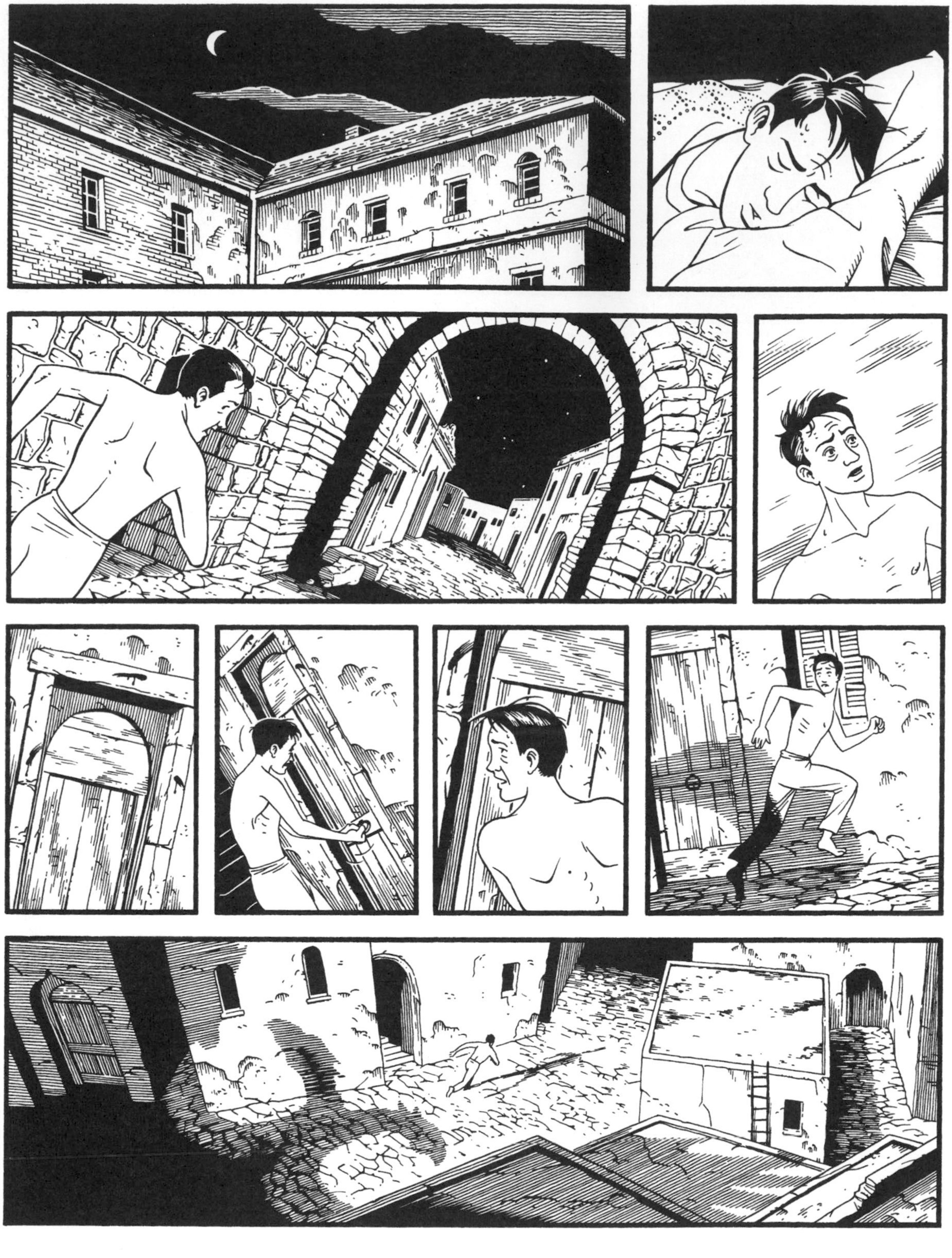

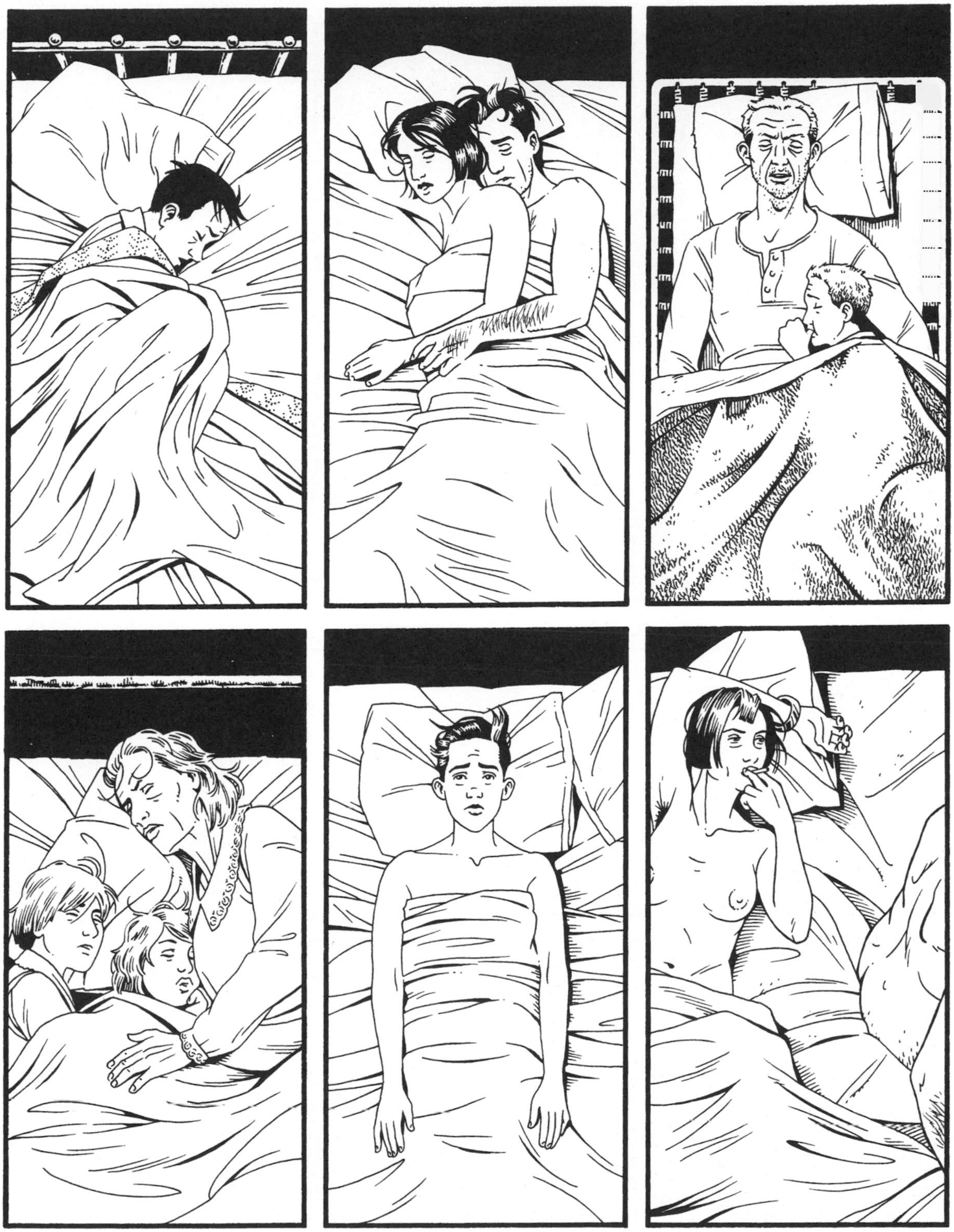

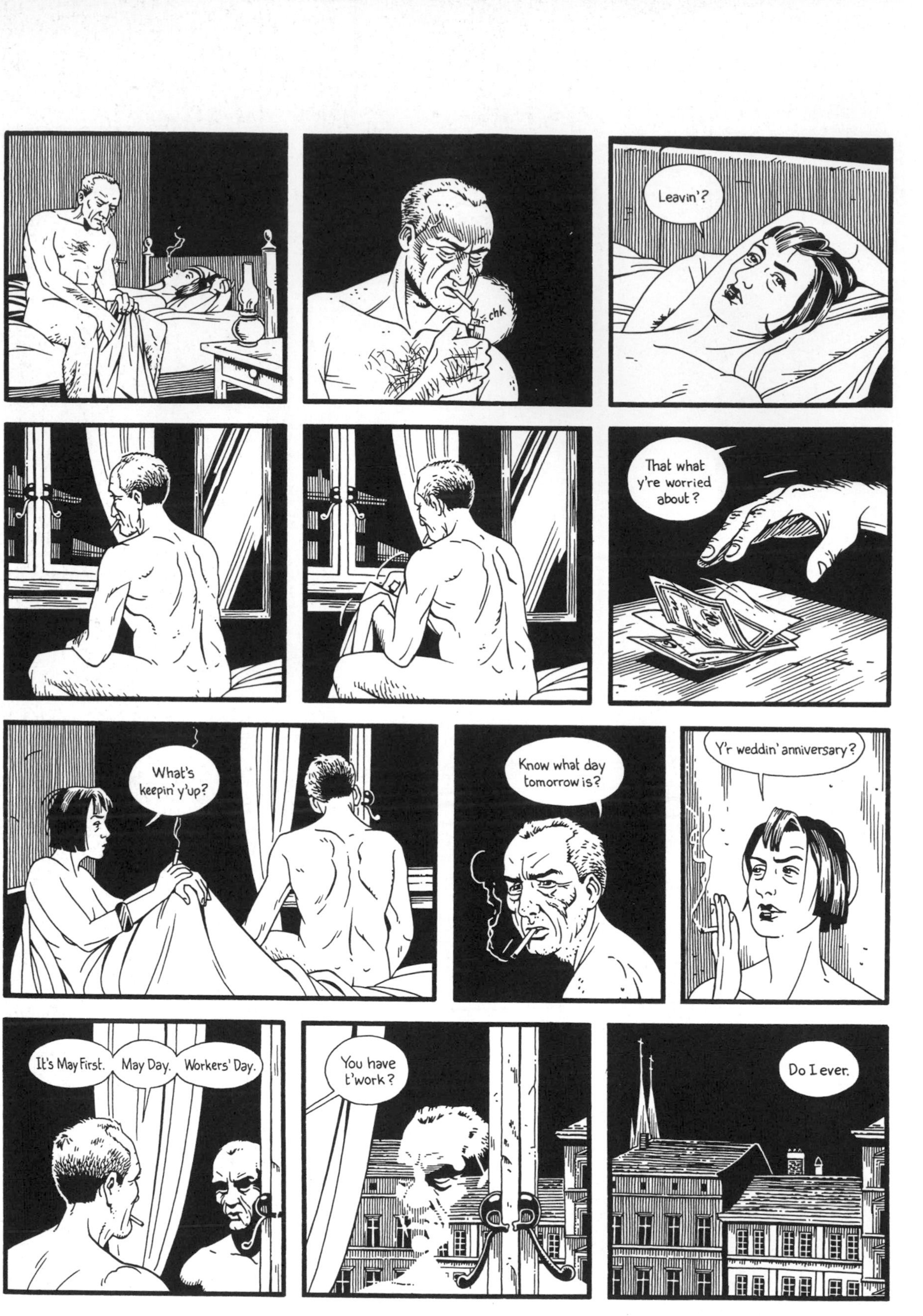
chk
Leavin'?
That what y're worried about?
What's keepin' y'up?
Know what day tomorrow is?
Y'r weddin' anniversary?
It's May First.
May Day.
Workers' Day.
You have t'work?
Do I ever.

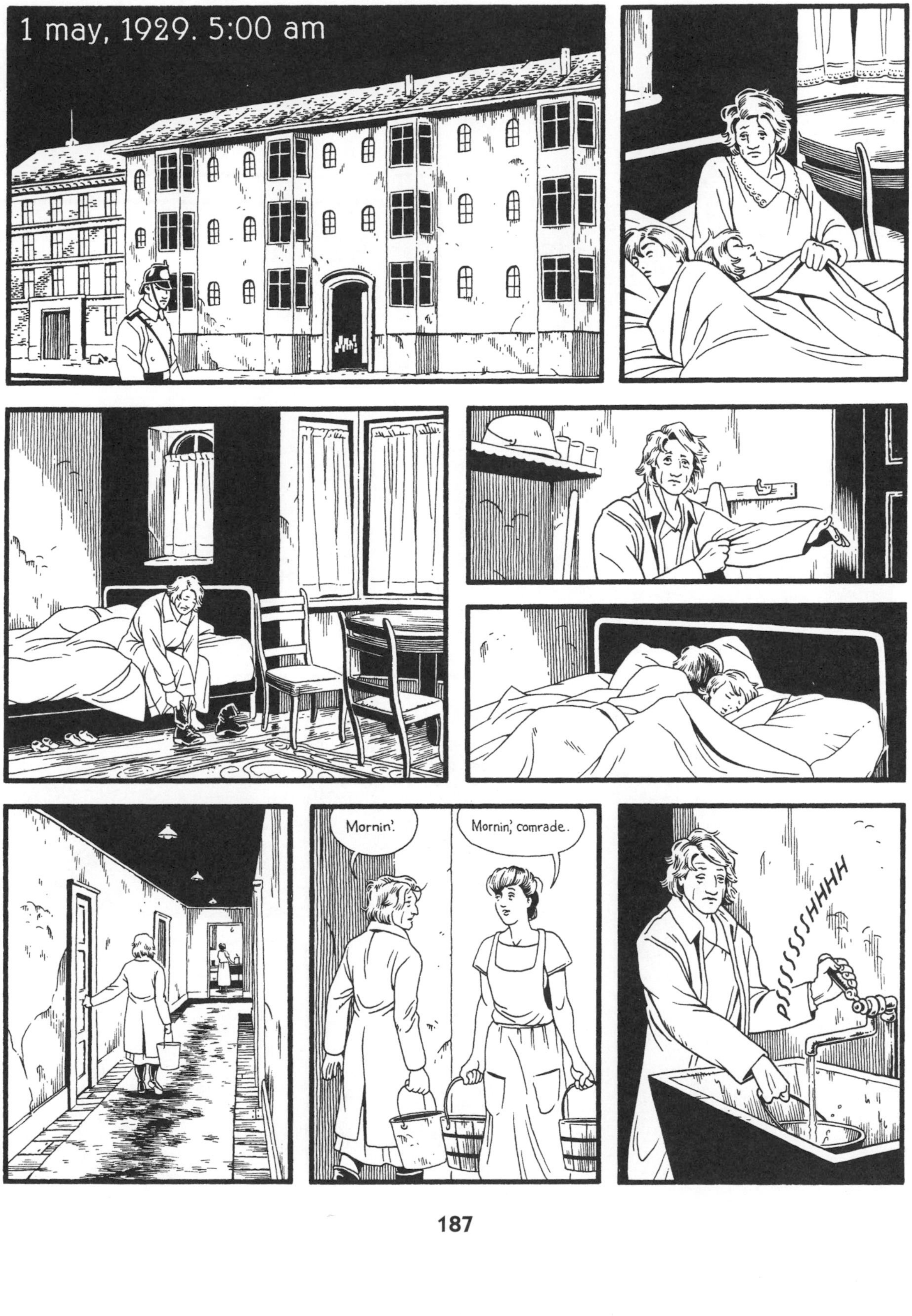
1 may, 1929. 5:00 am
Mornin'.
Mornin', comrade.
PSSSSSSSHHHH

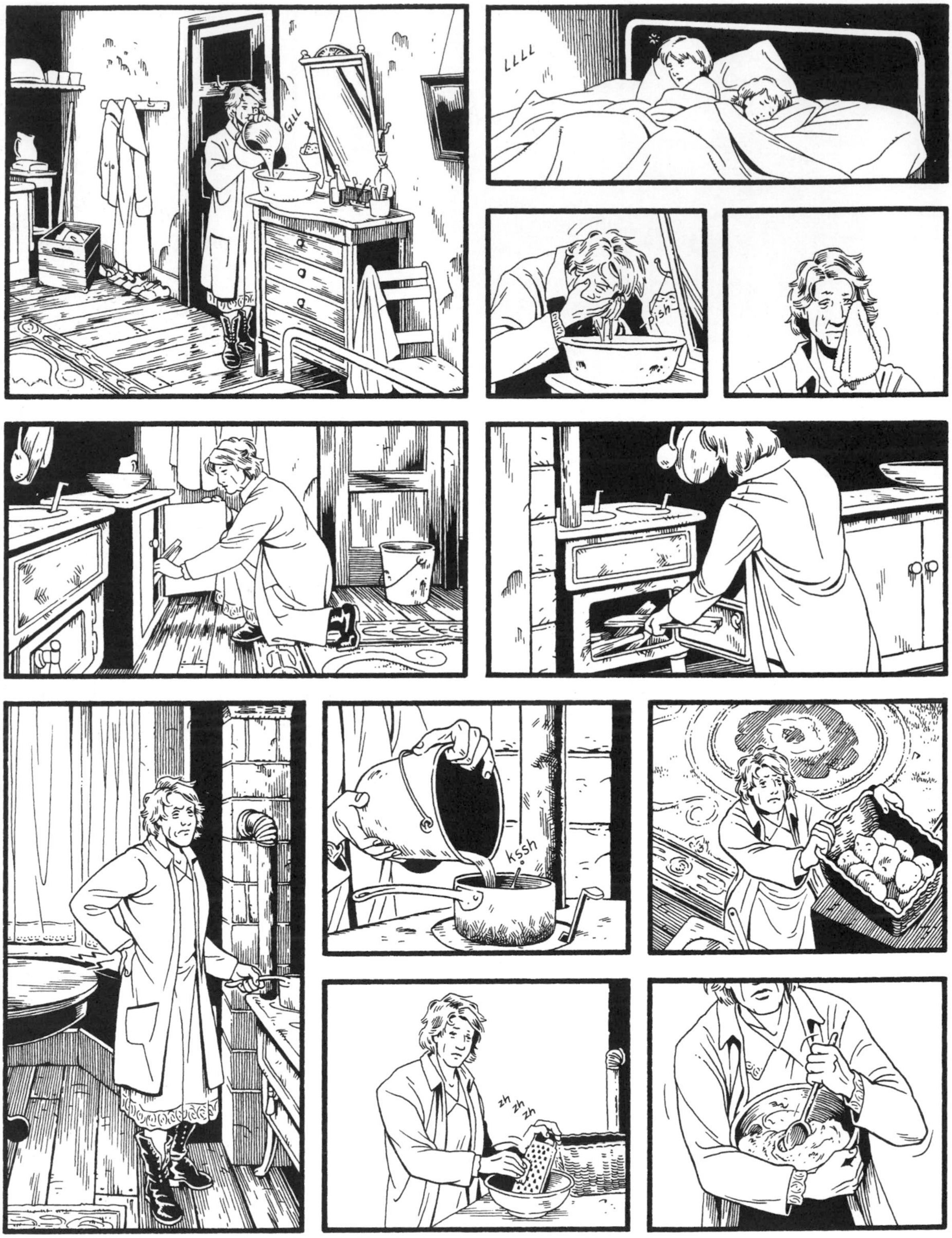
GLLL
LLLL
pish
kssh
zh zh zh

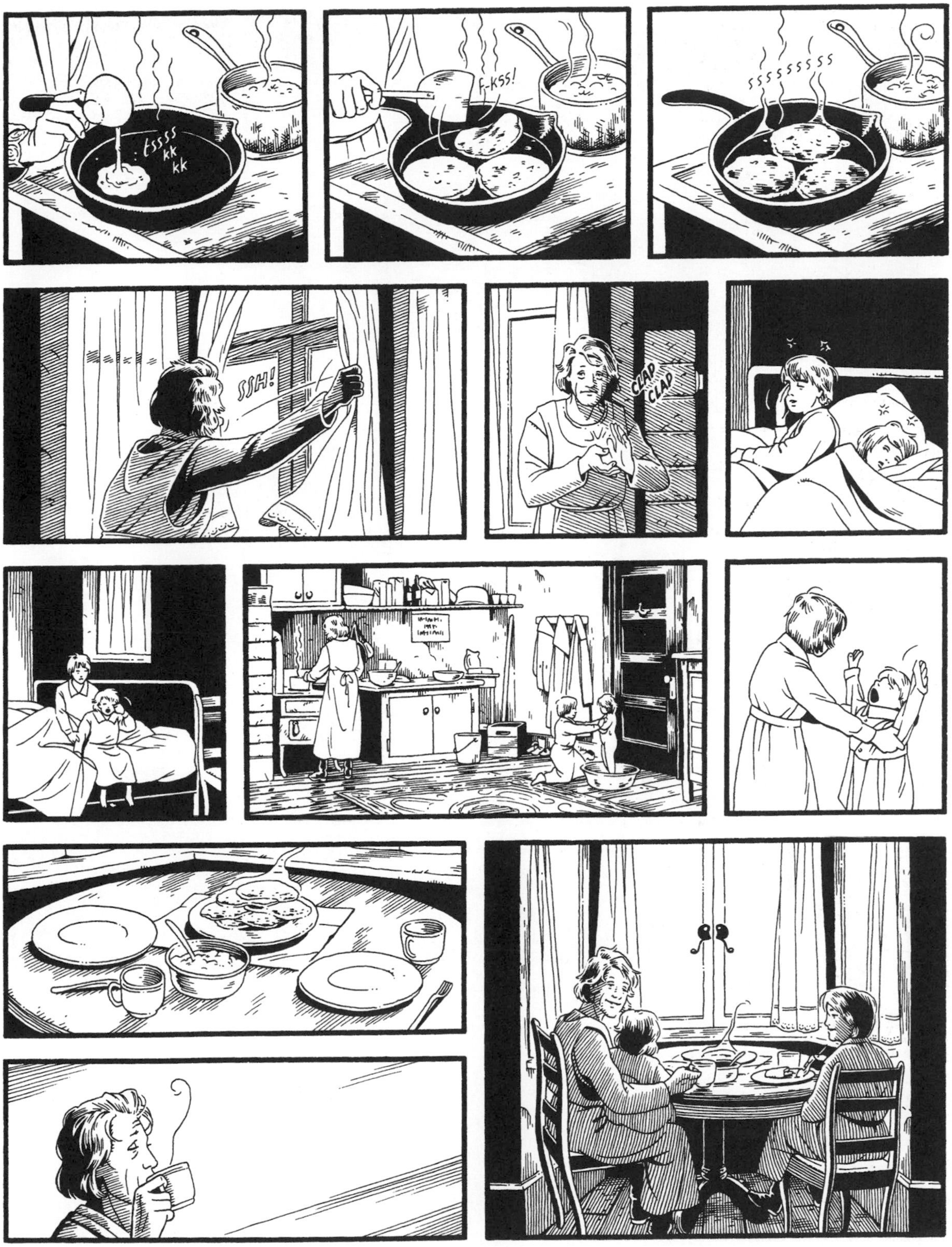
tssss
kk
kk
F-KSS!
SSSSSSSSS
SSH!
CLAP
CLAP

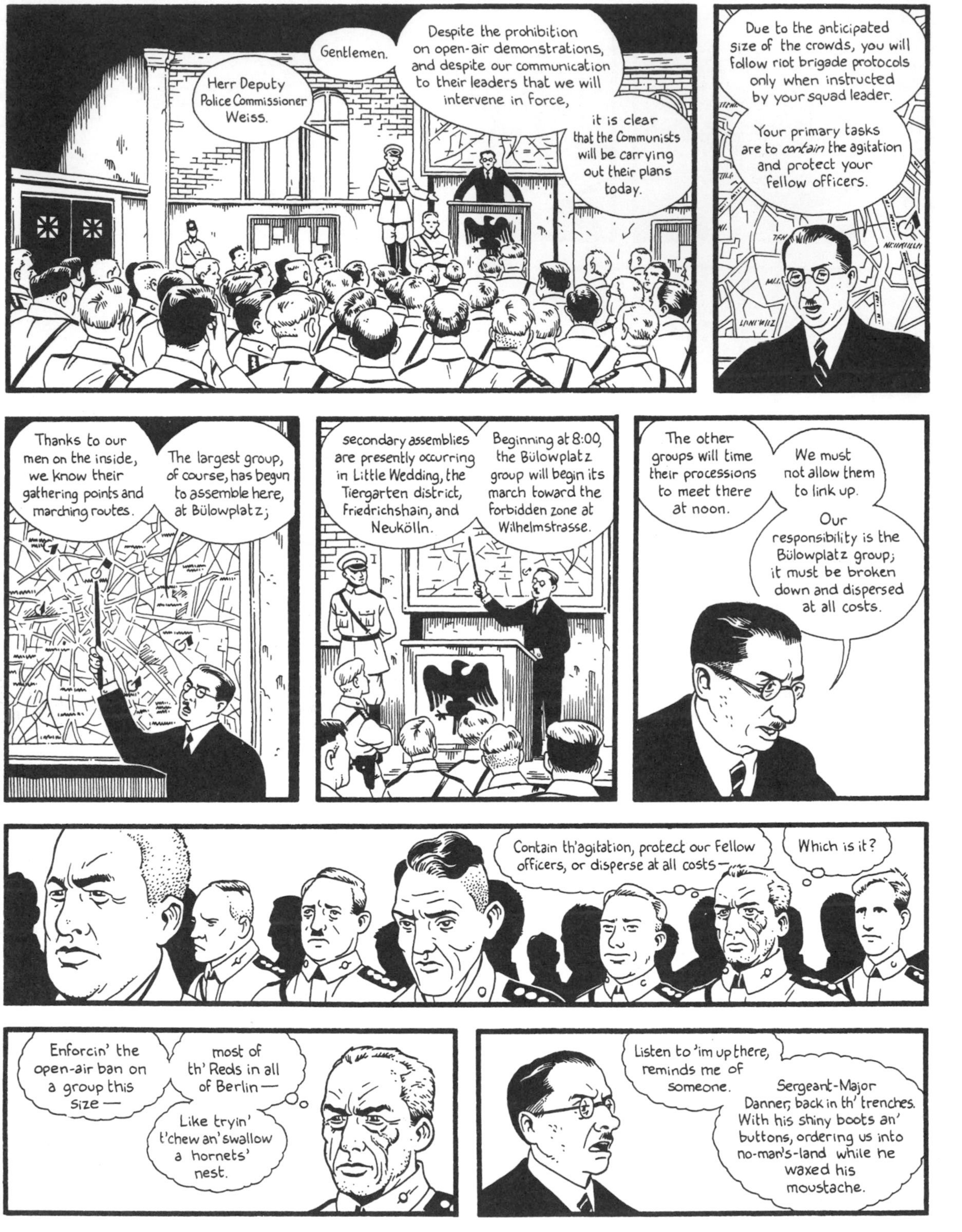
Herr Deputy Police Commissioner Weiss.
Gentlemen.
Despite the prohibition on open-air demonstrations, and despite our communication to their leaders that we will intervene in force,
it is clear that the Communists will be carrying out their plans today.
Due to the anticipated size of the crowds, you will follow riot brigade protocols only when instructed by your squad leader.
Your primary tasks are to *contain* the agitation and protect your fellow officers.
Thanks to our men on the inside, we know their gathering points and marching routes.
The largest group, of course, has begun to assemble here, at Bülowplatz;
secondary assemblies are presently occurring in Little Wedding, the Tiergarten district, Friedrichshain, and Neukölln.
Beginning at 8:00, the Bülowplatz group will begin its march toward the forbidden zone at Wilhelmstrasse.
The other groups will time their processions to meet there at noon.
We must not allow them to link up.
Our responsibility is the Bülowplatz group; it must be broken down and dispersed at all costs.
Contain th'agitation, protect our Fellow officers, or disperse at all costs—
Which is it?
Enforcin' the open-air ban on a group this size—
most of th' Reds in all of Berlin—
Like tryin' t'chew an' swallow a hornets' nest.
Listen to 'im up there, reminds me of someone.
Sergeant-Major Danner, back in th' trenches. With his shiny boots an' buttons, ordering us into no-man's-land while he waxed his moustache.

An' these boys—
farmers an' th' sons of farmers—
too young t'have been *there*, strangers t'Berlin...
I need t'eat somethin', but I feel sick.
We must also anticipate the presence of other groups, including the National Socialists.
They may assist in disrupting the Communist ranks.
So...
To reiterate crowd-dispersal procedure:
In all street-clearing situations, your squad leader will call for warning shots to open a shooting zone; anyone left in the zone will be ordered to disperse again before being subject to fire.
Upon dismissal, you will receive standard issue for these circumstances:
Bayonet, pistol, and grenade for every man.
Carbine for every third man, as assigned within your squad.
Questions?
er Straße
Schönhauser Allee
Prenzlauer Allee
Greifswald

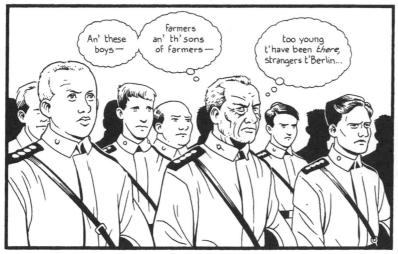

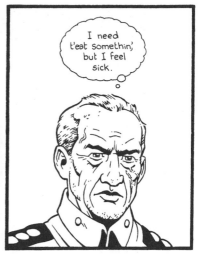

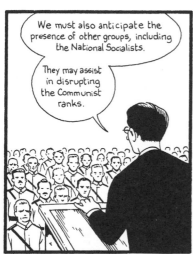

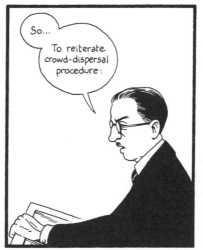

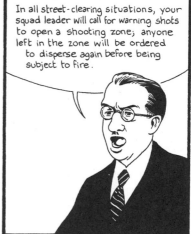

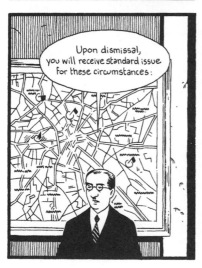

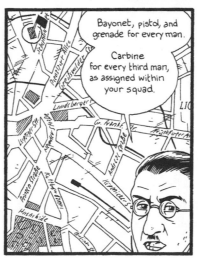

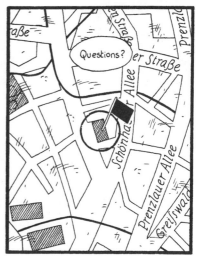

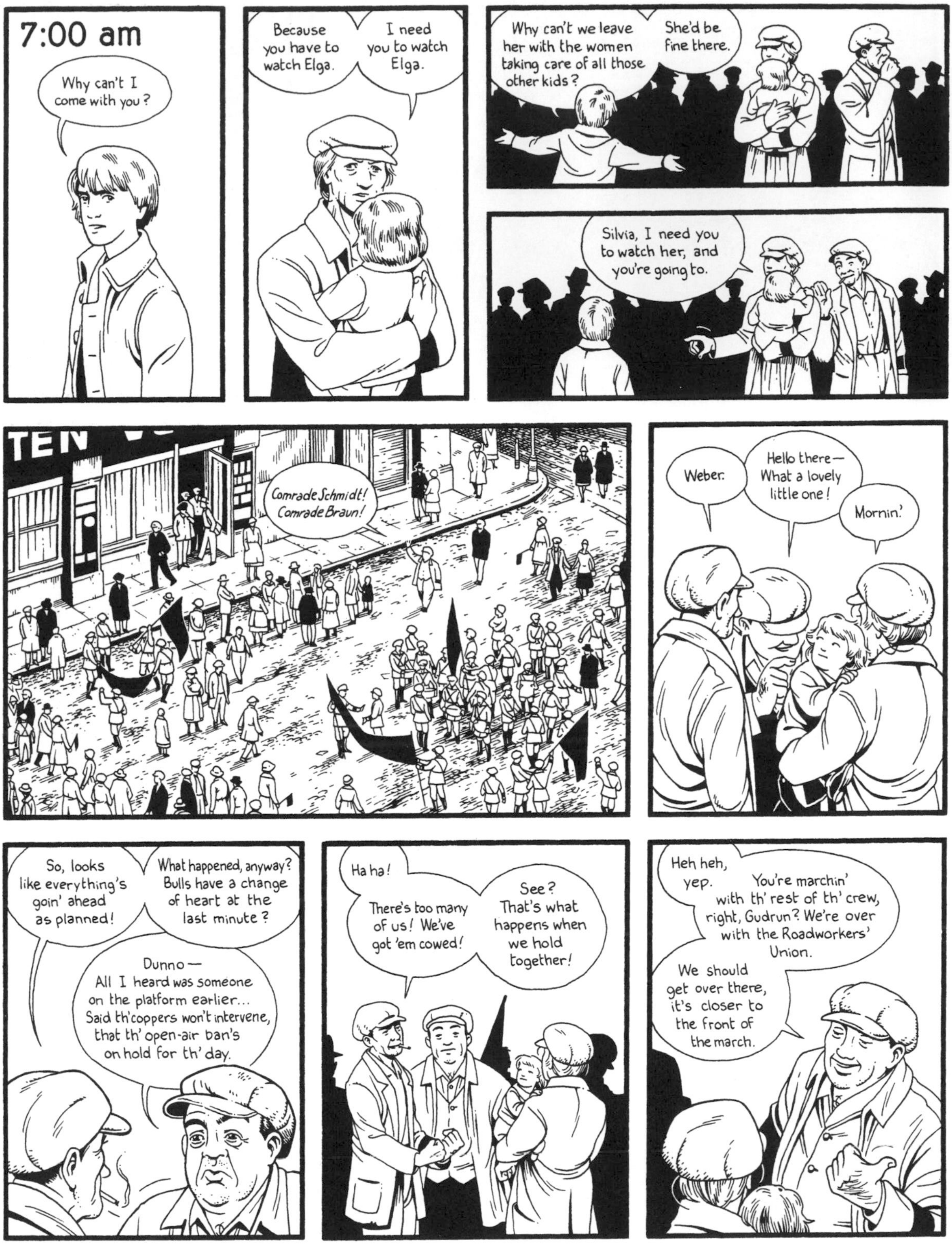
7:00 am
Why can't I come with you?
Because you have to watch Elga.
I need you to watch Elga.
Why can't we leave her with the women taking care of all those other kids?
She'd be fine there.
Silvia, I need you to watch her, and you're going to.
TEN
Comrade Schmidt! Comrade Braun!
Weber.
Hello there— What a lovely little one!
Mornin'
So, looks like everything's goin' ahead as planned!
What happened, anyway? Bulls have a change of heart at the last minute?
Dunno— All I heard was someone on the platform earlier... Said th'coppers won't intervene, that th' open-air ban's on hold for th' day.
Ha ha!
There's too many of us! We've got 'em cowed!
See? That's what happens when we hold together!
Heh heh, yep.
You're marchin' with th' rest of th' crew, right, Gudrun? We're over with the Roadworkers' Union.
We should get over there, it's closer to the front of the march.

There's half a loaf of bread an' some powdered beef broth in th' cupboard for lunch.

You can play in th' courtyard, but stay off th' street.

An' don't let Elga out of your sight!

I'll be home by three, all right?

She's a good girl, Silvia is. Smart girl.

Tough, too. Takes after her mother.

RED FRONTFIGHTERS

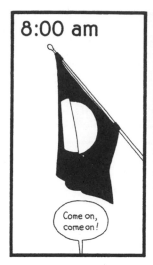

8:00 am

Come on, come on!

Hurry up or we're liable t'miss 'im!

Who once made GERMANY the PROUDEST and HAPPIEST country in the world?

Who sacrificed two million of our best far away on the battlefields?

Who fought and starved and suffered during the war?

It was US GERMANS...

WHO has besmirched our honor and stolen our money?

WHO owns our mines and railways today?

Poppa! Who're we tryin' t'see?

The Gauleiter of all Berlin! Our leader!

Up you go!

WHO has made a PROFIT out of our MISERY while we STARVED and SUFFERED?

It was our ENEMIES — JEWS and the SERFS of Jews!

UUURRRRRAAAHRH
arren
Cigar
AND WHAT FORCE THREATENS THE WORKING PEOPLE OF BERLIN — OF GERMANY THIS DAY ?
BOLSHEVISM!
CREATION OF THE JEWS!
RUAAH
TODAY WE CHALLENGE MARXISM TO A SHOWDOWN!
TODAY WE SHOW THAT JEWISH DEPUTY COMMISSIONER OF POLICE THAT THE STREETS ARE OURS!
FOR WHOEVER CONQUERS THE STREETS CONQUERS THE MASSES, AND WHOEVER CONQUERS THE MASSES THEREBY CONQUERS THE STATE!
RAAAHRH
arren
HEIL HITLER!
arren
HEIL HITLER!

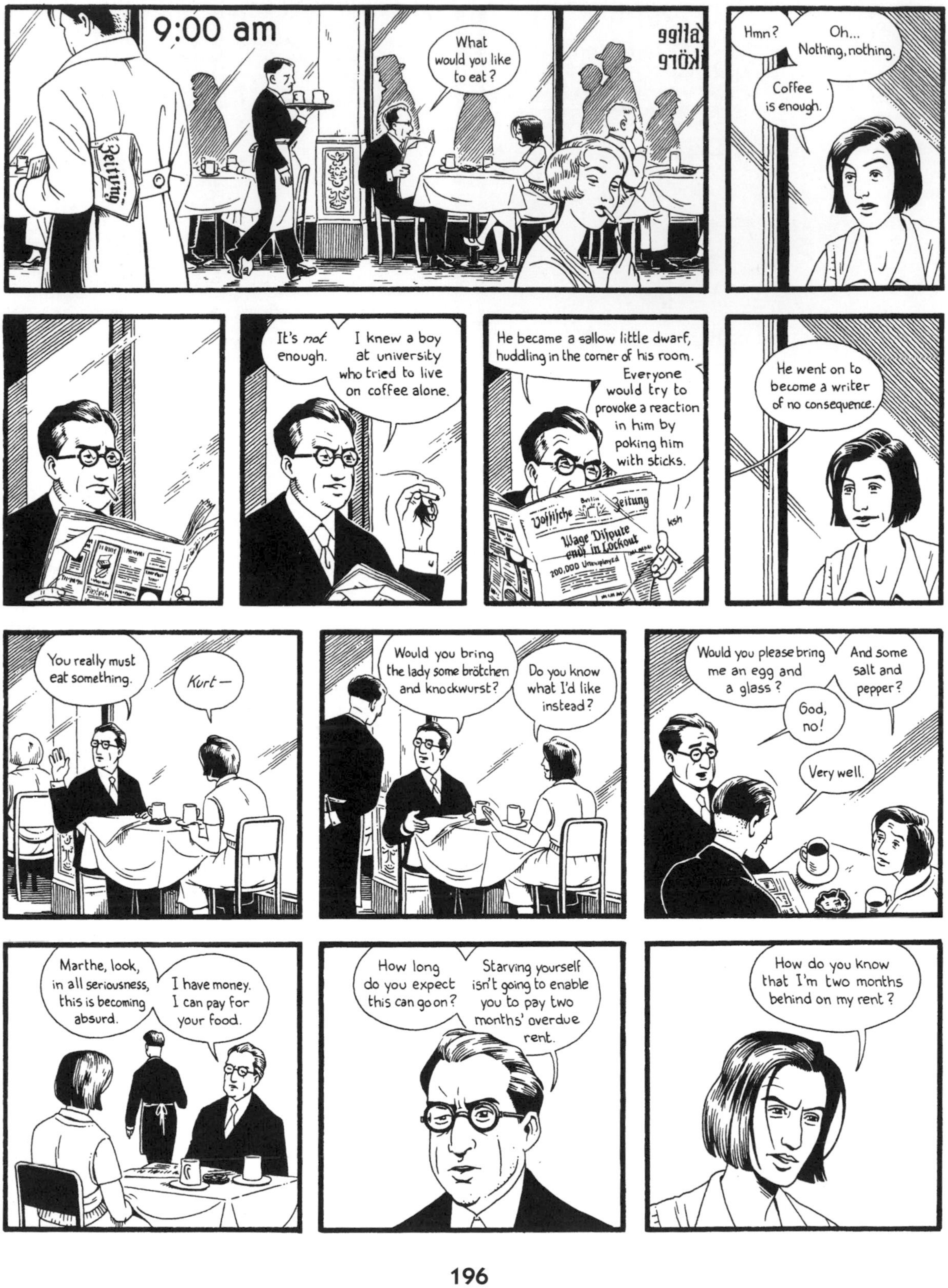
9:00 am
What would you like to eat?
Hmn?
Oh... Nothing, nothing.
Coffee is enough.
It's *not* enough.
I knew a boy at university who tried to live on coffee alone.
He became a sallow little dwarf, huddling in the corner of his room.
Everyone would try to provoke a reaction in him by poking him with sticks.
Vossische Berliner Zeitung
Wage Dispute ends in Lockout
200,000 Unemployed
ksh
He went on to become a writer of no consequence.
You really must eat something.
Kurt—
Would you bring the lady some brötchen and knockwurst?
Do you know what I'd like instead?
Would you please bring me an egg and a glass?
And some salt and pepper?
God, no!
Very well.
Marthe, look, in all seriousness, this is becoming absurd.
I have money. I can pay for your food.
How long do you expect this can go on?
Starving yourself isn't going to enable you to pay two months' overdue rent.
How do you know that I'm two months behind on my rent?

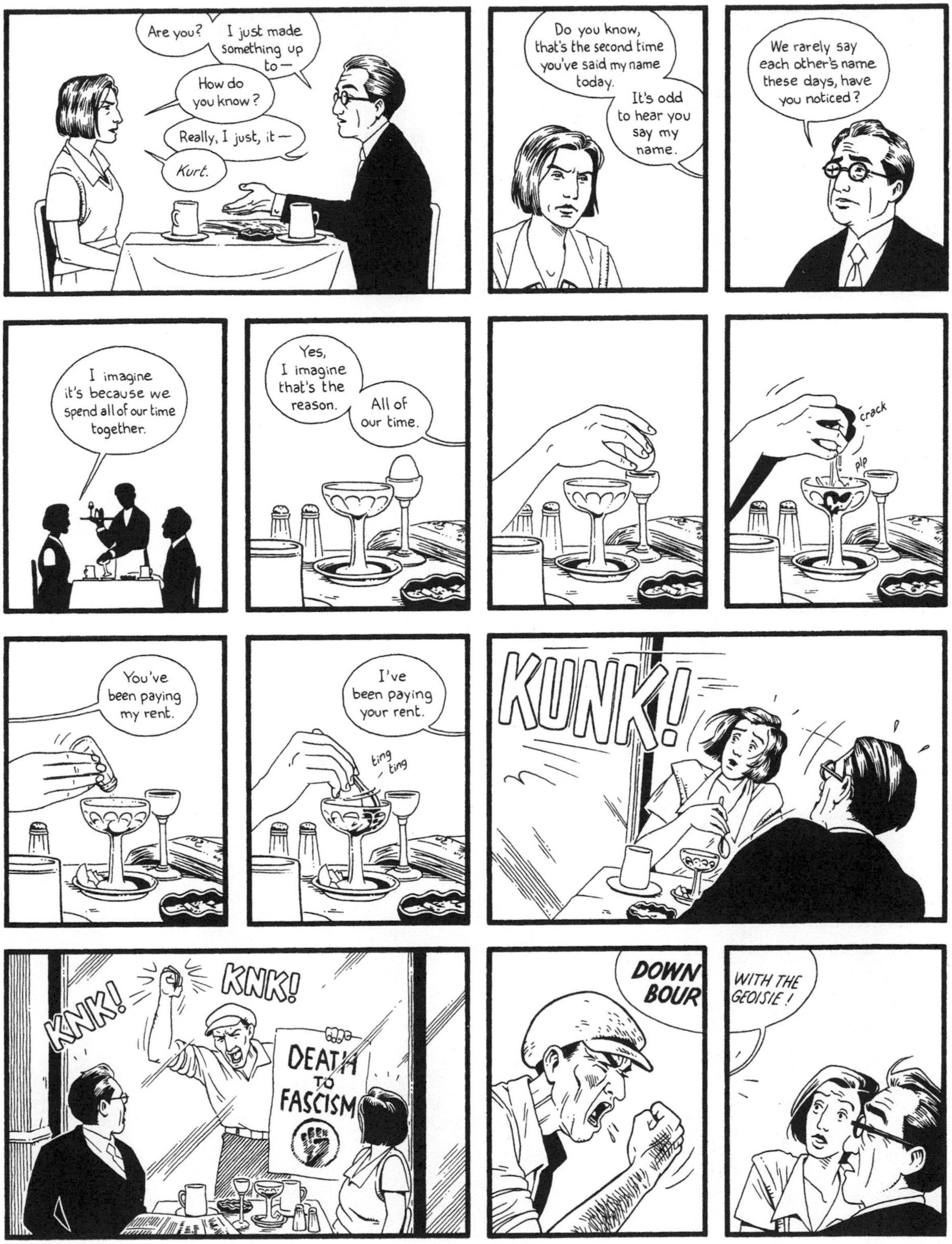

Are you?
I just made something up to—
How do you know?
Really, I just, it—
Kurt.
Do you know, that's the second time you've said my name today.
It's odd to hear you say my name.
We rarely say each other's name these days, have you noticed?
I imagine it's because we spend all of our time together.
Yes, I imagine that's the reason.
All of our time.
crack
plp
You've been paying my rent.
I've been paying your rent.
ting ting
KUNK!
KNK!
KNK!
DEATH TO FASCISM
DOWN BOUR
WITH THE GEOISIE!

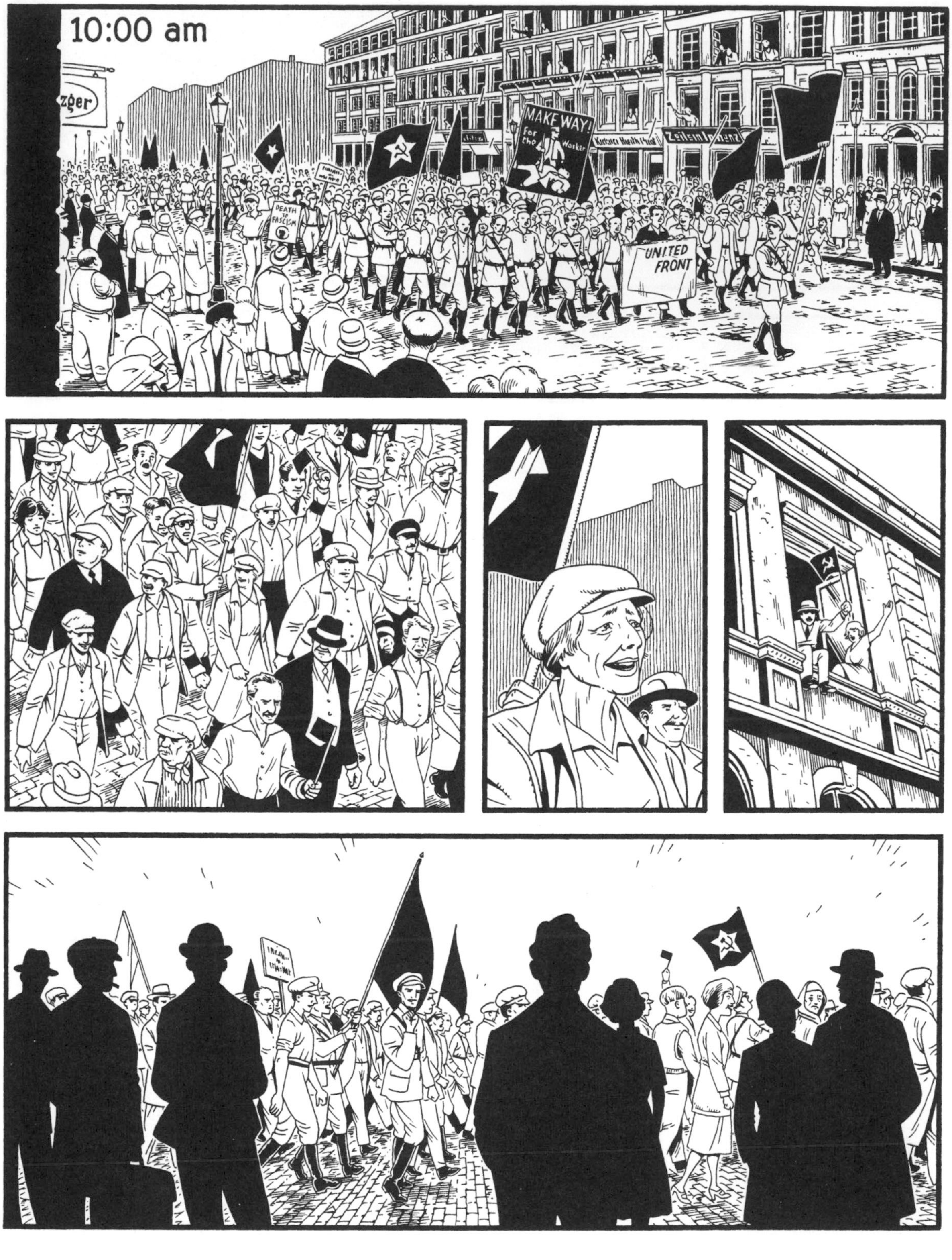
10:00 am
MAKE WAY!
for the Worker
DEATH TO FASCISM
UNITED FRONT

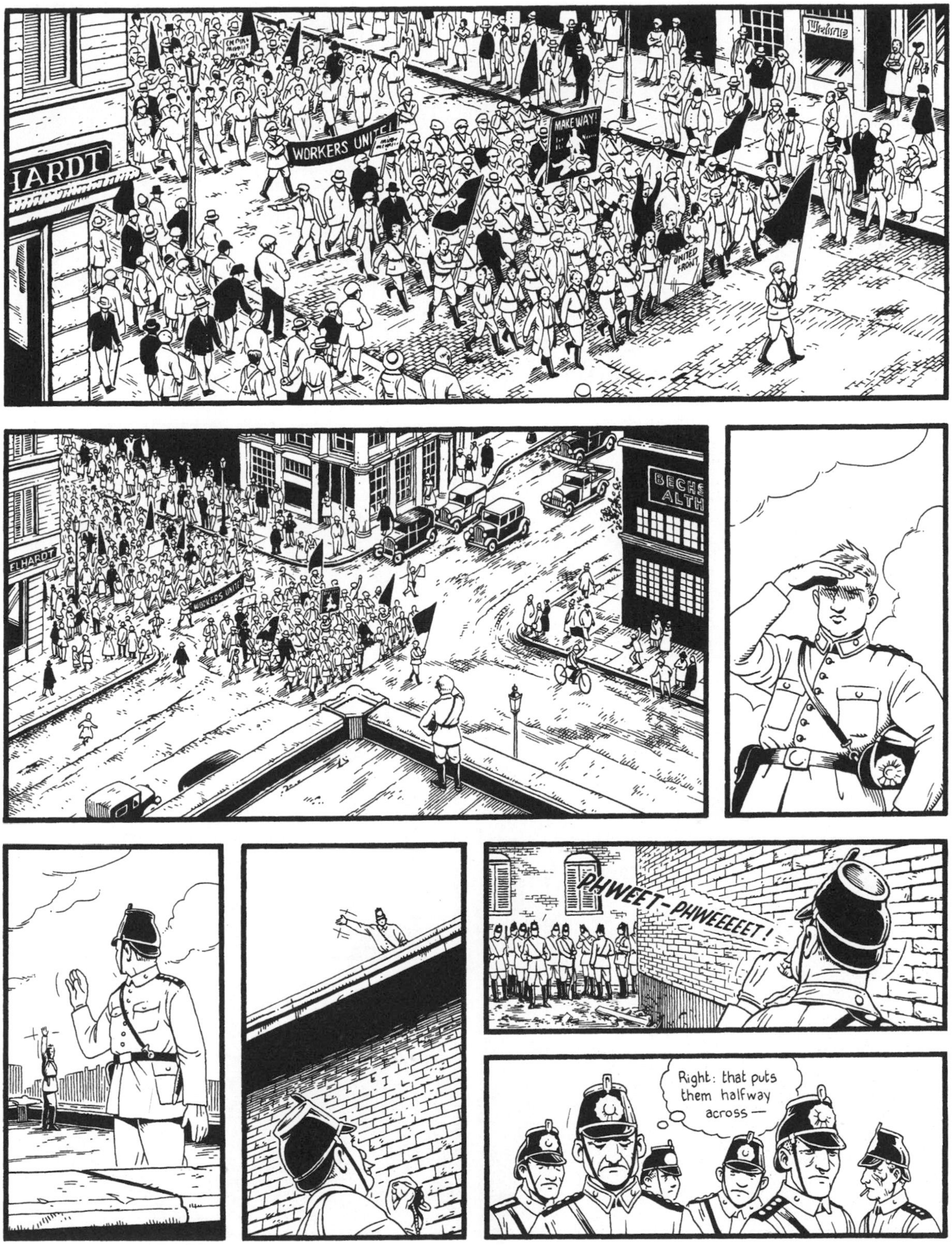
WORKERS UNITE!
MAKE WAY!
UNITED FRONT
PHWEET-PHWEEEEEET!
Right: that puts them halfway across —

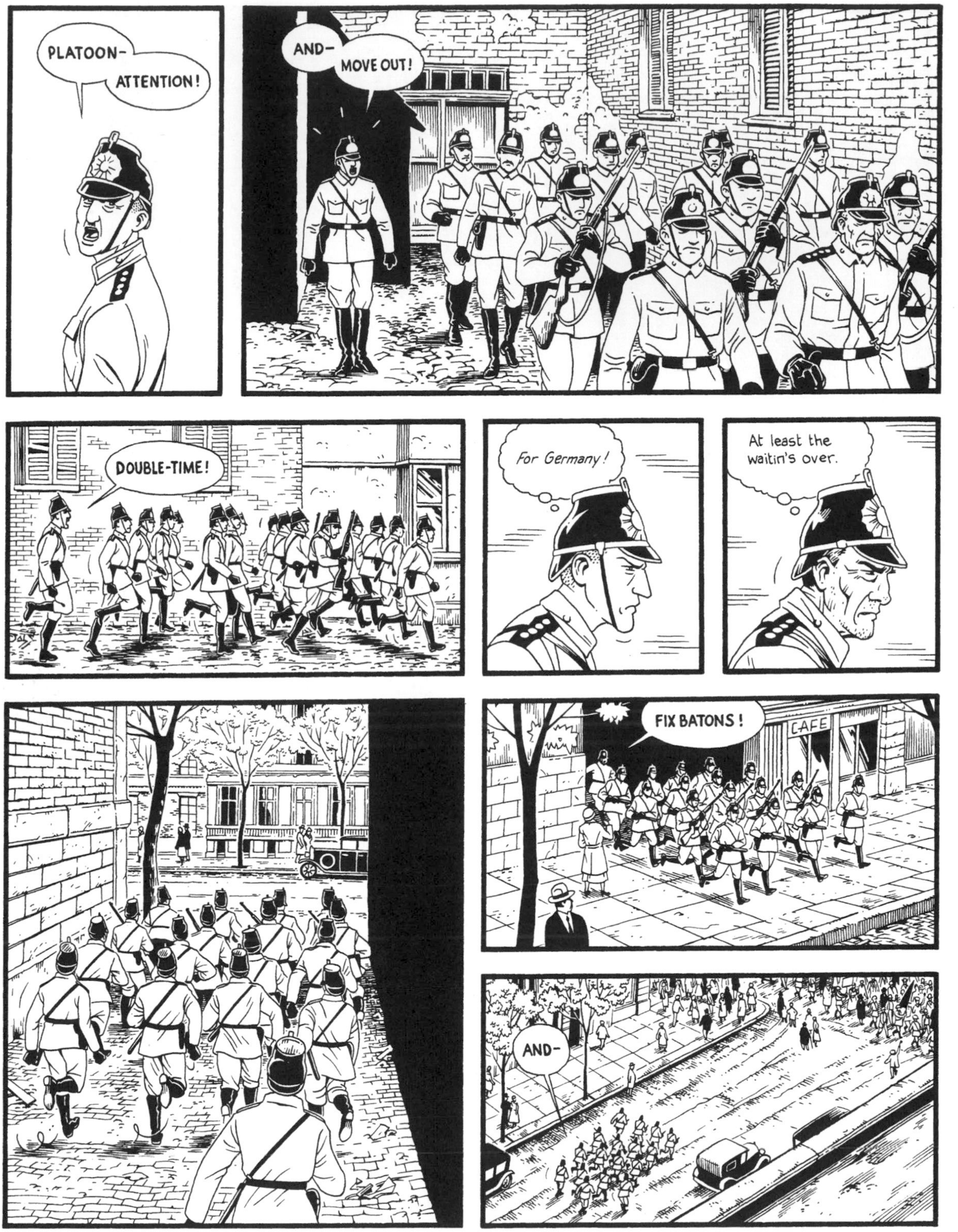
PLATOON-
ATTENTION!
AND-
MOVE OUT!
DOUBLE-TIME!
For Germany!
At least the waitin's over.
FIX BATONS!
CAFE
AND-

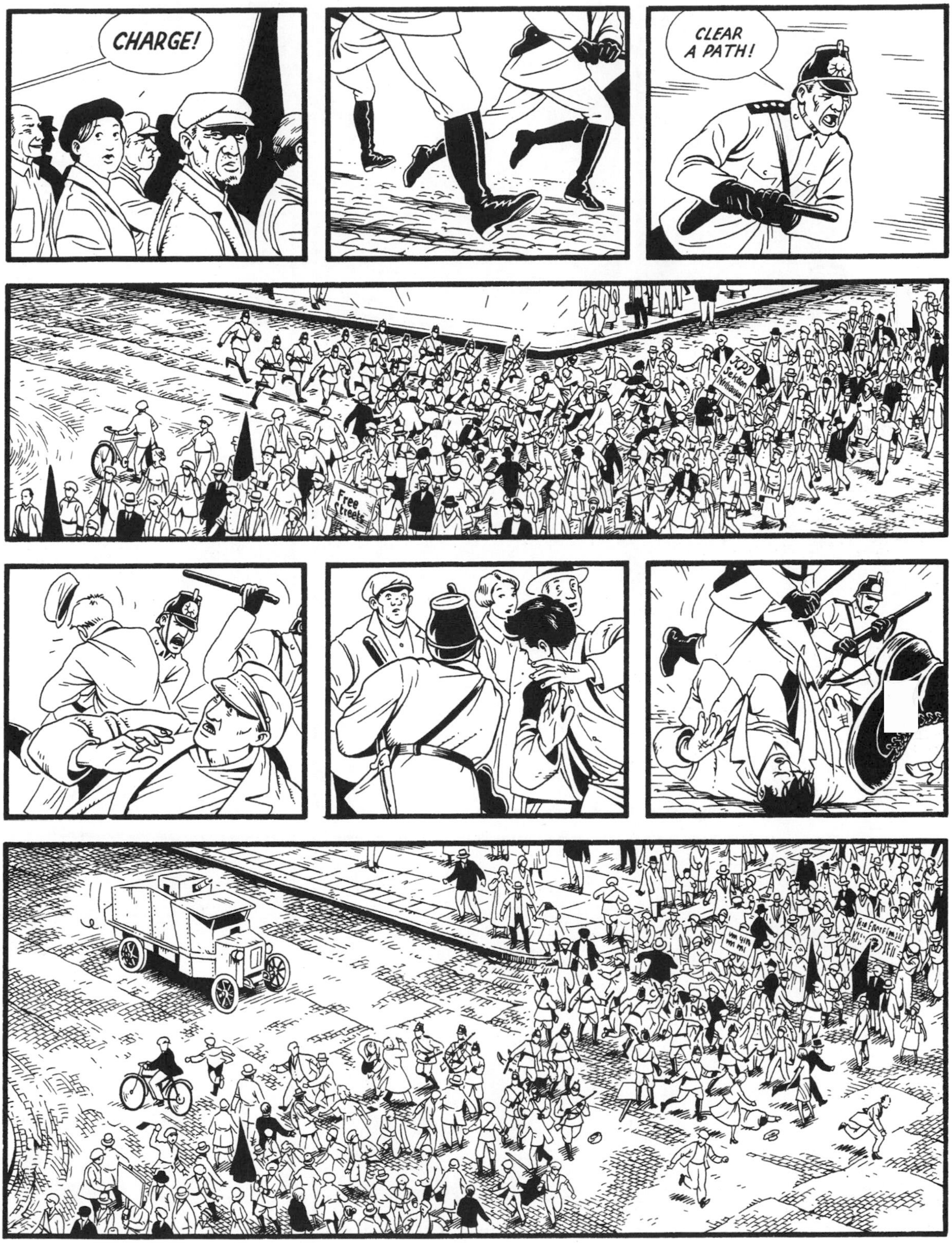
CHARGE!
CLEAR A PATH!
KPD Sektion
Free Streets

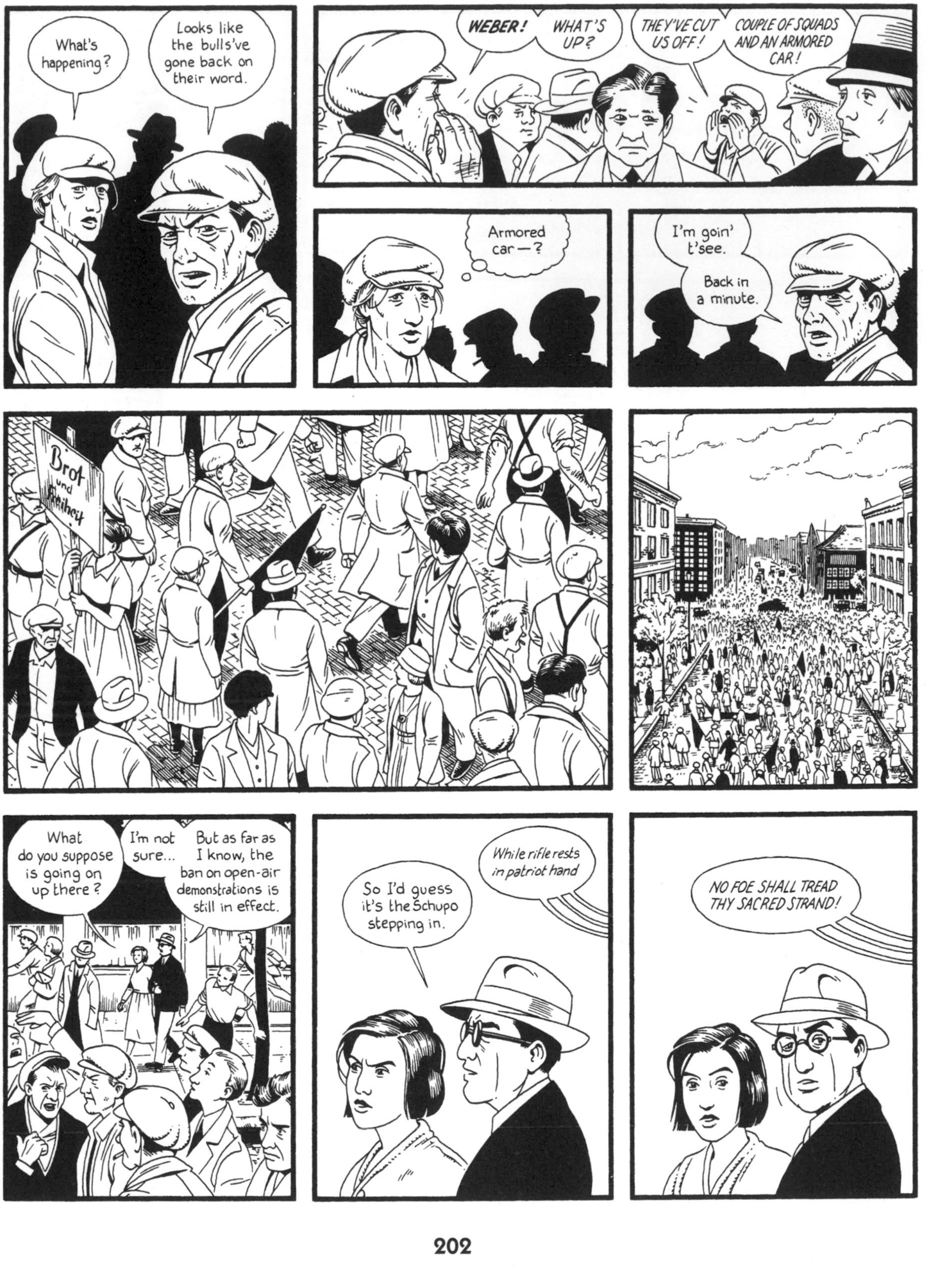
What's happening?
Looks like the bulls've gone back on their word.
WEBER!
WHAT'S UP?
THEY'VE CUT US OFF!
COUPLE OF SQUADS AND AN ARMORED CAR!
Armored car—?
I'm goin' t'see.
Back in a minute.
Brot und Freiheit
What do you suppose is going on up there?
I'm not sure...
But as far as I know, the ban on open-air demonstrations is still in effect.
While rifle rests in patriot hand
So I'd guess it's the Schupo stepping in.
NO FOE SHALL TREAD THY SACRED STRAND!

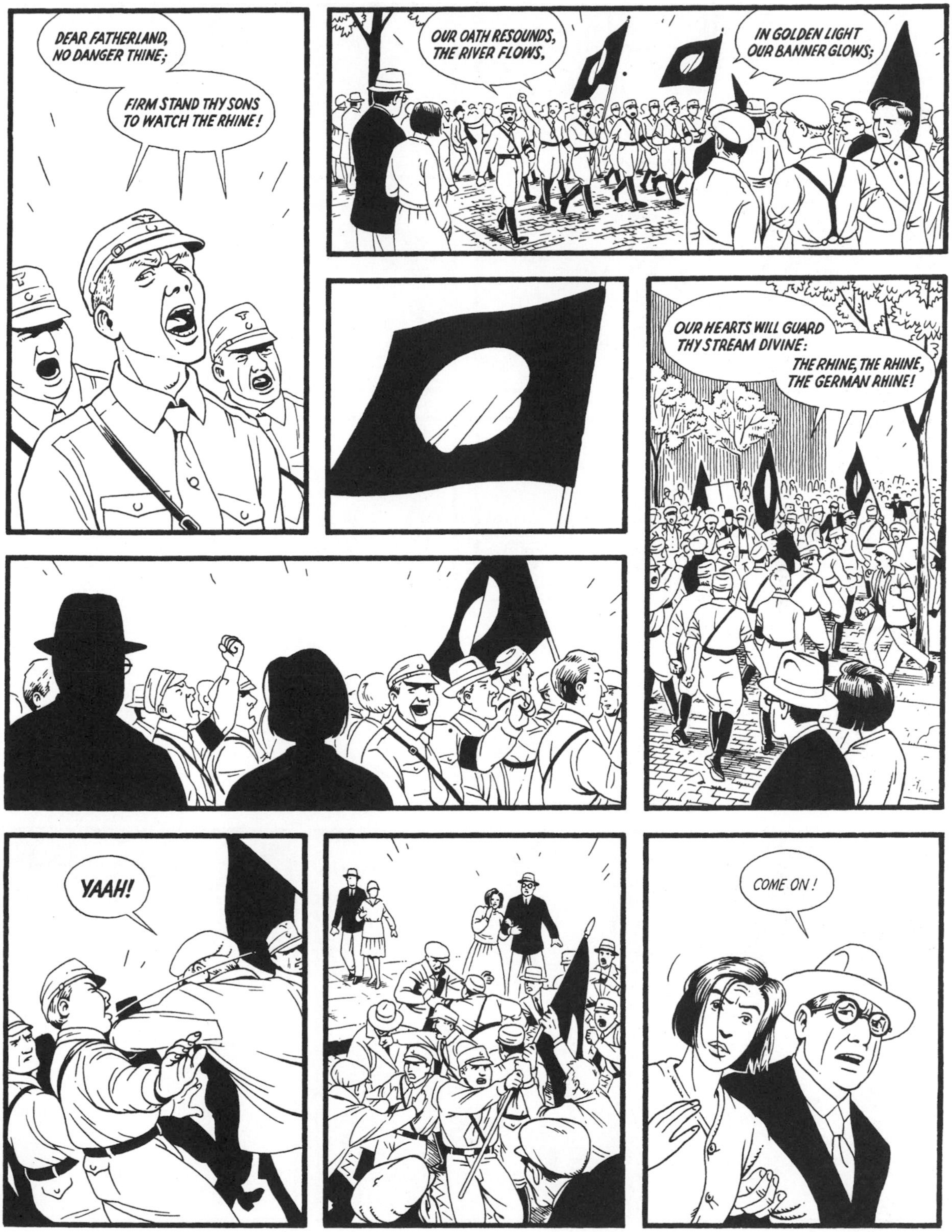
DEAR FATHERLAND, NO DANGER THINE;
FIRM STAND THY SONS TO WATCH THE RHINE!
OUR OATH RESOUNDS, THE RIVER FLOWS,
IN GOLDEN LIGHT OUR BANNER GLOWS;
OUR HEARTS WILL GUARD THY STREAM DIVINE:
THE RHINE, THE RHINE, THE GERMAN RHINE!
YAAH!
COME ON!

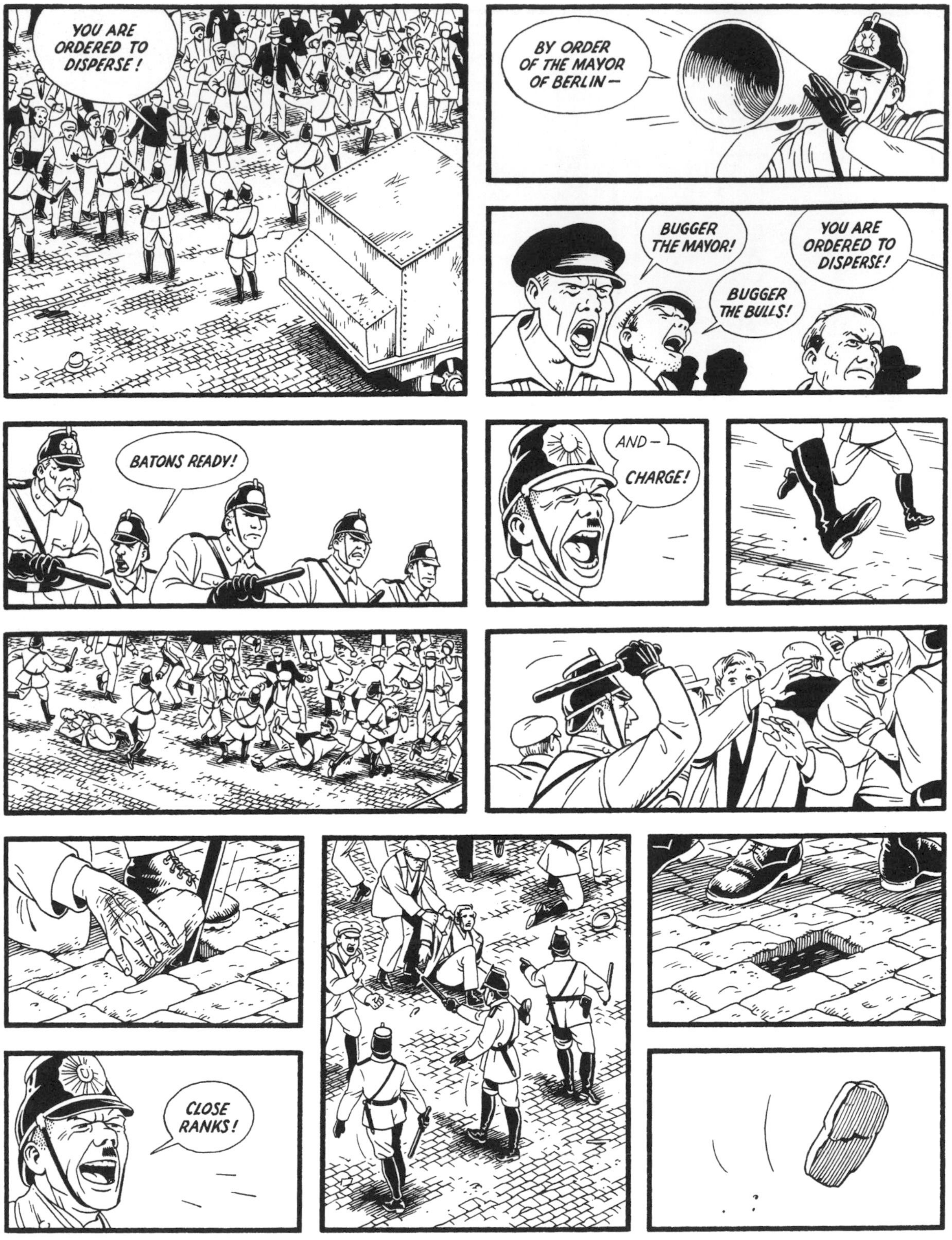
YOU ARE ORDERED TO DISPERSE!
BY ORDER OF THE MAYOR OF BERLIN—
BUGGER THE MAYOR!
YOU ARE ORDERED TO DISPERSE!
BUGGER THE BULLS!
BATONS READY!
AND—
CHARGE!
CLOSE RANKS!

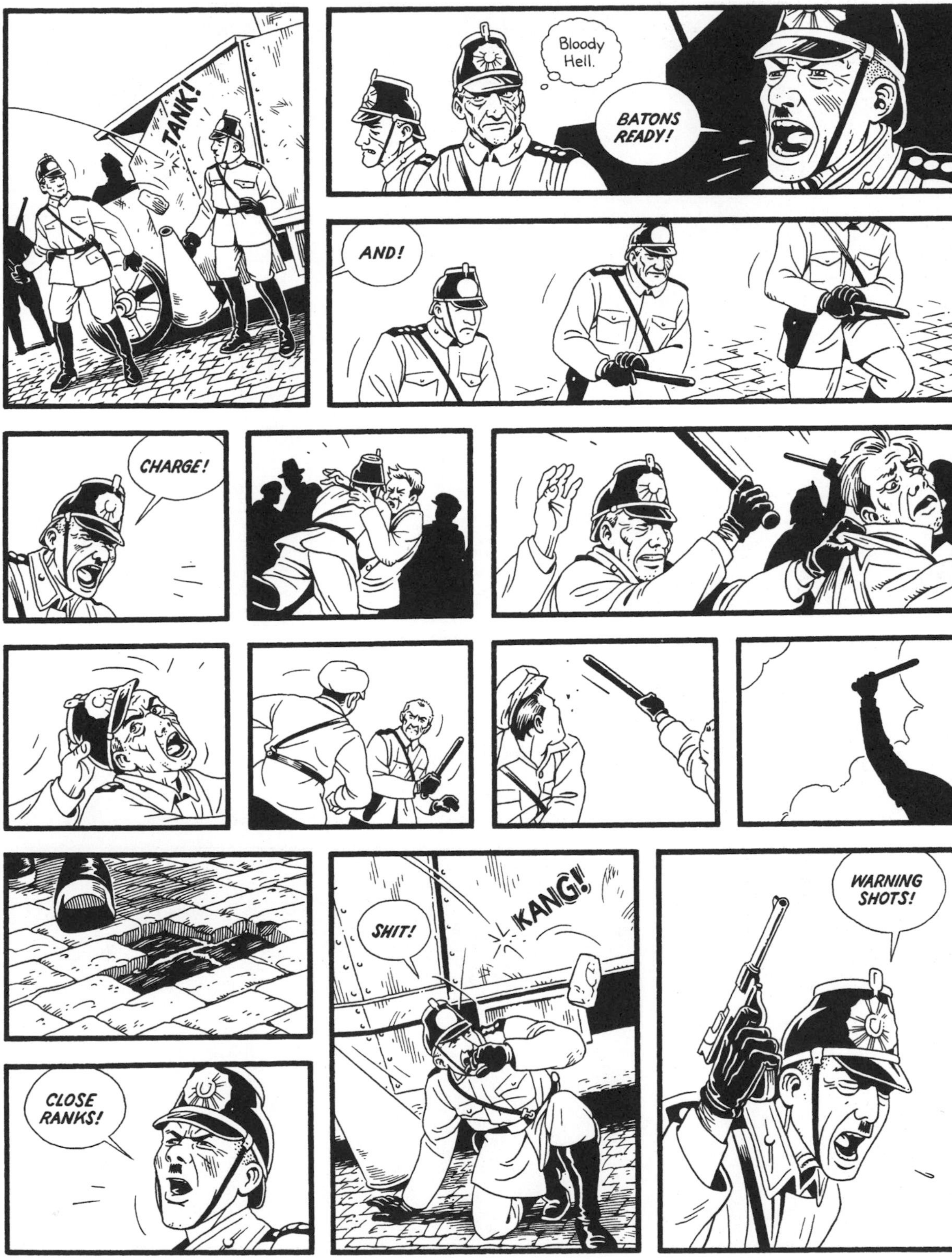
TANK!
Bloody Hell.
BATONS READY!
AND!
CHARGE!
CLOSE RANKS!
SHIT!
KANG!
WARNING SHOTS!

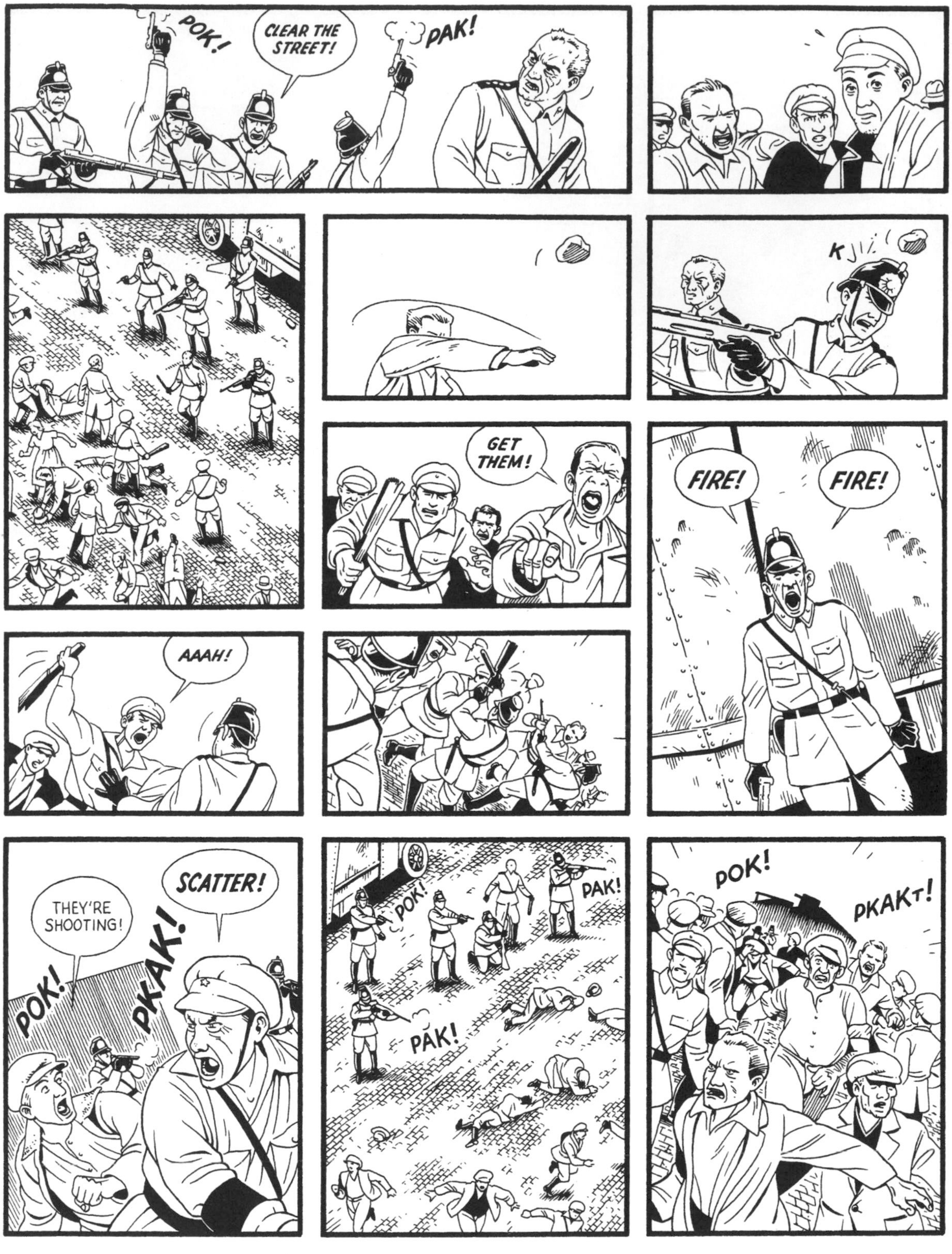
POK!
CLEAR THE STREET!
PAK!
K
GET THEM!
FIRE!
FIRE!
AAAH!
THEY'RE SHOOTING!
SCATTER!
POK!
PKAK!
POK!
PAK!
PAK!
POK!
PKAKT!

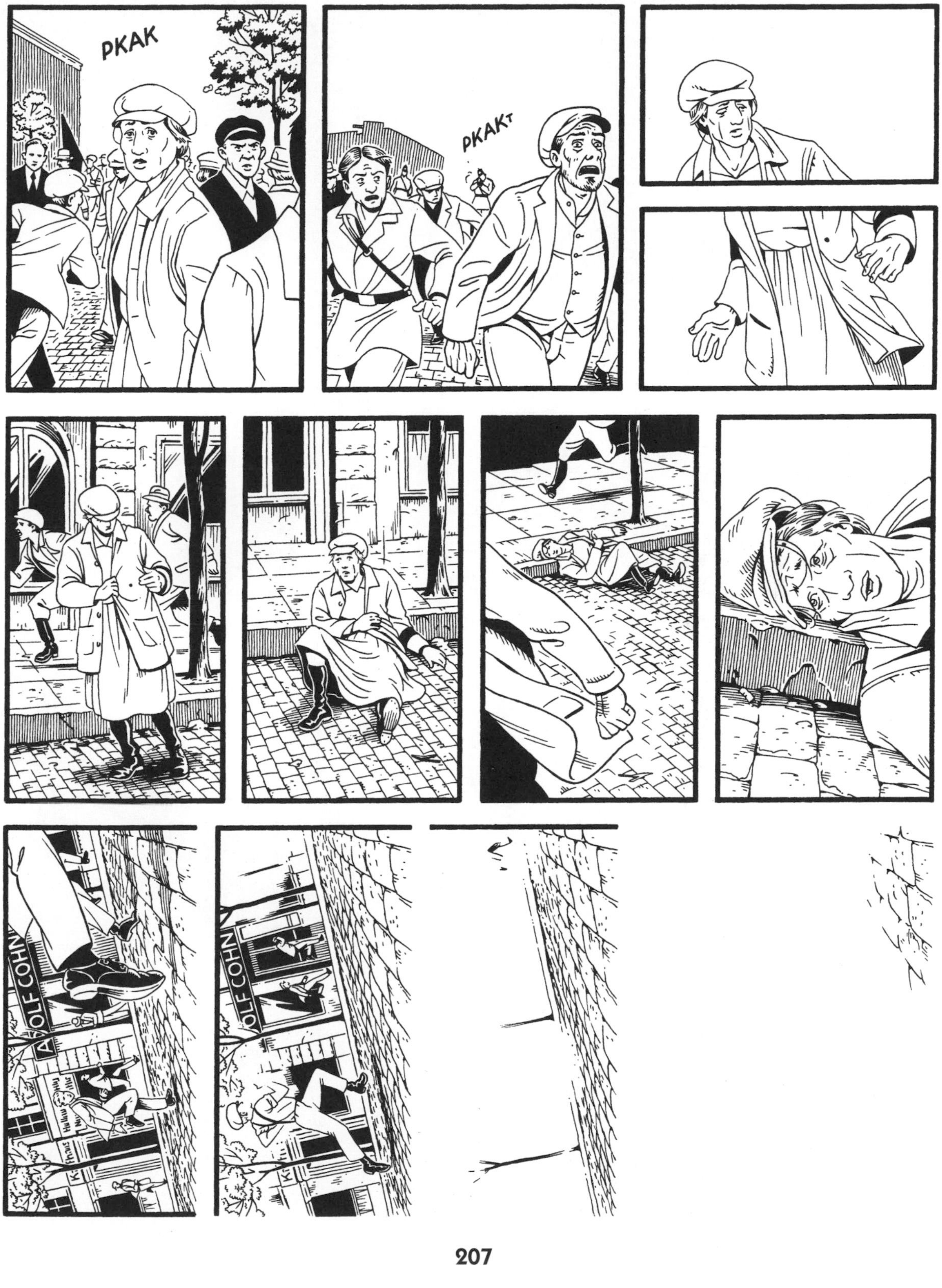
PKAK
PKAKT

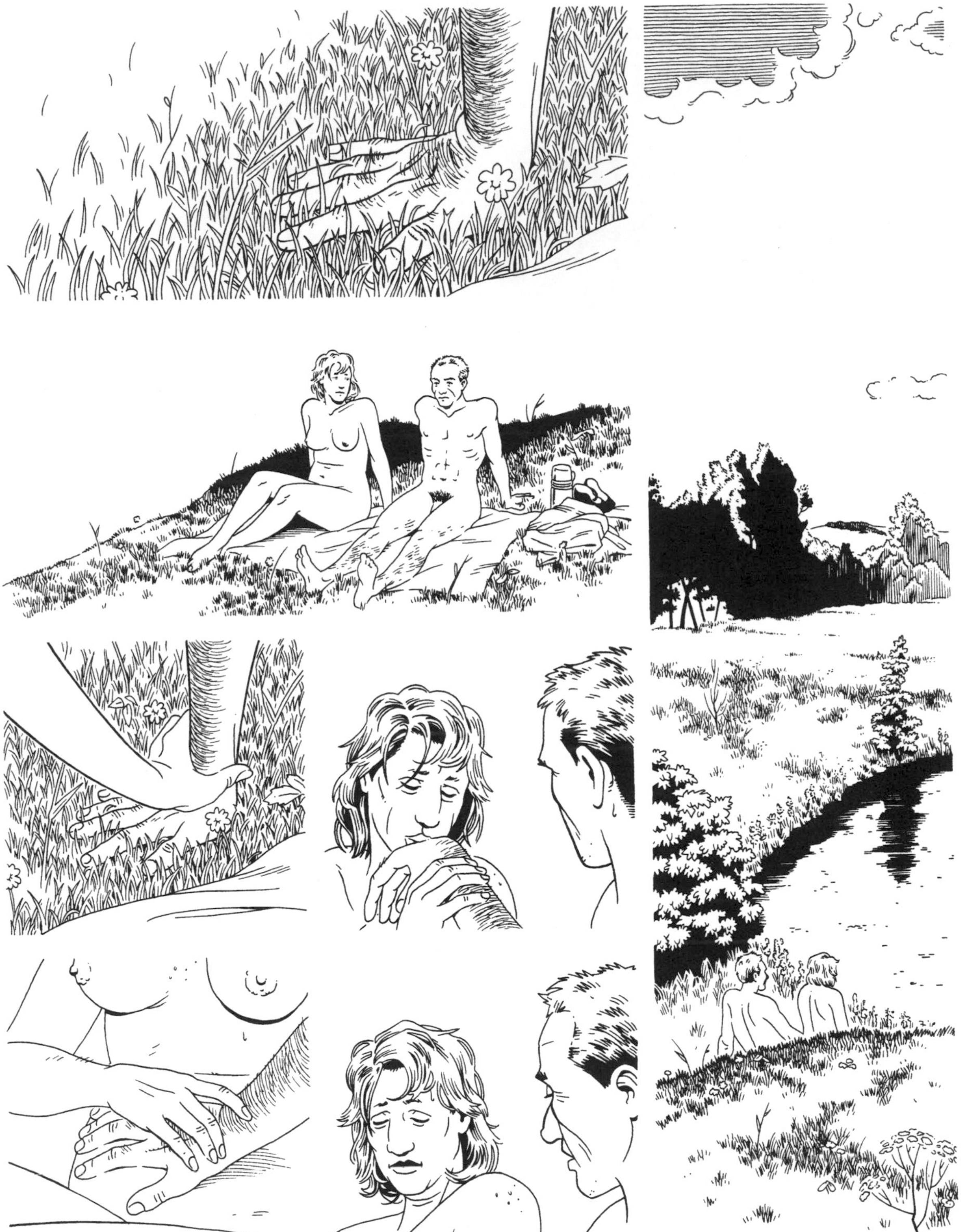

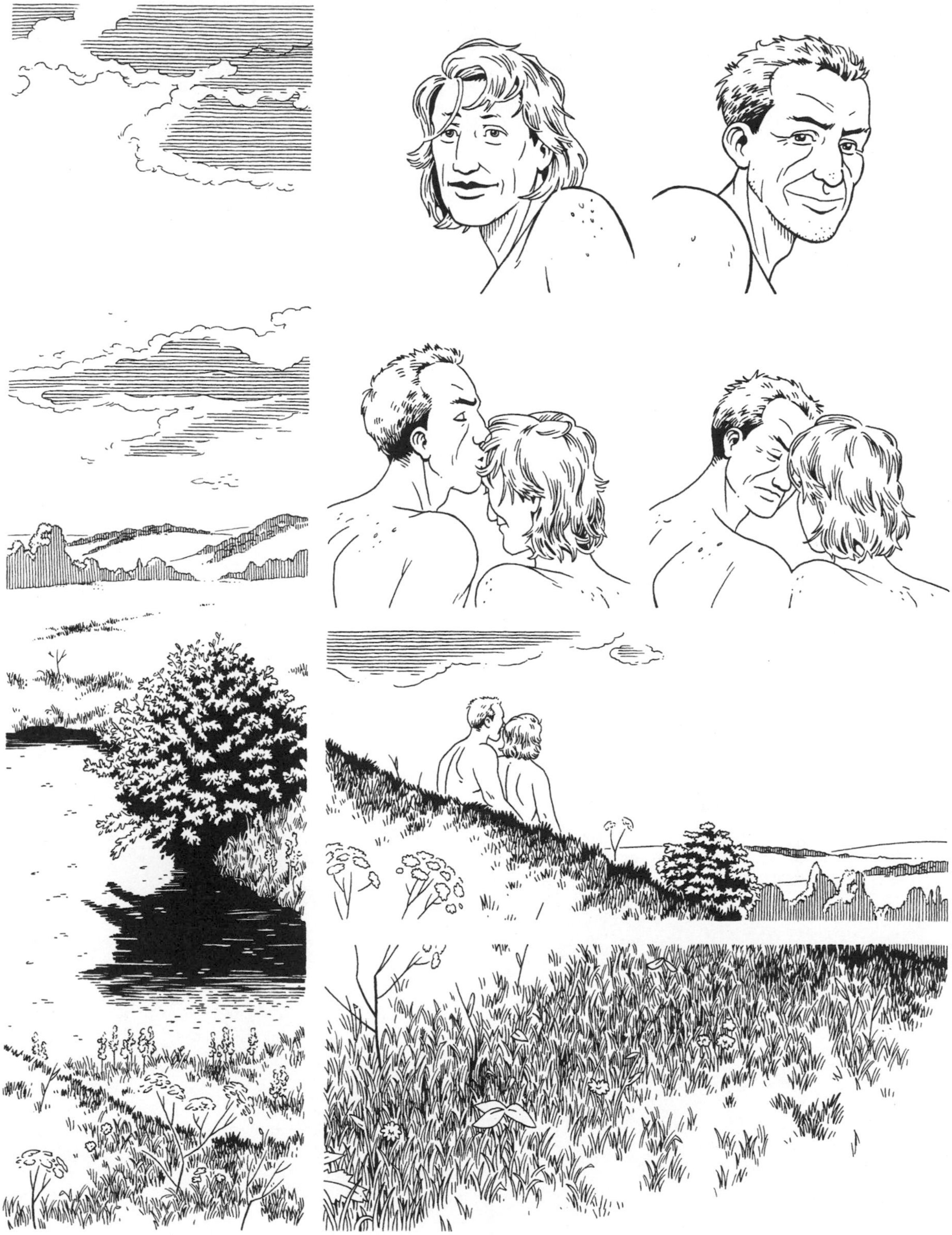

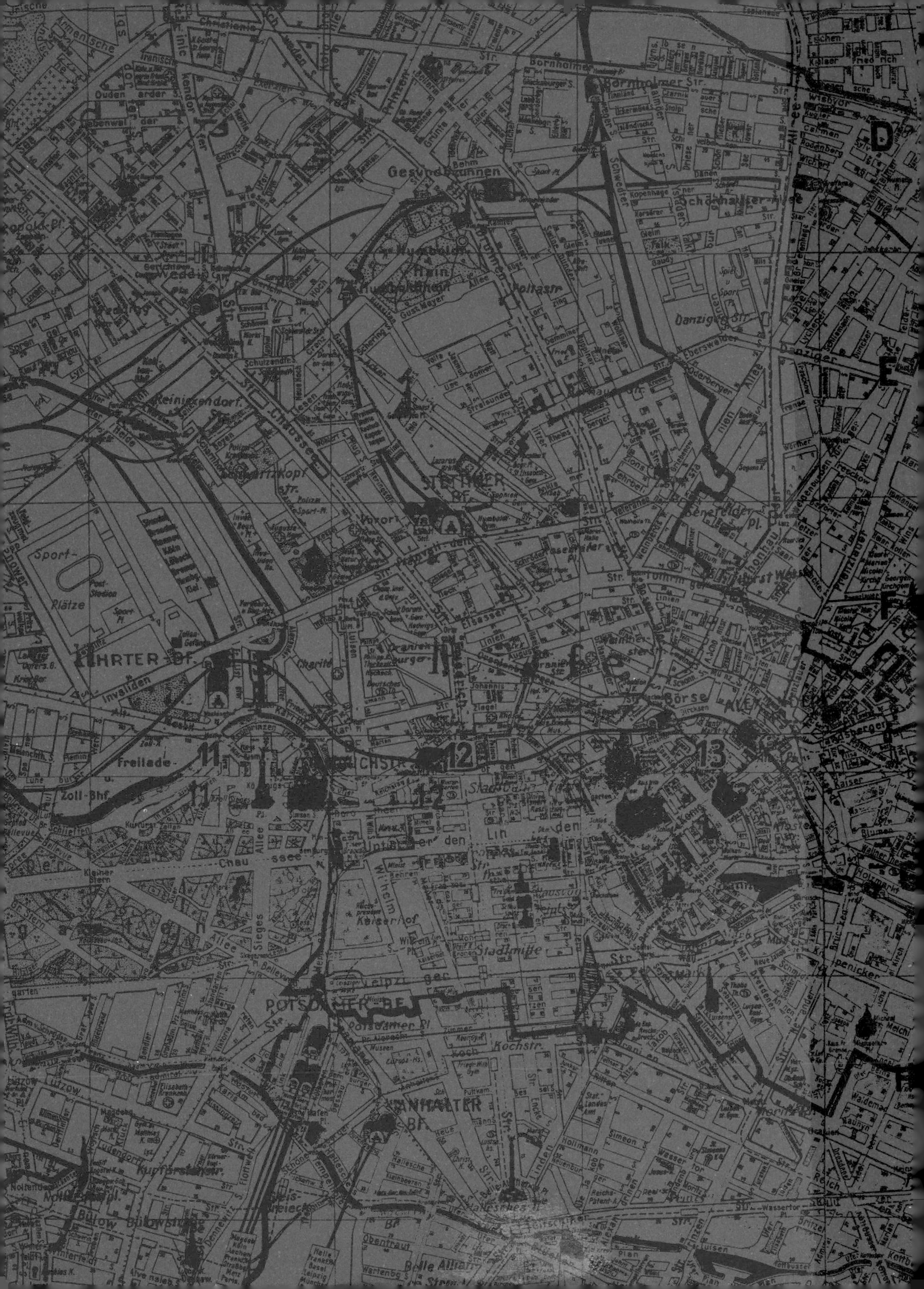

D
E
F
11
12
13
Bornholmer Str.
Gesundbrunnen
Humboldthain
Danziger Str.
Schwartzkopf
Stettiner Bf.
Reinickendorf
Chaussee Str.
Sport-Plätze
Lehrter Bf.
Invaliden
Charité
Freilade-
Zoll-Bhf
Börse
Unter den Linden
Kaiserhof
Stadtmitte
Wilhelm
Potsdamer Bf.
Potsdamer Pl.
Kochstr.
Anhalter Bf.
Kurfürstenstr.
Bülow
Landsberger
Holzmarkt